MEGAN EMMETT – Author

To combine in one person, a healthy dose of oestrogen and the ability to use a large calibre rifle accurately should only prove interesting! But guns and hormones generally don't feature a huge amount when one's passions primarily involve trees, birds, teaching and writing. Megan is best described as a naturalist with a creative bent and literary inclinations. With a conservation degree, a Masters degree in Environmental Management, and years of guiding and training field guides in her background, she has a solid grounding in all topics natural. But her career has been more eclectic than the traditional "bush-whacker" and has involved, amongst other things, creative expression through both written and visual media.

Currently, Megan is the Senior Producer on the 30-year old SABC environmental TV programme 50|50 and she has authored numerous natural history books including "If Trees could Talk" and a children's series on wildlife. Megan is most at home behind her pair of 10x32 binoculars stalking an "LBJ" or snapping a macro shot of something obscure that someone else might have stepped over. When she's not gallivanting in the bush for whatever reason, she is most probably enjoying a glass of Sauvignon Blanc in the company of her good friends or encouraging the keys of her Yamaha concert piano to produce a tune.

Game Ranger in Your Backpack
All-in-one interpretative guide to the Lowveld

Game Ranger in Your Backpack
All-in-one interpretative guide to the Lowveld

Megan Emmett

Sean Pattrick

Published by
BRIZA PUBLICATIONS
CK 1990/011690/23

BRIZA

www.briza.co.za

PO Box 11050
Queenswood 0121
Pretoria
South Africa

First edition, first impression 2010
First edition, second impression 2011
First edition, third impression 2012
First edition, fourth impression 2013
First edition, fifth impression 2014
First edition, sixth impression 2015

Copyright © in text: the relevant author
Copyright © in photographs: Sean Pattrick and other photographers as credited
Copyright © in illustrations: Penny Meakin
Copyright © in published edition: Briza Publications

Icons in Trees section used with permission of Anne Stadler. Illustrations of animal spoor in Mammals section used with permission of Burger Cillié.

All rights reserved. No part of this publication may be reproduced or transmitted in any form or by any means without written permission of the copyright holders.

ISBN 978 1 920217 06 8

Project manager: Reneé Ferreira
Illustrations: Penny Meakin
Cover design: Annalene Rautenbach
Inside design and typesetting: Annalene Rautenbach
Printed and bound by Craft Print International Ltd.,
9 Joo Koon Circle, Singapore

Contents

Acknowledgements 6
Introduction 7

The Lowveld region: the catena and formation of the Lowveld 8

Mammals 12
The Big Five 14 • Common mammals 36 • Predators 94 • Nocturnal mammals 116

Birds 126

Reptiles and amphibians 184

Insects and other invertebrates 222

Plants 252
Trees 254 • Grasses 312 • Small plants and wild flowers 320

Tracking and field signs 332

References & further reading 344
Index 345

Acknowledgements

Megan Emmett

My greatest thanks goes to my parents John and Ingrid Emmett for their patience, kindness and moral and financial support without which this project would never have happened. My deepest appreciation to them also for introducing me at a young age to the bush and inspiring in me the deep love and appreciation I have for wildlife. My thanks also to my sister Kate for her support and for being so energetically herself.

Thanks to Reneé Ferreira, Christo Reitz, Annalene Rautenbach and the rest of the team at Briza for believing in the idea of *Game Ranger in Your Backpack* and then making it happen.

A big thank you to Sean Pattrick for his images that help to make this book uniquely what it is and for his effort in making this project a reality. Special thanks to Hugh Chittenden, Mike Amm, Peter Lawson, Marius Swart, Jed Bird, Naas Rautenbach, Johan Louw, Frank de Villiers, Steve Roskelly, Braam van Wyk, Nico Smit and Ulrich Oberprieler for their photographic contributions.

Thanks is also due to all the friends and colleagues that so eagerly gave encouragement throughout the process. There are too many to mention each by name.

All praise and glory to Jesus Christ who made everything in creation so wonderfully well and who then made it possible for me to experience it and write about it in this book.

Sean Pattrick

A book is the accumulation of years of work, observation, lessons learnt, reading and a genuine interest in your subject. Getting the shot comes about because you have missed so many in the past, you have learnt about plants, birds, insects and animal behaviour, and your skills with a camera are honed over time and with practice. Those lessons start early on in life and for some of us – the very lucky ones who live and work in the natural world – it results in an expression of who we are. That is this book for Megan and I.

Without the help and guidance of like-minded people since my childhood this book would not have come about. I would like to thank the following people: George Collins, one of those few teachers who understood that wilderness is a lesson in itself. Mike Byrne, for giving a young boy the opportunity to grow up as all boys should. The Begg family for all their encouragement and support. My parents, John and Maureen Pattrick, for their patience, support and love which has enabled me to do what I love most. My brother, Neil, for his unwavering belief in me. Finally, Megan Emmett , for putting our thoughts to paper and her support.

I would like to dedicate my contribution to my son, Ben Douglas Pattrick, that he and many like him will have a better understanding of our fellow creatures and cherish them for generations to come, because we are inextricably linked.

Introduction

A game ranger is a person responsible for the custodianship of wildlife and ecosystems and traditionally administrates game reserves and national parks (or parts thereof). It is a person who has intimate knowledge of the workings of the natural environment and someone who then applies that knowledge to the management of wildlife to ensure ecosystems continue to function healthily and sustainably. More recently the term 'game ranger' has also been applied to the naturalists who host guests on guided safaris. These guides are also known as field or safari guides.

Naturalism is a popular field of interest world over and across all age groups. In South Africa, the Lowveld region is considered a wildlife mecca and millions of local and international visitors stream into the region all year round to experience the sights and sounds of the bush and its inhabitants. Bookshelves are lined with books on the myriad wildlife topics that one may potentially encounter but often these are so comprehensive that they overwhelm the amateur naturalist, leaving their questions unanswered. Field guides provide detailed information on how to identify species but *Game Ranger in Your Backpack* is not that kind of field guide.

Consider a book which substitutes the presence of a personal guide or 'game ranger' and makes the practical, interpretative information on the most commonly encountered species in the Lowveld accessible at a glance, eliminating the need to have several different field guides piled on the seat beside you. *Game Ranger in Your Backpack* is just such a book, a compact companion that offers the most interesting information on topics including mammals, birds, reptiles and amphibians, invertebrates, trees, grasses, flowers and tracks and field signs.

How to use this book

The chapters have been colour coded for ease of reference. Simply flip to the desired section and choose the species about which you'd like to learn more. The interpretative images, the highlighted keywords and the flow-chart nature of each spread easily directs the reader's eye to the different topics on the selected species. Simply read whichever part is of interest to you. Blocked information is available in the mammals section and icons in the trees section, providing technical details in a concise form. Although this guide does not focus on providing detail about identification of species, it does offer hints about easy recognition traits to look out for.

The Lowveld region: the catena & formation of the Lowveld

Formation of the Lowveld

If the Lowveld is examined in cross section its geological composition becomes evident. The western limit of the Lowveld is demarcated by the Drakensberg Mountains or Escarpment. These are granite-based and preside over the valley that stretches eastwards toward the ocean. The eastern hem of the Lowveld is marked by the rhyolitic Lebombo Mountains. Between these two ranges from west to east lie plains of gabbro derived soils, the red sands of ecca shales and basaltic clays. These were laid down one upon the other over millennia and exposed when Gondwanaland broke up and tilted the continent eastwards towards the sea.

Cross section of the Lowveld

Granite covered the Lowveld region first, 3 500 million years ago. Over time, some parts of the granite layer were metamorphosed by heat and pressure to produce gneiss and scattered intrusions of gabbro (an intrusive igneous rock) appeared amongst this granite-gneiss base layer.

Three hundred million years ago a layer of sedimentary rock was laid atop the granite-gneiss layer. These ecca shales developed due to a particularly wet climate at the time. Then as the mega-continent of Gondwanaland first began creaking 200 million years ago, a great deal of volcanic activity began spewing firstly layers of basalt onto the surface of the earth and then layers of rhyolite (both extrusive igneous rocks).

Finally Gondwanaland broke apart (about 135 million years ago) and the whole section of continent that now comprises the Lowveld tilted so that the flat layers of superimposed rock types were exposed in cross section. The different properties of the assorted exposed rock types determined the rate at which they weathered and the nature of the resultant soils and landscape. Granite and gneiss, being hard and weathering-resistant, resulted in the towering Escarpment. The rhyolite of the Lebombos is also resistant to weathering but less so than granite. In between, the gabbro, ecca shales and basalt weathered into flat plains. The gabbro produced thick black-cotton soils which become waterlogged and sticky when wet but which supports nutritious veld, including marulas, knobthorns and palatable grasses. The ecca shales weathered into red iron-rich soils and the basalt produced fertile clay soils. The combination of geological events, their resultant soils and the climate of the Lowveld has resulted in a diversity of landscapes and hence habitats which support a myriad plant life and animal life.

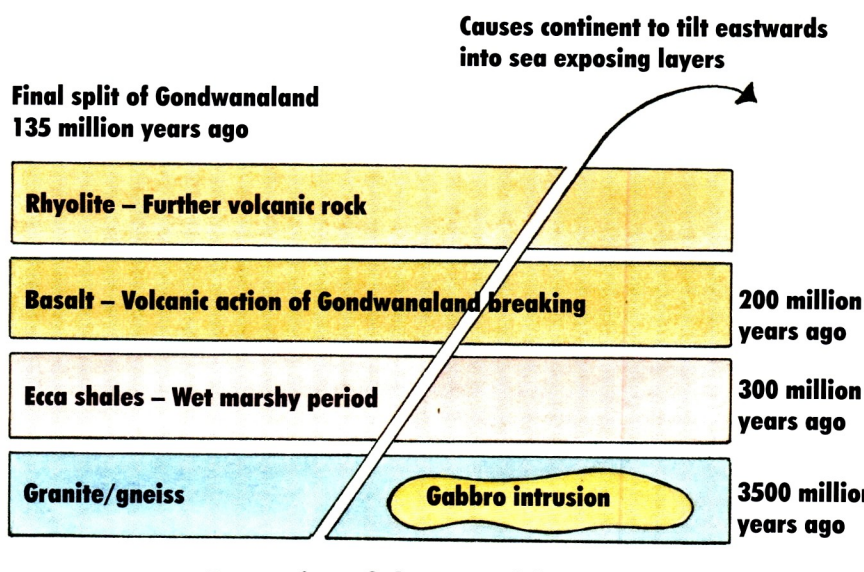

Formation of the Lowveld

The Lowveld region: the catena & formation of the Lowveld

Most of the Lowveld region is underlain with granite rock, some of the oldest in the world. **Granite is an intrusive igneous rock meaning it has formed from magma that has risen up under the ground and cooled below the surface of the earth.** Because it cools and solidifies under the surface, the cooling process is slow and the resultant crystals in the rock are large and noticeable. Granite has a coarse texture to it. Granite rock is eventually exposed through the erosion of the layers of earth above it, but once exposed it takes many thousands of years to weather away – often standing out against the rest of the landscape as boulder-strewn 'koppies' (small hills). Less quartz-rich (and hence softer) granite weathers into slopes produced as different-angled faces. These consequently support a diversity of plant life.

Granite primarily comprises three minerals: quartz, feldspar and **mica**. When granite does weather, the quartz forms coarse sand while the feldspar develops into fine-grained clay soils. (**Mica, a fine, platy, plastic-like mineral, breaks up to form shiny bits in both the sand and clay soils.**) The different consistencies of the resultant soil particles determine where they are found and the kind of plant life they support. The arrangement of these soils along a slope and the subsequent vegetation found there is referred to as a catena.

The Lowveld, for the most part, has a gently undulating topography and the **catena** repeats itself as a pattern across the landscape.

It should be noted that the catena is a dynamic arrangement as far as vegetation is concerned and localised soils as a result of geological features (like dykes and other geological intrusions) under the ground can cause apparent vegetation distribution irregularities. Like everything in nature, the catena is not a hard and fast rule but merely a pattern that can be detected along the undulating granite-based slopes. Many different species of vegetation occur along the catena.

The Lowveld region: the catena & formation of the Lowveld

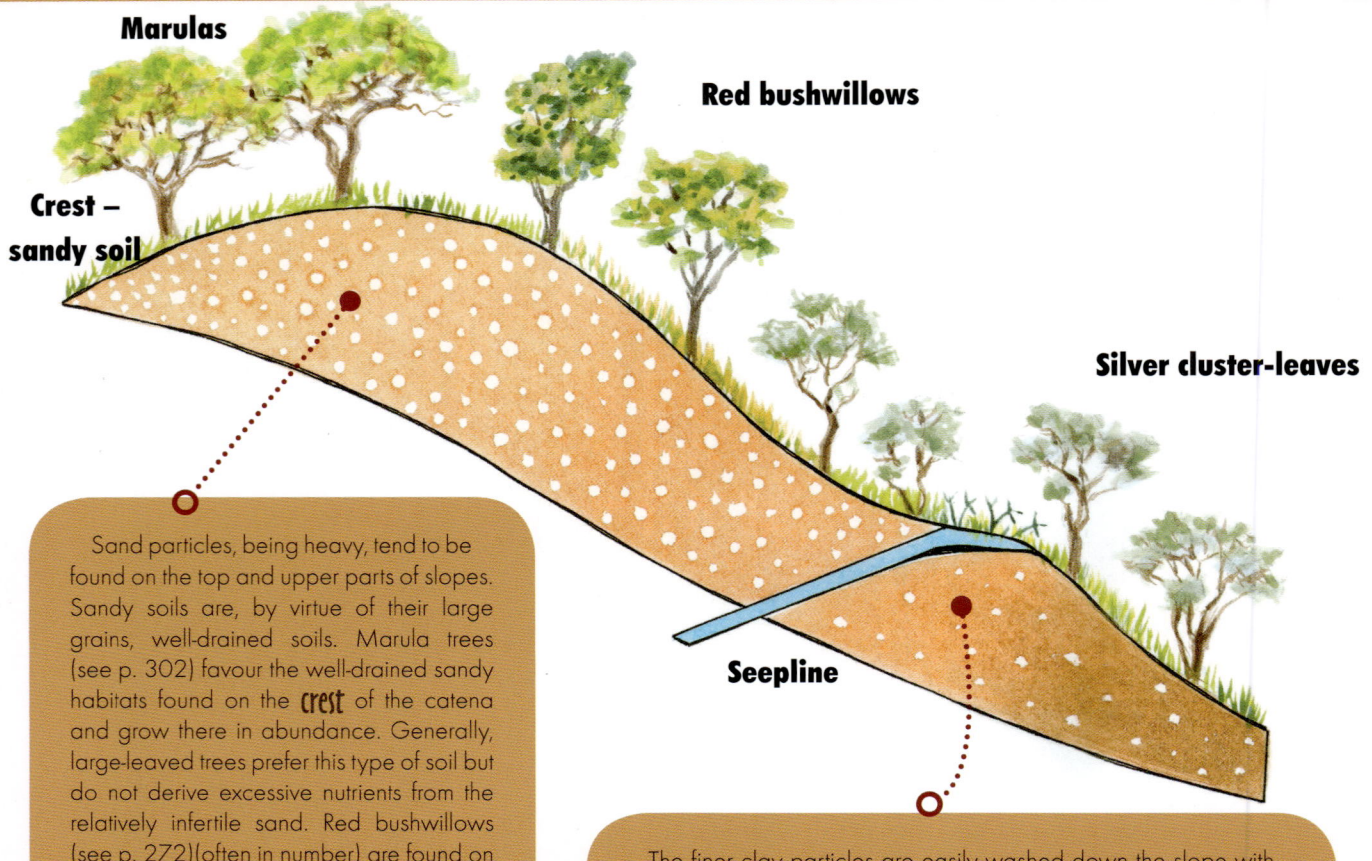

Sand particles, being heavy, tend to be found on the top and upper parts of slopes. Sandy soils are, by virtue of their large grains, well-drained soils. Marula trees (see p. 302) favour the well-drained sandy habitats found on the **crest** of the catena and grow there in abundance. Generally, large-leaved trees prefer this type of soil but do not derive excessive nutrients from the relatively infertile sand. Red bushwillows (see p. 272)(often in number) are found on the upper slopes of the catena but are not especially palatable. Often broad-leaved trees are targeted by insects as food and produce tannins and other secondary chemical compounds to dissuade overuse. Generally, less palatable grasses inhabit the upper slopes of the catena.

The finer clay particles are easily washed down the slope with rain and accumulate on the lower slopes and adjacent to the drainage lines or rivers. Where the clay soil and the sandy soil meet on the slope, is a band known as a **seepline**. Water (mostly in the form of rain) infiltrates the sandy soil and sinks easily into the earth where it runs downhill with the gradient. When it meets the denser clay soil (or sometimes even impermeable bedrock), the water is forced to resurface. This area, usually located on a contour midway down a slope, is waterlogged during the rainy season and supports a specialised community of vegetation that can handle these conditions. These plants are also considered 'indicators' of the seepline.

Most notably, silver cluster-leaf trees inhabit seeplines. They are quite obvious in the landscape for their grey-green shiny leaves and since they often form a dense band (see p. 308). Gum grass and herringbone grass grow on seeplines (see p. 319) as do sedges, grass-like plants that have no nodes, angular stems and prefer wet habitats. Animals rely on seeplines as these areas stay green for longer into the dry season. The waterlogged soils are very sensitive and should they be disturbed by, for example, placing a road through a seepline, they tend to dry out and consequently bush encroachment from the red bushwillows upslope tends to occur.

The Lowveld region: the catena & formation of the Lowveld

Clay soils do not drain as well as sandy soils due to their finer particles but are more fertile. These soils support fine-leaved woodland, especially members of the *Acacia* family. The trees are nutritious due to their fertile growing conditions and produce thorns as a defence against mammalian herbivores. The grasses growing on clay soils are generally nutritious and have high grazing value.

Acacias

Magic guarris

Riverine vegetation

Bottom of slope – clay soil

Sodic site

Drainage line

Sodic sites form at the bottom of catenas, often adjacent to drainage lines. Sodic sites are areas which support little to no plant growth (especially showing a lack of grasses) due to extremely hard sub-soils that prune the roots of all but the hardiest plants as they swell and contract. In the process of granite weathering, large concentrations of sodium are released. Both quartz and feldspar are primarily made up of sodium which is one of the most abundant minerals on earth along with oxygen and aluminium. Sodium particles accumulate in the bottomlands and the positively charged sodium ions subsequently repel one another rather than sticking together to form normal clays. This results in a highly erodable soil surface that is impermeable to water. Sodic sites are characterised by the growth of magic guarri bushes (*Euclea divinorum*, see p. 282) and are used by animals such as wildebeest bulls as territorial arenas. Sodic sites are extremely sensitive areas and should not be disturbed by, for example, driving over them. This would lead to severe erosion.

Drainage lines form along weaknesses in the underlying sea of granite that covers an area shaping the topography. These are often relatively straight lined and filled with coarse sand particles. Amidst these streams and rivers dark rocks are sometimes present as bands across them. These are usually exposed intruding dolerite dykes. Water can be found by digging into the sand on the upstream side of a dolerite dyke as when the drainage line flows, this is where the water banks up. The dyke below the surface prevents the water from draining away.

11

Mammals

Of all the creatures it is usually the mammals that the majority of people visiting the bushveld are most excited to see. Of these, the larger ones, known as 'mega-fauna', are particularly popular especially the 'Big 5' – historically the hardest animals to hunt, but nowadays the most exciting to capture on camera. The Lowveld region of South Africa is home to about 150 different mammal species (comprising 13 orders of a possible 21 orders in the world). The largest of these orders include the smallest of mammals, namely the rodents (Rodentia) and bats (Chirpotera). These animals (and a few others) have not been included in the mammals section as they are hard to view, except at a glance, and often even harder to identify. Instead, the space available has been filled with interpretative images linked in a flow-chart format to blocks of relevant commentary that explores the adaptations and behavioural traits of each of the larger mammal species most likely to be encountered during a visit to the bushveld. Highlighted keywords provide clues to the nature of the information, allowing the reader to select at a glance what is of most interest to him or her. The more technical details are given in a concise table format.

The Big Five
Lion • *Panthera leo*, page 14
Leopard • *Panthera pardus*, page 18
African elephant • *Loxodonta africana*, page 22
Cape (African) buffalo • *Syncerus caffer*, page 28
White rhino • *Ceratotherium simum*, page 32

Common mammals
Impala • *Aepyceros melampus*, page 36
Kudu • *Tragelaphus strepsiceros*, page 40
Nyala • *Tragelaphus angasii*, page 44
Bushbuck • *Tragelaphus scriptus*, page 47
Waterbuck • *Kobus ellipsiprymnus*, page 48
Steenbok • *Raphicerus campestris*, page 50
Common duiker • *Sylvicapra grimmia*, page 51
Klipspringer • *Oreotragus oreotragus*, page 52
Blue wildebeest • *Connochaetes taurinus*, page 54
Burchell's zebra • *Equus burchelli*, page 56
Eland • *Tragelaphus oryx*, page 60
Giraffe • *Giraffa camelopardalus*, page 64
Hippo • *Hippopotamus amphibius*, page 70
Warthog • *Phacochoerus aethiopicus*, page 74
Tree squirrel • *Paraxerus cepapi*, page 78
Rock dassie (hyrax) • *Procavia capensis*, page 82
Chacma baboon • *Papio cynocephalus ursinus*, page 86
Vervet monkey • *Cercopithecus aethiops*, page 90

Predators
Cheetah • *Acinonyx jubatus*, page 94
Wild dog • *Lycaon pictus*, page 98
Spotted hyena • *Crocuta crocuta*, page 102
Caracal • *Caracal caracal*, page 106
Black-backed jackal • *Canis mesomelas*, page 108
Dwarf mongoose • *Helogale parvula*, page 112

Small nocturnal mammals
Aardvark • *Orycteropus afer*, page 116
Civet • *Civettictis civetta*, page 118
Large spotted genet • *Genetta tigrina*, page 119
Small spotted genet • *Genetta genetta*, page 119
Scrub hare • *Lepus saxatilis*, page 120
Cape porcupine • *Hystrix africaeaustralis*, page 121
Honey badger (ratel) • *Mellivora capensis*, page 122
African wild cat • *Felis lybica*, page 123
Lesser bushbaby (lesser galago) • *Galago moholi*, page 124

The Big 5

Lions are the **largest African carnivores**. They are also the only social cats in the bushveld. By cooperating in prides, lions are able to kill bigger animals or improve the chance of a successful kill where there is little cover. They are also able to improve the survival of their young through cooperation.

It is commonly thought that a pride of lion comprises a single dominant male and his females, but this is not necessarily the case. A **territory is held by several males in partnership** – known as a coalition. There can be between two and five males in a coalition and their territory overlaps with a number of different, mutually exclusive female territories. Working as a team, it is easier to dispossess older lions of their domain and keep hyenas at bay, lions' chief competition. Collectively the males are a stronger force, can defend a larger territory and protect more females. They will split up to do patrols but rejoin as necessity requires. The coalition may be (but not always) made up of brothers. In this instance the cooperative effort serves the perpetuity of the family genes.

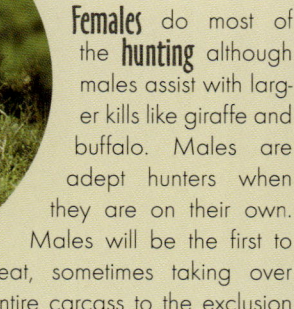

Females do most of the **hunting** although males assist with larger kills like giraffe and buffalo. Males are adept hunters when they are on their own. Males will be the first to eat, sometimes taking over the entire carcass to the exclusion of the females that killed it, or even their own cubs. The females tolerate this behaviour both because the males are larger and stronger and because the males afford the females protection by defending the territory against hyenas and other male lions. Foreign males that move into the territory will kill all the cubs in a pride under 1 year old. This infanticide is executed to bring females into heat quickly so that they might mate with the pride females and then spend their tenure as the territorial coalition defending their own offspring. Interestingly, the females will only conceive once the males have established themselves in the pride. This mechanism prevents wasted reproductive energy in that should the new males be displaced soon after takeover, a similar process will occur and the females will again lose their cubs.

Lion
Panthera leo

Size	Male: 1,2 m (at shoulder), Female: 1,1 m (at shoulder)
Weight	Male: 190 kg (up to 260 kg); Female: 130 kg Male attains maximum weight at 7 years, females at 5–6 years (declines with age)
Lifespan	10–14 years (maximum 18); females live longer, males killed or die at about 10 years old
Habitat & Distribution	Wide tolerance, even penetrate into deserts along dry river courses. Require barest of cover to stalk, and adequate medium to large-sized prey animals
Gestation	110 days (3,5 months)
# of young	1–6 (average 3)
Prey	Mammals from mice to buffalo (even elephants), birds up to the size of ostrich, reptiles, insects, fish and carrion. Common prey species: giraffe, wildebeest, zebra, impala, waterbuck, warthog and kudu
Predators	Hyenas and man; other carnivores and pythons take cubs

Lions have **protractile claws**. The claws can be pushed out by muscle contractions when the lion has need to fight or hunt but they relax back into a protective sheath when not in use which keeps them from becoming blunt while the cat moves around. There is a small dewclaw on a lion's wrist which is used when pouncing on prey to secure it.

Lions will drink water regularly if it is available. They fulfil the majority of their moisture requirements from the bloody meat they eat.

Mature male lions have huge manes of hair over their necks and shoulders. This makes them look large and impressive to contenders and to females. When male lions fight they do so head-to-head, raking each other with their claws. A dense mane of hair serves to protect their necks from a fatal blow.

Lions **roar to advertise their territory** or to locate other members of the pride. They do this mainly at night, as this is when they are most active but also because the air is stiller and sound carries further. It is estimated that the roar of a lion carries over 7 km depending on the time of year and weather. Lions recognise individual roars and will respond to one another if it is relevant to do so. Lions are able to roar so loudly due to the suspensorium, which is a 'voice box' device at the top of the windpipe suspended with cartilage. The larynx of other species is ossified in place. The cartilage allows for movement of the suspensorium and as a result the vibrations caused during vocalisation are significantly enhanced and thus louder and they project further. Of the African cats, the lion is most closely related to the leopard (also *Panthera* genus) because of their similar voice box structure. Lions also moan, purr, growl, snarl and the cubs meow.

After a day's resting and before they get active for the evening, a pride of lions will engage in **contagious behaviour** including yawning, grooming, defecating, urinating and communal roaring. This creates pride cohesion.

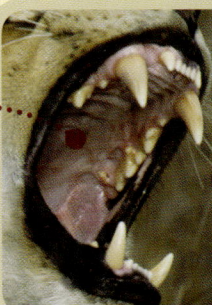

As it is the criterion to belong to the carnivore family, lions have a well-developed **carnassial shear**. The carnassials are made up of the fourth upper premolar and first lower molar. These teeth are laterally flattened and articulate against each other, acting with a scissor-like blade action to cut meat and sinew. The long, sharp canines are used to grasp and kill prey and are useless in feeding. The strong lower jaw is powered by well-developed muscles that attach to the massive skull. A lion's skull weighs over 3 kg.

Lions have extremely **rough tongues** and can actually separate meat from bone by just licking it.

Lionesses often **synchronise their breeding**. This is useful as all the mothers will then mutually suckle each other's cubs. However, if there are very new cubs in a pride as well as cubs 3 months or older, the mother of the younger cubs will keep her offspring away from the pride for longer than the usual 6 weeks. This is because the older cubs are stronger and have easier access to the milk on offer to the exclusion of the smaller cubs.

Mating in lions is a very intense affair. A pair will mate every 20 minutes for 4 days and nights with each bout lasting 1 minute. Lions have a low fertility rate and a very small percentage of mating results in conception. In fact, for every cub reaching 1 year old, the parents would have mated 3 000 times. The protracted copulations serve two functions. Firstly they stimulate the female to ovulate and secondly they provide the opportunity to confuse paternity. The male that begins mating with a female may become so exhausted by day 3 or 4 that another of the coalition members will take over. Since both believe the cubs to be his, both have a vested interest in protecting the offspring.

Although females often elicit mating by presenting their rumps (lordosis) to a male, by the end of a bout she appears irritable, turning to swat the male with her paw as he extracts. This is due to the fact that male lions have **barbed penises** and the extraction is extremely painful. The neck-biting and snarling that takes place during mating is ritualised.

Males determine that a **female is in oestrus** (ready to mate) by flehmen. They frequently smell the rump of the female or the area where she has recently urinated and then, pulling back the top lip in a grimace (called flehmen grimace), muscles on the palate are contracted to force the steroid hormones into the organ of Jacobsen. This chemo-receptive gland detects hormones that indicate reproductive status.

Lion cubs are born blind and weak (altricial). The gestation period is short (see box) since lionesses need to hunt in order to survive and provide for the pride. They would be severely disadvantaged if they were weighed down by heavy pregnant bellies for protracted periods of time. As a result, the cubs are **underdeveloped at birth** and need to be kept in hiding until they are strong enough to join the pride and hold their own. This is the converse to their prey. Antelope need only to eat grass to avoid starvation and a pregnant belly is no inhibitor to this. Once they are born, they must run to escape predators and so their young are born precocial (able to move and see immediately) but this comes of having longer to develop in the womb.

Lion
Panthera leo

All the **lionesses in a pride are related** and remain within the pride for life. They may split up into subgroups and operate in different parts of the territory but will join up from time to time. Young males are ousted from the pride in their third year and they must lead a **nomadic lifestyle**, keeping a low profile until they are able to contend for a territory from about the age of 5. They are fully mature at 7 years old at which time their manes are at their fullest. After tenure of a territory, ousted older males also resort to a nomadic lifestyle and are often killed or die from lack of pride support by 10 years old.

Lions are **extremely lethargic** for the majority of their lives, spending about 20 hours a day resting. This is necessary to recuperate from the intense periods they spend patrolling and hunting. Although lions may seem comatose at times, they are often alert and can be spurred to action in seconds.

Lions have **black tips to their tails and black behind their ears**. These are 'follow me' signs. The black tail is at exactly the right height for a cub to follow a female through tall grass. Cats **express their moods** with their tails and ears and so having these areas highlighted is valuable for communication and coordination during hunts. While the black is obvious from behind, from the front the animal remains completely camouflaged.

Lions are **opportunistic feeders**, eating mostly medium to large antelope but including anything from a mouse to an elephant. They will follow other predators or vultures to kill sites to steal food, including putrid meat, and they ambush animals by lying in wait at isolated waterholes. They may dig warthogs out of their burrows or pick off antelope lying up in the grass. They rid populations of their sick and weak members. They hunt predominantly under the cover of darkness but will hunt during the day if opportunity presents itself. Lions gorge themselves when they feed, leaving them almost immovable but food passes through their guts quickly to allow for a second meal soon after.

Lions are **super-predators** and dominate the bushveld predator hierarchy. They will steal food wherever they can from other predators and mutually kill each other's cubs. They may even kill smaller carnivores as food. Their only real competition is hyenas but only if these exist in significantly greater numbers and even a clan of hyenas do not stand much chance against a pride if males are present. Elephants chase and even kill lions to protect their young, as will herds of buffalo. The kills that lions make are attended by hyenas, jackals and vultures which will attempt to scavenge the leftovers.

Male lions seldom kill one another unless they are disputing a territory; rather they take great care to avoid confrontation. **Fighting** creates an immediate risk of injury and any injury could imply disability in **defending territory** or catching food. Instead lions spend a great deal of time advertising their position through roaring and scent-marking. Lions mark their territories by urine-spraying bushes and other obvious objects. They defecate conspicuously and scrape with their feet on the ground where they have urinated, transferring the scent to their feet to pass on while they patrol their boundaries.

Lions experience an exceptionally high cub mortality of up to 50%.

Lions are **expert stalkers**. They can use the barest of cover to get close to prey by holding the head and body close to the ground. With their eyes firmly fixed on the victim, they move carefully, freezing immediately if the prey lifts its head. Lions will get as close as possible to their prey before the final dash and pounce. Sometimes a chase is necessary but this is always short. **Lions can cover 100 m in 6 seconds in final chase**. The point of attack is usually the rump or shoulders of the prey and the sheer weight of the lion causes the animal to fall, at which time it is grabbed by the throat or muzzle for the final strangulation or suffocation.

Leopards are **master stalkers** and they will painstakingly approach to within 5 – 10 m of their quarry before launching an attack. They rely on the element of surprise and their powerful bodies to capture prey, which is grappled with the fore-claws and then bitten on the back of the head or around the throat.

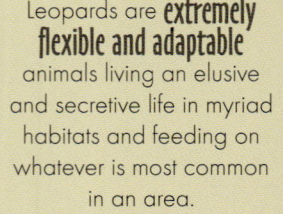

Leopards are **extremely flexible and adaptable** animals living an elusive and secretive life in myriad habitats and feeding on whatever is most common in an area.

Leopards are the **ultimate opportunists**. Although they are essentially nocturnal animals, they will not ignore hunting opportunities that present themselves during the daytime. They will generally eat small to medium-sized antelope (up to 70 kg) like impala and duiker but depending on circumstances will make use of 92 different food sources including unusual items such as winged termites, stranded fish, ground birds, rodents, reptiles, porcupine, aardvark, tree squirrels, dassies, mongoose, genet and even baby buffalo. They will also scavenge food from other smaller predators like cheetah.

Leopards are **solitary animals** except at times when females may be accompanied by their growing cubs. Both male and female leopards **defend territories that are same-sex exclusive**. The size of the territory depends on the availability of prey and varies between 5 and 100 km² (usually about 15 km²). Females choose territories based on prey density and available den sites. Males select territories based on the availability of females. Male leopards have larger territories than females and these encompass a number of female territories. In this way the males can locate and mate with females as and when they enter oestrus (come into heat). They detect females both by chemical clues left behind in their urine and through the constant calling of a female seeking a mate. Opposite sexes generally only remain in one another's company for the period of courtship and mating. They may share kills during this time but the male plays no part in raising the cubs.

In areas where leopards are regularly harassed by lion or hyena, they will **hoist their prey into a tree** where these large and clumsy scavengers are less likely to access it. **Hyenas will often wait beneath a tree** in which a leopard is feeding to pick up the scraps dropped. Sometimes large parts of the kill may come free and fall down to the opportunists below. Leopards feed on the ground in areas where there are few scavengers.

Leopard
Panthera pardus

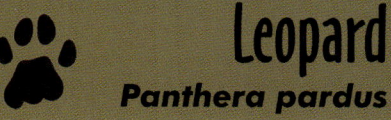

Leopards are **relatively fussy** eaters (although they are not averse to putrid carrion) and will typically pluck the hair or feathers off their food before consuming it. The intestines of larger prey are discarded and subsequently covered up to mask the smell so that other scavengers like lions or hyenas are not attracted to the kill site. The remains of a carcass may also be covered up with vegetation or soil to keep it safe should the leopard need to desert it temporarily.

Size	Male: 70-80 cm (at shoulder); Female: 60-70 cm (at shoulder)
Weight	Male: 60-90 kg; Female: 30-60 kg
Lifespan	11-15 years (maximum 20)
Habitat & Distribution	Wide tolerance – extremely adaptable but needs good cover to hunt and hide. Territories usually include rocky outcrops and densely wooded drainage lines
Gestation	100 days
# of young	2 or 3
Prey	Wide variety from mice, reptiles and fish to large antelope and small carnivores, mainly medium-sized antelope like impala, readily scavenges
Predators	Cubs killed by lions and spotted hyena

Male leopards are also known as 'toms'.

Another **visual territorial beacon is the clawed scrape marks** left on tree trunks along pathways. Leopards claw hard surfaces such as the bark of trees to maintain their claws. The friction removes bits of fraying claw-sheath. The resultant marks are often high up the trunk (the leopard rises up on its hind legs to claw the tree with its forepaws) and these are possibly to show off their size to would-be trespassers.

A leopard's vision is excellent and used to locate prey. **Forward facing eyes provide the binocular vision** necessary for gauging depth and distance. A high occurrence of rod cells (for black and white detection) in the retina of the eye makes it easier to see at night under conditions of light and shadow. Leopards also have a tapetum lucidum behind the retina of their eyes. This is a reflective layer that reflects light back onto the retina a second time to increase the stimulation of the retinal light-sensitive cells to improve vision in low light conditions.

Leopards have **excellent senses** and they use a combination of these to locate prey. These are also employed in the **exchange of information** between territory-holders and possible intruders. Both male and female leopards use urine to demarcate their territorial boundaries (only males spray). The scent of the urine as well as its strength carries messages such as the identity of the territory holder, the general time when it was last in the vicinity and hormone levels of females. Leopards also rub their faces against low overhanging vegetation along roads or other pathways and territory boundaries. In doing so they transfer secretions from their cheek glands which also carry olfactory messages. Male leopards scrape the ground during or after urination to transfer scent onto their feet to be left behind during patrols. The scrape marks are also visual beacons to intruders. They defecate in conspicuous places along territorial boundaries to ward off intruders. Leopards go to great lengths to advertise their territories to avoid physical confrontations with one another. As solitary hunters, they cannot risk injury by engaging unnecessarily with another leopard. Male leopards engage in deliberate patrols to reinforce their territorial limits while females concentrate more on finding food and only mark along active boundaries.

Leopards rely on their good sense of hearing when communicating over long distances. They **vocalise with a rasping call** that sounds like wood under a saw. Due to a suspensorium (non-ossified voice box that vibrates) like that of a lion (see page 15) leopards can send long-range messages to denote territory, make contact with offspring or locate mates. A female's call can be distinguished from a male's by being longer in duration and with a higher frequency of rasps.

Black leopards or panthers are in fact simple genetic variants of the normal spotted leopard. This black colouring is known as a melanistic form as it is caused by an excess of black pigment called **melanin**.

Leopards have intricate patterning all over their bodies. This pattern is unique to each animal. On the majority of the body black spots are arranged together to form rosettes. The back and flanks of the body are a golden colour and the underside almost pure white. In combination these **disruptive markings** and colours provide the leopard with **highly effective camouflage**. The patterning breaks up the shape of the body and allows the leopard to almost melt invisibly into any habitat. This is critical to facilitate hunting and to remain elusive from its own enemies.

Leopards experience a **high cub mortality** of up to 50%. Despite being hidden in heavy cover, caves or holes, young cubs are often found by other carnivores and killed. All mammalian **predators kill one another's offspring instinctively**, thereby reducing competition. Hyenas are a particular threat to leopards and in high numbers have the advantage over the individually powerful cat. Lions and hyenas will rob inexperienced leopards of their kills, as will other leopards.

Leopard cubs are left alone (although in hiding) for many hours while the adults hunt and patrol their territories. Whether on their own or in the company of siblings, these periods impulsively become times of play and exploration. **Play is a critical activity** as during these sessions muscles are honed and skills learnt that will be **required for survival** and hunting ability later in life. It is also during these long waits that these small predators first experience the lifestyle of every carnivore – feast and famine.

Leopards are **powerfully built animals** with strong necks and large skulls and jaws for executing kills. Older males develop particularly thick necks probably to appear more impressive to rivals and to facilitate fighting ability. High shoulders accommodate a rather depressed chest. This is an adaptation to dragging and hoisting prey, which drapes between the front legs at these times. **Leopards are able to hoist kills sometimes as heavy as their own bodies.** The dewclaws, placed higher up the wrist, are essential for climbing trees and hoisting heavy loads.

Leopards are **excellent mothers** and will leave their cubs secreted away in dense bush or up a tree in order to hunt for food to which they will then lead their offspring. They do this until the cubs are about 9,5 months old at which time they may accompany the mother on hunts executing their first kill at around 11 months old. Leopards cannot fend for themselves until they are at least a year old and the female will accommodate her cubs within the confines and protection of their territories for at least 18 months (if not longer) and even tolerate hunting visits by newly independent sub-adults which may not immediately be able to set up territories of their own. Where there are cases of females' territories overlapping, it is most likely between female relatives. They tend not to use the overlapping part of the range at the same time.

When leopards do come together to mate, it is an intense affair lasting 2 to 5 days with copulations occurring every 5 to 10 minutes. **Females are very flirtatious** at this time even leaving their own territories to actively seek out a male or calling and marking incessantly to attract one. The end of a mating bout is marked by a vicious paw swat aimed at the male's face. The female reels around in response to the painful extraction of the male's barbed penis.

Leopard
Panthera pardus

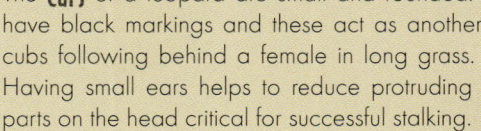

Leopards have **long whiskers** (also known as vibrissae). These are tactile sensory organs that indicate to the leopard whether it will fit through a particular sized gap. This is an important adaptation to moving around in the darkness.

The **ears** of a leopard are small and rounded. From behind they have black markings and these act as another 'follow me' sign to cubs following behind a female in long grass. Having small ears helps to reduce protruding parts on the head critical for successful stalking.

The long **tail is white-tipped** and stands out from behind. This is one of its **'follow me' signs** and when hanging relaxed is just at a height for young cubs to see and follow in long grass. The tail also indicates the mood of the cat and can be used as a non-vocal form of communication. Youngsters may target the white end of a parent's tail in bouts of play-pouncing. Leopards use their long tails for balance during hunting pursuits or when climbing trees.

Leopards often **roll in the dung** of other animals. It is not certain what the reason is for this but it has been suggested that the smell of the dung may mask the leopard's own scent during hunts or possibly even transfer the leopard's own scent onto the dung as a territorial act.

Gestation is rapid and cubs are born relatively undeveloped being completely helpless and blind (altricial). Female leopards cannot afford to be weighed down by a pregnant belly for too long, as this would affect their hunting ability. Instead, cubs continue to grow in a secret hiding place for 6 weeks and are suckled by the female for 3 months.

Leopards generally spend the **hottest hours of the day resting** to conserve the energy needed to execute kills and defend territories. They usually rest in the thick cover of a wooded drainage line or a leafy tree. Sometimes they may retreat into a cave. Leopards regularly make use of rocky outcrops as den sites, vantage points or to sun themselves during cold weather.

Leopards have a **large cultural significance** and capes made from leopard skins are worn as ceremonial dress to denote the status of the wearer. Sometimes stock thieving leopards are pursued and killed by young men seeking to prove their manhood to the community. Traditional medicine incorporates the use of a leopard's whiskers.

The African elephant is the **largest and heaviest terrestrial mammal** in the world. They are extremely intelligent and incredibly powerful animals that alter their surroundings to the benefit (and sometimes detriment) of whole ecosystems. Elephants are very adaptable creatures as they are able to vary their diet according to what is available and they easily overcome adverse conditions by simply moving to new areas covering long distances to take advantage of remote resources.

The **tusks** of an elephant are **modified upper incisor teeth** that grow continuously throughout life. Elephants use their tusks as weapons of defence against predators and other elephants and they are kept sharp for this function. They also use them as tools when foraging to clean soil off vegetation, to dig up items and to lever off branches or bark. Tusks vary between individuals with some adult animals developing massive tusks while others of the same age may have small tusks or none at all (this is caused by a recessive gene). Tusks may be broken and lost through injury or worn down through usage (generally more on the one side than the other as an individual will be left- or right-dominant). Older bulls use their tusks less as their competitive spirit wanes. These individuals may develop enormous ivory as their tusks continue to grow unchecked. The largest recorded tusk in the Lowveld weighed 64,3 kg. The longest tusk on record had a length of 3,55 m.

Telling female and male elephants apart can be tricky and is exacerbated by the fact that bulls have internal testes. Generally older adult bulls are significantly larger than cows and found alone or in small groups (cows are always in breeding herds). Younger males and females can be separated by looking at the forehead which is angled in cows and rounded in bulls. Males also have a straighter back profile than females. Cows have two enlarged mammary glands between their front legs (the only mammal other than primates to have these here) and bulls often relax their penises which hang down conspicuously.

Elephants **communicate** through body posturing or vocally by use of trumpeting or even screaming to indicate anger or excitement. Trumpeting originates in the larynx and is resonated in the trunk. Most communication takes place through **rumbling**, also produced by the vocal chords and possibly amplified in the upper regions of the trunk. Some of the rumbles (which sound like tummy-rumbles) are audible to humans but some are infrasonic messages that occur at low wavelengths and are inaudible. These infrasonic sounds can be detected by other elephants up to 12 km away and help to coordinate movements between animals out of eyeshot and even normal earshot of one another. It is suspected that elephants detect these 'vibrations' through their feet.

African elephant
Loxodonta africana

Size	Bull: 3 m (at shoulder); Cow: 2,5 m (at shoulder)
Weight	Bull: up to 6 tons (heaviest bull on record 6 569 kg); Cow: up to 4 tons
Lifespan	55–60 years
Habitat & Distribution	Every habitat in Africa with adequate food, shade and water including swamp, rainforest, woodland, savanna, desert, grasslands, hills, mountains and semi-desert
Gestation	22 months
# of young	1
Food	Herbivores – catholic diet that uses 90% of local plant species including grass, herbs, sedges, aquatic plants, bulbs, tubers, roots, fruits, flowers, bark, wood, pods, seeds, leaves and entire branches
Predators	Lions and hyenas prey on young; lions in some areas kill adults. Death also by parasites, disease and starvation

Elephants are **highly social animals**. Their complex society focuses on maintaining group cohesion and a strict discipline regime ensures social order at all times. Due to their enormous size, elephants could cause serious damage to themselves and each other if their social behaviour was not regulated and ritualised. Herd life predominantly revolves around guarding, rearing and teaching calves, activities engaged in by all herd members.

Since it takes 22 months for a calf to be born and the calving interval thereafter is at least 4 years, calves are family investments that are not easily replaced. For the first 2 years of its life, an elephant calf is intensively mothered but childhood is protracted and continued learning occurs. Amongst bachelor groups, young males keep the peace by ritualised tussling that establishes strength and therefore dominance amongst the males without the need to fight, and thereby injure themselves, except when an oestrus cow is at stake.

Elephants are a **keystone** species meaning that they influence the healthy functioning of ecosystems and even the survival of particular species. Due to their enormous size and energy requirements, elephants alter habitats. They are a **'driving force' in the maintenance of the bushveld habitat** type through the cropping of woody vegetation which prevents it reaching a forest climax (while fire keeps the grass at a competitive equilibrium).

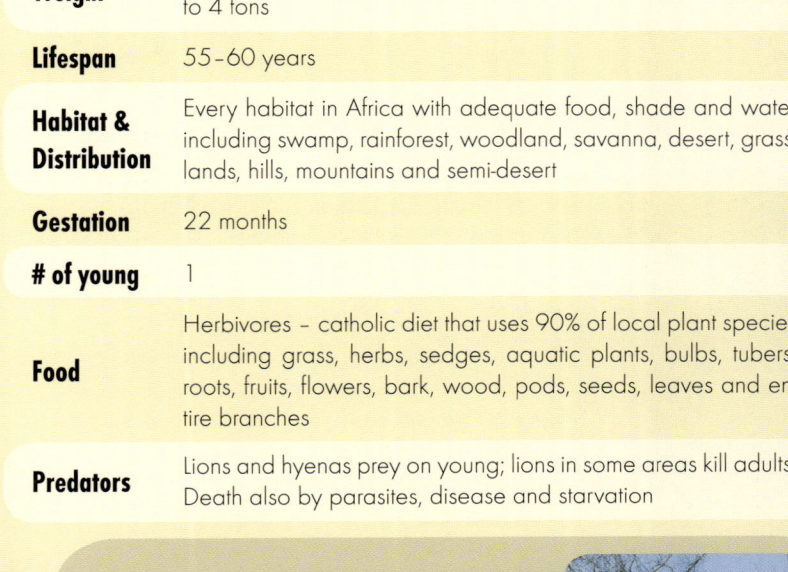

Elephants are **destructive feeders** and push trees over to access green leaves on the crown. They debark trees to access the inner cambium layer (vascular tissue), which contains the water and nutrients being transported up or down the stem of the tree (depending on the season). If debarking encircles the trunk (ring-barking), the trees can no longer transport nutrients from the roots to the leaves and will die. Even in social displays, bulls may push trees over to intimidate rivals.

These apparently **wasteful actions have positive ecological repercussions**. Fallen trees provide browse at ground level to smaller herbivores and they also create microhabitats for the breeding and survival of ground creatures like rodents, reptiles, small mammals and birds, especially once the grass grows up through the branches and creates a tangle impenetrable to larger predators. Nutrients from fallen trees are also recycled back into the soil through decay, as ash after fire or by termites which feed on the wood. Fruit knocked out of trees during an elephant's feeding activities becomes available to other smaller animals.

Elephants practise a **matriarchal society**. Females live in herds of related individuals with their successive offspring. The oldest cow, known as the matriarch, leads the herd. Because elephants are long-lived animals and **acquire knowledge through experience and learning** (much like humans do), the matriarch, being oldest, has the broadest cultural knowledge. She uses this to lead her herd. Migratory routes are passed on between generations and the matriarch leads her herd to traditional sources of food and water during different seasons and times of hardship. **Bulls leave the herd once they reach puberty** (at about 12–14 years old) to live alone or in small bachelor groups. Old bulls may be accompanied by a few younger ones known as askaris. These individuals may learn social skills from the older bull and may also afford him protection in his old age.

Elephants have **unique teeth** amongst mammals. Each tooth is large and oval in shape, flattened on the surface with transverse ridges of enamelled dentine (to which the generic name *Loxodonta* refers). They produce six sets of molars in a lifetime. Two are fully emerged at a time on each side of the mouth on both jaws. The molar in front is gradually worn down as the elephant feeds on an array of coarse material and the next molar then pushes from the back forcing the existing teeth forward to replace the eroding section. Every new molar is larger than the previous in proportion to the elephant's changing body size. Eventually only the final molar M6 remains. Once this tooth has worn away the elephant will slowly starve to death. This happens by 60 years of age, sometimes sooner if the elephant lives in an area where it is prone to eating large quantities of hard, woody material.

An elephant's trunk is a unique apparatus not shared by any other mammal. It evolved to assist the elephant with the processing of the large amounts of different kinds of food that it eats. It is formed by the merging of the nose and the muscles of the upper lip and it provides a sensitive organ which can be employed as an arm, a straw and a nose. Comprising thousands of muscles (between 50 000 and 100 000) the trunk can stretch to reach and grasp things or shrink to compact itself for travel. Air is breathed in through the trunk or it may suck up water (litres at a time) or dust to spew over the body or fruit to place in the mouth. The trunk is powerful enough to break stems or strip whole branches of their foliage but it is also dexterous enough to scoop up piles of small items from the ground or to grasp a single plum-sized berry with the finger-like protrusions at the tip. It also arranges the food inside the elephant's mouth to avoid damage from thorny branches. So complex is the fine control involved in operating a trunk that young elephants take some time to master the skill, clumsily flopping it around until they are about 3 months old.

Elephants have five toenails on their front feet and four on their hind feet. They **use their toenails when feeding**. Grasping a tuft of grass in the trunk, an elephant will slice it at the base of the tuft with the toenails to neatly sever the roots and adhering soil to ensure an earth-free mouthful. Elephants also use their feet to scrape together piles of fruit or to dislodge short grass which can then be scooped up with the trunk.

A particular kind of **tinaeid moth** only occurs in regions where elephants are found as they specialise in nesting in the sole of a dead elephant's foot. The hard curled-up sole is long lasting and provides a safe haven for the developing eggs. Once the eggs hatch, the larvae consume the dried leather before burrowing into the ground to pupate into adults.

Elephants walk on their toes. The 'heel' is supported with a cartilaginous pad that acts as a shock and noise absorber. The pad splays out when the sole of the foot makes contact with the ground and shrinks again when the foot is lifted. The forefeet are larger to support the enormous weight of the head, trunk and tusks.

African elephant
Loxodonta africana

The **ears of an African elephant are enormous** with a bull elephant having ears 2 m x 1,2 m and weighing 20 kg each. These have multiple uses. They are used for hearing with the large area acting like a satellite dish to channel sounds into the eardrum, the opening of which is in front of the flap. They are **used to express mood** during social interactions. They also **play a vital role in thermoregulation** (heat control), effectively dissipating three-quarters of the heat needed to maintain a constant body temperature. The ears comprise 20% of the elephant's entire surface area and the otherwise thick skin of the elephant is thinnest over the ears and well supplied with blood capillaries that run close to the surface. An elephant can **pump all of its blood through its ears every 20 minutes** (up to 12 litres a minute) and by flapping the ears or spraying dust, mud or water behind them, this cools the blood in the capillaries which then flows back into the body. On cooler days, elephants hold their ears close to their bodies conserving the heat in the capillaries, which has the opposite effect.

If elephant herds become too large they may split up, with a group of closely related cows and their young forming a new herd. The separated herds or **kinship groups remain in contact** with each other due to their relatedness. These groups are also linked to more distantly related herds in what are known as clans. Clans will frequent particular home ranges which are associated with the ranges of bull elephants. Within an area, bull elephants all recognise each other and a local hierarchy (abandoned during times of musth) is established from early in life through ritualised play fighting. These encounters continue until bulls are 40 years old and demonstrate, without risk of injury, a particular individual's strength.

Elephants have an **array of acute sensory perceptions** to compensate for (or possibly resulting in) relatively limited eyesight. Their eyes, which are the same size as a human's and appear dwarfed on their enormous heads, only permit clear focusing up to about 50 m. The large ears actuate **excellent hearing** and their sense of smell is sharp. They use their trunks to collect scents at various levels, often lifting them into the wind when investigating a particular intrusion. These scents stimulate the olfactory tissue but chemical clues collected simultaneously can also be placed into the **chemo-receptors** of the organ of Jacobsen on the palate, for deciphering.

From a relatively early age, **female elephants practise allo-mothering** or 'nannying' during which they guide calves assisting them over obstacles, teaching them what to eat (some calves even remove food from other elephants' mouths to learn what to eat) and protecting them just as the mother does. This provides a support network for the calves as well as important practice to the young cows for when they become mothers. While young female elephants practise how to become successful mothers, **young bulls spend time practising head-butting** and play mounting to establish rank between themselves and to develop skills that they will use to win dominance later in life.

The weight of an elephant's enormous head is reduced by **honeycomb-like** formations in the skull.

analene Rautenbach

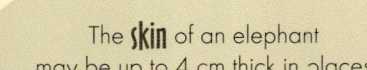

The concept of an **elephant graveyard** is much disputed. One explanation may be that elephants on their last set of molars spend lots of time at water where the food is softer and if they cannot eat then at least they can drink. Several old elephants may then die at the same waterhole if it is the only available water in an area, giving the impression of a graveyard.

The **skin** of an elephant may be up to 4 cm thick in places (legs, forehead, trunk and back). It is thinnest behind the ears.

Elephants are believed to **grieve their dead** as they movingly pick up tusks, skulls and bones of dead elephants carrying them around or scenting them with their trunks. Elephants will also go to the aid of sick or wounded members of the herd.

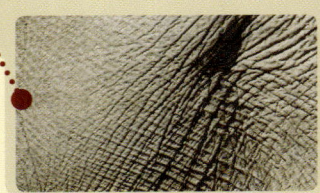

Elephants eat a variety of plants to meet their enormous dietary requirements. **An adult bull consumes 300 kg of food a day** (5% of its body weight). They also feed constantly (even through the night) in order to take in sufficient food. Elephants are hindgut fermenters putting all their food into a single stomach. The most digestible material is quickly absorbed while the more fibrous contents (accounting for 60% of what was ingested) are excreted.

Through-put is rapid (19 hours) and the expulsion of so much undigested material quickly makes room for more to ensure a constant flow of nutrients through the system. During times of drought when food quality is low, this allows the elephant ample opportunity to extract adequate nutrients and prevents time being wasted on the digestion of food that requires lots of energy to break down.

A bull elephant may expel up to 155 kg of dung in a day. This is utilised by dung beetles as well as baboons and birds which pick through the compost for undigested seeds and fruit. Some seeds (like those of the marula, *Acacias* and the baobab) that have passed through the stomach of the elephant are then more prone to germination due to the chemical and physical scarification of their seed coats, which allows better moisture penetration. These seeds then conveniently begin life in a pile of nutrient-rich compost.

Elephants practise **geophagia** (chew soil) to supplement mineral deficiencies in their diet. They use their toenails to loosen dirt and scoop it into their mouths with their trunk. They may also crowd at sodium-rich water supplies to access the salts they need.

Both bull and cow elephants have **temporal glands** on the sides of their foreheads. While bulls secrete from these profusely during musth, cows and youngsters also secrete from these glands when under stress. Elephants may **collect chemical clues** from one another during greeting ceremonies that involve the scenting of these glands with the end of the trunk.

In contrast to the bulls, female elephants may mate and conceive from as early as 8 years old. The **first mating may be fairly traumatic** for a young cow due to the large size difference between her, at about 1 200 kg, and the mature musth bull that mounts her and probably weighs in at 5 or 6 tons.

Although puberty in bull elephants arrives at about 12 years of age, they only get their first chance to mate from age 25, but usually closer to 35 years old. Elephant bulls must enter a **state of elevated testosterone** levels known as *musth* before they are permitted to mate with a cow. During musth an elephant bull **dribbles strong-smelling urine profusely**, discolouring the inside of his legs and penis, and **secretions from the temporal glands** stain the sides of his head. Bulls become relatively aggressive due to high blood testosterone and they impulsively **travel long distances** taking them away from the areas where they may be related to cows. Along the way they emit an **infrasonic musth call** to attract oestrus cows and they challenge any other bull that they may encounter.

Bigger, older bulls quickly suppress musth in younger males that they encounter and these give way to their superiors without much confrontation. This eliminates inexperienced bulls from the race. Equally sized bulls will fight (sometimes to the death) with powerful head and tusk clashes, twisting to expose the vulnerable throat and neck for attack with the tusks. The winner (holding the strongest and thus most desirable genes) then gains access to the oestrus cow in question, who will only mate with a musth bull. Young bulls only come into musth for short periods of a few days or weeks while older bulls may be in musth for months at a time.

African elephant
Loxodonta africana

Elephants are **creatures of habit** and although they need to feed constantly, they do follow a fairly regular daily routine especially during drier times of the year. Resting usually takes place during the hottest part of the day after a drink or mud bath at a favoured site. The whole **herd will take to the shade to rest**. Once the heat diminishes, they will continue feeding into the night and may take a second rest at midnight. Large elephants usually **sleep standing up or leaning against a tree** or large boulder but smaller animals will lie down on their sides to sleep. The herd will feed again during the early hours of the morning, continuing until they reach the waterhole again during the heat of the day.

Mud-wallowing or dust-bathing is another form of thermoregulatory exercise used by elephants. Applying a layer of moisture or dust to the sweat gland-free skin traps a layer of cooler air close to the skin and also prevents excessive exposure of the skin to the sun. Once the mud dries elephants will rub against hard objects like rocks or tree trunks to remove the itchy pieces. In the process they also work free parasites entombed in the dried mud. An elephant's habit of wallowing in mud has the ecological repercussion of creating or broadening depressions in the ground, which subsequently form pans that hold rainwater that can be used by other species.

Elephants are especially **partial to bathing and swimming** during which time they will either spray themselves down or submerge completely using their trunks as snorkels. Bulls especially are playful during swimming time and they engage in social dominance contests and play fighting while in the water. Bathing also helps to cool their large thick-skinned bodies down.

Elephants can be quite spread out and noisy while feeding but should danger threaten, the **whole herd will react immediately**, freezing to test the air before reassembling and slipping silently away. The alarm is raised by a trumpet or a scream and the young animals will head to the centre of the herd while the largest ones will position themselves promptly on the side of the source of danger, forming a barricade impenetrable to even large predators. Cows on the periphery may rush at lions or other threats to encourage them to depart. A very young baby always travels under the mother's belly between her legs to ensure its safety and in order for the mother to assist it over obstacles and to keep it cool. During normal activities baby elephants are seldom more than 1 or 2 m from an adult (and the mother is always nearby) and they are constantly touched as reassurance.

One of the elephants' major habitat requirements is access to water. Elephants **need to drink daily** to facilitate the digestion of the many kilograms of coarse material that they eat. They will take in between 100 and 160 litres of water a day, sometimes in one sitting. They are fussy drinkers and prefer to drink clean water, which they access by digging a hole alongside a muddy waterhole and allowing the water to filter into the excavation before drinking it. They are also able to smell underground water and frequently dig holes into which the subterranean water seeps and from which they can then drink their fill. These pools are available to other animals once the elephant is finished drinking, a valuable resource to the ecosystem during dry times. At times of shortage elephants **will travel long distances in pursuit of water** and are known to chase off other animals like zebra, sable, warthog and buffalo if limited sources are dwindling.

The Cape (or African) buffalo is an enormous and **formidable bovid** with a reputation for a dangerously moody temperament. Their size, strength and propensity to charge determinedly without warning have resulted in their inclusion in the Big Five – the top African animals to see in the Lowveld. It is also considered the most dangerous of the five to hunt.

Buffalo have **excellent senses**. Although sight and hearing are less well developed, their sense of smell is acute and they use it to find food or to detect predators. Buffalo are inquisitive and will approach sources of interest with their noses outstretched to pick up olfactory clues as to the object's identity. Buffalo also use smell to communicate socially. It is believed that the coordination of the numerous members within a herd is controlled by **olfactory cues** that afford recognition of individuals and allow the grouping of animals into sub-herds. In this regard **vocal communication** is also significant. Buffalo emanate cow-like bellows continuously as they move to maintain contact.

Because of the vast quantity of coarse material eaten, buffalo **depend on regular access to drinking water**. They drink daily, sometimes even twice a day during drier times. The approach of a large herd of buffalo to a waterhole in winter is a noisy and spectacular affair. They move resolutely in the direction of a waterhole during the late afternoon and the approach of the columns of fast-moving animals can be detected some distance off by the presence of an **advancing cloud of dust**. The herd will arrive and submerge belly deep in the water to drink. They may consume up to 35 litres of water at a time, drinking this up in mere minutes.

Buffalo are only moderately sexually dimorphic (i.e. the differences between the sexes are subtle). The older **bulls** are black and often caked with dried mud from wallowing. They have **massive horns** with bosses that meet in the middle to form an enormous 'helmet' used in combat. Younger bulls have hair on their bosses.

Female buffalo are more red-brown in colour and they have narrower horns and bosses. Juveniles also have a browner colour but can be discerned from the females by their hairy coating which becomes progressively sparser with age.

Both sexes have large, hairy ears that hang down below the horns.

Cape (African) buffalo
Syncerus caffer

Size	1,4 m (at shoulder)
Weight	Male: 800 kg; Female: 750 kg
Lifespan	23 years
Habitat & Distribution	Wide range – wherever there is suitable forage, access to water and shade
Gestation	11 months
# of young	1
Food	Bulk grazers – prefer long grass. Take small amount of browse in times of drought
Predators	Lions and humans

The **advantage of rank** within a herd of buffalo is that more dominant individuals feed ahead of and in the centre of the herd and they do not have to contend with trampled pastures. This privileged position also affords these animals the best protection from predators. High-ranked bulls benefit from better access to oestrus cows.

Rank in bull buffalo is a product of their **fighting ability** which is proportional to age and hence size. Although various forms of posturing generally keeps encounters between males civil, strength contests can quickly be settled through **head-on clashes**, the impact of which is absorbed by the enormous bosses. The impact of such combat can be likened to a car hitting a brick wall at 50 km/hour.

Very **old buffalo bulls** that have passed their reproductive peak (from 10 years old) are usually found alone or in small groups. These animals are sometimes nicknamed 'dagha-boys'. Dagha is the Zulu word for mud and refers to their pastime of wallowing in water or mud. These individuals often have skin diseases or old battle wounds and it is believed that the water and mud helps to soothe these aches and pains. Food surrounding the localised waterholes that they frequent is also likely to be softer and more easily digested. These animals lack the protection of a herd and are susceptible to attacks from lions. The cumulative result is that dagha-boys are extremely **temperamental** and dangerous if approached on foot.

Buffalo are very **heat sensitive**. To avoid excessive exposure to hot temperatures, buffalo will graze early in the morning or late afternoon and will often feed through the cooler night during hotter parts of the year. As soon as daytime temperatures rise too high, buffalo will **move into the shade to rest** and chew the cud (an important process to digest the coarse grass material they ingest). They also rest for parts of the night during which time they **lie down touching one another**.

Buffalo are **bulk grazers** taking large quantities of long grass while they continuously move through an area. A herd of feeding buffalo sound much like a gentle bushfire crackling through dry grass. They feed unselectively (despite being ruminants) selecting quantity over quality to sustain their large bodies. In the process of feeding, buffalo trample pastures and reduce long, less palatable grasslands to a height and quality (when it re-shoots) more easily utilised by zebra and subsequently wildebeest. This is known as **grazing succession**. Buffalo have a wide row of incisor teeth which they use in conjunction with their tongues to crop grass swiftly while they move. They lack the movable lips of more selective feeders.

Sometimes buffalo will **wallow** in mud to keep themselves cool during the hottest part of the day. This activity is, however, mostly practised by the bulls as it also plays a role in dominance displays. Bulls will roll in the mud or toss mud with their horns to denote their social status. Access to limited wallows depends on an individual's rank in the herd hierarchy – some bulls dominate others and all bulls are superior to cows.

Due to the necessity to find suitable grassy pastures and water on an ongoing basis, buffalo are **not territorial** although they do move within more familiar home ranges which more or less exclude other buffalo herds. Home ranges expand or shrink depending on the availability or shortage of resources.

When **threatened**, buffalo raise the alarm with a distinct distressed bellow to which members of the herd respond as a group. The calves and younger animals are sheltered alongside the cows in the centre of the herd while the adult males defend the flanks and rear. Since they are such large bulky animals, putting up a united front against predators is more effective than trying to flee clumsily. As a unit, buffalo will **mob** offending predators or **stampede** unexpectedly and they are often able to hold their own against even whole prides of lions. If they do flee, they run at a speed conducive to the herd remaining safely clumped together although an individual buffalo can reach **speeds** of almost **60 km/hour**.

The movements of a herd of buffalo are determined by specific individuals known as **'pathfinders'**. These are not necessarily dominant animals but they simply act as leaders to the herd. Each sub-herd within the major herd also has a pathfinder which will lead its members when the herd splits up.

Cape (African) buffalo
Syncerus caffer

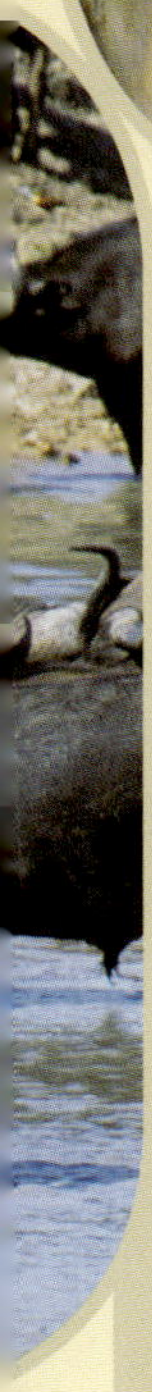

Buffalo bulls test the **reproductive condition** of cows through **flehmen** whereby urine particles are pumped into the organ of Jacobsen on the palate via a muscular facial grimace to detect the presence of steroid hormones. A cow in heat will be guarded by a bull but cows are uncooperative and their evasive activity attracts other bulls which subsequently replace the less dominant contenders. By the time the cow reaches the peak of her oestrus, the likeliest partner will by then be a dominant, gene-superior bull.

Buffalo are **gregarious** and live in mixed herds often numbering hundreds of individuals. These herds may increase or decrease in number seasonally. The **main herd** is subdivided into smaller, more closely related units or **clans** of cows and their offspring which cluster and move or rest together. During abundant summer times, the herds will segregate into these smaller units, joining up again when resources are isolated in the dry season. Cows are arranged within the sub-herds according to **rank**, which improves when they have young calves. Adult bulls are affiliated to and preside over the clans. Within the larger herd, a bull's status is delineated according to its size and age. When larger herds split, bulls may associate in age-related bachelor groups. Young bulls only get an opportunity to mate at 7 or 8 years old (in spite of reaching maturity at 5 years). By isolating in bachelor groups these youngsters are able to avoid the ongoing male power struggle within the larger herd for a time.

Buffalo usually **mate and calve** during the rainy season when there is an abundance of highly nutritious green grass to sustain the lactating cows. Cows will give birth in the presence of the herd but may be temporarily left behind while the calf gains the strength it needs to keep up. Although a newborn **calf is able to stand in just 10 minutes** it takes a few weeks for it to overcome its feeble sense of coordination and clumsy running ability.

White rhino are the **second largest land mammals on earth** and as such take their place amongst the Big 5 – historically those animals most dangerous to hunt but now the most sought after by tourists.

The wide muzzle (20 cm) comprises a more sensitive upper lip (which is used to manoeuvre grass clumps into the mouth) and a hard lower lip (against which the top lip presses to sever the grass). Both lips are swiped upwards to effect the neat cropping of grass.

No incisors are involved at all in ingesting grass but broad, intricately enamelled molars inside the cheeks provide a grinding surface for mastication. A rhino crops the grass continuously, moving its head in a semi-circle and then stepping forward to repeat the action. White rhino **maintain their own neatly cropped pastures** in stands of favoured grass species (like *Themeda triandra*, *Panicum maximum* and *Urochloa mossambicensis*) which are often well concealed amongst taller grass. They rotate the use of their favourite feeding areas so as not to obliterate them.

White rhino have large, elongated heads that terminate in a **set of broad, square-shaped lips**. The shape of the lips led to the naming of this rhinoceros as Dutch settlers referred to the 'wyd' mouth (meaning wide) and colonialists misinterpreted this to mean white.

Rhino have relatively **poor eyesight** and can only really see well at close range. They do, however, respond to movement at greater distances. To compensate, the **senses of hearing and smell are very well developed** and both are employed for the purposes of communication and detecting danger. A rhino's ears are constantly moving, rotating independently in all directions to collect auditory clues. When a sound is detected, both ears focus in that direction. The ears are conveniently placed on top of the long head to collect sounds, while the low-slung muzzle is optimally placed to smell.

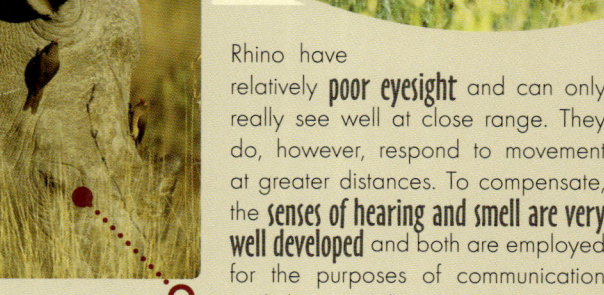

White rhino
Ceratotherium simum

Size	1,8 m (at shoulder)
Weight	Male: up to 2 400 kg; Female: average 1 600 kg
Lifespan	About 40 years
Habitat & Distribution	Flat undulating terrain with grasslands to feed, thick cover to rest up and water to drink and wallow
Gestation	16 months
# of young	1
Food	Selective grazer (certain species); prefers short, fresh growth
Predators	Humans; calves preyed on by lions and hyenas

The collective noun for a group of rhino is appropriately 'a crash of rhino'.

White rhino have massive necks with a large nuchal hump over the shoulders. The thick, short neck supports the **large head which is held low to the ground** in order for the rhino to feed on grass, the lowest-growing form of vegetation. Having its head close to the ground also facilitates the use of its nostrils to detect olfactory (scent-related) clues regarding territory and the location of other rhino. Rhino rely on their sense of smell since eyesight is limited. The powerful neck also provides the force behind the defensive horns.

The rhino's most **prominent feature is its horns**. They are weapons of defence used during bouts of combat or to protect itself and its offspring from predators. Horns are made of keratin (the same substance as fingernails) and grow 2–6 cm in a year and continue to grow throughout life. They are often worn down through usage and tend to be longer and thinner in cows, which do not engage them as frequently as do bulls. The record horn length for a white rhino is 1,58 m.

Rhino practise **geophagia** (chewing of soil) to supplement minerals deficient in their all-grass diet.

White rhino are fond of **wallowing in mud** in order to help them cope with excessive summer heat conditions. A good caking of mud prevents sunburn and keeps a layer of moisture close to the skin to assist with keeping cool. Once dried, the mud also acts as a parasite-removing wax treatment that the rhino will rub off their skin against trees, rocks or termite mounds. Rhino are prone to reusing their rubbing posts, which eventually become quite smooth and polished. They may also use these posts to scratch hard to reach areas such as the inner legs and belly. While they wallow in the mud, terrapins will also pluck parasites off the rhino's hide (see p. 192).

Because of the large quantity of fibrous grass that a rhino must consume to satisfy its energy requirements, it requires daily (if not twice daily) **access to drinking water** to assist with digestion. Rhino usually make their way to water late in the afternoon or even after dark. Because of their reliance on water, bulls that do not have a water source within their own territory will have to leave their turf and enter other bulls' territories in order to drink. So long as an intruding rhino behaves submissively, territorial bulls will tolerate water-related visits from neighbours. A bull rhino shows its submission by urinating in a stream (on his own territory he would spray). He may also flatten his ears and squeal to reassure the territory owner of his innocuous intentions. If water is scarce, rhino can go for up to 4 days without drinking.

When territorial bulls encounter one another along their boundaries, their responses are ritualised and posturing displays will satisfy one another of their independent status. However, when there is a new territory to claim or an oestrus cow in question, **bulls will fight**. Their primary weapons are their horns with which they will spar and attempt to hook one another. The skin over a rhino's shoulders is 25 mm thick to help reinforce this area against blows from an opponent's horn. Fights can be fatal.

Red-billed oxpeckers are almost always in attendance of rhino. They glean ticks and other parasites off the skin of the rhino, supplying themselves with a meal and their hosts with a free grooming session. The oxpeckers also perform the useful service of warning the sight-impaired rhinos of approaching threats by flying up noisily when disturbed. Oxpeckers can also be a useful indication to humans of the presence of rhino nearby.

To demarcate his territory a bull rhino employs a number of visual and olfactory signals. The bull patrols well-used paths to establish and reinforce boundaries. While patrolling, the bull will **urine-spray backwards** onto bushes and other conspicuous objects. Every 30 m or so, the bull will also **create visual scrape-markings** with his feet that simultaneously become impregnated with his urine. As he continues his patrol, the scent is laid in the form of an olfactory (smell) trail wherever his feet touch. This is also achieved by **kicking his dung** with his hind feet after defecating. Intermittently along the territory boundaries, large accumulations of dung (known as middens) are formed and constantly added to by the bull and even by his neighbour. Cows (and subordinate bulls) will deposit their dung on a bull's midden as and when they pass but refrain from breaking up their dung in the manner of the territorial bull. These sites provide important information to the territory owners such as when and who has passed through their turf.

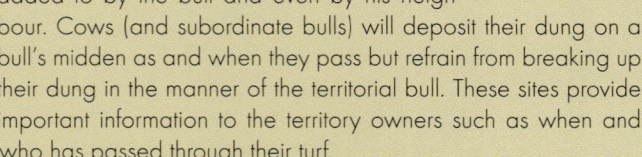

White rhino females are fairly gregarious (live with others of their own kind) and it is quite unusual to find a cow alone. A female is most often accompanied by her latest calf but sometimes the previous calf (who would have been chased off when the newest one arrived) will also accompany her. Cows without calves will often pair up and newly independent adults may form groups of the same (or even mixed) sexes of up to five individuals. Where there is good grazing or localised water, white rhino cows and their young may form aggregations sometimes numbering 10 or more. Most of the time female rhino live in undefended home ranges that overlap with one another. Sometimes these home ranges can coincide with the territories of up to seven different bulls. Where there is abundant food and water, these ranges may be as small as 6 km^2 but may expand to 20 km^2 during dry and difficult seasons.

White rhino **bulls are fiercely territorial** and are always found alone unless courting a female. Although they mature at around 4 years old, bulls are not usually able to contend with other bulls for territories until they are 12 years old. So long as they demonstrate submissiveness to the older and larger territory holders, younger bulls are tolerated. A bull rhino defends an area between 0,75 and 14 km^2 depending on the availability of resources. His territorial boundaries typically follow natural barriers like watercourses, topographical ridges and even man-made roads.

Rhino must surely hold the record for the **most protracted mating**. Copulation lasts a full 30 minutes and is achieved in only one mounting. Bulls find cows in oestrus by picking up hormones in the urine they leave behind when traversing a bull's territory. Rhino practise flehmen to check for the steroid hormones in the cow's urine. They do this by pumping airborne particles into the organ of Jacobsen on the palate by means of a facial grimace that turns up the lips. Once a cow has been identified as being on heat, the bull goes to great lengths to prevent her from leaving his turf and chases off any other males in the vicinity quite vociferously with snorts and shrieks. The cow may not be a willing captive and often the bull will be aggressively rejected. The male, however, **shows great persistence in herding the female** – chasing her, squealing and even clashing horns. Courtship can last 14–20 days and the pair will remain in each other's company for up to 6 days after mating.

White rhino
Ceratotherium simum

Although they seem quite ungainly, rhino are able to **charge at a speed of 40 km/hour** if they need to. Rhino that are stressed will show displacement behaviour which may take the form of curling up the tail, a nervous bouncy gait around the same spot, turning side on to the disturbance or rubbing the horn on the ground. Cows with young are especially protective. When a cow and her offspring flee from danger, the calf always runs in front.

Rhino are active throughout both the day and night and spend at least half their time feeding in order to satisfy the nutritional demands of their huge bodies. They prefer to **rest during the heat of the day** under the cover of dense bush. They also take refuge in thickets should the weather turn particularly cold or windy. When they sleep they do so relatively soundly, breathing heavily. During sleep the ears may be seen instinctively flicking in all directions and rhino can react to disturbing sounds with impressive speed if the need arises.

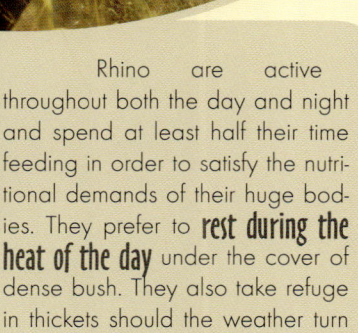

White rhino differ from black rhino in several ways. Black rhino are smaller overall. They have a shorter head which is carried higher up on the shoulders to accommodate their browsing (not grazing) habits. The **black rhino has a prehensile hook-shaped lip** to help it secure leaves and twigs (compared to the wide mouth that the white rhino uses to graze). Twigs are cropped at a 45° angle due to the shape of the black rhino's teeth and this angle is clearly identifiable in the twigs in their droppings. The ears of the black rhino are smaller and rounder and it lacks the large nuchal hump of the white rhino over the shoulders. The black rhino is one of Africa's top 10 most endangered animals.

Common mammals

Impala are **very common antelope** in the Lowveld but they are also one of the most **superbly adapted** species in this area.

Impala typically **inhabit ecotone regions** (the transitional zone between two types of habitat, in this case between grassland and woodland). Ecotones characteristically carry high parasite loads and in this regard impala need to be able to combat the effects of excessive ticks on their bodies. They employ several methods:

Impala are **fastidious groomers**. They spend a large amount of time seeing to their personal hygiene, evident in their shiny coats. For this job, they have modified teeth. Their lower incisors are slightly loose in their sockets and splay open to provide a comb as the teeth pass through the impala's coat, successfully hooking out dirt and parasites.

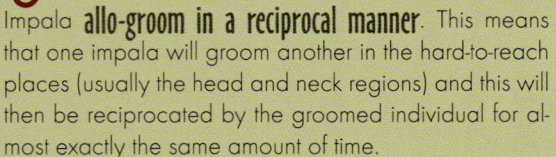

Impala **allo-groom in a reciprocal manner**. This means that one impala will groom another in the hard-to-reach places (usually the head and neck regions) and this will then be reciprocated by the groomed individual for almost exactly the same amount of time.

Impala are the smallest antelope that allow **oxpeckers** on their backs. These small birds act as grooming assistants removing ticks and other parasites from the impala's pelage (see p. 178). During the rut when males are too busy to self-groom and too territorial to allow allo-grooming, they accumulate six times the parasite load present on the herd females and as a result have many more oxpeckers in attendance.

Impala maximise on whatever food is available. Where most antelope are either predominantly browsers or grazers, impala are **mixed feeders** and will browse leaves and graze grass. They tend to browse more in winter when food is scarce and graze in summer as grass has more protein and less secondary compounds to digest when it is freshly sprouted.

Impala
Aepyceros melampus

Size	Male: ± 0,9 m (at shoulder)
Weight	Male: about 50 kg; Female: about 40 kg
Lifespan	Maximum 12 years
Habitat & Distribution	Bushveld ecotone species – woodland areas especially *Acacia* and mopane woodland, needs cover and water
Gestation	6,5 months
# of young	1 lamb
Food	Impala are mixed feeders: they browse leaves, graze grass, and also eat fruit and flowers
Predators	Large and medium carnivores, pythons, baboons, large birds of prey take young lambs

Impala are **water dependent** and will always be within a 5 km radius of a water source where they will drink daily.

Impala are often found **associating with other species** while they feed. Often in the case of other herbivores like warthogs, this is simply due to a mutually desired food source but animals in mixed feeding parties also benefit from shared vigilance and warning systems. Baboons and impala associate often. Impala pick up scraps of fruit or flowers dropped by baboons feeding in fruiting trees and while they feast, impala provide vigilance. There is seldom an impala in a feeding group that has not got its head up and watching for danger. As one head goes down to feed again, another pops up to watch while chewing a mouthful. Baboons also offer early warning to the impala for predators as they have better vantage from high up in the trees.

Impala have **excellent senses**. Their large ears detect sounds easily and their huge eyes provide them with excellent vision. Because an impala's most imminent survival threat comes in the form of predators, they (like most antelope) have side-positioned eyes which afford them excellent peripheral vision. Once danger of whatever form is detected, impala employ a loud alarm snort to alert the other members of the group. Although this seems very neighbourly, impala do this to spur the rest of the herd into flight and as they scatter explosively in all directions, the ensuing chaos works to shield the individual.

Pilo-erection is a technique used by mammals for different reasons. It refers to the ability of most mammals to raise the hair on their bodies, just like goose bumps in humans. Impala employ pilo-erection on cooler mornings and at this time their usually shiny coats take on a duller, darker appearance. **By raising the hair on their bodies** they trap a layer of air close to the skin, which warms up from the impala's body heat and in turn keeps the animal a little more insulated against the cold.

Impala females and young live throughout the year in **breeding herds**. Males associate with breeding herds and live in bachelor groups outside the rutting season. This group association is known as 'selfish herds' as they **provide safety in numbers**, basically reducing any single individual's chance of being the one that gets eaten! Impala, being the most common antelope in the Lowveld, have a host of predators including lions, leopards, cheetahs, spotted hyenas, jackals, caracals, pythons and even chacma baboons on occasion (the males catch the lambs).

Impala are **very athletic antelope** able to execute jumps of about 3 m high and 12 m long. This suits their wooded environment as they can jump over bushes instead of having to navigate around them. Impala also employ a gait known as 'the rocking horse' gait. This is where the impala rocks between its front and hind limbs in a slower canter as it flees. This gait is believed to indicate health and fitness to predators, demonstrating to the pursuer that it is not worth its while to try and catch that particular individual. Young impala also bound in this fashion, apparently in play. This probably serves a more vital function in the form of toning the muscles required for the athleticism key to their survival.

To further succeed as herd individuals, impala have **three black lines on the rump** which are 'follow me' signs. It stands to benefit one impala to have another individual running behind it should there be a predator in pursuit, and to have another in front of it should there be a potential ambush ahead. The effect of inducing others to follow automatically creates this 'middleman' safety effect.

Impala
Aepyceros melampus

Males mark the no-man's land between territories with **vast middens** of pelleted dung. These are often visible on the roads in the Lowveld. They also distribute these beacons randomly throughout a territory. Females will add to the middens when they pass by and in this way males gain olfactory information about the whereabouts of females within their turf.

The **black glands** on the ankles of impalas' back legs are unique to the species. They are called metatarsal glands and despite much investigation, the actual function of these glands is still uncertain. They are apparently activated when an impala kicks up its hind legs when running and it is thought that the resultant scent trail may play some sort of role in regrouping the herd after a threat has scattered them.

One of the impala's most successful tactics in remaining numerous is their **breeding strategy**.

At the end of January, shorter day lengths trigger an increase in testosterone in the males and they separate out of their bachelor groups and begin the arduous task of **setting up territories**. Ideally these need to contain good food and access to water – the resources that will lure the females. Rams rush about chasing contenders away, tails extended and they issue fierce roars that might confuse first-time listeners into believing the source of the noise to be more than a mere impala! Females too are herded into the territory in this fashion. More serious encounters between rams will involve **horn clashes**. The month of May is the peak of the rut and by this time, the males' cavorting has induced the females to come into oestrus. This is a short-lived period for impala ewes. Within about a three-week period all the females will be mated. This has the knock-on effect that by late November or early December, all the impala lambs in an area arrive within about a three-week period. This **flood of newborn impala** provides a glut for predators but even they cannot eat all the lambs and a large proportion survives to bolster the impala population. The intensity of the May rut is such that males are so busy herding females and warding off intruders that they do not feed or groom and they can thus only manage to hold territories for about 8 days. This ensures different genes are introduced into a given herd and that only the strongest contestants get to mate.

Impala use a **camouflage strategy** called counter-shading. They have a darker colour on their backs than on their flanks and the flanks are darker than the pale belly. This effect reverses the natural three-dimensional effect caused by sun falling on an object, i.e. sun from above illuminates the top of the object most, the sides slightly less and the underparts the least. The result is that to a predator that sees in hues of light and shadow rather than pure colour vision, the impala will appear two-dimensional and thus not stand out amongst the landscape as much as if it was three-dimensional.

There has long been a **myth** that impala are able to delay giving birth until conditions are favourable. This is not the case. Later births in areas with poor nutrition are caused by later conceptions. A full-term foetus of any kind needs to be evacuated from the birth canal lest it no longer fits. An animal cannot arrest the growth of a foetus. Some ewes will reabsorb foetuses during unfavourable conditions but this takes place very early on in pregnancy. Others may abort and these carcasses are seldom found due to scavengers.

Kudu are the **second tallest antelope in southern Africa**, the tallest being eland. They have remarkable athletic abilities and are able to jump easily over 2 m high fences. Some records show that bulls have cleared 3,5 m fences under extreme conditions.

When kudu take flight from a threat, they **lift their tails up** revealing the fluffy white underside. This provides a beacon in the dense bush for other animals, particularly young to follow. This is known as a 'follow me' sign. The white tail also acts as flash colouration. It attracts the attention of the predator which then focuses on the white tail as it pursues the animal. As soon as the kudu stops and drops its tail, the predator loses the obvious beacon it was following and will struggle to relocate its quarry.

Kudu live in **thicket habitats**. They are very secretive and tend to freeze if startled, allowing their disruptive colouration to blend them into their dappled environment. Disruptive markings are lines or marks that break the solid outline of an animal to camouflage them. The white chevron on the kudu's face and the creamy stripes down its back also resemble the shafts of light penetrating a canopy of vegetation such as would be present in the environment where they live. When threatened away from cover, their first response is to dart into thick bush where their camouflage works best.

Kudu are **gregarious** meaning they prefer to live together in groups. The females live in small groups of about half a dozen individuals made up of one or two cows and their offspring. Cows tend to have lasting associations with one another. Bulls associate in transitional bachelor groups where they can enjoy safety in numbers while not breeding. Sometimes they will be solitary or accompany a herd if in attendance of a cow in oestrus (even out of the breeding season). Herds of kudu may combine to create aggregations of 20 or so individuals in areas of good feeding.

Kudu
Tragelaphus strepsiceros

Size	Male: 140 cm (at shoulder); Female: 125 cm (at shoulder)
Weight	Male: about 250 kg; Female: about 170 kg
Lifespan	Male: 8–9 years; Female: 15 years
Habitat & Distribution	Thickets especially along rivers; home range is 3–25 km^2
Gestation	9 months (270 days)
# of young	1 calf
Food	Browsers: leaves, herbs, forbs, fruit, flowers, seedpods, succulents, tubers, (new grass)
Predators	Lion, leopard, hyena, caracal

When kudu bulls flee through thicket habitats, they lift their noses to allow their **horns to lie flat** against their backs and thereby prevent them snagging on bushes.

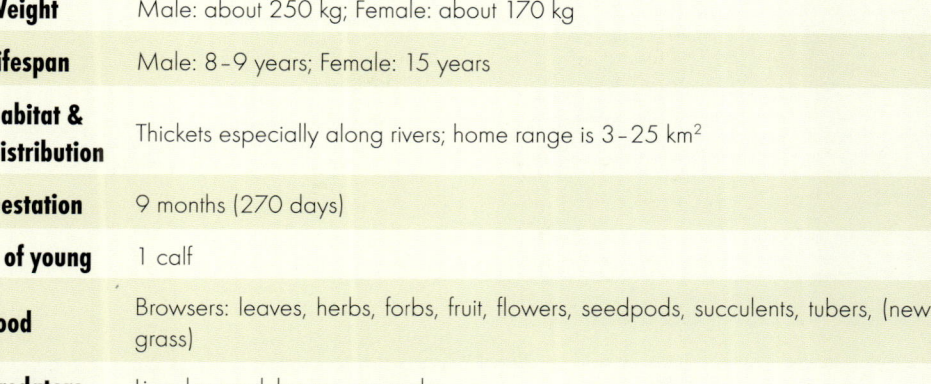

Since sound does not travel easily through dense mediums, **kudu have huge ears** to help them detect even the smallest of noises in the thickets where they live. When listening, kudu focus their ears in the direction of the sound stimuli and in the process take on a curious expression.

The impressiveness of the male kudu has developed to complement their **passive dominance system**. Kudu bulls do not maintain territories and for most of the time are tolerant of one another. But when it comes time to breed, bulls will weigh up their opponents by a show of their good looks. Like two boxers in a ring, opposing kudu will engage in lateral presentation, sizing each other up while marching in a circle head to flank with one another. Swollen necks, raised manes and a stiff-legged gait all serve to make the individual appear more impressive. The inferior contender gives way passively to the more superior. Only if the two animals are equally matched will they engage in horn-clashing combat.

There is a **well-developed sexual dimorphism** in kudu and this has to do with their breeding strategy. Sexual dimorphism means that the male and female look different to one another. The male has the most impressive horns of all the African antelope (record 1,76 metres, average 1,19 metres) and is larger than the female. Male kudu have pale yellowish legs and strong, thick necks with a beard of hair.

Kudu are not particularly water-dependent as they get a lot of moisture from the leaves they browse and the fruit and succulents they eat. They do, however, **drink regularly** visiting waterholes late in the morning when the temperature is usually getting hot.

Kudu have **small hooves** for their body size. Their hind feet step into the track where the front foot has just been. This is known as registering. It is an adaptation to walking quietly.

Wintertime is a stressful time of year for browsers to breed, as food reserves are low. To compound the **stress for rutting kudu bulls**, they only have a short and competitive window of opportunity to breed. Kudu bulls mature relatively late in life at about 5 years old (compared to 2 years maturity in females).

Understandably, the younger, newly sexually matured bulls are easily out-competed for females by the larger more impressive bulls (size increases with age and bigger, older bulls are dominant). The first real occasion for actual breeding by bulls then, only comes at about 7 or 8 years of age.

The late onset of breeding means that bulls **invest great amounts of energy** into displaying and then courting females (known as establishing a tending bond). In the case of equally sized individuals competing for the same cow in heat, serious fighting may occur which often leads to injuries. The energy investment, combined with the lack of nutrition, cold winter temperatures and possible injury, means that kudu bulls often die at the end of the breeding season at only 8 years old.

Kudu
Tragelaphus strepsiceros

Kudu **breed in the wintertime.** The reason for this is so that the calves arrive during the rainy season when there is plentiful browse for the lactating cows. Most calves arrive in February, which is when the grass is longest too. This is vital because kudu calves have a **lying-up period** where the young will hide in the long grass while they grow and gain enough strength to keep up with the herds. This may take between 1 and 3 months. The cows will visit the calves to feed them and keep an eye out for danger. The calves have no scent during this time and so long as they stay still and hidden, they are hard to detect by predators. The kudu cow will remove all traces of the afterbirth by eating it so as not to attract predators into the area where she has given birth.

Kudu are crepuscular. This means that their typical activity periods are early in the morning and late in the afternoon (dusk and dawn). Kudu are **remarkable adapters** and should they be disturbed significantly, they become nocturnal. This is often the case in areas where they co-exist alongside commercial agriculture.

Kudu make use of a very **loud, deep bark** as an alarm call since low frequency sound travels better in dense bush. Kudu make the loudest vocalisation of all antelope.

The common name of this antelope is derived from the **traditional Zulu word** for the animal, *inxala*.

Nyala are the **most striking of antelopes** and also exhibit the greatest sexual dimorphism (difference between the sexes). Females are red-brown in colour and characteristically striped along the ridge of the back with up to 18 white lines. These form the animal's camouflage, breaking up their solid outline and helping them to blend into their thicket habitats. The lines are known as **disruptive markings**. Males are slate grey with up to 14 white stripes along the back and white spots on the flanks and belly (also disruptive markings). The lower part of each leg is yellow in colour and contrasts strongly with the rest of the body. A **shaggy white-tipped mane** extends down the backs and a fringe along the under-neck and belly. Males have **spiralled horns** which females lack. The male's coat plays a vital function in social interactions with other males and is a form of visual communication whereby bulls express their individual impressiveness and superiority.

Because of the **great sexual dimorphism** in the nyala species, the smaller females are considered ewes while the larger males are called bulls. Any antelope the same size or smaller than a female nyala will have their sexes described as rams and ewes and any antelope the same size or larger than a nyala bull will have their sexes described as bulls and cows.

Young male nyala only begin to take on the slate-grey physical appearance of a bull from 14 months old. Up until this point the young males resemble females and are a rusty-red colour and without the mane and yellow legs. It takes a further 10 months before the youngster assumes the full adult pelage. This may be a tactic to reduce negative attention from more mature males or possibly the tawny coat (like the female's) affords the younger animals the better camouflage while they are growing up.

Mature bulls tend to be solitary but will interact with female groups as they encounter them to check whether any of the females are in heat (oestrus). If they are, the male will remain with the herd and try to court the ewe. Males do not defend territories and are tolerant of one another provided there is no oestrus ewe in question. Within a particular area, all males will fit into a local dominance hierarchy maintained by passive displays that prevents aggression when they encounter one another.

Nyala
Tragelaphus angasii

Size	Male: 1,1 m (at shoulder); Female: 0,97m (at shoulder)
Weight	Male: 110 kg; Female: 60 kg
Lifespan	15 years
Habitat & Distribution	Thicket in dry savanna woodland
Gestation	7,5 months
# of young	1
Food	Browsers, but take sprouting grass; strip bark and take fallen fruit, flowers and leaves
Predators	Any medium to large carnivore

Nyala live in **temporary associations** whereby members of the species join up and depart from one another's company freely every couple of hours. The only persisting bonds between nyala exist between a female and her offspring and these (including the most recent and previous calf) are usually found together in small groups. Sometimes family groups may combine temporarily to form slightly larger groups and aggregations of between 30 and 100 individuals form where there is a common resource such as a waterhole or a particularly good feeding site. At these times all but the members of the individual family units ignore one another, but they do all benefit from the collective vigilance such congregations afford.

Nyala will **drink water** whenever it is available but particularly during the dry season when they take a great deal of dry browse material.

Although male nyala do not defend territories, they do exhibit a **variety of status rituals** even in the absence of other nyala. The males gouge up soft soil with their horns and rub their faces and horns on bushes. They lack preorbital glands and no visible scent mark is left behind by these actions so their function is poorly understood. Sometimes males will demonstrate their strength or vent aggression by thrashing bushes, even simultaneously pawing the ground.

Due to their choice of habitat, nyala have developed a deep bark which is given in response to danger. Sound is easily absorbed in dense thickets but the **lower frequency of the bark** is less likely to be muffled by the vegetation. The alarm call of a nyala is also likely to set nearby impala into predator-avoidance action and vice versa. Nyala also react to kudu and baboon alarms.

Nyala regularly **follow troops of foraging baboons** and monkeys in order to benefit from their leftovers and other potential edible items knocked down from the trees. Nyala relish fallen flowers and fruit.

Nyala have **small hooves** for their body size. As they walk, the hind feet step into the position where the front feet have just been. This is known as registering and reduces the amount of noise made with each step.

Nyala
Tragelaphus angasii

The brilliant coat of the male nyala is used in a **visual dominance display known as lateral presentation**. This is a passive method of determining superiority based on physical impressiveness. The winner supersedes the loser with regard to access to oestrus cows. These displays occur at different intensities depending on the response of the contender. When two males engage in lateral presentation, the mane along the neck is raised (called pilo-erection) enhancing the size of the animal and its white colour contrasts superbly with the slate grey flanks and the yellow legs which are lifted slowly in an exaggerated high-step walk as the contestants parade around one another, head to tail. The tail is lifted over the rump to display its white underside and depending on the desired intensity the horns are either lowered and poised to attack (high intensity) or the head is held high (moderate intensity). The animal that **first becomes intimidated by his competitor's good stature** will break off and show his submissiveness by lowering his crest and tail and commencing feeding or grooming. An equal match may lead to actual contact whereby the bulls will engage head to head and push each other and clash horns, sometimes savagely.

Nyala ewes emit a **strange clicked vocalisation** when they come into oestrus. This and urine testing will convince a bull of her condition at which time he will attempt to convince her of his intentions by following her around and nuzzling her between the legs, often lifting her hindquarters right off the ground in the process. Ewes will avoid actually mating with a bull until the final few hours of their period of receptivity, which provides opportunity for the more dominant bulls to supplant the less favourable individuals.

The **thicket habitat** of the nyala provides ideal cover for the calves when they are born. Nyala experience a lying-up period for the first 2 to 3 weeks of their lives during which time they remain hidden to allow them to build up their strength before moving around with the adults. The mother visits her calf to feed and groom it. If it becomes threatened, the calf instinctively flattens itself onto the ground and due to its lack of scent at such a young age, can easily avoid the attention of predators this way.

The bases of the back of a **nyala's ears** are white as is the underside of the fluffy tail, which is raised when the animal takes flight. These devices are 'follow me' symbols that facilitate young in following after the adults. The flash of the white tail also provides a stark target to a predator but as soon as the nyala stops, the tail is dropped and the predator's focus is lost. The disruptive camouflage markings then come into play, further concealing the nyala from the predator's view so long as it remains still.

Bushbuck
Tragelaphus scriptus

Size	Male: 0,8 m; Female: 0,7 m
Weight	Male: 45 kg (maximum 54 kg); Female: 30 kg
Lifespan	12 years
Habitat & Distribution	Riverine forest and thicket adjacent to permanent water
Gestation	6 months
# of young	1
Food	Browsers but take some grass; eat buds, flowers and fruit
Predators	Any medium to large carnivore, especially leopard

Bushbuck are the **smallest tragelaphines** (spiral-horned antelope) in the Lowveld and in some areas are shy and secretive and in others quite common and conspicuous. In areas where there is a good supply of food and water, their home ranges can be as small as half a hectare and as a result bushbuck may exist at relatively high densities.

They are usually **solitary** or in small same-sex groups or pairs although they do sometimes aggregate in open areas abutting their usual riparian thicket habitats. They feed at night or early in the morning and late afternoon.

A **dominance hierarchy is maintained** between members within a given area and, like other tragelaphines, is established through lateral display. Although they do not defend territories, bushbuck are known to be aggressive with one another and with other threats, including humans, even killing them in extreme cases.

A loud, deep resonating bark raises the alarm. The sound is **not proportional to the size of the animal**. Because they freeze when in danger and rely on their crypsis to conceal them, the bark is ventriloquial to put predators off.

Bushbuck are remarkably **strong swimmers**. The calves have an exceptionally long lying-up period of 4 months.

The waterbuck is best recognised by the **white ring** around its rump. This has lead to its Afrikaans colloquial name of 'kringgat' meaning 'circle-bottom'. The white ring is a **'follow me' sign**. Waterbuck females and young live in herds and when startled will flee, often into water. The white ring induces animals in the group to follow each other and as altruistic as this may seem, it in fact serves to buffer the individual from danger. By having an animal ahead and one behind, the individual is spared attack from either direction. Obviously, the white ring has benefit for the young in that it serves as a beacon to follow when running behind their mothers to escape danger.

When one considers that animals' bodies comprise about 70% water, it is no surprise that African mammals all have had to develop tactics for keeping hydrated in a mostly dry and hot environment. Waterbuck are very **water-dependent**, being especially prone to dehydration. They are always found within a 5 km radius from water (but usually less than 2 km from water) and will drink several times a day.

Waterbuck have **glands in their skin** that release a musky odour. Territorial bulls are particularly smelly and the aroma can be detected up to 500 m away from the animal. It is not known what purpose this gland serves, but it has been suggested that the glands help with waterproofing the shaggy coat for the animal's water-loving lifestyle. It is untrue that these glands make the animals immune to predation by crocodiles and lions, and waterbuck are preyed on by all medium- to large-sized predators. Even humans can eat waterbuck meat but the skin must be carefully pulled away from the flesh to prevent tainting.

Waterbuck are **grazers** and feed on the medium to short grass pastures adjacent to waterholes. Their digestive systems are adapted to coping with a high amount of roughage although they do select the more palatable protein-rich grasses available. They also browse during dry conditions. Grass has lower moisture content than browse and waterbuck need to drink to help digest their food. Because they drink frequently their droppings are usually wetter than other ruminants' and the pellets tend to deform and stick together in clumps.

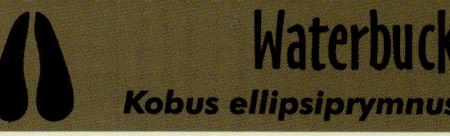

Waterbuck
Kobus ellipsiprymnus

Size	Male: 1,2 m (at shoulder); Female: shorter than male
Weight	Male: up to 270 kg; Female: 180 kg
Lifespan	About 11 years
Habitat & Distribution	Within 5 km radius of water and wherever there is good grazing
Gestation	9 months (280 days)
# of young	1 (twins occasionally)
Food	Grazers - feed on roughage. Favourite grass species: Guinea grass (*Panicum maximum*), Spear grass (*Heteropogon contortus*) and Finger grass (*Digitaria eriantha*)
Predators	Lion, leopard, wild dog, hyena, crocodiles

Young males band together in bachelor groups. They have no chance of securing territories for themselves until they are about 6 years old and banding together means they are afforded better safety from predators. They have to show submissiveness when in the vicinity of territorial bulls so as to pass through the territories of other males in order to get to food and water. Interestingly, youngsters will join a bachelor herd at less than a year old, as the territorial males will not tolerate the young bulls amongst the herds after they have been weaned. Within the bachelor group, a hierarchy is established through pushing contests. The older and therefore larger animals are always dominant. No old bulls are found in bachelor groups. From sexual maturity, they are territorial or in old age, solitary.

Waterbuck calves are unique amongst antelope in that they are relatively mobile during their lying-up period (2-4 weeks just after birth during which time they remain hidden away from the herd). After each visit from the mother to feed, the calves find their own hiding place under bushes but when threatened, they will often flee from the threat rather than lying still and trying to remain undetected. They are very vulnerable at this stage in their lives.

Waterbuck **males advertise their status** as the owner of a territory by standing in an obvious position with the head held high. **The white marks around his face emphasise his serious demeanour.** From the side, his thick neck is a caution to would-be contenders of his strength. The waterbuck bull's horns are used to good effect as weapons against intruders and waterbuck fight more frequently than other antelope, which often results in death. Remarkably, bulls do sometimes tolerate younger bulls (called satellite males) in their territory so long as they remain submissive to the territorial bull. These bulls do, however, assist with territorial defence. Sometimes these individuals may stand to inherit the territory should something happen to the dominant bull.

Waterbuck **bulls are very territorial.** Because they are always found near water, they are able to secure a resource-rich territory and remain sedentary without ill effect to themselves. Females move in their small herds (2-10 animals) between different bulls' territories, visiting the most favourable ones more frequently (i.e. the ones with best access to good grazing and drinking water). Bulls will herd the females and attempt to keep them in their territories for mating purposes. This social system is referred to as a harem.

Steenbok
Raphicerus campestris

Size	0,52 m (at shoulder)
Weight	Male: 11 kg (female larger)
Lifespan	10 years
Habitat & Distribution	Open country with scattered cover
Gestation	7 months
# of young	1
Food	Mixed feeders – eat mostly forbs; also grass, fruit, flowers, seeds, dig for bulbs
Predators	Medium to large carnivores, martial eagles

The following three species of **small antelope** are commonly encountered in the Lowveld bushveld. Often these antelope are mistakenly identified as being one of the other two species but simple variations in appearance, habitat and habits can help to tell them apart.

The steenbok is brick-red in colour with noticeable white underparts. Its colloquial name is derived from the Afrikaans word 'steen' which means brick because of its red-brown colouration. Male steenbok possess two pencil-like parallel horns which females lack.

The white underparts of the steenbok are noticeable when these small antelope run away. Their bounding gait is such that the rump bounces up exposing the white colour. This is possibly a form of **flash colouration** and offers a target to its pursuer. As soon as the antelope stops the white is no longer visible and the antelope blends in with its grassy habitat and becomes lost to the predator. Steenbok rely on hiding in long grass to escape notice as well. Where cover is limited they have been known to hide in holes such as those made by aardvark in the sides of termitaria.

Steenbok are **solitary antelope** except for females accompanied by a lamb or a courting male. The male and female reside in abutting, if not overlapping, territories of about 0,03 km² in extent which they defend from other members of their species with passive demonstrations (combat seldom occurs) and scent markings from the preorbital glands (in front of the eyes), pedal glands (between the hooves) and throat glands.

Steenbok urinate and defecate in **latrines** which they then take great care to cover up. Although buried, they still seem to play a role in territory demarcation as they are usually located on the perimeter of the territory.

Steenbok are **capable diggers** and will unearth bulbs and rhizomes to eat. They also utilise the scraps left behind after porcupines have excavated holes to reach roots. Because of the moisture content of this sort of food, steenbok do not need to drink and are water-independent. They further conserve moisture and energy by lying up in the shade during the hottest part of day.

Common duiker
Sylvicapra grimmia

Size	50 cm (at shoulder)
Weight	Male: 15-18 kg; Female: 16-21 kg
Lifespan	11 years
Habitat & Distribution	Savanna with bushy cover – home range 21 ha
Gestation	7 months
# of young	1
Food	Browsers – leaves, twigs, fruit, flowers, seeds, forbs
Predators	Medium to large carnivores, martial eagles

The common duiker has a **host of common names** including common, grey and Grimm's duiker. The name 'duiker' is derived from the Afrikaans word 'duik' meaning 'to dive' due to its characteristic porpoising flight pattern.

Common duiker are **identifiable** by their slate grey colour (which in some areas varies to include shades of red and yellow). They have a tuft of dark hair between the horns (or just on the head in the case of the females, as horns are absent) and a dark stripe down the centre of the face. The preorbital glands (in front of the eyes) are conspicuous and exude a tarry secretion probably used in scent marking. They tend to live in areas with lots of bushy cover, unlike steenbok who prefer open areas. It is into this cover that they dart and dive when disturbed. They have excellent hearing which alerts them to disturbances.

Common duiker are known to **consume unusual food substances** for antelope. There are several records of them eating nestling ground birds as well as records of reptiles, mopane worms and even mice in their diet. It is unknown whether these items were consumed accidentally during browsing or whether duiker purposely consume them as protein supplements. Aside from the usual browse material they eat, duiker dig for tubers and nibble bark off trees and shrubs.

Duiker are **solitary** in nature except when a female is in oestrus at which time she may be attended by a male. Babies are exceptionally precocial and within 24 hours they can run around energetically. They mature very rapidly, obtaining adult size by only 6 or 7 months old.

'Klip' means rock and 'springer' means jumper in Afrikaans and they are descriptive of this antelope's rocky habitat and its exceptional agility moving over such terrain.

Klipspringers are distinctly golden in colour but have a rough appearance. The hairs of the coat are generally pale but are individually tipped with colour that gives the coat its golden sheen. It is grizzled with black as a result of darker bands on the hairs. The **nature of the coat provides effective camouflage** amongst the rocks.

A klipspringer's **fur is hollow** and each strand is flattened and springy. This provides the device for thermoregulation in the otherwise exposed and harsh environment where klipspringer reside. Rocky areas can be both exceptionally cold and very hot. The unique pelage (fur coat) insulates the body from these temperature extremes and helps to conserve moisture. It protects the klipspringer from heat loss by trapping body-warmed air amongst the coat while the flatness and looseness of the individual hairs allow for increased heat reflection and loss when it is hot. The coat also provides protection should the klipspringer fall on the rocks with the hollow-filled hairs acting as miniature shock-absorbers. Historically klipspringer hair was used to stuff saddles and to make numnahs (saddle cloths).

In conjunction with the visual statue-pose display, klipspringer **demarcate their territories** by creating copious dung piles throughout their turf, most especially along boundaries. They horn bushes and take care to deposit **tarry secretions from the preorbital gland** (an obvious naked black slit in front of eyes) on the ends of twigs by inserting the twig right into the gland. The male marks most frequently and when the female marks, her mate will over-mark her secretion to reinforce it. This is also believed to reinforce pair-bonding.

Klipspringer
Oreotragus oreotragus

Size	50–60 cm
Weight	Male: 10–15 kg (female larger)
Lifespan	15 years
Habitat & Distribution	Rocky hills and outcrops
Gestation	6–7 months
# of young	1
Food	Browser
Predators	Leopard, hyena, caracal, baboon, black and martial eagles; lambs taken by jackal

Klipspringer have **unique feet** amongst ungulates. They actually walk on the tips of their hooves and their spoor impress as two round marks, the heart-shape facing the reverse direction to normal (i.e. the thicker edge faces forward). The hooves are essentially cylindrical with blunt tips. They are rimmed on the inside edge with a cartilaginous pad. This arrangement specifically modifies the feet for bounding unhindered up steep rock faces and from boulder to boulder. The hooves provide traction and grip, absorb the shock of each landing and enable klipspringer to change direction suddenly.

Klipspringer will defend their isolated resources by chasing intruders away but are **seldom aggressive** to one another and the presence of an animal standing conspicuously on a high point is often sufficient to repel unwanted visitors. Sometimes temporary associations of a number of family groups will form in areas where there are particularly good feeding grounds and klipspringer may even leave the rocks to exploit resources on nearby flats. Should any disturbance occur, each unit will flee back to the safety of its rocky retreat.

Klipspringer mostly have the advantage of seeing danger approach from afar. They **respond to distant threats** by freezing and allowing their colour and rounded-back shape to blend them into their surrounds. They may resort to using a **whistle-snort alarm** which can be heard up to 0,7 km away to alert the partner or offspring of danger. The pair sometimes duet this high-pitched sound repetitively and direct it at the predator so that it realises that the element of surprise has been lost and pursuit is not sensible. Klipspringer can easily outrun most predators in their own habitat.

Klipspringer form **monogamous pairs** (one male and one female exclusively) and remain together in a mutual territory. It is rare for mammals to form long-term monogamous alliances and only 5% of them do so. Klipspringer live in a very specific habitat. Rocky areas almost form islands amongst other inappropriate habitat and it can be extremely difficult and risky to find a mate. It therefore makes sense for them to team up with a partner for life. In this manner the effort of securing a mate with which to breed is limited to the first occasion only. Thereafter, the pair can focus their energy on defending an area with good resources and raising young. Klipspringer pairs are seldom far from one another and they even rest lying touching one another.

Klipspringer usually nibble from different plants as they **forage** seldom focusing on a single plant unless it is in fruit or flower. In such cases they will deftly pluck the desirable parts of the plant without damage to the rest of it. They may stand on their hind legs to access food up to 1,2 m high. Remarkably klipspringer favour the extremely toxic rubber euphorbia tree (see p. 284). They supplement mineral deficiencies (usually calcium and phosphorus) in their diet by practising both osteophagia (chewing of bones) and geophagia (chewing of soil, in this case accessed from termite mounds). They will drink from rock pools after rain but are not water-dependent.

The blue wildebeest is also commonly called the 'brindled gnu'. Its silvery-blue coat is lined with darker bands over the shoulders and flanks which provide the brindling and the **noise that the wildebeest makes sounds like 'gnuuu'.**

Blue wildebeest are **pure grazers** and selective at that. They do not select for species or specific parts of the plant like other selective feeders but rather wildebeest are 'site selectors' and will only take forage 15 cm long or less. In this regard they trample and maintain their own pastures and their wide muzzles are perfectly adapted to crop the lawn.

Telling male and female blue wildebeest apart can be tricky as both sexes have horns. The **females** are slightly browner in colour with a little russet on the forehead but **juveniles** also have brown on their faces so this could be confusing. If seen from the side, the male's penis sheath breaks the curve of his belly. Most reliably the horns of the two sexes differ slightly with the male's horns (which are slightly heavier) extending further than the end of the ear before curving upwards.

Courtship in wildebeest is somewhat persistent and often a cow not yet ready to mate will lie down to avoid the male's ongoing advances. If he does not get the required response, he will rear onto his hind legs as a display of his strength and dominance.

Blue wildebeest are **traditionally a migratory species.** When resources are depleted, individual herds form massive aggregations (especially in places like Kenya) and they 'breed on the run' so to speak. Where adequate food and water is available blue wildebeest are more sedentary and exhibit a **harem system** where the male selects and protects a demarcated territory containing the resources that females desire. When the females roam into his area in search of fresh grass or water, the male will herd them and attempt to keep them in his territory (especially during the rut when they are in oestrus). Females live in the herds in which they were born and young males band together in bachelor groups from the age of 2 years, as this provides them with safety in numbers until they can contest a territory themselves. In the meantime, bachelor groups are forced to use the fringes of territorial bulls' habitats. Breeding herds move in home ranges that expand in drought conditions (up to three times) and become fairly stable during favourable times.

Blue wildebeest
Connochaetes taurinus

Size	Male: 1,5 m (at shoulder); Female: 1,35 m (at shoulder)
Weight	Male: 250 kg; Female: 180 kg
Lifespan	15 years
Habitat & Distribution	Open woodland, scrub and grassland, must have access to water and fresh pastures, not found abundantly where there are cold winters
Gestation	250 days
# of young	1
Food	Pure grazer preferring fresh growth less than 10–15 cm long
Predators	Lion, hyena, leopard, wild dog, cheetah, crocodiles

Blue wildebeest **feed** during the cooler parts of the day and into the night. During the hottest parts of the day they will **seek refuge in the shade** and if this is not available, they will face into the prevailing breeze and allow the wind to cool the blood flowing through the bosses of their horns.

Blue wildebeest have bodies that are modified to accommodate their migratory habits. The **slanted back** is a result of shoulders that are positioned high on the body and long front legs. This structure allows wildebeest to canter for long distances. The **canter** is an energy-efficient mode of locomotion that allows wildebeest to follow the signs of distant storms (thunder and lightning) at a pace faster than a walk but less tiring than a full out run or trot.

The **calf** of the blue wildebeest is one of the most precocial (developed at birth) of all antelope species. The calf can stand within a few minutes and can run within a mere five minutes. It is able to keep up with the herd within the day. This adaptation probably developed to accommodate the wildebeest's migratory inclinations. Wildebeest calves have a fawn colour and look like a separate species to the adults. At eight months old the horns develop their upward curve.

A **typical blue wildebeest territory** is usually positioned in the direct vicinity of water and somewhere nearby a sandy area that can be used as a stomping ground. Wildebeest have pedal glands (glands between their hooves) and they rake the ground with their feet to release the scent into the sand. They also release this smell wherever they walk. They make large dung middens on their **stomping patches**. Wildebeest bulls will engage in horn rubbing against bushes or on the ground often becoming covered in mud, in order to transmit preorbital (below the eyes) glandular secretions. Sometimes prominent rubbing posts develop within their territories. Bulls that have territories spend much time as **solitary animals** (until females pass through and can be herded) and in this regard they are vulnerable to predators but since only territorial bulls will sire offspring, this is a risk they are willing to take. Bulls will chase intruders out of their territory and will wrestle on their knees with any offender that does not comply.

Wildebeest are **very water-dependent** and they will drink daily even satisfying their thirst on muddied waters (unlike zebra). In areas where they can no longer migrate to follow seasonal supplies, they will always be within a 15 km radius of a permanent water supply. Wildebeest can be quite influential on ecosystems surrounding water sources and in areas where they have become sedentary because of artificial water supplies they have been known to trample and alter longer grass pastures to the exclusion of long-grass specialists like sable and roan antelope.

Blue wildebeest have a **fixed breeding season** in the Lowveld mating in early winter so that there is a synchrony of births peaking in mid-November to December, the start of summer when lots of green grass is flushing. This peak is a strategy to saturate predatory activity and hopefully more calves survive than if the births were staggered throughout the year.

Each zebra has a **unique stripe pattern**, a barcode or fingerprint so to speak. When young zebra are born, the mare will screen her foal from any other zebra until her own stripe pattern has imprinted on the youngster, ensuring recognition.

The Burchell's Zebra has characteristic **'shadow stripes'** between the black and white stripes of the rump which gives the body a dirty chestnut colour.

The **tail** of a zebra is an incessant fly-swat. The whisk of black hair on the end is a useful device in this regard.

Telling male and female zebra apart is fairly difficult. The **males** have a narrow black stripe running vertically between the legs and under the tail. **Females** have a broader black wedge between their hind legs and under the tail.

Zebra are unselective bulk feeders. Eating a lot of fibre means that they require a regular supply of water to facilitate digestion. Zebra must drink daily and are seldom further than 10 km from water. They are **fussy drinkers** preferring clean water and in this regard they may scrape a hole next to a waterhole and allow clean water to filter through before they drink or they may carefully skim cleaner water off the surface. Their reliance on water is the driving force behind zebra migrating when supplies are inadequate. Since they must move to find water (and good grazing), they are not territorial and different groups will aggregate together in favourable areas.

Zebra are hind-gut fermenters. Lacking the four-chambered stomach of a ruminant, zebra pile all their often fibrous food into one gut which digests via fermentation. The breakdown of cellulose is less effective than with a ruminant but they can digest larger amounts of food faster. **Large quantities of gas** are released as a by-product and this inflates their bellies so that they always look fat and healthy. It is also the cause of the flatulence experienced when zebra take fright and run away.

Burchell's zebra
Equus burchelli

Size	1,35 m (at shoulder)
Weight	320 kg
Lifespan	20 years
Habitat & Distribution	Open woodland, scrub and grassland. Home range: 110– 220 km² (in KNP)
Gestation	One year (360–390 days)
# of young	Single foal
Food	Grazers; occasional browse, herbs and burnt twigs of mopane and kiaat
Predators	Lions and hyena prey on the adults (16% of lions' diet KNP); foals taken by lion, hyena, leopard, cheetah

Because even sick and weak zebra appear fat due to their gaseous digestive process, the most reliable way of determining the health of zebra is by looking at its **mane** on its neck. Usually the short hair stands erect but under stress this will flop over.

Zebra have **black muzzles** equipped with a **strong movable upper lip**. They use the upper lip to push grass between their incisors and then snip it off.

There has been some suggestion that the **stripes of a zebra** are a form of camouflage. True camouflage is the interruption of an object's solid outline such as the effect created by alternating black and white stripes. In certain light conditions this may be true and effective, but camouflage or disruptive markings generally work best against a mottled background and usually zebra are found more in the open. Furthermore, camouflage works best when combined with silence and motionlessness. Zebra are active and noisy. Predators also see in predominantly black and white (low light vision that detects movement easily) so surely black and white are most obvious colours to them?

Zebra are well known for the fact that they **eat grass in open country** where they can keep an eye out for predators. They have excellent senses of smell, sight and hearing. Zebra prefer shorter, green grass such as that which flushes after a fire or the first rains but they do also readily take tall, coarse growth. Taller grass is cropped and made more suitable for the foraging habits of blue wildebeest and other antelope in a process known as grassland succession. Wildebeest prefer very short grass and are often found in association with zebra for this reason and to benefit from their excellent vigilance.

Even though zebra are strictly **grazers**, they have been known to browse occasionally, most probably at the hardest times of the year when there is little else available. They also dig up the rhizomes (underground stems) of grasses that are often more succulent than the above ground parts, particularly in winter.

57

The **stallion is the harem's defender**. Equipped with an exceptionally powerful kick and the tenacity to inflict nasty bites, the stallion will run behind his harem when threatened. The mares and foals bunch together and flee as a unit to ensure that they enjoy the protection of the stallion's rear-guard. The contrasting black and white stripes are thought to facilitate the cohesion of the group at times of trouble. Black and white are the most visible colours to the zebra (who do not have colour vision), particularly in the low light conditions in which they are usually attacked.

The **foal** of a zebra is remarkably precocial, standing on its own after just 10 minutes of its birth. It can walk within 30 minutes and runs within the hour. The protracted year-long gestation ensures the foal is born well developed since it must be able to run to escape danger almost immediately in order to survive.

Males practise flehmen to check the reproductive status of the mares. This is the process whereby liquid or air-borne chemicals from the mare's urine are pumped into an organ on the roof of the mouth known as the organ of Jacobsen (or vomeronasal organ). A facial grimace whereby the upper lip is pulled back, relaxes the opening of the glands allowing the chemicals to enter. The hormonal content of the urine is thus evaluated and the stallion consequently determines whether a mare is ready to mate or not.

Burchell's zebra
Equus burchelli

Zebra are **keen dust-bathers** and frequently roll in loose dirt, probably to help with parasite control and thermoregulation. Zebra are able to roll over on their backs completely, a trait not shared by antelope. Zebra also enjoy a good rub of the head and shoulders on objects like rocks or termite mounds. They may even queue up in rank order to perform this apparently pleasurable task.

Amongst the mares there is a **strict rank hierarchy** which is linked to age but initially also to the 'first wife, second wife' arrangement. Whichever filly was abducted first becomes the dominant mare. The groups bond through allo-grooming (mutual grooming).

Zebra **do not have territories**. Instead, the defended resource of a stallion is his four to six mares and their foals. **A stallion practises a true harem system** (one male with a number of females), which is bought at an incredible price. Colts leave the natal herd of their own accord at 2 years of age but between 4,5 and 12 years of age, they will approach other herds with the intention of **abducting fillies**, one by one, to form their own harems. This is no easy feat as each existing harem is defended valiantly by the stallion, which will not let the young bachelor merely lure his fillies away – through a protracted period of sometimes a year, he is forced to prove himself.

Often this is done through **vicious fighting** between the contender and the filly's father as well as other suitors. If the young stallion can get it right to mount and impregnate a filly during her annual five-day oestrus period, the filly will become his and she will remain faithful to him. He will then pursue another. This protracted courtship ensures that only the fittest stallions prevail.

Zebra **sleep** a fair amount, enjoying a midday siesta when it is hot (while standing). They also snatch a full 7 hours after dark. This they do lying down, even on their sides (especially the foals). Usually one animal will remain standing and alert to watch for predators.

One **theory regarding why zebra have stripes** suggests that the confusion caused by a group of zebra fleeing simultaneously (as they do bunched in a group and followed by the stallion) creates a screen for the individuals' escape. The blur of black and white supposedly makes it difficult for predators to separate out an individual target. Although predators do still catch zebra successfully and regularly, this may have some bearing as a defence technique since it depends on the individual being part of the fleeing unit.

The weaker, older or slower members of the group may lag behind and generally it is the isolated members of the population that are picked off by predators first. Zebra are however **group-orientated animals** and will attempt to rally around their weaker individuals during times of threat.

When alarmed, zebra make a high-pitched and repeated 'kwa-ha-ha' sound, an iconic call of the African bushveld.

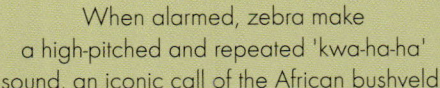

Eland are unusual antelope in the bushveld in that they are **nomadic** and as such do not defend territories. They move around following the best feeding resources, sometimes in **aggregations numbering a thousand animals**, and their breeding is governed by a system of seasonal temporary association.

Eland are the **largest antelope** in the Lowveld and indeed in southern Africa. This southern-occurring species is superseded in size only by their north-west African relatives, the Giant or Lord Derby's eland as the largest antelope in the world.

The name 'eland' comes from the Dutch word for elk.

Older bulls take on a blue-grey colour and have spectacular dewlaps and impressive thick necks. These strong necks give eland bulls the power that they need to twist and push one another off balance during fights for access to females on heat. They have a mop of hair on their heads between their horns which covers a glandular region and this region is regularly coated in mud and is smelly from rubbing it where females have urinated or from plowing up soft ground. These actions as well as the thrashing of bushes with their horns and loud bellowing are demonstrations of dominance. Eland bulls are able to snap tree trunks 4 cm thick with their horns to display their aggression.

During the **breeding season** females, sub-adults and mature bulls (up to six) occur together in herds. After breeding is over, the males separate out from the herds and occur as bachelor groups or alone. The females separate from the younger animals which stay together in nursery herds and seem to be more closely bonded to one another than to their mothers. The females and nursery herds join up again at the next breeding season and are subsequently joined by the males at this time too. A **system of rank** determined by size and age exists to keep some order amongst the groups. Males are always dominant over females and older (and hence larger) animals over younger. The hierarchy is maintained by subtle ritualised threats which, if not responded to appropriately by an inferior animal, are followed through with persuasive jabs of the horns. Males in a herd will automatically size each other up and give way to stronger-looking animals without question. Equally matched bulls will fight over females in oestrus, sometimes to the death, by horn-locking and pushing and twisting.

Eland
Tragelaphus oryx

Size	Male: 1,7 m (at shoulder); Female: 1,5 m (at shoulder)
Weight	Male: 700 kg (maximum 840 kg); Female: 460 kg
Lifespan	20 years
Habitat & Distribution	Versatile
Gestation	9 months
# of young	1 (very occasionally twins)
Food	Mixed feeders
Predators	Lion and man; young potentially taken by hyena, cheetah, leopard and lion

Although **newborn eland calves** can stand almost immediately and are able to walk and follow an adult after 3 or 4 hours, they engage in what is known as a lying-up period. During the first 2 weeks of its life, the calf will hide in long grass or shrubbery. It is visited by its mother to suckle. The lying-up period affords youngsters some time to grow and develop strength before they have to deal with the pressure of keeping up with a moving herd.

Adult eland (especially bulls) **produce a characteristic 'click'** noise as they move. This supposedly emanates from their knees although it is poorly understood what causes it and why it happens.

Eland are **athletic jumpers** and can easily clear fences 2 m high from a standing position.

Eland **walk extremely fast**. The rate is so quick that humans cannot keep up with them on foot. Their trotting gait also allows them to cover ground very rapidly. These are probably both adaptations to being nomadic.

Both sexes in a herd of eland practise **urine testing and flehmen** (facial grimace which pumps steroid hormones into the organ of Jacobsen on the roof of the mouth). This is unusual as usually only the male of the species uses these techniques in order to determine a female's readiness to mate.

Members of a herd of eland **allo-groom** (mutual grooming) one another on the head, neck and rump areas, all the places that are hard to reach themselves. They are also meticulous about grooming themselves and regularly rub their heads and bodies against trees and other objects at the right height. Like the cattle they so closely resemble, eland are followed by cattle egrets, which benefit from the insects kicked up by the antelope as they move and also remove parasites from the antelopes' bodies.

Adult eland are **almost immune to predation** due to their enormous size but the young are more vulnerable. Eland females are renowned for their tendency to cooperatively protect their young chasing off large predators to give the smaller animals a chance to bunch together and run to safety. Although adult eland **run away readily from disturbances** and can cover distance very quickly at a gallop, they do tend to stand their ground against predators that they probably would not outrun, bunching heads-together and presenting the offender with a wall of powerful, kicking legs with which to contend.

Eland
Tragelaphus oryx

Eland are **ruminants** (have four-chambered stomachs) and as such they need to be somewhat selective in what they eat to accommodate their **fibre-sensitive systems**. In summer when grass is the most nutritious source of food around, eland will eat mostly grass. They are often found in newly burnt areas or where grass is newly shooting. In winter, browse holds its nutrient and moisture contents more successfully than grass and eland switch to browse at this time of the year, particularly favouring protein-rich species like mopane and even eating the dried leaves of such trees for nutrients (see p. 269). They are adept at using their horns to twist-snap off branches of trees with foliage out of their reach. Once hanging down or broken off, other eland can then also feed off the stem (providing the animal in attendance is not more dominant!). When food is abundant, eland tend to be more sedentary and less nomadic.

Eland are adapted to **living independently of water** supplies. They do not have to drink regularly (although they do where water is readily available) but rather get the moisture they need from the food they eat or from other simple water conservation techniques. Eland feed during the day but they also feed at night when the moisture content of foliage is higher. They produce very concentrated urine and dry faecal pellets so as not to discard of moisture unnecessarily. They will stand in the shade on very hot days and have the ability (like gemsbok) to allow their body temperature to rise by a few degrees dissipating the heat after dark when it is cooler. Eland breathe deeply and slowly to conserve the moisture in their nasal passages.

The giraffe is the world's **tallest land mammal** and has some curious adaptations to accommodate its lifestyle.

The only other member of the giraffe family is the okapi, which is found in the Democratic Republic of Congo.

Giraffe do **lie down** to rest at some point during the night but they generally only sleep curled up in five-minute instalments as they are very vulnerable during these times.

Giraffe
Giraffa camelopardalus

Size	Male: average 4–5,5 m (at shoulder) (maximum 6 m) Female: average 3,5–4,5 m (at shoulder)
Weight	Male: 970–1 400 kg; Female: 700–950 kg
Lifespan	About 25 years
Habitat & Distribution	Open woodland, dry savanna, sometimes light forest and desert areas but not high mountains or forested country
Gestation	15 months (457 days) The only ruminant with a gestation period of more than one year!
# of young	1
Food	Feed on deciduous foliage in the rainy season and rely on evergreen species at other times; consumes 34 kg/day
Predators	Lions and hyena (especially the young)

Giraffes' **long necks** give them a height advantage and they can access a 2 m band of vegetation out of reach to all other herbivores except elephants. The biggest bulls can reach almost 6 m high. Because of the height difference between sexes, male and female giraffe feed in different zones and therefore do not compete for food with one another. Bulls tend to feed higher up, stretching themselves to their height limit while cows tend to utilise lower browse. Bulls will also take to taller, denser woodland than cows. The feeding techniques of giraffe can affect the growth form of trees. Continuous pruning of young trees can stunt their growth and in favoured species of taller trees, giraffe may be responsible for creating a waistline around the middle of the tree giving their favourite trees telltale hourglass shapes.

Giraffe are **classic browsers**, their long necks giving them access to the highest of foliage. They do, however, bend down to ground level in order to pick up bones or soil that they chew to supplement calcium and phosphorus that is lacking in their diet. This is called osteophagia and geophagia respectively.

Because of their **height advantage** and **good eyesight**, many other animals will associate with giraffe and respond to early signs of danger given by these 'lighthouses'. Giraffe are also very curious animals and will stare at predators lying in the grass or any other intruder, giving shorter animals (and even humans) a clue to the fact that there may be carnivores in an area.

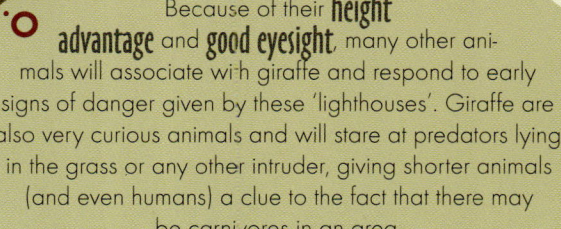

Giraffe are believed to be the **mammal pollinator** of the knob thorn *Acacia nigrescens* (see p. 252).

Both sexes of giraffe have **horns**. In the case of the **males**, these are stouter and hairless on the top. **Females** have more elegant, tufted horns. Males possess 'a third horn' known as a median horn in the centre of his forehead. This enlarges over his lifespan as calcification takes place from impacts while necking. Other calcified knobs also form on the forehead for the same reason. Horns are present right from birth although at the time of birth they are not attached to the skull, to assist with an easy exit from the womb. As the calf grows, the cartilage horns ossify onto the skull and become solid bone.

The **unique patches** that wallpaper a giraffe's body break up its outline and thereby provide camouflage to the animal that has only to stand still to disappear into its surrounds despite its size. The patches are created by a simple variation in the colour of the fur. Patches darken with age, particularly in males and they vary between individuals, each animal having a unique coat. All animals have mechanisms to thermoregulate (control temperature) and the patches of a giraffe are believed to scatter heat falling on the giraffe's body.

The general arrangement of patches on giraffe also varies between isolated populations and in spite of some debate there seems to be at least six different **recognised races** of giraffe in southern and east Africa.

The **narrow muzzle** with its lithe upper lip enables giraffe to pick individual leaves from between thorns. Since giraffe are selective feeders needing to consume high-quality forage to accommodate their ruminating digestive system, this is an important trait. Horny papillae (bumps) protect both the lips and tongue from pricks from thorns.

Giraffe
Giraffa camelopardalus

Giraffe have **long eyelashes** which protect their eyes when they push their heads into the thorny or twiggy canopies of trees to get their food.

Giraffe have a **modified atlas-axis** joint at the base of the skull that allows them to tilt their heads vertically to reach upwards for forage.

Males are usually **darker** than females and taller sometimes by a full metre. The penis-sheath of the male breaks the contour of his belly and his large scrotum is obvious.

The length of a giraffe's **tongue** is 45 cm and it can extend a great deal beyond the mouth. This gives giraffe an additional height advantage. The tongue is prehensile (able to grip) and this enables giraffe to use different feeding methods. They are able to strip whole branches of their leaves by wrapping their tongue around a branch or they might grip and pluck a particular bunch of leaves or leaf. The tongue is very rubbery and not easily penetrated by thorns. It is also coated in profuse saliva.

Giraffe have some **special adaptations** that suit them to feeding high above the ground and on thorny vegetation. The evolutionary arms race that exists between herbivores and their 'plant-prey' caused the trees that grow in more fertile clay soils (that line the band lower down the slope) to produce thorns (see p. 11). These trees, such as *Acacia* species, are highly nutritious because of their growing conditions and therefore sought after by herbivores. Thorns are most effective against large herbivore mouthparts (over other options like chemicals) and deter herbivores from feeding excessively on any given tree. Herbivores have developed mechanisms for getting around the discomfort of feeding on thorny plants and the giraffe is an expert in this field.

Giraffe may drink every 2 or 3 days if there is water around but they get most of the moisture they need from the green leaves they eat. **When giraffe do drink**, the **process is a complicated** one as bending down potentially subjects their brains to an overload in pressure. A giraffe's brain sits up to 5 m above ground and almost 2 m away from its heart, which circulates 60 litres of blood every minute. To counteract a potential flood of blood to the brain, giraffe have a network of small capillaries that dilate and constrict to control the flow of blood to the brain when the giraffe bends down and subsequently the flow of blood back to the heart when it stands up again (to eliminate the chance of a giant head rush!). They also possess valves in the neck to assist this process.

Many people believe giraffe to be mute but although they are generally silent they do have a **number of vocalisations** that they use to communicate with one another or sound the alarm. These include snorts, bleats, mews, bellows and coughs.

A **newborn giraffe** weighs 100 kg and can stand within 15 minutes of birth. Although many people believe that the foal's almost 2 m drop at birth consequently starts their hearts, this is not the case. The foal itself is large and it exits the birth canal head and front feet first (almost spatch-cocked). The cow squats as much as possible and the foal's feet touch the ground before the rest of the body and hind feet exit, helping it to brace the fall. To start life, the calf spends most of its time lying up, hidden by its camouflage and propensity to lower its neck if danger threatens. The mother **remains nearby most of the time** to keep guard and provide nourishment but she herself may need to find food or drink and so may be absent for hours at a time. Later on youngsters group together in crèches for protection in numbers and to relieve the pressure of individual parents to be on 'guard duty'.

Giraffe manage to stay out of harm's way by being large animals with excellent day and night time vision and by possessing a **powerful kick**. They are not, however, immune to predation and some lion prides specialise successfully in hunting giraffe by chasing them over a medium that causes them to trip. Youngsters are vulnerable which is why they remain concealed for the first part of their lives and until they can run fast enough. Cows watch over and defend their offspring from harm commendably. Youngsters concentrate most of their food intake on growing, out of harm's way. A calf grows 1 m in the first 6 months of its life and doubles that in the first year.

Giraffe
Giraffa camelopardalus

Giraffe have very **loose social structures** known as temporary associations. Within a period of hours, the individuals making up a group will fluctuate and no lasting bonds exist between members (except initially between mothers and calves). Giraffe are gregarious and still prefer to be around members of their own kind even though the make up of the group fluctuates. Bachelors generally associate with other bachelors and maternity groups or crèches tend to form, but any combination of sex and age may be found. The vantage point created by the giraffe's height allows separated individuals to maintain visual contact. The **skin behind their ears is white** and obvious from behind, a lofty 'follow me' sign and contact beacon well suited to giraffe.

Bull giraffe are generally solitary and move from one temporary association to the next seeking cows on heat. Giraffe are not territorial and a local status hierarchy develops according to age and size. This is established through **ritual necking encounters amongst bachelors** from an early age. Duels are not violent unless two equally matched bulls are contending for the same oestrus cow. Necking rituals are synchronised and seem like a graceful dance but the ultimate intention is for one bull to thrust his neck sideways making well-placed blows with his horns and knobbly head on the opponent's body while the two stand side on, head-to-rump. The opponent does his best to avoid blows and reciprocate the attacks and a rhythmical movement ensues.

Giraffes' **species name** *camelopardalis* means camel-like leopard. The leopard (*pardalis*) refers to its colouration while the camel-like similarity exists in the way giraffe walk, moving the two legs on the left side, followed by the two legs on the right side. This pattern of walking helps to prevent the long legs tangling with each other and the neck assists with balance. When giraffe gallop, the front and back legs operate like those of a hare. The hind pair exceed where the front pair have just landed between them. Giraffe can reach 50–60 km/hour when galloping.

Hippos **bask** in the sun to warm themselves up, particularly during cooler times of the year.

Hippos **save a great deal of energy** by being in water. Their large barrel-like bodies are buoyed up by the water and consequently, hippos do not need to eat as much as expected. An adult consumes only 15–40 kg of grass in a night, a mere 1,5% of its body weight. Usually large mammals need to eat about 5% of their body weight to sustain their nutrient requirements.

Hippos have **unique skin**. The fine epidermis renders the skin extremely sensitive to dehydration, up to seven times that of other mammals. For this reason they while away the hottest hours of the day submerged in water without which they would overheat. If exposed to excessive heat and radiation the hippo will react firstly by secreting a red fluid from mucous glands on the skin (which is not blood) that acts as a sunscreen and thereafter the skin will dry and crack. In times of drought, hippos pack together in mud pools to remain hydrated. This leads to a great deal of conflict and they may then travel vast distances seeking permanent water. Females have been observed dribbling saliva over exposed calves.

Hippos have enormous, **powerful muzzles** that can stretch wide open. Their lower canines are modified into huge tusks that grow continuously and may reach 30–50 cm long. A hippo will defend itself and its young with these well-adapted weapons and is well able to bite a 3 m crocodile in half.

Hippo
Hippopotamus amphibius

Size	140 cm (at shoulder)
Weight	Male: 2 000– 3 000 kg; Female: 1 400 kg
Lifespan	About 35–40 years
Habitat & Distribution	Permanent water that abuts grasslands
Gestation	8 months
# of young	1
Food	Hippos are unselective grazers
Predators	Hippos are mostly immune to predation due to their large size. They cluster together in the water to protect the young from crocodiles. Lions and hyenas do occasionally attack hippos when on land at night

Hippos harbour the bilharzia parasite in their bodies. This does not seem to cause them any ill effect.

A hippo's **eyes, nostrils and ears** are situated high on its head and this enables the hippo to keep its heat-sensitive body submerged while all its vital senses are above the water to keep a look out for trouble.

Hippos can **remain submerged** for 5–6 minutes. They are able to close their nostrils and ears to prevent water from getting inside them. Young (2-month-old) hippo can hold their breath for only about 40 seconds.

Hippos are **clumsy on land** and cannot jump or navigate over obstacles. They are, however, able to reach speeds of 36 km/hour if provoked.

Hippos take to the water immediately if **threatened**. They use well-worn pathways to and from the water and if disturbed will charge headlong down these pathways to return to the safety of the water. In this way, many humans that have come between a hippo and the water have lost their lives. There is a myth that hippos stamp out fires but this probably stems from fleeing hippos running through fires made at camps set up beside the river, in an effort to get back to the water.

Hippos **walk on the bottom** of rivers or dams and do not swim per se. They can create negative buoyancy by breathing out before submerging and this allows them to walk underwater. They will also push themselves off the bottom with their feet and do a kind of ballet-gallop through the water. As they move, hippos create pathways through underwater vegetation which is a valuable ecological service and is necessary to keep waterways flowing. Hippos must surface in order to breathe.

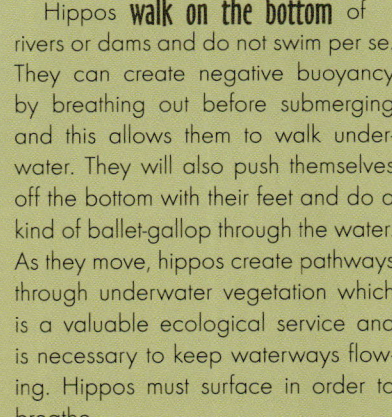

Hippos have **unique feet.** They are the only ungulate to possess four toes. Because they have an even amount of toes (like antelope, which have two claws or toes) they belong to the order Artiodactyla, i.e. even-toed ungulates.

Calves are born in the water, albeit shallow enough so they do not have to swim to breathe. They are able to walk and swim within minutes. They suckle underwater which is made possible by the folding ears and closing nostrils that also allow them not to drown when submerged normally. The calf pinches the female's teat between its tongue and the palate of its mouth. Females are fiercely protective of their babies, even against other hippos, including the bull.

Hippo calves lose heat much quicker than the adults. If it is cold, a calf will lift itself onto its mother's back to bask in the sun.

Hippos are **grazers** (they eat grass). They are not selective of which species they eat or which part of the plant they feed on. Their broad muscular lips allow them to pluck short grass which they 'mow' repeatedly or taller swathes of grass. They are noisy feeders. Sometimes hippos will eat water plants growing in the waterways where they reside.

Hippos **come out of the water at night to feed**. They leave the water in the late afternoon and split up to forage solitarily through the night. They follow well-used paths and generally do not stray further than 1-2 km from water, returning to it before the sun gets hot. During stressful conditions hippos can travel 15 km in a night to find food.

Hippo
Hippopotamus amphibius

The iconic and impressive **honking** of hippo bulls serves to advertise territory and ward off would-be intruders. Hippos do, however, produce other sounds from growls to grunts to squeals. These probably fulfil an array of social uses.

Hippos practise a **harem system** where bulls occupy well-defended territories that contain nursery herds of females and their young. Pods of hippo can range from 2 to 200 animals but typically contain 7 to 15. Bulls are especially grumpy and do not tolerate one another and often even young bulls are slashed on the head and shoulders with their sharp teeth. Dominant bulls typically display their status through wide-mouth yawns that exhibit their formidable canine teeth – instruments of defence, not feeding. These are continually sharpened by abrasion with the pair on the opposite jaw and can easily penetrate the 6 cm thick hide of a contender and do some serious damage to him. Only the most serious opponents will engage in combat as this can lead to death. Usually they signal their disapproval of one another with showers of dung sent scattering by a paddled tail-action. Territories are marked on land in this way too, especially favoured pathways leading from the water.

Hippo bulls have little tact when it comes to **mating**. There is no courtship ritual to speak of and the male will simply locate an oestrus female by parading through the pod smelling their rear ends. A female on heat is then chased into the water where the bull will force her prostrate, even snapping at her should she come up for breath!

Hippos have **internal testes** like elephants. This makes it difficult to tell males and females apart. Generally males are larger than females.

The fact that hippo **defecate** in or near the water has an important ecological benefit. They are adding nutrients to the system which can then be utilised by members of the food chain like fish and invertebrates.

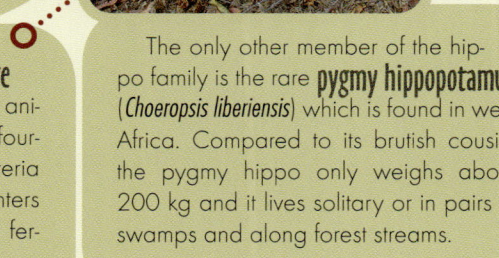

The only other member of the hippo family is the rare **pygmy hippopotamus** (*Choeropsis liberiensis*) which is found in west Africa. Compared to its brutish cousin, the pygmy hippo only weighs about 200 kg and it lives solitary or in pairs in swamps and along forest streams.

Hippos have a **unique digestive system** amongst ungulates (hoofed animals). They are neither ruminants (four-chambered stomach with microbacteria in the foregut) nor hindgut fermenters (single stomach with microbacterial fermentation occurring last). Hippos have three-chambered stomachs and practise foregut fermentation. This means that their food is exposed to microbacteria that can break down the cellulose plant cell walls early on in the digestive process. They do not, however, chew the cud as in ruminants and are essentially bulk grazers, like hindgut digesters.

Hippos often **nibble carcasses of dead animals** floating in their waterways or lying on the banks. Some theories suggest that this behaviour stems from the omnivorous traits of their pig ancestor. Other theories suggest that hippos do not have mouths suited to pulling off flesh and chewing it and that this behaviour is rather linked to kin recognition. Hippos are believed to be trying to cognitively recognise the deceased creature through the use of the chemo-sensitive organ of Jacobsen located on the roof of the mouth.

The name 'warthog' comes from this swine's obvious **facial warts** which are made up of thick skin and cartilage. Females have a single pair of warts just below the eyes while males have an additional pair just above the tusks. The warts on boars are much larger and this, as well as the additional pair on the cheeks, helps to protect their faces and eyes from opponents' tusks during times of combat.

The name given to a group of warthogs is a **'sounder'**.

Warthogs are mostly hairless but what hair they do have serves vital functions. The **mane** of long, rough hair along the back is erected (called pilo-erection) when they are stressed. This probably serves to make the small animal look more intimidating to opponents or predators. The pronounced **cheek whiskers**, particularly present in juveniles, are a clever form of mimicry. The white hair imitates the adults' fearsome tusks while they are still developing in the youngsters and serves to deter would-be predators even though the piglets are essentially defenceless.

A warthog's **tusks are formidable defence weapons**. They are modified canine teeth that grow sideways out of the warthog's mouth and the upper tusk can reach lengths of about 60 cm and the lower about 13 cm. Although the lower tusks are the smaller ones, these are the ones that can cause serious injury to unwary enemies. The lower tusks articulate against the inner groove of the upper tusks and each time the warthog's mouth opens or closes, the lower tusks are honed and become blade-sharp. In old females the upper tusks curl over the snout more than in males.

When **fleeing danger**, warthogs **erect their tails** which comically look like navigational aerials. This action is in fact an involuntary muscular reaction activated when the pigs take fright and run away. The tail acts as a 'follow me' sign to the piglets and other members of the sounder, especially necessary when running through tall grass.

Warthog
Phacochoerus aethiopicus

Size	65–84 cm (at shoulder)
Weight	Male: average 80 kg; Female: average 65 kg
Lifespan	18 years
Habitat & Distribution	Only 'pig' adapted for grazing in savanna habitats. Prefers open ground: grassland, vleis, areas around waterholes, open woodland and scrub; avoids forest, dense undergrowth and desert. Drinks and wallows daily (where water is available). Home range: 64–374 ha (average 174 ha)
Gestation	160–170 days
# of young	2–3
Food	Wet season: grazes mostly on lawn-like swathes of grass. Dry season: underground rhizomes of perennial grasses and sedges; also eats bulbs, tubers, herbs, shrubs and fruits (fallen figs, marulas and monkey oranges)
Predators	Lion, leopard, hyena, wild dog; piglets taken by pythons, cheetah, jackal, raptors and any other medium-sized carnivores

Because warthogs have typically hairless bodies, they make regular use of **mud-wallows** to help regulate their body temperature on hot days. The thermoregulatory 'bath' also aids in parasite removal and warthogs are prone to rubbing themselves on any convenient post to remove caked mud and concurrently the encrusted ticks. Warthogs are further aided in parasite-removal by red-billed oxpeckers. They are the smallest ungulates attended to by these useful birds who frequently warn them of danger. Warthogs rely on and respond to these and other animals' alarm calls as they are both short-sighted and short-legged!

Warthogs are **highly diurnal** meaning they are only active during the day and they will retreat into holes – usually the disused excavations of aardvark – before nightfall. On cold, wet or overcast days, warthogs come out of their burrows much later than usual. The more stable microclimate inside the burrow affords their naked bodies critical protection from the weather conditions. In summer they will also use burrows for shade during the extreme midday heat.

Without much subcutaneous fat, **piglets are especially sensitive to cold and wet conditions** and up to 50% of warthog young die in their first 6 weeks due to sudden temperature fluctuations (and predation). To help overcome these risks, warthog sows excavate their burrows with an internal shelf that serves as a 'bunk-bed' to keep the young off the floor in the event of flooding. If the shelf is absent from a particular burrow, the piglets will sleep on the sow's back.

Using their forefeet, warthogs **adjust holes to their own specifications**, moving the loosened dirt with their shovel-shaped snouts. They prefer to use large burrows that have numerous entrances as this offers more escape options should a predator try to dig them out. For this reason as well, warthogs usually **reverse into their burrows** so that their weapon-like tusks are facing any potential danger. They are very careful when leaving their burrows, hesitating to listen for danger first but less cautious about entering holes which they may have to bolt into to escape a threat! The juveniles typically pile in first while the adult turns around at the last minute to reverse and thereby creates a cloud of distracting dust. A sounder of warthog may use up to 10 holes alternately within their home range, and neighbouring sounders may even share homes on a first-come-first-serve basis.

Warthogs have a **specific mating season** and the beginning of the dry season produces some entertaining warthog shenanigans. Boars will wait at the entrances to burrows to seek sows on heat. Once they locate a suitable sow they follow them around strutting to show their dominance. If other males dare intrude, boars become very aggressive, rushing at one another – sometimes even sideways – manes erect and pawing the ground or head butting while on their knees. The winner then continues to pursue the sow with a bouncy, hip-swinging strut while chomping his jaws and salivating.

By October there are usually **warthog litters** secreted inside burrows. The young remain in their underground homes for the first 6 weeks of their lives, suckled by sows that produce profuse milk due to the coinciding spring grass flush. Between the ages of 3 and 6 weeks, the young are suckled a remarkable 12 to 17 times a day at about 40-minute intervals. The first piglets usually emerge into public view early to mid-November at between 3 and 6 weeks old to begin grazing or to move burrows. Occasionally younger piglets can be spotted being carried in the sow's mouth to a new den. This is generally done if the existing burrow becomes parasite-ridden. Although there are usually 2–3 piglets in a litter, larger groups may be found in the case where abandoned piglets join another sounder due to the female being killed by a predator.

Warthogs have a **matriarchal society** in which one sow or sometimes a couple of sows and their related offspring associate together and are only attended by a boar during the rut (breeding season). The usual number in a sounder is up to five members but they can reach up to 16 members during wetter, more productive times of the year. They are not strictly territorial and home ranges are shared by bachelors, solitary males and maternity groups. Both sexes tend to remain in the area where they were born and as such warthogs in a given area are usually clans of relatives. Members of a particular sounder may be bonded through successive seasons for up to 3 years and will allo-groom one another by running the mane hair through their front teeth or over their lips.

Warthogs are **generally silent animals** but they do grunt and snort to keep contact with the group or if aggressive. Piglets squeak if under stress. By far the most amusing sounds made by warthogs are the jaw-chomping noises produced by a boar courting a sow. These sounds can be heard 50 m away from the mating couple.

Warthog
Phacochoerus aethiopicus

Warthogs are hindgut fermenters. Where antelope process their food in a complex four-chambered stomach, this ungulate (hoofed animal) has only one stomach into which it piles relatively coarse-textured plant material. The transit time through its stomach is faster than in ruminants, which must first refine their food by chewing the cud. A warthog's meal is only subjected to the microbacteria that can break down the cellulose of plant cell-walls towards the end of its digestive process (in ruminants this takes place first to ensure the thorough digestion of food).

The result is that a warthog **defecates fortuitously** and its dung has larger bundles than the pellets produced by antelope. It also comprises material that is still fairly coarse textured. The advantage of this 'less-effective' type of digestion is that they can put **larger amounts of food through their bodies relatively quickly** and as a result extract adequate nutrients at harder, dry times of the year. To facilitate their digestive systems, warthogs feed selectively, choosing more nutritious plants and parts of plants. They are also exceptionally water-dependent and must drink daily.

Warthogs are **well equipped for their dietary habits**. They have large, flattened molars and a modified jaw articulation perfect for grinding grass (in summer) and the harder bulbs, tubers and rhizomes unearthed during the dry season. The head is flat and downward-facing, terminating in the rounded cartilage snout that encloses the nostrils and is hardened on the upper side. This acts like a shovel to dig for tasty tit-bits up to 10–15 cm deep under even hard earth. The warthog's short neck gives leverage to the spade-like head when the warthog is grovelling. To further improve this action, warthogs often kneel down on their front 'elbows' (carpal joints of the wrist), which are calloused from birth for this reason.

Warthogs have some **peculiar eating habits**. They exhibit osteophagia (the chewing of bones), geophagia (the chewing of soil) and coprophagia (the consumption of faeces). They chew bones and soil to supplement nutrients that may be deficient in their usual diets. The young consume the adults' dung to colonise their guts with useful digestive microbacteria. They also ingest dung to reprocess plant material that has not necessarily been completely digested the first time round due to their 'poor' hindgut digestive system. There are records of warthogs eating carrion, which may be attributed to the omnivorous habits of the pig family generally although it is unclear whether warthogs actually eat meat off carcasses or merely the stomach contents of herbivores typically discarded by predators.

Squirrels **sleep and nest in hollow cavities in trees**, which they line with grass and leaves. These abodes are called 'dreys'. During nesting the females clean out their nests regularly to prevent the build-up of parasites. During these occasions, young may need to be moved. The female moves her offspring by holding one of their back-legs. The youngster clings to her shoulders in a 'sack-of-potatoes' manner.

Tree squirrels are named as such for their habit of living in savanna woodlands and nesting in holes in trees. They are frequently found in abundance in mopane woodland as these trees are prone to having natural cavities and the squirrels are therefore also **called 'mopane squirrels'**.

Tree squirrel
Paraxerus cepapi

Size	Overall length 35 cm (tail about half the length)
Weight	200 g (males slightly heavier)
Lifespan	8 years
Habitat & Distribution	Woodland (especially *Acacia* and mopane woodland) which have copious natural holes
Gestation	53–57 days
# of young	1–3 (average 2)
Food	Vegetarians with insects eaten as a secondary constituent. Their diet includes flowers, seeds, berries, bark and grass
Predators	Snakes, raptors, wild cats, mongoose

The squirrel family is known as the Sciuridae and *skiouros* is the Greek word for **shady tail** referring to the bushy tail that is used as an umbrella by some species.

Newborn squirrels are altricial (blind, naked and helpless). The parents are particularly attentive and the female remains with her young in the nest for the first few days grooming and caring for them. Even the male assists with grooming duties and remains attentive of his family throughout the breeding process. The young wean quickly and at this point the food supplied by adults dries up immediately. This is to encourage the young to follow the adults and learn for themselves what to eat by observing what the adults feed on. At a mere 10 months old, squirrels become sexually mature and may then leave their natal groups.

Tree squirrels live in **family groups** that recognise one another through a common smell. They are **meticulous groomers** (a necessary trait in small animals that cannot afford to lose energy in the form of blood to parasites) and the group odour transfers between members during allogrooming (mutual grooming) stints or from sleeping together. They also mark one another by dragging their anal glands over their mutual group members. Any animal which does not have the correct smell is chased away.

Family groups are **territorial**. They designate their turf with chattered vocal declarations coinciding with tail-flicks and with scented markers, including urine deposits and secretions from lip and anal glands. The territory is primarily defended by the male who holds the highest rank in the group hierarchy. When a female is on heat she will vocalise with urgent, high-pitched chatters. These attract any male within earshot to come and attend to her. Understandably the territorial male does not approve of all the intruders and males spend a great deal of time chasing one another around noisily at these times for access to the female. Her chatters also seem to induce other females to enter oestrus simultaneously and so the male has his hands full. This paternity competition may be a mechanism designed to facilitate the mixing of genes.

Although squirrels nest and overnight in trees, they are as much terrestrial (ground-dwelling) as they are arboreal (tree-dwelling) when it comes to foraging. They spend a **large portion of the day on the ground** picking up seeds (and the occasional insect) and eating grass. While they forage they are cautious and walk in a jerky manner, often with their tails flicking nervously. Tree squirrels forage alone and must rely on their own vigilance to keep them alive. Their sense of hearing and sight are both acute and given even the slightest provocation, the squirrel will bound into the safety of a nearby tree. They take cover in tree holes or lie flat against a branch. They often circle the trunk of the tree, keeping the threat on the opposite side of the trunk to itself. If need be tree squirrels can scamper between trees very rapidly, bounding easily across 2 m gaps.

Tree squirrels do **cache food supplies** to be used at a later time but their pantries are never quite as substantial as European squirrels. They dig small holes into which they deposit seeds and other food debris and then pat the soil down with their chins. This is always done in private, but food thieving is nonetheless common among squirrels.

Tree squirrels are **diurnal** and forage during daylight hours only. They are most busy during the cooler mornings and afternoon periods and generally they will rest up during the heat of the day.

Tree squirrel
Paraxerus cepapi

Tree squirrels are extremely dextrous and **manipulate tiny objects like seeds with expert skill**. They routinely hang from their hind legs to reach food just out of arm's reach or they may even jump and grab, repeating the procedure until the item is obtained. They may clamber over the flimsiest of branches to access fruits. Squirrels usually **sit in an elevated position** while they feed to enable them to look out for danger at the same time.

Although tree squirrels are endothermic (warm-blooded), being small they lose heat rapidly and at colder times of the year are **avid sunbathers**. They may spend a couple of hours in the mornings basking in an elevated spot to warm up before they move off to feed. On return to the nest site in the afternoons, squirrels will again sun themselves to gain heat before the chilly night begins. Sunning sessions usually coincide with grooming sessions. The young receive a compulsory grooming from their mother which holds them down to prevent their escape, much like human children need to be constrained at bath time!

Tree squirrels are **extremely vocal** and their bird-like alarm rattles are a common sound in the bushveld alerting observers and other wildlife to the presence of danger, be it in the form of a snake, raptor or larger carnivore. The noise becomes more intense as the situation progresses and absolute fear is indicated by a higher-pitched whistle. Other squirrels within earshot of the alarm-raiser will rally together at the source of the danger to mob predators like snakes or contribute their own alarms from a safe vantage.

Rock dassies are remarkable for the fact that they colonise an otherwise fairly **inhospitable habitat** – rocks. Rocks are cold when the temperature is low and are extremely hot and exposed when the sun is high.

The colour and stout, rounded body of a dassie is such that it is hard to distinguish it from the often stone-strewn nature of the rocky areas where it lives. This is a form of **camouflage**. Furthermore dassies sit still for long periods of time either sunning themselves or resting. This helps their 'concealment' even further as predators will only recognise them as prey once they are seen moving.

Dassies practise a **heat-sharing activity** known as 'heaping'. This is where layers of huddling dassies form one upon the next and up to four layers deep. Each layer arranges itself such that their rumps face inwards and their heads outwards (to allow for breathing). The young are often on the top. As a result of the close personal contact, all the members of a group develop a common odour. This identifies them to one another and any strangers without the communal smell will be chased off. Newborn babies crawl onto the backs of the adults shortly after birth in order to obtain the group scent.

Under extreme circumstances, dassies are able to **travel up to 20 km** from their usual retreats to seek food. Usually it is only the young males ousted from their natal groups that do any travelling. Sometimes older males are also displaced and must seek new residences. During these travels they are extremely vulnerable to attack and these young and old individuals are primarily the ones preyed on by black eagles.

Dassies **live in harems**. The males are very territorial and do not tolerate other adult males in their turf whatsoever. The male even drives off his own male offspring when they are just over a year old attacking them with his sharp teeth if they do not comply. Each male defends a group of females numbering up to 17 depending on the size of the rocky outcrop and the amount of food available in the area.

Rock dassies (hyrax)
Procavia capensis

Size	50-55 cm long
Weight	3-4,5 kg (female slightly smaller than male)
Lifespan	12 years
Habitat & Distribution	Rocky hills and outcrops
Gestation	7,5 months
# of young	1-6 (average 2-3)
Food	Vegetarian mixed feeders, they take grass and browse even aromatic and poisonous substances
Predators	Caracal, birds of prey especially black eagles, leopard

Dassies are equipped with **sharp incisor teeth**, one large pair on the upper jaw and two pairs on the lower. These teeth are modified for use as defence weapons. They have triangular tips which are sharpened by articulation against the opposite pair. These are especially well developed in the males, the upper pair overlaying the bottom lip and being visible when his mouth is closed. The incisors are sometimes used to strip the bark off trees during spring when the inner bark is rich in moisture and nutrients being transported to the leaves. Usually, however, the majority of the dassie's food is cropped with its cheek teeth, which develop a sharp outer edge through wear and tear. There is a relatively large space between the incisors (there are no other front teeth) and the row of cheek teeth. This arrangement is similar to a rhino's teeth.

Dassies are **strictly diurnal** and will return to their dens before sunset and only emerge well after sunrise unless the temperatures are particularly warm (in which event they may remain out for slightly longer). Because they live in isolated habitats and rely on bolt holes for safety, dassies tend to utilise their available food heavily with the result that only **poor quality forage** is available to them much of the time.

Since making forays further than 500 m to nearby riverine areas for food is too dangerous, they have developed a unique way of saving energy to reduce their intake requirements. Dassies are thermolabile meaning that they can **regulate their own body temperature**. By allowing the body temperature to drop a few degrees, they can save metabolic energy and then they regain the heat through basking in the sun which they do religiously everyday. On cold days, dassies may remain in their dens and huddle to share body heat. They also save energy by spending very little time (only 5%) actively feeding or moving around. Dassies do not handle lengthy exposure to heat well and will retreat into the shade when the sun gets too hot or may spread out their bodies with sides or bellies against the rocks to dissipate heat via the rocks.

Dassies take **refuge** from predators, cold and by night in crevices and holes in the rocks. By day they are seldom further away from such a refuge than 15 m and will take to it as soon as the alarm signals danger from the skies. Black eagles are their primary predators. Usually an older female plays the role of sentinel. Sometimes suitable hiding places are limited and it is thought that this is one of the reasons that dassies live in groups.

In parts of southern Africa dassies provide an essential source of meat and their skins are dried or made into karosses.

The **name dassie originates from the Dutch** word 'das' meaning badger. It was given to the rock hyrax (as it is more technically known) by the Dutch settlers who arrived in the Cape in the 1600s when the area was riddled with dassies. They had never seen dassies before and the closest comparison they could make was with a European badger.

Because dassies are **always on the lookout for black eagles**, they have **highly modified eyes** that are thought to allow them to look directly into the sun. A device in the eye known as the 'umbraculum' acts as a shield. The pupil of a dassie's eye is kidney-shaped. This is orientated horizontally with the concave edge on the top and may also have something to do with their unique vision capabilities.

Dassies are insulated from the cold by a **double layer of fur**. The fur closest to the skin is woolly and warm while the outer layer closes this in with a thicker, rougher layer or guard coat that protects and streamlines the animal. Amongst its normal pelage all over the body are **long tactile** (touch-sensitive) hairs that may protrude by 7 cm. These act like whiskers and help dassies to orientate themselves in the darkness of rock crevices. They also have 10 cm long whiskers on their faces to help with this.

Dassies confine their excretions to **latrines** which may become exceptionally large and stained from protracted usage. Crystallised dassie urine is believed to possess medicinal properties and has been commercially supplied as 'hyracium'.

Dassies have a **well-developed vocabulary** comprising 21 different vocalisations including growls, grunts, wails, squeals, snorts, whistles, twitters and a sharp bark that warns of danger. Repetitive barking is used to advertise territory. Teeth gnashing is used as a non-vocal form of communication.

Rock dassie (hyrax)
Procavia capensis

Dassies **groom themselves** with a specialised grooming claw present on the inner digit of both hind feet. They may also use their lower incisors for this function. Grooming is done regularly to rid themselves of external parasites and dassies will engage in grooming after a bout of sunning. The heat of the sun probably makes the parasites move around making it easier to find and remove them. They may take dust baths to help with parasite removal too.

Dassies have a **unique intestinal tract** amongst mammals. Beyond the stomach is a large sack that contains the bacteria for the fermentative digestion of cellulose. This joins onto the caecum (where bacterial fermentation usually takes place in simple-gut mammals) via a short extension of intestine. The caecum possesses two horn-shaped processes, a design usually found in birds. The caecum is involved in manufacturing fatty acids that serve as an additional source of energy to the energy-conservative dassie.

Dassies **drink when water is available** but they have very efficient kidneys and can extract most of their moisture requirements from the food they eat. If they only have dry material on which to feed, they do rely on dew or succulent plants for moisture.

Dassies, like elephants, are near ungulates. This is the term used to refer to animals that **do not have typical hooves** like antelope or buffalo (ungulates), but which also do not fit into the carnivore or primate groups (which also have specific foot structures). Dassies have four stumpy nailed digits on their front feet and three on the hind feet. The **soles of their feet are naked and padded** to help with traction on the rock faces. Glandular tissue in the feet supplies permanent moisture to the soles, which also improves traction. Although their limbs are short, dassies are most adept at navigating steep and often slipper surfaces and are agile jumpers. They are also good tree climbers and use their front feet to manipulate vegetation.

In the middle of the dassie's back is a patch with longer hair than elsewhere. This is the **dorsal spot** and it **covers the dorsal gland**. The exact function of the gland is unknown but it is suggested that it plays a role in individual recognition especially since during huddling and heaping individuals' noses come into close contact with another's patch. The hair of the dorsal spot is erectile and during bouts of aggression involving growling and the baring of teeth this hair is erected. Aggressive displays are used to displace individuals from favoured sunning spots or to gain access to food. The displaced or submissive individual keeps its dorsal hair flat. These interactions prevent actual fighting which may result in injury.

After a **protracted gestation** period young are born precocial (fully haired with their eyes open). They are capable of agile movement within a day. It is essential that young spend a longer time within the safety of the womb so that they are born well developed and are immediately able to evade danger. Helpless young would quite literally provide 'sitting ducks' to the dassies' predators.

Chacma baboons have a characteristic kink in their **tails**.

Baboons have a **dog-like shaped head** to which the species name *cynocephalus* refers, literally meaning 'dog-head'.

Baboons have **three priorities in a day**. These are to find enough food and water, to find time to play and groom and to avoid predators.

Baboons can **see in colour**. This adaptation supposedly enables them to identify ripe fruit (although they are prone to taking green fruit as well). The fact that they have colour vision means that visual advertising is possible during the female's oestrus period. A male baboon will simply recognise the readiness of a female to mate from the **scarlet colour of the sexual skin around her rump** (ano-genital swelling). This changes to different shades of pink throughout her cycle, being brightest when she is on heat.

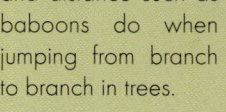

Baboons sleep **above the ground at night**. As with humans, colour vision works better during the day than at night and because they are rendered vulnerable at this time, they sleep in tall trees along rivers or up against cliffs. Baboon troops may not necessarily return to the same roosting site every evening but they do have favourite sites that they frequent and may even defend against other troops if roosting places are in short supply. At night they will perform a racket if disturbed, even urinating and defecating upon the source of the disturbance below. Favourite sleeping sites smell strongly and are stained by baboon excrement over time.

Female baboons can be very promiscuous and will mate up to 100 times with various males when they are on heat. This a female solicits from males by flashing her white eyebrows at them or simply presenting them with her rump. When she reaches the peak of her oestrus, at which time she is most likely to conceive, she will only mate with a dominant male.

Baboons have **forward-facing eyes** that allow them to see with binocular vision. Binocular vision is vital in animals that need to gauge depth and distance such as baboons do when jumping from branch to branch in trees.

Chacma baboon
Papio cynocephalus ursinus

Size	Male: 1,5 m including tail (much larger than female with distinct mane across shoulders) Female: 1,1 m
Weight	Male: 30 kg (up to 40 kg); Female: 15 kg (up to 18 kg)
Lifespan	About 20–30 years
Habitat & Distribution	Wide distribution in a large variety of habitats; they flourish where there is trees to sleep in and water to drink, including semi-desert to woodlands, mountainous areas, but not forest
Gestation	6 months
# of young	1
Food	Omnivores: fruit, grass, seeds, bulbs, invertebrates, small mammals and birds
Predators	Leopard, crocodiles and eagles – possibly lions and hyenas

On the inside of a baboon's mouth there are **cheek pouches** with the capacity to hold as much food as their stomachs do. This is an insurance device that allows baboons to stuff their mouths full of food at resourceful sites. Should they need to evacuate the area due to danger, they can then chew and swallow the food at a later time while safely up a tree or elsewhere out of harm's way.

Baboons are known to **associate with many other herbivores**. Impala benefit from being around baboons as they respond mutually to the other's alarm calls. Impala as well as kudu, bushbuck and civet pick up the scraps of fruits or shoots that baboons knock or drop out of trees. Baboons are undeterred by buffalo and elephants in an area. These large herbivores trample areas and open up feeding grounds for the smaller primates. Baboons also dig through elephant dung to extract tasty morsels of fruit or seeds that have passed undigested through the elephant's gut.

When they are born, **baby baboons** are black with pink faces and ears. The troop members are always fascinated by the small baboons and in many a social dispute may even attempt to use these infants as bargaining leverage by grabbing them. Understandably this creates mayhem amongst the troop and the godfathers perform an important role in protecting these youngsters from any kind of boisterous activity. Godfathers have also been known to care for orphaned babies so long as they are older than 6 months and weaned.

For the first 5 weeks of their lives, the babies cling to the mother's belly where they have an on-tap supply of milk and can be transported safely whenever danger threatens. At 5 weeks old, the babies can walk and at this stage they begin to ride **jockey on their mother's backs** using the kinked tail as a backrest.

Baboons have a **basic daily routine**. They wake early and come down from their roosting sites to sun themselves. During these early hours, important social activities take place in the form of grooming, playing, mating or fighting. Once these are taken care of, the troop will move off to forage. They may take a midday siesta if it is hot. Feeding in the afternoon generally takes them on a circuit back towards a favoured roosting site, timed to reach it before dark so that they can engage in further social activities before retiring to the trees or a cliff face for the night.

Baboons are **long-lived animals** that exhibit a great deal of intelligence, a criterion for animals that practise complex social systems. The young are born altricial which means they are rather helpless for some time after arrival. They grow slowly and through various stages including infant, juvenile, adolescent and adult. **As they grow, they learn,** much like human children must, the subtleties of life in the community. They learn what to eat by watching other more experienced baboons as well as where to find food, refuges and water.

For a **young male baboon**, rising up the ranks within his natal troop is extremely difficult. Young males will usually emigrate at 6 or 7 years old (after puberty) and they will join another troop of baboons where they have no genetic ties. These youngsters act aggressively and quickly rise in seniority. Males may move more than once until they find a troop where they stand the best chance of becoming dominant and hence winning access to females to breed.

Baboons are **not territorial**. Because of their tendency to roam (sometimes up to 15 km) in search of food and water, they do not limit themselves to a particular defended area. Often troops' home ranges will overlap with one another in an area and although a great deal of shouting may ensue when they meet up, it is only really sleeping sites (a valued resource to escape danger at night) that are defended by barking, chasing and branch-shaking.

Baboons are one of few animals with the dexterity to **dig for water**. In this regard they perform a useful ecological role, opening up pits in dry river beds and drainage lines that can subsequently be accessed by other animals like antelope especially during the dry times of the year. Another animal that does this is the elephant. Baboons are **very water-dependent and need to drink daily**.

Baboons have **dexterous hands** with opposable thumbs. These are used to manipulate various food substances while foraging and feeding. This may take the form of peeling tough skin off fruit or overturning rocks in search of scorpions, insects or slugs. The fingers are nailed to assist with digging. They will dig up clumps of grass which they shake free of loose dirt before eating or they may patiently dig to unearth a juicy bulb up to 30 cm below even hard ground.

Baboons spend a fair deal of time sitting while they are feeding and they have subsequently developed **built-in cushions on their buttocks**, called ischial callosities. In females these are separate but in males they fuse to form a band below his anus.

Chacma baboon
Papio cynocephalus ursinus

The **social system** practised by baboons is known as an oligarchy. What this means is that baboons have a band of dominant males that work cooperatively to defend the females in the troop and they thus share the breeding resource. Baboons do not have a harem system where only one male is dominant although there is a strict status hierarchy within the troop with young, prime individuals (usually the immigrants) being most aggressive and hence dominant. Males visually advertise their dominance by a display of their impressive canines.

Baboons are **terrestrial primates** and they spend the majority of their day on the ground. This is unusual for a member of the monkey family, most of which are confined to safer tree habitats. Baboons will take to trees to sleep, to look for or escape danger or if the trees are fruiting. There are risks to living in the open and moving away from the refuge of trees. To overcome these risks, baboons live together in large troops. There is an element of safety in numbers because of this as well as shared vigilance (lots of eyes and ears looking for danger). If danger threatens, the alarm is barked most noisily and contagiously. The dominant males then act cooperatively in the interest of defending their troop. They are large, formidable animals and have canine teeth that rival even a lion's in size. A predator would place itself at grave risk should it take on such a defensive band.

Living in a group has its disadvantages. Amongst a troop of baboons there will be competition between individuals for food (or other social rights). The most dominant animals automatically get access to the best spots but by persuading more dominant individuals to form an alliance with it, a lowlier ranked baboon can enjoy first class feeding sites and other privileges too. Baboons **build relationships through grooming**.

Within the troop, smaller sub-groups or cliques form through grooming. These individuals will usually sleep together, feed together and males (known as godfathers) will come to the rescue of the females that groom them (and their babies) should they be harassed by other baboons. All males are dominant over females but there is a dominance hierarchy amongst females too and it is particularly useful to have a male around to settle inter-female disputes. Females remain in the troop where they were born for life and they inherit the status of their mothers. This status does change temporarily depending on her reproductive condition, with mothers with infant black babies being especially elevated in rank.

Baboons are **omnivores** meaning they eat both plant and animal materials. Most of their diet comprises fruit, seeds, bulbs, rhizomes, the thick bases of grass stems and invertebrates. They are extremely resourceful and will eat almost anything except rotting meat. They even hunt. Baboons will capture small mammals and birds opportunistically including rabbits, birds like Egyptian geese, and lambs of small antelope. It is usually the more dominant males who will hunt and eat meat.

Baboons have a **broad vocabulary** including screams, squeals, barks and chatters. The 'ba-hoo' of a dominant male is a well-known sound in the bushveld as it echoes off cliff faces and down valleys. Vocal communication is used to maintain contact while foraging, to alarm for danger or to demonstrate mood in social contexts. Baboons have very expressive faces and rely on the use of their lips and brows to communicate visually as well. The combination of both vocal and visual signals significantly enhances their social communication repertoire.

Vervet monkeys are almost exclusively the **only monkeys** found in the Lowveld (there may still be few isolated patches where samango monkeys are found but these are rare).

Vervets are attractive monkeys with an all-grey pelage and striking black faces. The fur fringing the face is tinged white to **highlight the facial expressions** during social encounters. A vervet monkey wishing to intimidate another will raise its brow to reveal the white eyelids which contrast sharply with the black face conveying an unmistakable message to the recipient.

Groups of about 20 vervets make up a **troop** in which there is a strict **hierarchy of rank** amongst the males and amongst the females. All males outrank females and the status of an infant is inherited from its mother. There is usually one male which dominates the troop overall and he (and a few other high-rankers) is generally most in demand as a mate to the females. Dominance benefits females by allowing them the best access to prime feeding and sleeping sites.

Vervet monkeys (unlike baboons) are **territorial**. They demarcate their defended area by dispatching scent from the cheek and chest region onto the branches of trees. Where many vervets are found together in a large group, there usually is a particularly sought-after common resource like a tree in fruit or a source of water. Although they will all make use of the resource, they do not necessarily do so amicably and once done will separate into their usual separate troops.

Vervet monkey
Cercopithecus aethiops

Size	Male: 114 cm (tail 65 cm); Female: 100 cm (tail 58 cm)
Weight	Male: 5,5 kg; Female: 4 kg
Lifespan	12 years
Habitat & Distribution	Arboreal, especially riparian vegetation (i.e. along rivers)
Gestation	5,5 months
# of young	1
Food	Diet varied, includes fruit, flowers, leaves, buds, seeds, pods, gum, insects, bird's eggs and nestlings, occasionally reptiles. Feed in trees or on the ground
Predators	Birds of prey, snakes especially pythons, leopard (and other medium to large carnivores) and baboons

Vervet monkeys have an **impressive vocal repertoire** with 36 calls recorded but there's a probability more exist. At least six different alarm signals have been identified and are used to indicate the presence of different types of predators be it an aerial threat (i.e. bird of prey) or a prowling leopard. When distressed, vervets will alarm call constantly and stare in the direction of the source of disturbance making it possible for humans to locate predators by following the gaze of the alarming animals.

The vervet monkey **status hierarchy works to absorb aggression** within the troop. If a dominant animal should attack a lower ranked individual in a display of status, the subordinate will not react to the attacker but rather will vent its frustrations on an even lower ranked member of the troop. As a result, the lowliest of the social community can easily be picked out of the troop by a prevalence of bite marks at the base of its tail.

Vervet monkeys are **gregarious and social creatures**. Animals which live together are known as gregarious animals but not all gregarious animals are social. Sociality depends on whether the animals within a group interact with other members of the group. Vervet monkeys use tactile communication in the form of allo-grooming (mutual cleaning) to forge relationships and elicit favours amongst themselves. Females groom the most and lower ranking individuals always try to curry favour with higher ranked animals through grooming. Visual displays are important and the raising of an eyebrow might convey a threat while the baring of teeth or the bobbing of a head could mean aggression for the recipient. Within the group, more closely related individuals interact more intensively and rally together to support each other during disputes. The majority of social interaction takes place during the rest period in the heat of the day.

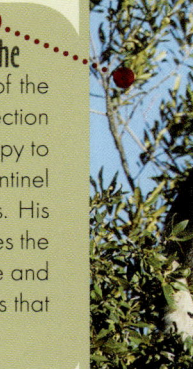

Because of their vested paternal interest in the troop, the more **dominant males perform the service as sentinel** most reliably and raise the alarm more frequently than the other members of the group. At the alarm, the other vervets will look immediately to the sentinel to determine the direction of the threat. In the case of a bird of prey, the troop will take to the densest part of the tree canopy to hide. In the case of a snake, they may rise up on their hind legs and chatter agitatedly. The sentinel also provides a **passive alarm system by occupying a conspicuous perch** while the troop forages. His white belly is obvious to the members of troop and the presence of the male on his perch assures the foragers that the coast is clear. Should the sentinel abandon his post, the entire troop will notice and quietly slip into cover. By not raising the alarm, the troop can escape the attentions of predators that may not yet have noticed them. Vervets also respond to the alarm calls of birds.

In order to discern ripe from unripe fruit, vervet monkeys have **colour vision**. The most favoured and productive of resources for vervet monkeys is a tree in fruit. Since fruit makes up a large proportion of their diets it is imperative to be able to tell when it is ripe. While it is still green, fruit contains tannins and alkaloids which often taste bitter and are sometimes even toxic. Once they ripen they lose the distastefulness and become rich in healthy sugars. Sometimes, however, vervets do eat the fruit while it is still green.

Vervet monkeys have **eyes** which face forward and the fields of vision overlap to enable them to gauge depth and distance. This is known as binocular vision and is imperative for a lifestyle that involves jumping between branches of trees.

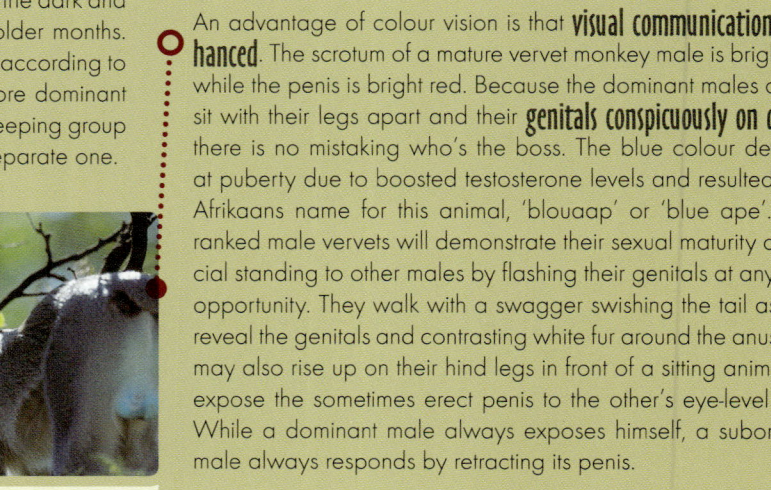

Colour vision assists with detecting ripe fruit and in dominance displays by the males but a higher incidence of cones (colour cells) to rods (light-sensitive black and white cells) in the eyes means that night vision is compromised. Before nightfall, vervets **take to the trees** (the larger the better) where they hide in dense foliage to escape detection by nocturnal predators. They huddle together while sleeping for assurance in the dark and for warmth during the colder months. Generally vervets group according to rank at night with the more dominant individuals forming one sleeping group and the subordinates a separate one.

An advantage of colour vision is that **visual communication is enhanced**. The scrotum of a mature vervet monkey male is bright blue while the penis is bright red. Because the dominant males always sit with their legs apart and their **genitals conspicuously on display**, there is no mistaking who's the boss. The blue colour develops at puberty due to boosted testosterone levels and resulted in the Afrikaans name for this animal, 'blouaap' or 'blue ape'. High-ranked male vervets will demonstrate their sexual maturity and social standing to other males by flashing their genitals at any given opportunity. They walk with a swagger swishing the tail aside to reveal the genitals and contrasting white fur around the anus. They may also rise up on their hind legs in front of a sitting animal and expose the sometimes erect penis to the other's eye-level gaze. While a dominant male always exposes himself, a subordinate male always responds by retracting its penis.

Vervet monkey
Cercopithecus aethiops

Vervet monkeys have **very sharp canines to use as weapons of defence** and aggression or as tools to forage. The teeth are kept sharp because the edge of the upper canines occludes to the edge of the lower premolars and every action of the teeth refines the cutting surface.

Vervet monkeys have **long tails** which are important instruments of balance. The tail helps to steady the monkey during leaps through the branches of a tree and assists with balance when they run along vertical branches. The tail is prehensile meaning it can be used to grip things and acts as an additional limb while the monkey moves and forages in precarious positions in the trees.

Babies are carried clinging to the mother's stomach and chest. The paired mammary glands are situated between the front legs and the baby can conveniently suckle while in transit. Babies are looked after by all the females in a troop, including younger members and any and all members of the troop will rush to their defence if they are threatened.

Vervets have **long whiskers** which are tactile sensory organs and assist them with navigating around trees.

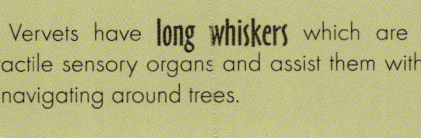

Vervets have **hands with dexterous digits** and opposable thumbs which facilitate grip when climbing and jumping in trees and also the manipulation of food objects. They also use their fingers adeptly when allo-grooming one another's fur, fingering through the pelage of a troop mate and deftly removing bits of dead skin, salt and ectoparasites.

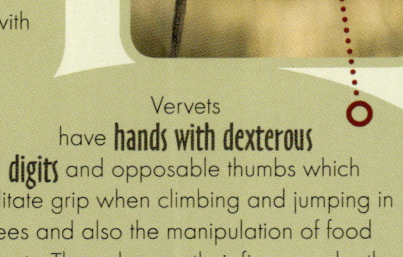

Females spend their entire life in the troop where they were born. Males leave the troop and join another as this improves their chance of rising in rank and ultimately breeding. **Brothers band together** and depart as a group once they reach sexual maturity and they usually time the departure with the onset of the breeding season. The automatic departure of young males at this time also helps to reduce aggression within the natal troop, as the dominant males then need not exert discipline on the newly mature individuals. Sometimes older males may also disperse but these tend to join more distant troops and it is thought this behaviour contributes to healthy genetic exchange amongst a population.

Play is an important mechanism of learning. Young monkeys learn skills and hone the muscles they need to become independent of their parents and fend for themselves amongst a troop. Young animals learn how to integrate socially through play and mimic the older animals' actions in the process of learning what to eat and which alarm signals denote which predators.

Predators

Cheetahs are predators **specialised for speed**. Clocking a record speed of 112 km/h, they are undoubtedly the fastest land mammals. Generally cheetahs only accelerate up to between 75-100 km/h at a full sprint and this lasts only a few hundred metres before they tire.

Cheetahs have **long legs**, long, flexible spines and wasp-like waists that in combination effect the long strides necessary to run quickly.

The **tail** is long and acts as a rudder to counterbalance the cheetah when it has to change direction quickly.

The **chest** of the cheetah is deep set to accommodate its large lungs and heart, the internal powerhouse of the sprinter.

Cheetahs are not considered social cats like lions but they do prefer to live in **family groups** (i.e. a female with her most recent litter) or in the case of the males, to cooperate as **coalitions** (usually groups of about three brothers) to reinforce their sway against other males. Males have smaller territories than females, which they demarcate with urine and faeces and these overlap with areas regularly used by females although males will only accompany females when they are actually in oestrus. Males use ritualised threat displays to chase intruders away but will fight over females in heat with slaps of the front paws.

Although cheetahs are relatively large in size, they generally **do not attack large ungulates** (hoofed animals) like wildebeest, zebra or buffalo. This is due to the fact that pulling these powerful animals down requires great strength, which the cheetah lacks and in the process would **risk injury** to itself. Coalitions of males may cooperate to pull down larger prey but usually they target younger animals of these species.

Cheetah
Acinonyx jubatus

The cheetah is easily recognised by the presence of two black **'tear marks'** running down the sides of its nose from the corner of the eyes to the corners of the mouth. They also have black spots covering the body rather than the rosettes characteristic of leopards.

Size	2 m head to end of tail; 0,8 m at shoulder
Weight	40-60 kg
Lifespan	16 years
Habitat & Distribution	Open plains and savanna woodland without thick undergrowth
Gestation	95 days
# of young	1-6 (average 4)
Prey	Medium to small antelope or young of large antelope, also wide range of ground birds and small mammals including guineafowl, bustards, ostriches, hares and porcupine
Predators	Lion, leopard, hyena

The **head** is small and streamlined with small ears. The teeth are smaller than other similar-sized predators as these make the skull heavy. The reduced dentition also makes room for bigger nasal cavities to improve oxygen intake while in full sprint and to facilitate breathing when suffocating captured prey. Cheetahs also have aerodynamic nostrils to maximise the flow of air over them while running.

Cheetahs are **picky eaters** skimming meat neatly off the surface of a carcass. They may eat the heart and liver but the other innards are discarded. Bones and skin are also discarded due to their toughness and the cheetah's diminished dentition and small jaws. They only scavenge occasionally and usually when displacing another predator is not required.

In order to be successful, cheetahs must get close enough to their quarry before embarking on the final sprint and are thus **accomplished stalkers**. They hunt in open areas, making use of any available cover to stalk or they may simply walk directly towards the prey freezing immediately should the animal raise its head. Cheetahs will try to get within 100 m of their target before chasing it and they typically choose animals isolated on the skirt of a herd. Once the **chase is underway**, cheetahs will pursue the animal for a short time only and its marvellous sprinting ability must enable it to gain on the prey almost immediately in order to trip it up with a paw and then secure a throat grip (thus depriving the prey of already depleted oxygen reserves) or else the cheetah will abandon the chase. Once a kill is made, the cheetah is too exhausted to feed immediately and rests to catch its breath first. Prey is eaten where it falls or dragged to nearby shade if possible.

Because cheetahs are so **over-specialised for speed** they are almost totally defenceless against larger predators like lion, leopard, hyena and even vultures. As a result they are **very susceptible to losing kills** to larger predators. After making a sprint to kill, cheetahs are typically exhausted and cannot begin to feed immediately. To avoid the attentions of largely nocturnal carnivores, cheetahs hunt during the day (i.e. are diurnal predators). However, all predators are opportunistic and should they become aware of a kill, they will scavenge regardless of the time of day.

Cheetahs regularly make use of elevated **vantage points** when resting or hunting. They are poor climbers but will take to sloping tree branches or climb atop termite mounds in order to better view their surroundings, looking out for prey or enemies like lion.

Although they are **diurnal predators** (i.e. active during the daytime), cheetahs still prefer to use the cooler morning and late afternoon hours to hunt and move, resting up in the shade during the hotter parts of the day (somewhere with a view of their surrounds). If it is cold, cheetahs like to sun themselves before becoming active later than usual.

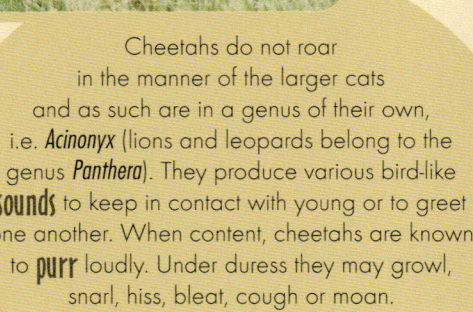 

Cheetahs do not roar in the manner of the larger cats and as such are in a genus of their own, i.e. *Acinonyx* (lions and leopards belong to the genus *Panthera*). They produce various bird-like **sounds** to keep in contact with young or to greet one another. When content, cheetahs are known to **purr** loudly. Under duress they may growl, snarl, hiss, bleat, cough or moan.

At some point in their recent history (about 10 000 years ago), cheetahs went through a **population bottleneck** resulting in the fact that there is very little genetic diversity amongst all the cheetahs in the world.

A recessive gene in cheetahs occasionally causes a deviant colour form in which the usual spots of the cheetah merge to form lines down the body and flanks of the animal. So impressive is this varied colouration that these animals have been dubbed **'king cheetahs'**.

Cheetah
Acinonyx jubatus

Cheetahs are considered attentive mothers and **cubs**, which are born in tall grass or other cleverly hidden sites after just 3 months' gestation, will **regularly be moved** to remain undetected and free of parasite infestations. The female painstakingly moves her cubs one at a time, pinching them by the scruff of the neck which relaxes the nerves in that area and calms the cubs as they travel. The female brings meat back to her litter when they are still as young as 5 weeks old and in just 3 months the cubs are completely weaned and by 8 months old will **begin to hunt** and make their own kills.

Cheetah cubs **gain independence** and begin fending for themselves at just 18 months old. Before reaching an age at which cheetah can secure choice territories or settle into fixed home ranges, they become nomadic and wander great distances, putting themselves at great risk to attack by other large predators. Survival during this period is also compromised by competition with other cheetahs and similar-sized carnivores for food.

Leopard	Cheetah
Stocky, powerful build	Slender, slight build
Large head and skull, strong neck and body	Small head, long tail, slender waist and long legs
Powerful attacker – master of camouflage for stalking	Sprinter lacking strength – catches prey by oxygen starvation through fast chase and subsequent suffocation
Prey can be hoisted up trees to evade other predators or scavengers	Always feeds on ground usually where the prey falls or in nearby shade, often loses kills to other predators or scavengers
Feeding commences immediately	Needs to catch breath before feeding
Rosettes	Black spots
No tear-marks	Tear-marks down sides of nose
Very adaptable to many habitats and whatever is most common to eat, even formidable prey	Requires open plains for hunting where there are low lion densities. Takes small to medium-sized antelope, never big or dangerous species
Solitary males	Coalitions of males
Scavenge readily	Fussy eaters, prefer fresh meat
Retractable claws	Only semi-retractable claws

Young cheetah cubs (up to 3 months old) have a **mantle of grey fur** along the saddle of their backs which at quick glance resembles the colouration of the formidable **honey badger**. This mimicry is believed to deter larger predators from attacking the defenceless cubs as predators mistake them for the more ferocious and generally avoided badger.

Adult cheetahs also have a crest of hair down their backs but this generally lies flat and is only erected when the cheetah wishes to appear larger. Males in confrontation with other males or individuals threatened by enemies will **pilo-erect** the longer hair on their backs to accentuate their size and thus **appear more formidable** or intimidating.

Although it is commonly thought that cheetahs cannot 'retract' their claws at all, they do in fact have **semi-retractable** claws but these are unsheathed and so appear to be permanently protruding. This is an adaptation to assist with traction during the chase. Pads on the underside of the feet are hard and often ridged, which also assists with traction and improves their braking ability.

Wild dogs are **cooperative breeders**. They live in packs of about 12 but sometimes up to 30 dogs. Remarkably only one pair, the alpha pair, breeds. All the other dogs cooperate to hunt and to support the breeding effort. Collectively the relatively small dogs are better able to catch more and bigger prey and can successfully raise more pups than if each dog tried to do so alone.

There is a **beta male and female** which sit next in the hierarchy to the alpha pair. If something happens to one of the alpha dogs, the beta animal will automatically take over. Sometimes the beta pair will mate and breed but the alpha female will either kill or steal the beta bitch's puppies.

Adults in a **founder pack** of wild dogs are same-sex related. All the males are brothers and all the females are sisters. They leave their natal packs as same-sexed groups when they disperse, joining up with an opposite-sexed group. The **breeding alpha male and female act as representatives from each gene line**. All the other adults that support the breeding pair are supporting the perpetuation of their own genes. This is known as 'kin selection'. Obviously, as litters are produced they are incorporated into the group and too have vested genetic interest in assisting their parents raise further litters.

Non-breeding individuals in the pack take turns to **perform different functions**. 'Den-guards' stay at the mound where the young pups are hidden to protect them from any predatory passers-by. Other dogs join the hunting group and help to secure food to provide for the pups and any sick members left at the den. All the adults will help to clean the pups and prevent them from straying.

Wild dog
Lycaon pictus

Size	75 cm (at shoulder)
Weight	20-30 kg (male larger than female)
Lifespan	6-12 years
Habitat & Distribution	Savanna woodland and broken hilly country with open plains
Gestation	70 days (2+ months)
# of young	Litter up to 21 pups (average 7-10)
Prey	Favourite prey is impala but also take small to medium antelope including kudu, duiker and steenbok and occasionally wildebeest, zebra and even buffalo
Predators	Lion, leopard, hyena

Wild dogs time their **denning period** to coincide with the end of the impala rut (breeding season). At this time there are a number of out of condition rams exhausted by intense territorial defence and breeding stress. During the dry season there are increased concentrations of game at the waterholes and the veld is more open, providing improved visibility for hunting (wild dogs hunt by sight). These ideal hunting circumstances mean that the puppies can be well fed and develop quickly so that the pack can return to their nomadic lifestyle quickly. The pups leave the den by 2,5 months old. They may straggle behind during hunts but they follow the adults by scent and the adults come and fetch them once the kill is executed.

Wild dogs make use of disused aardvark burrows as **dens**. The pups are born blind and helpless (altricial) and need the safety of the burrow to develop. The holes are lined with grass and leaves and if the dogs are disturbed in any way or if parasite loads build up, the female will move her pups one by one to a new site. She does this by casually gripping them by a leg or any part of the body.

The pack carries meat back to the den in the safety of their stomachs where they will **regurgitate** whole solid chunks for the puppies and babysitter. There is a great deal of excitement around feeding time and the returning hunters yip enthusiastically to summons the pups, which beg instinctively to induce the regurgitation. Adult dogs may also assume infantile begging to get food. This is accompanied by whining and the licking and nudging of the other dog's face.

Wild dogs have **heavy skulls** with strong muscles to power the massive lower jawbone. As a result, they have a **very powerful bite**. The upper incisors are modified and wear down into sharp canine-like weapons which are used in gripping prey. The carnassial shear (blade-like cheek-teeth) of the wild dog is reinforced with a sectorial (lower first molar) to enhance its cutting ability.

Lycaon pictus means 'painted wolf' and refers to the wild dog's **mottled coat**. This is uniquely patterned in each dog.

Wild dogs have **large round ears** that actuate acute hearing, performing a similar sound-collecting function to a satellite dish. Sometimes when wild dogs are resting during the heat of the day, all that is visible above the grass are the super-large twitching ears.

The wild dog is one of Africa's **most endangered carnivores**, second only to the Ethiopian wolf. Their misunderstood hunting techniques led them to be considered vermin and historically they were eradicated by farmers and game wardens. Nowadays there is inadequate habitat to support their nomadic lifestyles and populations suffer huge blows from diseases like rabies and canine distemper.

Wild dogs have obvious **white-tipped tails** which provide an effective following mechanism in tall grass. They are also used in communication, being an indication of a particular animal's mood. A relaxed dog hangs its tail downwards or curves it up during social attractions. If the tail stiffens, this indicates aggression and if it curls between the legs it represents submission.

Wild dog
Lycaon pictus

Wild dogs **hunt by coursing**. This is the process whereby the hunter walks directly up to its prey (no stalk involved) and begins chasing it relentlessly for a protracted time. Wild dogs can achieve speeds of 50-60 km/h for several kilometres. The prey becomes exhausted at which point it is disembowelled. This kills an animal extremely quickly and is not as brutal as often thought. In fact, disembowelment terminates a life faster than the supposedly more 'humane' suffocation tactics of the cats.

Wild dogs **eat very quickly** dispatching of an adult impala carcass in just 15 minutes. They do this to avoid the attentions of other large predators like lion, leopard and hyena all of which will attempt to deprive them of their kills. Wild dogs will stand up to other predators if packs have adequate numbers, treeing leopards and driving off lone hyena.

In order to follow abundant game herds and avoid confrontation with lions (which steal their food and kill both adults and puppies), wild dogs are **nomadic** occupying ranges in excess of 450 km^2. They become sedentary for the 3 months that they den between May and July. They do not defend territorial boundaries of any sort but they will defend their den. The **alpha pair scent-marks their current home range through anal-dragging** and all members of the pack mark their environs with urine and body-rubbing.

There is **little aggression** within a pack of wild dogs due to a **ritualised greeting ceremony**. The puppies in the pack are the most privileged individuals and from their begging process, this infantile appeasement ritual has developed whereby dogs lick each other's faces, nuzzle the corners of the mouth and whine. Every dog submits to the dominant pair.

The wild dog makes a characteristic and very **excited bird-like twittering** call before embarking on a hunt and again once prey has been captured. They also make contact amongst themselves with a musical 'hoo' or growl-bark an alarm.

Because they engage in lengthy hunting chases, wild dogs have well-developed **nasal passages** which facilitate breathing during this exertion.

The spotted hyena is arguably the **most successful large carnivore** in Africa because it is both a proficient hunter and scavenger exhibiting resourcefulness and stamina in its foraging pursuits. It is the only mammal able to digest bone, which it crushes easily in its powerful jaws and thereby extracts calcium and protein unavailable to other animals. Hyenas are extremely mobile and will travel up to 70 km in a night to access food if need be.

Although its physical appearance would have us believe that it is related to dogs, the hyena is in fact more closely related to cats. Among the carnivore families, this **unique animal enjoys its own family** known as Hyaenidae and is neither cat nor dog. There are four species in the Hyaenidae family including the spotted hyena, brown hyena and aardwolf (which are found in Africa) and the striped hyena (found in Asia).

Hyenas have **exceptional senses** with sight (especially night vision), smell and hearing all being excellent. A hyena's olfactory capabilities are remarkable and animals may follow scent trails that are already 3 days old.

The spotted hyena is a large carnivore with massive forequarters modified for carrying heavy carcasses. The large head and neck are well equipped with muscles to actuate the kinds of crushing and tearing jaw actions that hyenas use. The enlarged forequarters give the hyena a sloped appearance and the front feet are larger than the hind to accommodate the extra forward weight. This **body structure** is also an adaptation to the loping energy-efficient gait used by hyenas when they forage.

Hyenas have a **crest of hair** that runs down their neck and shoulders. This is erectile and pilo-erection is used to make the individual appear larger to intimidate rivals or predators.

The bizarre female genitals are the focus of the hyena **greeting ceremony** whereby two hyenas from the same clan stand head to tail and lift their legs to **expose the erect genitals to the other's nose.** Only animals familiar with one another will engage in this greeting ceremony and males (the less dominant sex) are particularly reluctant to expose their most vulnerable parts to the powerful jaw of a female. This ritual is a **form of social bonding amongst clan members** that need to have good cohesion to perform team activities like attacking prey or lions and defending the territory.

Spotted hyena
Crocuta crocuta

The spotted hyena gets its **common name** from the irregular dark spots on its pelage. Females gradually lose these markings with age. Young hyenas are usually darker in colour than older ones.

Size	85 cm (at shoulder)
Weight	Male: 60 kg Female: 70–80 kg (larger of the two sexes)
Lifespan	20 years
Habitat & Distribution	Wide tolerance (except forest and desert)
Gestation	16 weeks
# of young	2
Prey	Usually young of large antelope like wildebeest but opportunistic and will take almost any mammal, bird, fish, reptile as well as vegetable matter, carrion and even garbage (eats 3,8 kg of meat a day)
Predators	Lion, other hyenas (diseased animals)

The **genitals** of a female hyena **closely resemble those of a male**, making hyenas extremely hard to sex except that adult females are larger than adult males. On close examination, the pseudo-penis (which is actually a pseudo-scrotum and an enlarged penis-like clitoris) lacks the triangular glans (tip) of a male's penis. Hyenas are not hermaphrodites as myth has previously suggested. The strange female genital **contains the opening to the birth canal**. The penis-like organ develops due to exposure to high androgen levels in the womb and female hyenas possess much higher testosterone levels than one would expect of a female animal.

A hyena's **skull is as massive as a lion's** with a female's skull weighing in at 3 kg. The large skull provides ample attachment for the muscles that action the powerful jaws which subsequently actuate the hyena's powerful bite. The hyena's teeth equip it well for its lifestyle. The canines, assisted by the upper outer incisors, are heavy and provide lethal grip. The molars are adapted to crushing the densest bones and the carnassial shear (the flattened blade-like molar-premolar tooth arrangement common to all carnivores) enables hyena to slice through cartilage and tough skin.

Hyenas **have 14 calls** including whoops, grunts, groans, lowing, giggles, snarls, yelling and whines. The 'whoop' is the most conspicuous as it travels a great distance and is often heard at night as hyenas advertise their presence or rally their clan members to assist with territory defence or the hunting of food. Like lions, hyenas recognise one another's calls and respond accordingly. Spotted hyenas are notorious for their giggled vocalisation. This is emanated while feeding together on a kill as a sign of deference or included amidst a cacophony of different vocalisations during frantic encounters with lions.

A hyena's **droppings are very conspicuous** and turn white on drying. This is as a result of the high calcium content from eating bones. Leopard tortoises sometimes eat hyena scat to benefit from this calcium content to bolster their bony shells. Hyenas make use of well-visited latrines as part of their territorial demarcation.

Hyenas **live in clans** dominated by the larger, more aggressive females. Each clan defends a territory of about 130 km². Females have a rank hierarchy amongst themselves and all females (and their female cubs) are dominant over all males. **Female cubs inherit their mother's status** and they form coalitions around her in which they operate (i.e. hunt together). These coalitions, especially if lower ranked, will sometimes break away to form new clans where their status is improved. Young males leave the clan at 2 years of age to be inducted into a new clan which will give them a slightly elevated status as they are genetically vigorous. They will work hard to gain social favour in order to mate with females. Sometimes males will simply remain alone.

The focus of a hyena clan centres on a **communal den** (usually a disused aardvark hole with multiple entrances for easy access) where all the females keep their young. Unlike lions they do not mutually suckle each other's young but like lions, they come and go as they please, members separating and reuniting randomly. Adults seldom go inside the den where the cubs typically dig small tunnels to escape into if danger threatens. They remain at the entrance where they suckle their young on the **richest milk of any terrestrial carnivore**. The cubs remain within the confines of their maze-like den being fed on only milk for a protracted time (they only wean at 14-18 months old). The hyena's strategy is to keep their young safe by leaving them at the den and thus out of harm's way for as long as possible and to avoid the attention of competitors like lions by taking food back to them in the form of milk rather than actual meat.

Spotted hyena
Crocuta crocuta

Hyenas are coursers, hunting by chasing prey until they or the prey exhaust. They form the **vital ecological function** of eliminating sick and old animals from populations, the easiest targets. They choose a victim by blundering into the middle of a herd of animals and do not stalk in the manner of cats. Hyenas are more successful as hunters than similar-sized predators due to their remarkable endurance. They are able to chase prey at a speed of 60 km/h for over 2 km and have been known to follow herds of animals almost 30 km before making a kill. They may hunt alone or in cooperative groups.

Hyenas **scent-mark their territories** by wiping an everted anal gland over a shaft of grass, thereby depositing a strong-smelling secretion on it. This is known as pasting. Cubs as young as 4 weeks old begin practising this.

Hyenas will dispossess lions of their food if they have the advantage of four hyenas to one lioness.

Hyenas typically **regurgitate pellets** of indigestible material such as hair and antelope hooves.

Since hyenas **scavenge** so readily, it is thought that they play a role in the **natural control of diseases** like anthrax by disposing of carcasses. The degree to which hyenas scavenge depends on the concentration of lions in a given area. Where lions are numerous, hyenas scavenge more often. Where hyena numbers are high and lion numbers low, hyenas hunt more often (and lions then scavenge from them).

Giving birth is no easy task for a hyena mother. The birth canal traverses the pseudo-penis and is twice as long as in other mammals. The umbilical cord disconnects from the placenta while the cub is still inside the birth canal, the opening of which is far smaller than the cub's head. As a result first-time mothers often produce stillborn cubs due to oxygen starvation. Due to the uro-genital opening splitting, subsequent births are a little easier.

Hyena **cubs are very playful** and make for entertaining viewing. They chase each other around, clamber over the adults and pick up objects like sticks during their games. These activities all help to hone developing muscles as well as the lifestyle skills they will require as adults.

Unlike other carnivores, **hyena cubs are born with their eyes open**, canines fully erupted and aggressive tendencies intact. The female usually gives birth to twins, which in the case of two female cubs, means that the battle for dominance begins immediately and one cub usually dies. If one of the cubs is male, the female naturally dominates him and there is no need for fighting.

Cats use their **ears to demonstrate their mood**. Caracals' ears as well as the striking black and white facial markings (which are present from birth) are used to emphasise their expressions. Being territorial, caracal **prefer to live alone**. Their markings come in useful when they interact with an intruder and the ears are then used as a signalling system, the black tufts perfectly highlighting their position. Caracals in visual display will face each other, move their heads side to side and flick their ears to show hostility to each other. By warding off potential contestants without actually engaging in combat reduces the risk of personal injury.

The **black ears** are also used as 'follow me' signs to youngsters following behind in long grass. The black stands out against the tawny grass and the tawny cat but because it's behind the animal, it doesn't give away the camouflage.

Caracals have a reputation worldwide for their speed and agility in executing **aerial bird kills**. They have a propensity for ambushing sandgrouse and doves at waterholes and will often secure two birds from a two-pawed swat in just one leap. An ancient Middle Eastern sport even used tamed caracals to this end and hence originated the expression 'to put a cat among the pigeons'.

Caracal prefer to **hunt by night** which affords them the best cover but a degree of kills do take place during the day on cool or cloudy days. The give-away black ears are tucked back when the cat stalks, presenting only the sandy fur along the leading edge in the direction of the victim. It's imperative that a caracal is not detected prematurely as its success depends on an unexpected pounce or a blinding dash over the last few metres. The **killing blow** takes the form of a bite to the neck or throat. Birds are consumed entirely bar a few feathers. Other carcasses are eaten from the rump without the innards removed. Clumps of fur are plucked around the feeding site and the meat is neatly sheared away from the skin.

Caracal are **formidable predators**. They can take down prey the same size as leopards, including female kudu, adult springbok and grey rhebok – species twice their own weight.

Caracal
Caracal caracal

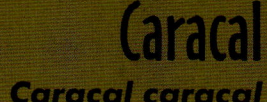

Size	± 0,45m (shoulder height)
Weight	8 – 13 kg (female); 12 – 19 kg (male)
Lifespan	Approximately 10 years
Habitat & Distribution	Open areas, especially arid bush. Uses plains, vleis, rocky areas, mountains and mixed woodland. Must have woody cover for hunting or danger evasion. Endangered in the northern reaches of their distribution which extends throughout Africa and Asia. Home ranges sometimes extend up to 50 km².
Gestation	78 days
# of young	2 or 3 altricial young (up to 4)
Prey	Dassies (53%), antelope like grey rhebok (up to twice its weight), hares, rabbits, rodents, birds, monkeys, reptiles (1%) and small carnivores; flush sandgrouse from waterholes
Predators	Larger carnivores, pythons, birds of prey (take young)

Caracal are superb **jumpers** and can jump 4 – 5 m into the air from sitting. This is possible due to the power of huge **hindquarters**. The characteristic short stubby tail steadies them during these acrobatic leaps.

Large paws house heavily built, **protractible claws** that make no sound as the caracal moves. The dew claws are nifty devices too. Higher up the wrist and not imprinting in the spoor, these are used as securing apparatus, especially useful for climbing trees, when pulling down prey or even for use on an opponent when posturing proves inadequate.

Caracal **kittens** have their characteristic pronounced facial markings from birth. They also have a pronounced vocabulary communicating initially with high-pitched twitters which quickly develop into full-blown feline purrs, hisses, growls and spits. Hunting instincts are also present from early on. Like many other mammals, youngsters use the time while parents are away hunting or guarding territories to play – stalking things like lizards and insects and thereby honing muscles and practising skills they will need later on in life to survive.

Juveniles stay with their mothers until they are about 10 months old and then they disperse into a solitary existence of their own up to 180 km away from their natal turf.

Caracal are excellent **climbers** and like leopards, they use trees to cache prey or to ambush sleeping birds of **prey** like tawny eagles. They also use their climbing and leaping ability very successfully when pursuing a favourite rock-dwelling food source, dassies, (see p. 182).

Caracal respond to danger by making a **speedy dash** into hiding without a backward glance.

What do caracals do for farmers?

Caracals are notorious stock thieves and cause farmers a great deal of trouble and financial loss annually. However, these cats also offer farmers a service in pest control. Rodents are a favourite food type, to which the caracal's ability to launch from sturdy hindquarters up and upon prey is well suited. Dassies are another favourite and are easily snapped up off rocky outcrops thanks to the caracal's adept climbing and jumping skills. Even jackal pups make for an occasional meal. Caracals do more than benefit farmers by their choice of prey species; they play a pivotal role in keeping ecosystems balanced and other wildlife populations in check.

The black-backed jackal **gets its name** from the saddle of long, dark hair on its back. The similar looking (albeit rarer) side-striped jackal lacks this dark saddle and has a white tip to its tail. The black-backed jackal has a black-tipped tail.

Jackals may **rest out of sight** during the hotter parts of the day using dense vegetation, holes or rock crevices to secret themselves away. Sometimes on cold nights they will sleep on top of flattened piles of elephant dung or on the vast patches of impala middens. The dung has insulating properties that helps to conserve warmth.

Marius Swart

Being smaller carnivores, jackals will characteristically use elevated sites such as rocks or compacted vegetation to deposit their scat. This serves as a **territorial marker** but is also believed to convince intruders that the territory holder is larger than it really is as the dung is higher up. Sometimes jackals will deposit their scat, seemingly defiantly, on top of larger carnivores' scat.

Jackals can be seen moving around at a **bouncy trot**. This is an energy-efficient gait for covering ground while on patrol. They will walk slowly if seeking sensitive prey such as rodents and insects.

Black-backed jackal
Canis mesomelas

Size	40 cm (at shoulder); 1 m long
Weight	7-10 kg
Lifespan	10 years
Habitat & Distribution	Wide range – highly adaptable. Prefer to forage and rest in open where there is a good view of the surrounds
Gestation	2 months
# of young	1-6 pups (born Aug-Oct)
Prey	Insects, rodents, small antelope and antelope lambs, birds, fruit, carrion
Predators	Lion, hyena, leopard, pythons, large raptors

Jackals are monogamous (*mono* meaning one and *gamous* meaning marriage). A male and female **pair for life**. They share the duties of defending a territory, the male dealing with male offenders and the female with female offenders. So established is their bond that should one of the pair be killed, the other is likely to lose the territory and may possibly even die.

Jackals live in **extended family groups**. Pups from the previous year's litter will stay on in the parent's territory and assist with raising the next litter. They perform duties including regurgitating food for the pups and lactating mother, guarding the den and playing with or grooming the pups. These 'helpers' offset the need to locate mates, establish territories and raise litters of their own until they are older and more experienced. Gradually young animals will make excursions further and further away from their natal territory until they find a niche for themselves.

Jackals **make use of the holes** created by burrowing animals like aardvarks, to house their pups. The existing cavity is modified to include a large main chamber between 1-2 m across and is equipped with several escape routes. Jackals change their den sites regularly to prevent the build up of parasites or if there is pressure from predators in a particular area. The den is used only while the pups are reliant on the adults for food. By 3 months old, the pups are weaned and can forage with the adults.

Jackals are extremely **resourceful feeders**. They are omnivores and will eat whatever is available even changing their menu seasonally. They will even cache food to eat at a later occasion. Usually they focus on insects and rodents but remarkably for carnivores they will eat quite a large percentage of fruit and are responsible for the naming of the jackalberry tree (see p. 280) whose fallen fruits they are known to relish.

Black-backed jackals are remarkable for their **adaptability** and they adjust and survive in varied and even harsh environments. They are exceptionally resourceful animals and are renowned for their ability to acquire and share knowledge of how to avoid danger and still thrive as a population.

Interspecific (between species) competition occurs between jackals and caracals which keeps both carnivores' populations in check. It would appear that in an area of high jackal concentration, lower populations of caracal exist and vice versa. Jackal may overuse the prey in a given area and the caracal may then move out in search of new resources. Because jackal and caracal mutually prey on each other's pups and kittens, at high densities of one or the other, the likelihood of coming across the opponent's young increases and further puts pressure on that species to leave the area.

Jackals are adept and **bold scavengers**. They have been known to rush in and grab meat off carcasses that still have the offending predator in attendance. Although they defend mutually exclusive territories, forays by neighbouring jackals into another's turf for access to food such as a large carcass that needs dispatching, are tolerated. They are, however, also capable hunters and using the typical canid (dog family) technique they will leap up with an arched back to pin down quarry such as rodents or hares, biting them across the back to snap the spine. Larger prey is run down, sometimes cooperatively in a relay fashion, until the prey is exhausted. Jackals are vital ecologically for removing sick and injured animals from the bush. Jackals play an important ecological role in controlling rodent and dassie populations.

Black-backed jackal
Canis mesomelas

Jackals have **erect and pointed ears** which facilitate excellent hearing. They rely on this sense to detect large kills kilometres away or to pick up the give-away rustles of rodents and insects.

A jackal's **teeth** are superbly adapted for its catholic omnivorous diet. The upper canines are long and curved with a sharp ridge running up the back. These, assisted by the canine-like upper, outer incisors are ideal for catching and holding prey. The carnassial shear (a modified molar-premolar tooth arrangement in all carnivores) is scissor-like and adapted for slicing and shearing meat off the bone. The molars are broad for crushing and grinding up smaller items like insects or fruit.

The **wailing call** of a black-backed jackal is characteristic of the species and iconic to the bushveld. This is one of the ways that territories are advertised and late in the evening, particularly at the start of the breeding season, pairs can be heard answering one another as they reinforce their stakes. Family groups that are separated during the day while foraging will regroup by making use of a 'yipping' vocalisation.

Dwarf mongooses are the **smallest carnivores** found in the Lowveld. They are also often the most numerous carnivore found in the bush due to their gregarious nature. They live together in cooperative groups of about 12 individuals but these groups may sometimes expand to include up to 30 members.

Dwarf mongooses are **extremely social** cooperative breeders and within their community they show **great organisation of roles**. The group is dominated by an alpha pair that is solely responsible for breeding and for leading (alpha female) and initiating defence (alpha male) of the group. The other members of the group – which may be the successive offspring of the alpha pair or immigrants totally unrelated to them – perform duties that range from guarding, grooming and protecting the group to babysitting, playing with, warming, transporting and raising the young or caring for the sick or wounded.

The assistance of the group produces a **collective effort that improves the survival of the individual** (more eyes and ears allow for a coordinated warning system) and allows for maximum breeding success that would otherwise be compromised if the animals paired off without helpers. The alpha female (and mother of the litter) is free to feed while up to three mongooses 'babysit' her brood and this augments her milk production. Sometimes, despite being sexually suppressed by virtue of their subordinate status in the group, other females may also lactate to help feed the young.

Dwarf mongooses utilise **home ranges of about 1 km²**. Within the area they require a network of **termite mounds** (with exposed ventilation holes) and other small refuges (like shallow burrows or tree hollows) to act as night-time stopovers and bolt holes when threatened by predators. During the day, dwarf mongooses forage through piles of leaf litter or under fallen vegetation and progressively work from one sleeping site to the next covering the extent of their home range in a rotation lasting about 3 weeks. In this way, they are able to reduce the pressure on their food resources and remain in their home range on a sustainable basis.

Dwarf mongoose
Helogale parvula

Size	40 cm overall (body 20 cm, tail 14-18 cm)
Weight	300 g
Lifespan	6 years
Habitat & Distribution	Dry, open woodland with adequate hiding places, e.g. termite mounds
Gestation	63 days
# of young	2-4 (average 3)
Prey	Carnivorous - termites, snails, locusts, beetles, centipedes, scorpions, reptiles and eggs
Predators	Birds of prey, small carnivores, snakes

Dwarf mongooses are territorial but will **defend sleeping sites** more vehemently than territorial boundaries. Territorial markers include both **cheek and anal gland secretions** and sleeping sites are obvious by the accumulation of the entire group's scat in a nearby latrine. Vertical objects are collectively marked by reversing backwards up the post to get the scent as high as possible. The smell lasts about as long as it takes for the group to circumnavigate the home range and may also serve as a marker to the group as to when last they visited the area. If a neighbouring group attempts to overtake a particular sleeping site, the groups will mutually charge one another aggressively with bristled tails and biting advances and the larger group generally displaces the smaller (without injury) and thus quickly settles the dispute.

Rank in the group is determined by age with the **alpha pair** (which remains mated for life unless one dies) dominant to all others. This rule varies with very young babies which outrank even the higher ranked adults. **Females dominate males** and the alpha female is the largest in size of all the members. Subordinate members always defer to their superiors, especially where food access is concerned, and they indicate their submission by crouching low or rolling onto their backs while twittering softly. Status can be improved by performing important functions like babysitting, especially regularly. Immigrant animals, which possess fresh genes, quickly outrank resident mongooses although joining a new pack may first be fraught with weeks of difficulty to gain acceptance.

Dwarf mongooses are **strictly diurnal** only leaving their night-time refuges well after the sun is up and entering the new one before the sun goes down. Being small animals, they are susceptible to getting cold at night and they ritually **sun themselves first thing in the morning.** The alpha female is always first to emerge and she will check that the coast is clear before summonsing the rest of the group to emerge. The pack will engage in social activities during this time. They groom themselves and each other, assiduously transferring saliva and scent amongst themselves so the whole group shares a unique smell. This identifies them to each other and separates them from other packs.

The **Shangaan name for the dwarf mongoose is 'machiki-chorr'** an onomatopoeic name that refers to their constant vocalisations. These develop from contact peeps to churrs, twitters and rolling chatters as different stimuli and situations take place. The dwarf mongoose vocabulary includes subtle changes in sounds to denote different kinds of predators (e.g. aerial vs. terrestrial threats) and may even indicate to the group the nearness of a given threat. This differentiation is necessary because being small animals they are virtually defenceless against aerial predators and must rely on darting into cover to overcome these threats. Some terrestrial threats can be dealt with through group cooperation and mobbing attacks.

Dwarf mongooses are **accomplished hunters** and use many different techniques to capture their prey, which comprises mostly of insects but includes formidable creatures like scorpions, centipedes and snakes and even some small mammals. Most typically, dwarf mongooses use their **sharp claws to dig** up prey that they detect underground. Sometimes while digging intently their heads may even disappear completely into the excavation. This necessitates the good guarding system. They are **astute pouncers** and either jump to snatch airborne insects or bound upon terrestrial ones, consuming these head first. Mice are dispatched in a similar manner, being pinned with the forefeet and bitten upon the head. Larger prey, like lizards, are killed with multiple bites and a canid-like death shake. Snakes are bitten behind the head, shaken and then dropped repeatedly. Larger snakes may be tackled cooperatively with some members shaking the snake by its tail while it is gripped behind the neck by another mongoose. In order to avoid the stings of certain insects, these will be chewed with the lips held away from the teeth. The stings of scorpions do not seem to pose a problem and those of smaller scorpions are even consumed by dwarf mongooses.

Once **the alarm is given**, a group of mongooses will **freeze** as an initial response. This allows them to escape detection through lack of movement (a stimulus used by many predators to catch prey). They may then rise up onto their hind legs using the tail as a prop, in order to have a better look around. When the members of the group are satisfied that the threat is no longer pending, they will continue feeding. If imminent danger looms, the pack will dart for the nearest boltholes (of which they have an intimate knowledge within their territories). Dwarf mongooses (especially the alpha male) are renowned for their brave rescue attempts to retrieve captured members.

Dwarf mongoose
Helogale parvula

Yellow-billed and red-billed **hornbills regularly forage with dwarf mongooses** to benefit from insects flushed up but missed by the mongooses. The hornbills return the favour by alerting the mongooses to danger. They even sound the alarm for raptors that are not a threat to themselves but are a danger to the mongooses. This valuable warning service relieves the pressure on the mongoose pack to be especially vigilant and fewer individuals need take time out of feeding to act as sentinels when the hornbills are around. So mutually beneficial is this relationship that the hornbills will wait at the mongooses' night-time refuge for them to emerge in the morning (often becoming impatient and calling down the holes to rouse them) and the mongooses may delay their departure from a sleeping site if the expected hornbills are late.

Although the alpha pair is essentially responsible for the reproductive effort, sometimes **subordinate individuals may also breed**. The onset of oestrus in the alpha female stimulates other females to come into heat and the alpha male may then mate with other females after he has completed mating with the alpha female (usually after a remarkable 2 400 mountings). Only a few young are produced in this way and it is thought that young born to subordinates are killed by the alpha female (known as infanticide). Dwarf mongooses breed in summer when insects are plentiful and by 4 or 5 weeks old the babies begin to forage with the rest of troop, each one being escorted by a caretaker to show it what and how to eat. Until then, the helpless babies are carried between night-time mounds by the alpha and other females.

Dwarf mongooses have **excellent senses** and prey is detected by smell and sound. Their vision is adapted for spotting aerial predators via horizontally elongated pupils that allow for an enlarged visual field.

If an alpha animal dies, the next high-ranked member of the troop will take over the role. Where there is a dispute as to the heir, a grooming contest ensues during which time the two contenders may groom one another for up to 4 days constantly until one is proved more persistent. By this time they will both be drenched in saliva.

Dwarf mongooses are very **agile and athletic**. Typical locomotion involves a bounding run with bounces that may take the mongoose up to 90 cm off the ground. They change direction easily even at full speed and are adept climbers, their slender bodies easily fitting through small spaces.

Dwarf mongooses spread out when they feed but **maintain contact amongst themselves** with constant 'peeping' noises. **Sentinels** are posted on vantage points both ahead of and behind the foraging group and they too emit 'all clear' sounds every few seconds so that the feeding individuals need not waste time looking up from their excavations. The guards will rise up on their hind legs using their tail as a tripod balance in order to gain the best view of the surroundings. Sentinel duty lasts only about 15 minutes each and as soon as a relief guard is set up (usually once the group has foraged about 60 m from the rearguard) then the individual that has been on duty will resume feeding. It must scamper the 60 m distance to catch up with the group and is exceptionally vulnerable to predators during this dash. If the group becomes very spread out or particularly preoccupied in a good feeding area, additional guards will be set up. Guard duty is shared amongst the pack but the subordinate adult males engage in it most often and some individuals more than others.

Small nocturnal mammals

The aardvark is unmistakable by its **strange shape**. It is an ant and termite specialist and is **superbly adapted** for this.

Facial bristles protect the aardvark's eyes while it burrows and may even help it to detect the tiny vibrations of its prey.

The **large ears,** which can rotate, are an adaptation to hearing prey and detecting predators but can be conveniently folded away to keep them free of sand.

Aardvarks have only a few reduced **peg-like teeth**, as they do not need to chew. Instead their stomachs are adapted to grinding, much like the gizzard of a bird.

The **short tail** tapers to a point and leaves drag marks in the sand where the aardvark has walked.

The aardvark's **tongue** is long and covered with copious amounts of saliva to which ants and termites stick and are thus taken up into the mouth.

Powerful digging claws are present on the front feet to enable the aardvark to excavate for its food.

Aardvarks are **exceptional diggers** and are able to dig into the cement-like substrate of the hardest termite mounds. In sandy soil, aardvarks can dig themselves out of trouble digging faster than men with spades. They push the dirt backwards with their feet and sweep it away with the muscular tail. Aardvarks do not only dig for food or to escape predators but they also excavate burrows in which to live. These burrows begin with a tunnel just wide enough to accommodate the aardvark's body so that larger predators cannot pursue them down their holes. They cannot be dug out of their holes as they generally dig faster than their pursuers. The tunnel may be up to 10 m long depending on the substrate and opens into a wider chamber which serves as the aardvark's sleeping and breeding quarters, as the microclimate here is stable. The earth excavated out of the ground is left in a heap at the entrance and sometimes soil remains on the floor of the tunnel. This is pushed back and forth when the aardvark enters or leaves the burrow and is used to seal the aardvark into the safety of its burrow and close intruders out.

Aardvark
Orycteropus afer

Size	1,5 – 1,7m long (tail 50 cm); 0,4 m shoulder height (50 cm at highest point)
Weight	40 – 60 kg
Lifespan	About 20 years
Habitat & Distribution	Broad habitat tolerance – open woodland or grassland (also in rainforest in central Africa and in arid zones). Needs sufficient termites for food and prefer sandy areas where digging is easier but do make use of other habitats too **Endemic to Africa**
Gestation	7 months
# of young	1
Food	Ants and termites
Predators	Lion, hyena, leopard, python and humans

Aardvarks have **unique droppings** which are small oval pellets that comprise of termite heads and the excess soil they cannot help but swallow while foraging. These are seldom found, as the aardvark defecates in a shallow scrape and then covers its dung.

Aardvarks are **solitary animals** coming together only to mate. While their sense of smell is well developed they do not see particularly well and are especially cautious when they leave their burrows in the evenings, pausing and sniffing to ensure there are no imminent threats. Although aardvarks are usually back in their burrows before dawn, they may occasionally come out of their underground world to catch some sun after a particularly cold night.

Aardvarks **feed** mainly on ants in the dry season (while termites are mostly inactive) and feed on termites during the wet season (when termites are especially active). They will forage in a seemingly random manner zigzagging across the veld and smelling out columns of termites moving above the ground or ant nests below it. They utilise the same mounds repeatedly, opening up old excavation wounds and marking favoured feeding sites with a secretion from glands in the groin. Although the excavations of aardvarks do open up termite mounds to invasions by Matabele ants (the termites' biggest predator), the aardvarks themselves do not eradicate whole termite populations when they feed. They favour the eggs and larvae of their prey and worker termites are preferred to soldiers as they have higher calories and fewer toxins, but to get at these the aardvark must dig past the soldiers' defences, which do not seem to faze them in the least. Ants may cover the aardvark's face completely and it will only show the faintest irritation by shaking its head once in a while.

The **disused burrows** of aardvarks are utilised as homes by no less than 17 mammal species, two reptiles and a couple of birds. These include bats, cats, civets, hyenas, jackals, porcupines, warthogs, wild dogs, monitor lizards, owls and kingfishers. The feeding excavations of aardvarks greatly benefit the aardwolf, which does not have the same digging capabilities and will feed in the wake of the aardvark.

Civet
Civettictis civetta

Size	1,3 m
Weight	11,25 kg
Lifespan	14 years
Habitat & Distribution	Dense woodland with hiding places and surface water to drink regularly
Gestation	60-65 days
# of young	up to 4
Prey	Omnivore - eats grass (including rumen content of dead antelopes), insects, small rodents, fruit, birds, reptiles, frogs, fish, carrion, invertebrates including poisonous millipedes and snakes like puff adders
Predators	Lion, leopard, hyena

Civets are stocky animals that resemble cats but are closer to dogs in size. They belong to neither of those carnivore families but rather are part of the Viverridae, the same **family as mongooses**. The viverrids all have well-developed **anal glands for scent marking** and the civet is no exception. The dark secretion from a civet's anal glands is known as civetone and is most pungent in smell. It is used to mark territory by wiping the everted gland against smooth objects. Civets may reverse backwards up a rock or tree to deposit the secretion as high up as possible. This may be a ploy to make themselves seem bigger to intruders as the smell is so elevated. They also use their anal gland secretions as a chemical defence against predators. It has a long-lasting smell (lasts for 3 months), which led to the substance being used as a fixative in women's perfumes.

The civet's **striking black and white colouration** is aposematic meaning that it is obvious to night-vision animals and warns such predators of the civet's chemical tactics, cautioning them to stay clear. The white patches on the civet's face highlight its facial expressions when it encounters other civets.

Civets have an **extremely diverse diet** which is accommodated by teeth modified for both tearing and crushing. Civets eat plants and fruit which they gather on the ground or by clambering weakly on low branches. They eat the meat of many kinds of small animals which they catch with a pounce-bite-shake method. They eat various kinds of poisonous food including insects, puff adders and millipedes. Civets are one of very few animals that can eat millipedes as their generalist digestive systems can deal with the cyanide found in these invertebrates. Civets regularly raid rubbish bins and seem to process items such as plastic bags without any ill effect. They will scavenge readily and eat the grass in the rumen of dead antelope. It may not be a coincidence that civets, which eat poisonous and other rather unusual items, produce such noxious secretions.

Civets **live alone**, hiding in holes or in dense undergrowth by day. They are shy and freeze when threatened and then slip silently away. Civets also display **pilo-erection** when under stress, raising the longer-haired crest of fur along their backs and standing side-on to the predator or intruder to seem larger and more intimidating.

The presence of civets in an area is more commonly betrayed by their **vast middens**, which are made near the paths they use to forage and are littered with millipede rings, berry kernels and seeds. Civetries, as the middens are known, are used as territorial markers in conjunction with their scent marks and are important centres for seed dispersal. Remarkably, the dung of a civet is enormous relative to its body size and is comparable in cylindrical shape and coarse consistency to that of a baboon.

Genet
Genetta tigrina & Genetta genetta

Size	Small spotted genet: 94 cm
	Large spotted genet: 98 cm
Weight	Small spotted genet: 1,9 kg (female 1,8 kg)
	Large spotted genet: 2 kg (female 1,8 kg)
Lifespan	13 years
Habitat & Distribution	Woodland and scrub. The small spotted genet also penetrates deserts along rivers. The large spotted genet also occurs on forest fringes
Gestation	70 days
# of young	1-4
Prey	Insects and invertebrates (spiders, scorpions, millipedes), small mammals including lesser bushbabies, golden moles and bats, birds, eggs, reptiles, fruit, crabs, frogs, occasionally scavenges
Predators	Minor part of the diet of larger carnivores

There are **two species** of genet in the Lowveld, the large spotted genet (*Genetta tigrina*) and the small spotted genet (*Genetta genetta*). The easiest way to tell these two very similar looking animals apart is by **looking at the tip of the tail** which is black in the large spotted genet and white in the small spotted genet. This is quite a reliable method since these animals are shy and often seen fleetingly as they run for cover.

Like the civet, genets belong to the carnivore family known as Viverridae which use **anal glands extensively** in the marking of their territories. Genets' anal gland secretion has a musky smell which retains its scent for up to 9 weeks. They also make use of middens which are usually near their dens and easy to recognise because their droppings contain copious insect fragments. During the day, genets shelter in holes or in thick cover.

As with civets, the **white patches below their eyes** and up the forehead are used to enhance their facial expressions when engaged in social interactions. These encounters are rare due to their predominantly solitary lifestyles but essential nonetheless when dispelling intruders or finding mates. Genets, remarkably, also have seven different vocal signals with which to communicate.

Although they are **agile climbers**, genets generally forage on the ground stalking, rushing and pouncing on prey in the manner of a cat. They will take to trees if searching for birds, eggs or fruit or **if they are frightened**. They may also engage in pilo-erection, raising the crest of long black hair along their backs to appear larger and more intimidating.

Scrub hare
Lepus saxatilis

Size	50 cm (females slightly larger than males)
Weight	2-3 kg
Lifespan	8 years
Habitat & Distribution	Woodland and scrub
Gestation	42 days
# of young	1-3
Food	Grass, roots, tubers
Predators	Jackals, Verreaux's eagle owl, pythons, caracal, leopard, lion

Ulrich Oberprieler

Scrub hares are the most common lagomorphs in the Lowveld. They live above the ground and **do not make use of warrens** in the way rabbits do. During the day scrub hares hide out in thick undergrowth vegetation. While sleeping they flatten themselves and the vegetation where they have been lying typically takes the shape of their bodies. Consequently, the 'dens' of scrub hares are known as 'forms'. Because scrub hares live above the ground and have no 'safe-house' to escape into when pursued by predators (as rabbits would have), they are equipped with **long powerful legs for running** and long ears for enhanced hearing. Their young (known as leverets) are extremely precocial (fully furred, eyes open and can move from birth) as they need to be able to escape danger immediately on being born. Remarkably, leverets will be totally independent of their parents within 1 month. The young of rabbits (known as kittens) are typically altricial (eyes closed, helpless and reliant on parental care) as they have the safety of a warren in which to develop after birth.

Steven Roskelly

When scrub hares **flee from danger**, they are able to reach speeds of 70 km/h. They **run in an irregular zigzag manner** which makes it difficult for the predator to follow. They may even allow an insistent pursuer to gain on them and then at the last moment diverge causing the predator to overshoot and thus have to abandon the chase. At night, if scrub hares are caught in the headlights of a vehicle, they may instinctively employ this strategy and continuously flee down the road possibly deflecting at seemingly the last moment. Often they get tunnel vision from the lights and cannot see where to dart off to so they keep following the illuminated area. It is always the most sensitive thing to dip your headlights and slow down to allow scrub hares to move away.

Scrub hares are **vegetarians** and eat grass, roots and tubers which are digested by a hind-gut fermentation system (all their food is digested in a large central stomach and only exposed to cellulose-decaying microbacteria late in the digestive process). This means that digestion is quick but not as effective as it could be. For this reason, hares **practise coprophagia** (eating dung) to maximise on the undigested nutrients still in their dung. Hares produce vitamin-rich soft green faeces during the night (called caecotropic faeces), which are immediately eaten directly from the anus to extract the moisture and additional nutrients in the dung and to replenish the microbacteria in their guts. Then the following day, hares produce the more familiar hard pellets, which are discarded. This process is known as refection.

Cape porcupine
Hystrix africaeaustralis

Size	700 mm long; 25 cm at shoulder
Weight	12 - 19 kg
Lifespan	30 years
Habitat & Distribution	Broad tolerance but prefer broken country
Gestation	94 days
# of young	1 - 3 young
Food	Predominantly vegetarian, including poisonous plants, bark, bulbs, tubers, roots, fallen wild fruit (marula, figs)
Predators	Lions, leopard

The Cape porcupine is the **largest rodent in southern Africa** and is characteristically equipped with long, **sharp quills** (that are actually modified hairs), which it uses in defence against predators or other porcupine intruders. Contrary to popular belief, porcupines do not shoot their quills out but rather, when threatened, raise their quills (pilo-erection) and run backwards into the offender. The quills pull free of the body easily and if the porcupine makes contact with the predator or if a predator takes a swipe or bite at the porcupine, the quills may penetrate their skin deeply, sometimes causing fatally septic wounds. The **end of the tail is modified** into a rattle comprising hollow quills that produce a loud sound when shaken. To put predators or intruders off porcupines will rattle their tails and erect their quills menacingly, raise the crest of hair on the neck to appear bigger, stamp their feet and emit a low-pitched roar.

Porcupines **live in family groups** comprising an adult male and female and their offspring from previous litters but only the adult pair within the group breeds. Breeding in porcupines is an understandably tricky task so it is remarkable that the monogamous pair actually mates daily. The physical contact is necessary to stimulate the female's ovarian cycle and while in the family group, other females are suppressed in this way and must disperse in order to have a chance at breeding. Copulation barely lasts a couple of minutes. The female moves her tail out of the way and backs into the male who stands on his hind legs. In spite of the daily interaction the female only conceives once a year.

Martin Harvey / AfriPics

Although porcupines live together, occupying disused aardvark burrows as their homesteads, they **forage alone**. The adult male and female will initially escort youngsters and help defend them from predators but by 5 months old the young will forage alone too. Porcupines are predominantly vegetarians but they have extremely tough digestive systems and can process even poisonous materials like the bark of tamboti trees. They regularly **practise osteophagia** (the chewing of bones) as they have high calcium requirements to maintain their coat of spiny quills and their large, continuously growing incisor teeth. Bones are often found strewn around the sites where they den. Porcupines are noisy and destructive feeders, sometimes damaging more than they eat. They do play an ecological role in this regard, ring-barking trees and contributing to the balance of woody and grass plants in the savanna system.

Unlike other rodents, **porcupine babies** are born precocial with their eyes open, their incisor teeth and some spines fully erupted. The female suckles her young with teats positioned on her flanks so that she need not roll onto her quills. The young develop their defensive foot stamping and aggressive behaviour quickly.

Honey badger (ratel)
Mellivora capensis

Size	95 cm long; 26 cm shoulder height
Weight	About 12 kg
Lifespan	20 years
Habitat & Distribution	Wide habitat range, except desert and forest
Gestation	6 months
# of young	2
Food	Bee larvae, honey, wide range of small animals including a large percentage of mice, scorpions, spiders, lizards, snakes, some larger mammals and grubs. Scavenges occasionally
Predators	Not many due to its ferocity!

Mel means 'honey' and *voro* means to 'devour' and the genus refers to the honey badger's **habit of eating bee larvae and honey**. Contrary to popular belief, it is actually the honeyguide bird that follows the honey badger to bee hives (not vice versa) to access the site once the badger has opened it up.

The honey badger has a well-developed **reputation for its ferocity**. It is a relatively small animal with the temperament of a large one and even large predators would be taking a risk by trying to kill a honey badger. The honey badger has a tough, thick skin particularly over its shoulders (probably an adaptation to resisting bee stings) and this enables the animal to turn right around when gripped in this area and attack its own attacker. It has sharp canines, a powerful jaw and an unrelenting grip. Honey badgers have been known to go for the groin area of larger animals that may threaten it.

The honey badger is part of the carnivore family Mustelidae shared by the otters and polecat. Like civets and genets (of the family Viverridae), they have well-developed anal glands which open into an anal pouch and produce very **strong foul-smelling secretions that are used to mark territory or expelled in self-defence**. The black and white 'warning' (aposematic) colouration of the honey badger's coat alerts predators to its chemical defence. If the ferocity of the badger or its chemical defence is not sufficient to put predators off, honey badgers will practise thanatosis (feign death). Predators often will not attack animals that are already believed to be dead.

Jed Bird

Honey badgers have **short limbs** which give them a comical appearance as they lumber around. The limbs, however, are very powerful and terminate in long, blade-sharp claws which effect the honey badger's **digging ability**. They dig up prey out of their burrows or excavate hardened balls of dung to get at the fat dung-beetle grubs inside. They are able to completely demolish rotten logs to access various forms of larvae. They make headway digging into sandy ground in just 2 minutes and dig new der daily to accommodate their sometimes nomadic habits. Honey badgers rely on their sense of smell to locate their prey or food and this is subsequently their most developed sense. Their lack of substantial ears indicates that hearing is probably of little value to them especially since they have little to fear!

African wild cat
Felis lybica

Size	Male: 90 cm; Female: 85 cm
Weight	Male: 5 kg; Female: 4 kg
Lifespan	15 years
Habitat & Distribution	Wide tolerance
Gestation	65 days
# of young	2–5
Prey	Rodents, birds, lizards and insects
Predators	Larger carnivores, birds of prey, pythons

The African wild cat looks **just like a domestic cat** but has longer legs, more reddish ears and it sits more upright than a domestic cat. The similarities are no coincidence as domestic cats originated from wild cats. They were first domesticated 5 000 years ago in Egypt. The people of the time were agriculturalists and stored the grain that they harvested annually in baskets.

These abundant stores naturally attracted mice which, in turn, attracted the local wild cats. Because of the favour the cats provided humans by controlling the grain pests, they were encouraged to stay around by leaving out treats of fish. With a constant supply of food, no harassment from people and no natural enemies to threaten them around human habitations, cats quickly habituated. **Gradual genetic mutation resulted in the approximately 100 domestic breeds we find today.** Sadly the true form of African wild cat is being lost through hybridisation with domestic cats in many areas.

Frank de Villiers

The African wild cat is a **solitary creature** which has well-developed senses to apply to the pursuit of rats, mice, small birds, lizards and insects. Both the males and females spray urine to mark their territories and scat is buried in the manner of a domestic cat. Kittens are born in summer when there are lots of rodents around.

Johan Louw

123

Lesser bushbabies are **small nocturnal primates** which are predominantly insectivorous and enabled to catch their prey by an extremely well-developed sense of vision, hearing and jumping ability.

Bushbabies have **enormous eyes** with expanding pupils that allow for the collection of light in poor light conditions. Their eyes are so large that they are immovable in their sockets and to compensate bushbabies can rotate their heads 180 degrees (much like a bird) to look over their shoulders. They are able to bulge their eyeballs to gain focus of an object. There is a highly reflective layer called the tapetum lucidum in the back of the eye, which shines reddish in a spotlight. This also facilitates night-time vision. Remarkably for nocturnal creatures, bushbabies have a high percentage of colour cone cells on the retina.

Bushbabies have **long whiskers** (vibrissae) near the eyes to help them detect nearby objects and so protect the eyes while foraging in the dark.

The bushbabies' brilliant **leaping ability** is effected by enlarged powerful hind legs and the long tail is used for power and balance. Primate-like hands and feet with nailed fingers and dexterous thumbs and toes assist with grip. The ends of the digits are padded with soft friction pads and so are the palms of the hands and the soles of the feet. These also help with grip and with capturing prey. They are able to land and grip with just their feet to keep their hands free for grasping prey. Bushbabies can leap horizontally up to 4 m and vertically almost 2 m. They cover many metres in just a few seconds and more than a kilometre in a night with these impressive leaps and bounds. On the ground, bushbabies hop like miniature kangaroos.

The **membranous ears** are also moveable and can be swivelled independently or simultaneously to pick up sounds or can be folded back out of harm's way. Bushbabies have acute hearing and they are able to locate insects on sound alone, even snapping gnats out of the air with their hands. They in fact jump upon prey with their eyes closed so as not to get flailing insect parts in them.

Apart from insects, bushbabies also eat the gum of particularly *Acacia* trees, which is extruded when the tree is damaged. This gum is high in dissolved carbohydrates and also contains proteins and minerals like calcium. To harvest the gum off branches, bushbabies have the front teeth on their lower jaw modified into a scraping mechanism. Although they do eat gum all year, it is eaten more in winter when insect numbers drop.

Lesser bushbaby (lesser galago)
Galago moholi

Size	37 cm (female slightly smaller) Adults generally 17-20 cm (without tail)
Weight	150-200 g
Lifespan	14 years
Habitat & Distribution	Savanna woodland (especially *Acacia* woodland), not forest or grassland; home range of 4-23 ha
Gestation	124 days (4 months) – twice a year
# of young	1-2 (twins frequently)
Prey	Insects and gum
Predators	Eagles, owls, genets, snakes

Bushbabies **hide by day** inside tree cavities, dense vegetation or self-built nests. They sleep together in small family groups (except for the males which sleep apart). At night they split up and forage alone, provided the weather is not foul. Before leaving to forage, bushbabies, like other primates, take some time to wake up, stretching and grooming. A **special curved grooming claw** is present on the second digit of the hind foot. This is also known as the 'toilet claw' and is used particularly to groom the head, shoulders and ears. The toothcomb (also used for scraping gum) is used to groom their fur. A sharp fleshy comb under the tongue is then used to clean debris out of the **toothcomb**.

Bushbabies mark their territories and their dominance in a process known as 'urine-washing'. By **urinating into a cupped hand** and then rubbing this on the feet, bushbabies spread their scent wherever they move. This may also be rubbed onto the chest of the male as a sign of dominance or onto a female in courtship. Bushbabies also have chest glands which are utilised in mating and dominance rituals. Bushbabies will fight to ward off intruders, sitting up on the hind legs and **holding the fists up ready to 'box'**. Fights can be vicious and involve wrestling and biting so intense it sometimes proves fatal. Young bushbabies start practising their **wrestling skills** from just 6 days old. Older youngsters will comically hang upside down by their feet while they cuff and wrestle.

While some primates have rather expressive faces, bushbabies do not. They rely on the **chemical communication** of urine-washing to transmit social messages as well as on vocalisations. Bushbabies have a **vocabulary which includes at least 25 different sounds:** grunts, clicks, moans, crackles, chattering, twittering, shrill cries, 'tchak-tchak' sounds and even ultrasonic sounds. Predators are identified with species specific calls and young bushbabies 'speak' differently to adults.

Young bushbabies leave the nest for the first time at just 10 days old. The mother carries them around so that they are not vulnerable to predation while she is away. She carries the young by the scruff of the neck just like a carnivore and does not have them cling to her like monkeys. She moves them between nest sites regularly so that parasites do not build up. When she forages **she leaves them clinging to a branch nearby, which is known as 'parking'**. By 4 weeks old, the young resist going back to the nest and the female then rolls them around until she can get a grip on the nerves under the skin on the scruff of the neck, which relaxes (paralyses) them into submission.

Birds

The diversity of body sizes and shapes, beak and feet designs and colours of feathers that occur within the bird class is astounding. These traits along with the ability to fly have made it possible for birds to occupy a very broad range of habitats and particular niches within those habitats. A good 900 species of bird have been recorded in southern Africa of which about two-thirds occur within the extent of the Lowveld. This plethora of variety gives the bushveld a biodiversity uniqueness of its own. When game-watching is slow or the weather is less than ideal, there is always an assortment of birds to watch. In this vein, bird-watching is fast becoming a popular hobby in South Africa. Since there are numerous field guides available on the identification of birds and because there are really too many species to cover individually in detail, the approach taken here is of imparting the intricacies and fascinating facts of bird biology by using the common species as examples. Colourful, interpretive images assist with the identification of these and as easy references to the topics. As the reader learns about the behaviour of birds, so they learn interesting facts on particular species. Some of the popular groups of birds like owls, kingfishers, woodpeckers, vultures and nightjars have been allocated their own spreads and in these sections particular attention has been given to the physiological and behavioural adaptations of the species, facilitated by the mind-map flow of pictures and text.

Bird song, page 128
Colour in bushveld birds, page 130
Feather hygiene, page 132
Bird party, page 134
Food and feeding, page 136
Cooperative breeding in birds, page 140
Brood parasites, page 144
Monogamy: the royal pair, page 146
Nests, page 148
Precocial and altricial, page 153
Symbiotic relationships in birds, page 154
Raptors, page 156
Vultures, page 160
Owls, page 164
Nightjars, page 168
Ground birds, page 169
Ostrich, page 174
Oxpeckers, page 178
Kingfishers, page 180
Woodpeckers, page 182

Bird song

Swainson's spurfowl

Yellow-billed duck

Birds **sing to advertise their territories** and to attract mates and subsequently build bonds with those mates. Birds sing most earnestly in the morning when the air is clear and still and sound travels furthest and loudest. This is known as the 'dawn chorus'. They also utilise the dawn chorus to remind their neighbours that in spite of a night of darkness since last they called, they are still very much in attendance of their turf. Birds call in the late afternoon again to establish ownership of an area before they sleep.

Individual species of birds may have **more than one signature sound**. Different sounds have slightly different functions. A call is the contact communication used between both sexes of bird all year round. It may alert an individual as to the location of its chick or the whereabouts of its other flock members. It may also help birds to identify one another, as each 'voice' is unique. Alarm calls alert other birds in the vicinity of danger. A song is usually a longer, more melodic and repeated tune that advertises a male's territory and status and attracts females. Interestingly, the message a particular song gives to an intruder is different to the message the same song might give to a potential female mate. Males typically use song to serenade their mates to sustain their bond throughout the duration of their relationship.

Black-shouldered kite

Birds make their calls by means of an apparatus called a **syrinx**. This is a cartilaginous device located at the base of their windpipes just above the lungs. The syrinx receives a bronchial tube from each lung and the opening is manipulated by fleshy membranes. When a bird wishes to vocalise, it contracts its lungs sending a jet of air through the syrinx and by vibrating the fleshy membranes it controls the pitch and tone of the sound. Birds create complicated tunes by vocalising using both tubes simultaneously and producing different sounds from each side. The **crested barbet** is able to sustain its incredible ongoing trill by vocalising with predominantly the one tube and using the other to breathe. Other birds may take shallow breaths and expel air from each side of the syrinx while the other side continues to vocalise. In this way they may also continue calling uninterrupted for minutes on end.

Bird song

Some birds **use duetting to reinforce their pair bond**. This usually occurs between the members of a monogamous pair like black-collared barbets that stay together for years and need to maintain their relationship and mutual territory on an ongoing basis. A duet is a synchronised call where the one member of the pair completes the call of the other member so precisely that the resultant tune appears to be only one song. **Black-collared barbets** have excellent rhythm and the split-second 'du-' of the one bird is instantly responded to with a '-pudley' by the other to create the trademark and strident 'du-poodley...du-poodley...du-poodley...' that denotes their territory. Crested francolins also duet in this rhythmical manner and it is suggested that they repeat 'beer and cognac...beer and cognac...etc'.

Some birds attempt to impress potential mates by **copying phrases of songs** and sounds belonging to other species of bird in a process known as mimicry. The fork-tailed drongo and **robin-chats** are **experts at mimicking**. The complexity of the assembled tune is suspected to be an indication of fitness to females. Males that are able to remember and knit together long sequences of phrases are considered better partners. A strong mimicked vocal signal also may intimidate rivals and convince them of the singer's superiority. Indigobirds are brood parasites and mimic the calls of their hosts in order to find their nests as well as find one another.

Hugh Chittenden

Some birds use sounds other than vocalisations to establish communication. Bearded woodpeckers are **masters of tapping**, choosing resonating logs on which to drum with their sturdy bills to declare territory and attract mates. Other birds such as storks (especially **marabous**), helmetshrikes and the black-backed puffback **use bill snapping** in their mating displays and the wing claps of some species of bird in flight are also strong communication techniques used during courtship.

Colour in bushveld birds

In order to survive in the animal kingdom, an individual must find enough food to sustain itself while avoiding danger in the form of predators. But **survival is about more than staying alive**, it's about being able to find a mate and reproduce successfully to ensure personal genes are perpetuated. Within the bird class, species are divided between these two 'schools of survival' and both have their costs and benefits.

Three-banded plovers

Having bright colours, such as the **lilac-breasted roller**, makes a bird an appealing mate. His visual attire is further enhanced by **exhibitionistic displays**. The 'roller' gets its name from its propensity to noisily take to the sky, flying upwards until it reaches an imaginary summit from whence it shoots downwards rocking side to side on its wings or 'rolling' all the while vocalising in a less than songful manner.

Birds such as doves and sparrows select less for colour and more for **tones that blend them into their environment**. Remaining undetected by predators is the priority and they will rely more on courtship rituals and song to locate a partner and maintain pair bonds. Some of these duller species have hidden crests that can be erected to impress the females, such as the **red-crested korhaan**. This bird will only introduce its colourful headrest when needed for courtship. Some birds take blending in to the extreme and species such as nightjars, sandgrouse and **scops-owls** use cryptic colouration to mimic their surrounds so perfectly that they are almost undetectable.

Southern grey-headed sparrow

There are **two main pigments found in birds**. The primary pigment is **melanin**. This is the pigment responsible for the colour black. It not only provides pigmentation but also fortifies the feathers. This reinforcement is especially important in the primary and secondary feathers of a bird's wings, the feathers used in flight.

The second main pigment group found in birds is the **carotenoids**. This gives feathers the colours of yellow, orange or red. The weavers are a common family of birds adorned with this pigment. Small **yellow-fronted canaries** are also commonly seen yellow birds that occur in the Lowveld. Small flocks can often be seen flying up from beside the roads where they collect seed.

Black crake

Colour in bushveld birds

Glossy starlings are some of the most striking birds spotted in the Lowveld. Their feathers have an **iridescent sheen** that shimmers with hues of blue, green and purple depending on how the light falls on the bird. Remarkably, this effect is not caused by pigmentation and in fact glossy starlings have no colour pigment in their feathers at all. There is some melanin – the dark pigment that adds strength to the feathers. The colourful effect is created by the manner in which the keratin (the structural material that makes up the feathers) is layered. As light falls on the feathers, these keratin layers reflect different wavelengths of light differently resulting in the spectacular iridescence. The underlying melanin absorbs other colours and in poor light makes the whole bird appear black.

The well-known, noisy **hadeda ibis** has iridescent shields on its wings.

The **turaco family has some pigments that are unique** to them. This includes a green pigment called turacoverdin and a red pigment called turacin. The green in the turaco's feathers is the only green caused by an actual pigment. All other greens in birds' feathers are caused by either tyndal scattering (in the presence of yellow carotenoids) or a combination of yellow and black pigment in the feathers which produces the olive colours of bush-shrikes and thrushes.

The **bright blue of the kingfisher's feathers** is caused by a concept known as tyndal scattering. Once again the keratin of the feathers comes into play but instead of the layering alone affecting the reflection of particular wavelengths of light (as with iridescence), small air spaces interfere and also scatter the light. Scattering of the shorter wavelengths result in the spectacular blues of kingfishers and rollers.

Grey-headed bush-shrike **Purple-headed turaco**

The bright greens of **bee-eaters** and bushveld parrots are also produced by tyndal scattering when combined with the presence of carotenoids in the feathers.

When all the light falling on a pigmentless feather is scattered, the feather may appear white or in the presence of melanin, grey.

131

Feather hygiene

Filoplumes are sensory feathers and are found in between the contours. They are long and filamentous and used to detect changes in air currents.

Feathers are the things that **make birds unique** among all other members of the animal kingdom. Birds have feathers to enable them to fly, another feature virtually unique to them amongst warm-blooded creatures (except for bats). **A bird's feathers are specially adapted to accommodate a number of different functions.**

Specialised feathers may include the rictal bristles found around the mouths of birds such as nightjars. They are also sensory in function and help to direct insect prey into the wide gape of these aerial hunters. Other modified feathers include the water-collecting breast feathers of the male double-banded sandgrouse and the feathers that make up the facial discs of owls and are used to direct sound into the ear drums.

Johan Louw

Contour feathers (tectrices) 'contour' the bird's body giving it a streamlined shape to facilitate movement through the air.

The **remiges** are the sturdy flight feathers that make up the wings and are commonly known as primaries and secondaries. These are usually reinforced with melanin (black pigment). The bases of the remiges are covered with covert feathers.

The **retrices** are the tail feathers and are used in steering and stabilising the bird during flight. They are also usually blackened for strength.

Down feathers are situated at the base of the contours. They are soft and without rigid structure and are used to insulate the bird.

Many birds **bathe in water to clean themselves** or cool down. Most land birds appear to physically enjoy water and watching a bird bathing can be most entertaining. The bird carefully balances the extent to which its feathers become soaked so as not to impair flight should it suddenly need to escape a predator. For aerial feeders like swallows and bee-eaters that have weak legs and hence poor get-away speeds from the ground, it is too dangerous to bathe at the water's edge. They will dive and dip into water mid-flight to bathe. Even waterbirds bath by flushing water over their backs or dipping head and shoulders under the water. After a good wash, birds will shake their feathers to dry them and then apply preen oil and preen.

As important as a well-maintained aircraft is to a pilot, so too are well cared for feathers to a bird. Flight feathers and contours are bound in their aerodynamic shapes by barbs and barbules, tiny hooks that hold the vanes together. Wear and tear from flight and weather, upset these vanes and a bird is then required to re-latch its feathers by drawing them through its beak in a process known as **preening**.

Yellow-billed duck

Herons and **egrets** combine the preening of their feathers with the **application of powder** from the fraying edges of powder-down feathers on their bodies. The powder absorbs the dirt and grime accumulated in the process of feeding on fish or frogs in often murky water. The birds then strip the downy-dirt off with a pectinate (comb-like) claw and re-oil their feathers with preen oil at the end.

The uropygial gland (or preen gland) is situated on the lower back of a bird, just above the tail. This **gland secretes oil** which is used to coat the feathers during preening to make them supple. The preen oil also serves a number of other functions. It protects the feathers (and skin) from bacteria and fungal infestations and strips excess fatty residue off the plumage. It also helps with waterproofing.

Feather hygiene

Preening the hard to reach areas such as the head and neck is problematic for most animals and birds are no exception. To overcome the problem, many birds allo-preen. This is where **one bird preens another** and then the preened bird reciprocates. This behaviour is often practised by monogamous species and serves the dual function of pair-bonding.

Black-headed oriole

Shaking in birds is a common form of feather hygiene. By lifting or rousing the feathers and then shaking vigorously, the bird not only gets rid of moisture after a water bath but also dislodged dust and parasites.

Anting is a poorly understood hygiene method used by birds. It is thought to be a part of preening and apparently may be active or passive. Using ants of the family Formicinae that squirt formic acid in self-defence, a bird will rub the ant over its feathers (active anting) or lie where the ants will crawl over it (passive anting). In both instances the ant is encouraged to squirt formic acid on the feathers, often facilitated through shaking of the bird's wings. It is thought that the formic acid may possibly act as a pesticide to kill parasites or dislodge ticks and mites which are then removed in preening. Another suggestion is that it soothes the bird's skin during moulting. Anting may also help to rid the bird of old preen oils.

Sunbathing is popular amongst many species of birds that assume a variety of postures to best expose their feathers to the sun. The sun is used to dry feathers after a bath or rain shower. It also has the effect of softening old oils and getting parasites to move around. As soon as this happens, birds will begin to preen, ridding themselves of these unwanted contaminations. The ultraviolet light also kills bacteria and helps to restore the shape and structure of feathers dishevelled from flight.

Red-billed hornbill

Because the **rigours of flight** may damage feathers beyond the kinds of repair that preening can achieve, all birds moult their feathers once to a few times annually to replace the entire set, especially the retrices. Female hornbills use the opportunity of being incarcerated inside their sealed-up tree cavity nests to shed the full set all at once. This helps to make room inside the nest chamber and furthermore, the female is safely secreted away from harm during this time. By the time the female is ready to leave the nest chamber, she has replaced her full set of feathers. Most other birds lose and replace a few feathers at a time so that the ability to fly is not interrupted. This usually takes place after the breeding season.

Some birds **dust bath** to clean themselves. Ground birds like **francolins** and guineafowl use this technique regularly. They wriggle their bodies into patches of loose bare earth and flick fine dust over their bodies with their wings. The dust is supposed to help dislodge parasites. It also sticks to excess preen oil, much like powder down, and can then be preened off more effectively. African and green wood-hoopoe fledglings take a dust bath immediately on leaving the nest for the first time due to unsanitary conditions in the nest (a defence against predation).

Bird party

Dark-capped bulbul

Birds of different species frequently associate in mixed feeding parties and are found together in what is known as a 'bird party'. Generally the species in a bird party are predominantly insect eaters and each level or strata of birds feeding in the vegetation **benefits from the habits of the one above it,** be it that they reap what the birds above them drop or that they inadvertently 'herd' insects into one another's grasp.

The collective feasting effort of a bird party affords all the birds in the area **shared vigilance** and many eyes and ears are better able to look out for danger and provide early warning of it. In the case of predators like a snake or small raptor, many different species of bird may then cooperate to mob it and chase it away.

Although most species attending bird parties are insectivorous, seed-eaters like blue waxbills and doves also frequently form part of the action, as do some frugivores (fruit-eaters) and omnivores (meat and plant-eaters). **A common food resource generally attracts** the birds to form mixed parties and in the case of fruiting or flowering trees, not only will the frugivorous and nectarivorous birds be drawn to the location but so too will insects. In turn, the insect-eating birds arrive (and possibly also a predatory bird species occasionally). While the birds in the higher levels of vegetation move and feed they may knock seeds down to the smaller seed-eaters below.

Bird parties are a type of interspecific (between species) **allelomimetic behaviour**. Allelomimetic behaviour relates to 'copy-cat' behaviour practised predominantly by gregarious bird species. For example, **blue waxbills** form monogamous pairs but during the day they feed together in flocks for greater protection, keeping constant contact with each other through high-pitched 'tswees'. If one bird suddenly flies off, the entire flock will also fly away.

Red-billed queleas take this to the extreme and droves of literally thousands of birds respond to a change in direction by just one of their members and collectively they manage the most perfectly synchronised flight, appearing as ever-changing dark shapes over the bushveld.

Cooperative breeders (see p. 140) such as **arrow-marked babblers** call in an allelomimetic fashion – one bird begins and the others join in, contagiously producing a loud group vocalisation that rises and then descends in volume. As far as bird parties are concerned, one or two birds begin feeding earnestly and other species notice this and join in 'mimicking' the original birds' behaviour until a large party forms.

Bird party

Bird parties are the ideal find for avid birders as they provide concentrated viewing of varied species. The commonest species typically found associating in bird parties in the Lowveld include the birds illustrated on this page as well as brubru, green-winged pytilias, golden-breasted and cinnamon-breasted buntings, white-bellied sunbird, orange-breasted bush-shrike and Retz's helmet-shrike.

Blue waxbill

White-crested helmet-shrike

Yellow-billed hornbills

Red-billed firefinch

Black-backed puffback

Long-billed crombec

Dark-capped bulbul

Grey-headed bush-shrike

Arrow-marked babbler

Yellow-fronted canary

Fork-tailed drongo

Southern black tit

White-browed scrub-robin

Spotted flycatcher

Chin-spot batis

Laughing dove

Emerald-spotted wood-dove

Natal spurfowl

Food and feeding

Doves

Doves are **seed-eaters** and are often found feeding on gravel roads in game reserves. The reason for this is twofold. Roads are open areas where doves are afforded a good view of their surroundings and are able to flee danger if it threatens. Seeds are also knocked off grass stems onto the roads by the traffic of moving animals and vehicles that use them. Because eating seeds is much like eating dry biscuits without any milk, doves are very water-dependent and can be found in droves at waterholes early morning and late afternoon.

Hamerkop

The hamerkop specialises in eating frogs and tadpoles, particularly platannas. They do this by wading in shallow water **stirring the mud** below with their feet and probing in the water with their sturdy bills until a frog moves, giving itself away at which point it is snapped up. Hamerkops do also eat a small amount of fish and invertebrates and occasionally forage by snatching evident morsels from the surface of water while in flight.

Marabou stork

Marabou storks are exceptionally opportunistic. They make a living by **scavenging food** that vultures work free of carcasses as they cannot cut meat themselves with their straight bills. They also typically monopolise on the abundance of catfish that become trapped in drying pools towards the end of the wet season. They use their feet to stir up the shallow muddy water to disturb the fish, which they then locate by sight or feel and stab viciously at them with sharp beaks. The fish are swallowed head first so that scales and fins are aligned correctly and do not cause the stork to choke. Marabous have the unsanitary habit of urinating on their legs to cool down, leaving them characteristically whitened.

Hornbills

Hornbills (specifically yellow-billed, red-billed and grey) are predominantly **insectivores** and they especially favour dung beetles. They utilise their huge bills to dig and manoeuvre objects on the ground to access their prey, which is usually relatively large in size and sometimes hairy in the form of caterpillars. The large bill helps them handle their prey at a safe distance away from the vulnerable facial area and eyes. Aside from insects, hornbills are fairly carnivorous catching and eating lizards, nestling birds, bats and rodents. They also eat berries such as those found on the velvet corkwood (see p. 266). The enlarged portion on the upper mandible of the male hornbill's beak is called a casque.

Food and feeding

Dark-capped bulbul

The dark-capped bulbul is a **frugivore** or fruit eater. It has a solid bill for plucking and cutting fruit which often has a hard rind. Bulbuls tend to move around in groups moving wherever there are fruiting plants. They have shortened guts that allow seeds to pass through their systems rapidly and when they subsequently deposit the ingested seeds, they facilitate dispersal. Bulbuls will sometimes supplement their diet with nectar.

Cuckoos specialise in feeding on hairy caterpillars.

Openbill stork

The openbill stork's bill is another of the avian world's unique creations. The bill is **open between the upper and lower mandibles** creating a space about 6 mm wide and touching only at the base of the bill and at the tip. This is an adaptation to processing molluscs and provides structural reinforcement. The openbill stork locates a snail or mussel by probing, bill ajar, in the mud. On locating a morsel, it pins it down with the upper mandible and expertly uses the lower one like a knife blade to remove the soft tissue from the shell without breaking the shell.

Herons

Herons have **spear-shaped bills** that they use to spear fish. Theirs is a game of patience and green-backed or grey herons are often observed standing statuesque for hours in quiet backwaters waiting for a fish to come within striking range. The flexible neck, reinforced with strong muscles, then reacts lightning fast to power the strike and spear the unsuspecting prey.

Grey heron

Green-backed heron

Food and feeding

Bee-eaters
Bee-eaters have **tweezer-like bills** and wide gapes that they use effectively to snap airborne insects out of the sky with spectacular aerobatic manoeuvres. They have long, narrow wings, forked tails and small, streamlined torsos which all facilitate their acrobatics; small rictal bristles (hair-like feathers on the face) help to channel food into their mouths. Dangerous insects such as bees are commonly caught and dispatched by beating the prey against a perch until the sting comes free and it is safe to swallow the food.

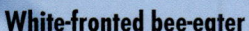

White-fronted bee-eater

African spoonbill
Spoonbills have unique bills which are **spatulate in shape**. The rounded disc at the end is used to filter mud to get at small fish and invertebrates. It forages slowly sweeping the bill from side to side while slightly submerged in the water.

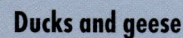

Ducks and geese
Ducks have **flat bills** which are used for sieving edible particles out of the water. Many ducks up-end or dabble, partially submerging their upper bodies in order to access food below the water. The food they consume includes various parts of aquatic plants, insects, detritus in mud, algae, crustaceans and other invertebrates.

White-faced ducks dabble for food but may also dive fully under the water to obtain something they desire. They are fairly unique among ducks for their tendency to also feed at night on grass, seeds, grain and even fruit. The characteristic three-syllabled whistle makes these attractive ducks easy to recognise in flight. They are often heard in the evenings as they fly over on their way to forage.

Egyptian geese are **true grazers** flying to open areas to feed on grass, seeds and grain, leaves and even young crops early in the morning or late afternoon.

Food and feeding

Yellow-billed stork

The yellow-billed stork is most usually seen with **head down and beak ajar** in the water. As it moves, its feet disturb prey which the stork snaps up in its slightly decurved bill that is super-sensitive to the movement of the fish as they try to escape.

African fish-eagle

The fish-eagle is a **piscevore** (fish-eater) and is specialised for this difficult task. It has long, sharp talons to effect a tight grip on its slippery quarry as well as spicules under the feet which also assist with grip. Typically the fish-eagle will remain perched for most of the day hunting for only 1% of its time. On sighting a fish or possibly a swimming reptile (like a monitor lizard, snake or terrapin) it will stoop down off its perch and plane low over the water and then, throwing its talons forward, it will snatch up the prey off the surface in a well-executed single movement. It never dives deeper than 30 cm and prey of 2 kg is easily carried away. Larger fish are caught but must be planed or paddled to the shore. Fish-eagles do take other food including birds, mammals, reptiles and occasionally frogs and they are particularly accomplished pirates (especially the younger birds) robbing other birds of their food or harassing birds like herons until they disgorge their crop contents. Like marabou storks, fish-eagles monopolise drying pools for the trapped fish. They are also astute nest-robbers pulling weavers' nests to shreds to get at the nestlings.

Cooperative breeding in birds

Cooperative breeding is a system employed by many species of birds (and a few mammals; see pp. 98 and 112) which has developed over evolutionary periods of time because these species breed more successfully if they cooperate their breeding efforts than if pairs attempt to breed on their own.

Cooperative breeding occurs where there is a flock of birds living together but where **only one pair within the flock breeds** (the dominant or alpha pair) and all the other members of the group perform the role of 'helpers'.

Depending on the species, the **founder flocks** may be formed by a monogamous pair of birds that then integrate their offspring into the flock or it may form when a group of dispersing male birds joins up with a group of dispersing female birds. In the latter instance, the birds will select a representative from either sex as the dominant member whose role it will be to breed on behalf of the gene line. In both scenarios, the principle of kinship selection is at play. The individuals are exerting less energy into the breeding effort than they would if they bred individually and yet their genes are being perpetuated through a family representative.

Cooperative breeders **experience several benefits**. The breeding pair are assisted by the 'helpers' in the functions of collecting nesting material, incubating eggs, defending the nest site and chicks, and finding food. The 'helper' birds get to perpetuate their genes with minimal effort and in some instances may be gaining valuable information on how to raise young of their own in a cooperative context. It goes without saying that living in flocks improves vigilance and renders the individual bird less vulnerable to predation.

Some common cooperative breeders found in the Lowveld include white-crested helmet-shrikes, green wood-hoopoes, ground hornbills, **arrow-marked babblers** and oxpeckers.

Cooperative breeding in birds

White-crested helmet-shrike

White-crested helmet-shrikes are small black and white birds that live in flocks of 7–30 and are often seen flitting in a butterfly-like fashion between trees where they **feed on insects**. As soon as they land, the flock re-establishes communication in a chattered tone and with bill snaps.

These cooperative breeders have an **alpha pair that bonds for life** and this bond is maintained by allo-preening (mutual preening). The alpha pair selects a nesting site in a cryptic position in a fork of a tree but the **construction of the nest** is done by all the flock members. Thin bits of bark is stripped off trees by the helpers and bound together with spider's web that the helmet-shrikes collect on their head feathers. These feathers, which give the birds their characteristic 'helmets', are erectile and modified for this exact purpose. Cobweb is added to the nest by the helpers throughout the nesting period.

Helper birds take turns to incubate the eggs and changeover of **incubation duty is highly coordinated**. The bird on the nest will call to the rest of the flock when it is

ready to be relieved and the whole flock will fly and settle around the nest site as if foraging. The sitting bird will fly up and another will take its place as the whole group moves off again without attracting unwarranted attention to them. Helmet-shrikes are **socially cooperative** outside of the breeding season and will roost bunched together on a branch, share territorial defence tasks and move in unison when feeding. Young may either remain with the flock (if viable) or disperse in single-sexed units.

141

Cooperative breeding in birds

Green wood-hoopoes

The Zulu word for a green wood-hoopoe is 'iNhlekabafazi' which means 'cackling women' and refers to the **raucous chattering call** characteristic of this prominent species. The constant and contagious calling exhibited by green wood-hoopoes is known as allelomimetic behaviour and is exhibited by many cooperative breeding species as a means to maintain group cohesion. In green wood-hoopoes this behaviour is enhanced by **group displays** whereby the whole flock sways their bodies and flicks their tails while vocalising. This is taken a step further in a process known as 'flagwaving'. One of the dominant birds may pick up a twig in its bill and wave it at an offending neighbouring flock or predator while being supported vocally by its own flock.

There is a **distinct hierarchy** amongst the members of green wood-hoopoe flocks. This is maintained by mutual feeding and grooming. The breeding male and female are the oldest and most dominant and thereafter males dominate females and older birds dominate younger ones. If one of the breeding pair should die, the next highest-ranking individual of the appropriate sex will assume the dominant role.

Green wood-hoopoes are **secretive nesters**. Making use of natural holes in trees, the whole flock will get involved in prospecting for suitable sites, which must have narrow entrances that are mostly inaccessible to predators. Only the dominant female will incubate the eggs but the male and the helpers all get involved in feeding her and the chicks when they hatch. Sanitation at the nest is poor and helpers do not remove eggshells and the chicks defecate against the side-walls of the hole, resulting in a smelly environment. This is believed to play a role in repelling predators. Chicks also sway and hiss to mimic snakes when threatened in their hole, poking their beaks dangerously at the source of the disturbance. They may even spray the offender with liquid excreta or foul-smelling fluid exuded by the preen gland. In order for the female and helpers to see the chicks in the dark to feed them, hatchlings have prominent white projections on the sides of their gapes which create an obvious white circle when they open their mouths to beg.

Fledging birds are cared for most attentively by the flock helpers who compete to feed, preen, guard and lead them to the roost sites at night. Young are integrated into the flock to become helpers themselves for the successive brood or may leave in single-sexed parties to form new cooperative units.

Green wood-hoopoes have fairly **voracious appetites** taking items such as beetles, termites, grasshoppers, caterpillars and millipedes off the trunks and branches of trees where they are found foraging. They clamber awkwardly and restlessly using their zygodactylous feet to cling and their tails as props much like woodpeckers do.

At night wood-hoopoes **roost inside cavities** and in this regard they are territorial. Appropriate roosting sites are a scarce resource but a critical habitat requirement. The availability of roosting cavities will determine the distances they will venture to forage and in the case where holes are limited, flocks tend to be bigger (up to 12 birds) as young birds are less inclined to immigrate and risk not having a nocturnal safe haven. When it is time to retreat for the evening, the birds will create a decoy for predators by pretending to roost at a given location and then when the coast is clear they will silently slip into the actual hole.

Cooperative breeding in birds

Ground hornbills

Ground hornbills are **conspicuous by their size** and their striking black plumage and red wattles. They habitually occur together in groups of 4 to 5 birds (but up to 8 or 9) and spend much time in the open scouting for their prey which comprises lizards, insects, small mammals, snails, birds and venomous snakes. They are specialists at feeding on tortoises that they are able to break open with their strong bills.

Ground hornbills are **long-lived birds** and only reach maturity at 6 years old at which time female birds will leave their natal flocks and join up with a group of males to form new flocks. The dominant pair within the flock mate for life and the cooperative group defend a territory of about 100 km^2 advertised with a booming 'hoo hoo hoo-hoo' duet that carries over 4 km in distance. They will also chase offending neighbours in flight.

A **dominant female** can be recognised by the patch of blue amidst her red throat patch. Juveniles have drably coloured faces that turn red at about 3 years old.

Ground hornbills' **nesting sites** are hard to come by. They require large tree cavities at least 40 cm wide and located 4-7 m above the ground. These are found only in the largest of trees such as jackal berries and baobabs (see pp. 280 and 260) and are becoming scarcer due to logging, local wood collecting and elephant damage. They do not close up the entrance to their nests in the manner of the yellow-billed or red-billed hornbill.

The female will enter the cavity when she is ready to breed and the male and the **helpers bring nesting material** and food to the female. They continue this ritual throughout incubation as once the first egg is laid the dominant female will not leave the nest except to defecate. One or two eggs are laid but the second chick normally does not survive as the first chick is much further advanced by the time the second hatches, and the second is quickly outcompeted. The second egg is produced as an insurance policy should the first not survive.

Chicks are altricial (blind, helpless and nest bound) and the **breeding process is particularly protracted**. The incubation of the eggs takes 40 days and the nestling period continues for sometimes over 85 days. The chicks only start to feed themselves at 6-12 months old but are supplementary fed by the members of the flock for 2 years at which point their development is far enough advanced for them to become helpers themselves.

Breeding is irregular in ground hornbills and thought to be linked to rainfall. Generally flocks produce a chick once every 6 years and for this reason the species is **quite endangered** as viable populations can only be sustained if birds survive for a minimum of 28 years.

Traditionally the ground hornbill is considered a sacred 'wise spirit'. Damage to a hornbill can only be atoned through the sacrifice of a calf and the bird is not spoken of for fear of retribution. Their distinctive call is supposed to indicate rain and in some countries their skulls and bills feature in hunters' headdresses.

Brood parasites

Brood parasites are birds that make **use of host parents to brood and rear their young**. They do not build nests of their own nor do they play any parental role in raising their offspring.

Only about 1% of all birds use brood parasitism as a breeding technique. Having a host family raise their chicks means that brood parasites expend less energy on the breeding effort themselves thus **improving their own chances of survival**. But more importantly, brood parasites are able to produce many broods in one season which is not possible for birds that raise their own offspring.

Brood parasites and their young **use a number of different techniques** to ensure that the host parent gives the intruder the attention it requires. Tactics used by brood parasite chicks are innate and instinctive. The chicks are driven to behave the way they do from hatching, as it is fundamental to their survival.

The parent bird or chick (once it hatches) may **evict the host's eggs** or chick in order to replace them with their own. Some cuckoos have scoop-shaped backs to facilitate this. Removing eggs or other chicks affords the brood parasite the undivided attention of the host adult and completely removes all competition for resources. Sometimes only a single egg is removed as this helps to trick the host so that it does not notice the sudden addition of an egg. Some hosts will expertly recognise foreign eggs and kick them out the nest. To compensate, the colour of the eggs laid by the brood parasite will often match those of its host precisely, especially the more host-specific parasites.

Brood parasites' chicks are usually larger than their hosts and quickly outgrow and **out-compete their host siblings** to their own advantage and often to the host's offspring's demise. Some species trample and smother the other chicks in the nest due to their larger size while other species (like indigobirds and whydahs) are simply reared alongside the host's brood. The honeyguides are especially intentional about getting the competitive edge and their chicks are equipped with a bill hook on hatching which they use to lacerate and **destroy their host's chicks**.

In southern Africa there are **five different groups** that practise brood parasitism. These are the cuckoos, honeyguides, indigobirds, **whydahs** and the cuckoo finch (part of the weaver family). Honeyguides are the only family where the entire family is brood-parasitic.

Brood parasites

Once it has overcome the competition, the brood parasite still needs to **ensure that the host parent will feed it** as it grows more obviously different every day. To induce this, the brood parasite chick has the same colour gape with similar markings (palatal spots) as the host chicks. The colour or pattern of the gape revealed during begging is unique for each species and is what induces the adult to feed the chicks.

Although brood parasites never meet their own parents and are completely raised by a host species, they **still know their own songs**. The call of a brood parasite is inherited in its genes and is not a learned skill. In this way they will attract the correct species of mate later in life.

Brood parasites may be very **host specific** in their choice of species to brood their young. For example the **village indigobird** will only parasitise the **red-billed firefinch**, even mimicking its call to enable it to get close enough to the firefinches to locate the nest and lay a matching egg. Other species are less host-specific but may use bird hosts that exhibit similar nesting habits, for example the scaly-throated honeyguide parasitises hole-nesting species such as woodpeckers and barbets. Diderick cuckoos and greater honeyguides are very generalist using 24 and 35 species of hosts respectively.

The survival of a brood parasite chick is further enhanced by the fact that invertebrate parasites that infest birds and their nests are also host specific. The parasitic fledgling will be **immune to infestations of pests** that affect the host birds.

Host birds do not comply willingly and will invest a great amount of energy into chasing and mobbing brood parasites when they are spotted. Hosts have co-evolved with brood parasites in an arms race where the development of a particular exploitative tactic on the part of the brood parasite is countered by the host in the development of an avoidance strategy. An example of this would be the size of some weavers' nest tunnels. These are large enough to accommodate the weaver parents but not quite large enough to accommodate a diderick cuckoo (a common weaver parasite). There are records of cuckoos getting stuck and dying in the just-too-tight tunnels of weavers' nests. The arms race is, however, ongoing and as the hosts evolve so too do the parasites as their survival too is at stake.

Monogamy: the royal pair

Ninety percent of all bird species form breeding pairs that consist of just one male and one female. This is known as monogamy (*monus* meaning one and *gamous* meaning marriage). Birds have to catch food and feed their chicks directly as they have no internal source of nourishment like the mammary glands of mammals. This is time-consuming and costs energy. By **forming a paired alliance**, both sexes invest equal time and energy into the relationship and parental duties and are subsequently able to rear offspring more successfully than should one bird be left to do so on its own.

Pairing may happen once off as in the case of African fish-eagles, **saddle-billed storks** and various ducks and geese which **pair for life** or it may occur seasonally as in the case of migratory birds which only have short periods in which to complete the breeding cycle. Owls change their partners annually.

Fulvous duck

The monogamous **male bird must defend a territory** full of resource and sing and display attractively to convince a female mate that he is the best candidate to care for her and her offspring. Once he has acquired a partner, a male will guard and attend to his female partner attentively to ensure paternity in return for his faithfulness. The pair defends the territory together and spends much time maintaining the bond between them through allo-preening, nuptial gifting, song and ritualised displaying. Comparatively, in polygamous birds (i.e. birds with many mates) most of a male's energy is directed into the process of continuously attracting and mating with different partners.

Monogamous birds do not exhibit a great degree of **sexual dimorphism** (physical differences between the male and female sexes) as the emphasis is not so much on being attractive to mates, as in more colourful or dimorphic species, but rather on maintaining the pair bond and raising young. Because both sexes are intimately involved in the nesting process, they need to be equally inconspicuous. Egyptian geese, doves, ducks and storks are good examples of birds with little to no sexual dimorphism (also called sexual monomorphism). Reverse sexual dimorphism occurs in raptors where the female is the larger of the sexes because of her role in producing and incubating eggs. The male is smaller so that he is more agile to capture prey to provide for his partner and brood.

Monogamy: the royal pair

Egyptian geese are noisy birds which are conspicuous for their courtship and pairing activities which involve chasing flights, jump flights (takes off and lands immediately) and affectionate allo-preening (mutual preening). They are **extremely successful breeders** and outside of the breeding season they congregate gregariously in great numbers near water. Aside from the dual effort of the monogamous parents to care for the offspring, the reason they are so successful is their generalist approach to nesting sites. Egyptian geese are not fussy about where they nest and they use a multitude of sites including the ground, holes, cliffs, disused hamerkop, heron, raptor and crow's nests and even buildings. The location is lined with down to provide bedding for the eggs which are also covered with down when the female is not in attendance. The chicks are exceptionally precocial (well developed, feathered and eyes open at hatching). They will leave the nest within 6 hours of hatching, literally responding to the summons of the mother goose by jumping out of their nest even if it is positioned metres above the ground. The female will lead her brood to water where she and her male partner care for and protect the chicks.

Species that do not practise monogamy are called **polygamous** (*poly* meaning many and *gamous* meaning marriage). Birds such as whydahs and weavers are generally polygamous and both groups **invest a great deal of time and energy** into the attraction phase of breeding. They must convince females that they are worth choosing as mates irrespective of the fact that after mating they will abandon the females, leaving them to take care of the offspring alone.

The **paradise whydah** grows a long, impressive tail and develops stunning plumage which it shows off in display flights as an exhibition of gene superiority. The whydahs subscribe to the theory known as 'the handicap hypothesis' which states that having an impressive tail is essentially a handicap and if they are still able to outsmart predators with these impediments, then they are to be considered genetically fit by females.

Some of the **weavers** build homes to impress females into mating with them. At least half the preparation for chicks is thus completed before the male moves onto another mate leaving the female to care for and raise the chicks.

Polygamy where the male has more than one mate is called polygyny (*poly* meaning many and *gyna* meaning woman). Polygamy where the female has more than one mate is called polyandry (*poly* meaning many and *andry* meaning man) and this is practised by African jacanas and painted snipe.

The **red-crested korhaan** is a polygynous species and to attract females, the usually well-concealed male puts on an exhibition for the ladies rivalled by none. The bird starts with guttural clicking sounds which then develop into well-paced whistled notes that gradually become louder and more urgent turning into a piping 'pippity' note. He then takes off from the ground and flies diagonally up into the sky to just above the skyline where he stalls – folding his wings and flashing his black underbelly upwards – before dropping out of the sky like a half-brick. Just before the imminent crash landing, the male korhaan opens his wings and lands gracefully.

The **black-bellied bustard**, also polygynous, is not as exhibitionistic as its relative the red-crested korhaan but relies on an equally novel tactic to impress females and denote territory. The black-bellied bustard produces a guttural 'quark' sound from within his erect but bloated neck that shows off the black and white throat and then quickly retracts the neck into the shoulders before stretching it straight up again and emanating a 'pop'. The overall effect resembles the uncorking of a champagne bottle.

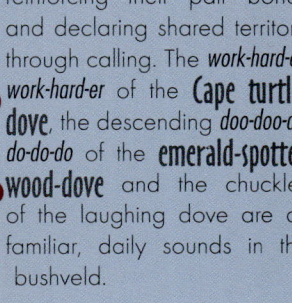

Doves spend much time reinforcing their pair bonds and declaring shared territory through calling. The *work-hard-er, work-hard-er* of the **Cape turtle-dove**, the descending *doo-doo-do-do-do-do* of the **emerald-spotted wood-dove** and the chuckles of the laughing dove are all familiar, daily sounds in the bushveld.

Nests

Weavers

To attract females, male weaver birds go to extreme lengths. Since the ultimate selection of a mate is usually up to the female, the male weavers leave nothing to chance in their construction of delicately and **expertly woven homes**. These they show off to passing females, flagging them down with vigorous displays and their brightly coloured costumes. Females will inspect the nests and finding them to their satisfaction, will begin to line the interiors as an indication of their approval. Mating will follow. If a nest is continually rejected by female passers-by, the male will destroy it and begin again. It is critical that the material used is fresh and green and that the quality of the weave is masterful.

Some species of weaver build their nests in colonies over water where they are afforded a degree of protection from predators. Others like the red-headed weaver are fairly resourceful, often making use of telephone wires or electric pylons. **Red-headed weavers** have the untidiest of all the weaver nests but they are constructed of twigs rather than fine grasses and palm leaves.

Red-billed buffalo-weavers live communally in large stick constructions built and defended by a single dominant male. These nests are sturdy and last many years as the material used can be up to four times the size of the builder. Within the nest, individual chambers are constructed connecting to the outside by a tunnel. The male invites many different females to occupy each of these chambers by fluttering his drooped wings for them. If a female should comply, the pair will mate and she will line her portion of the nest with greenery and proceed to incubate and care for her offspring alone. Copulation in red-billed buffalo-weavers is unique amongst birds for it can last for up to 2 minutes (for most species it takes just seconds). The male birds have a permanently erect phalloid organ which enlarges further during the breeding season and seems to facilitate the process although it is not a penis. The nests of the buffalo-weavers are usually positioned on the western or north-western side of a large tree and can be used to help orientate oneself in the bush on a sunless day. Verreaux's eagle-owls and white-backed vultures may also benefit from these nests using them as ready-made platforms for their own nesting needs.

Nests

Hamerkop

Hamerkops are esteemed for their **enormous nests** which may contain material including sticks 1,5 m in length and assortments of human debris such as bicycle tyre tubes. The nests are usually built in the main fork of a large tree near water, which is where the hamerkops earn a keep **specialising on feeding on frogs** and tadpoles. The giant sized mansion is constructed as a territorial marker to indicate to intruders that the region is occupied. Since it is constructed in a team effort by male and female, it may also serve to reinforce their pair bond.

The nest begins as a V-shaped cup in the fork of the tree and the sides are gradually built up basket-like around an internal cavity. The **roof is the real masterpiece** and is constructed with one bird inside and one bird outside the nest. Sticks, reeds and grass are added vertically and horizontally until the network is solid and a metre thick. So expert is the roof construction that it can support the weight of a fully grown man, let-alone the usurpers such as **Verreaux's eagle-owls** which often occupy the roofs of hamerkop nests, using them as their own nests.

The **internal chamber** is lined with mud to provide insulation for the eggs and chicks while the parents are frogging. A mud-lined upward-facing tunnel leads to the entrance which faces centrally outwards to make it inaccessible to predators. The 80 cm wide chamber can accommodate both adults and youngsters during the night. Early in the morning the birds shoot out of the tunnel like erupting corks, returning late afternoon with an upward dive, folding the wings at the last minute.

The **finished structure** weighs anywhere between 25 kg and 50 kg. It is up to 2 m high and 1,5 m wide. The construction takes 6 weeks (sometimes longer) to complete with 50–60 trips made in an hour to collect material. In spite of the amazing building statistics, hamerkops may choose to rebuild the following year or even build again the same year. Some remain in the same home for years. Many creatures, including barn owls, eagle-owls, Egyptian geese, comb ducks, tree squirrels, genets, monitor lizards, snakes and bees, make use of the valuable real estate provided by hamerkops irrespective of whether they are disused or still occupied.

Nests

Grey hornbill

Red-billed hornbill

Hornbills

Hornbills (specifically yellow-billed, red-billed and grey) have a remarkable nesting strategy. After the summer rains when there is adequate mud around, the **female secretes herself away** in a natural cavity in a tree which is lined with mud for insulation and the entrance is completely sealed off with mud and excreta bar a slit for her bill to receive food from her mate. Once inside she moults her tail and flight feathers to line the nest and make space for her brood. During her incarceration she is completely reliant on her partner to care for her and should he neglect his duties, she may die.

Such 'trust' is built up before the nesting season through **elaborate and incessant courtship displays** and pair bonding. For this reason hornbills have only one mate for the season (i.e. are monogamous) onto which they mutually lavish all their attentions. Pairs will feed together prior to mating and the male will bring nuptial gifts to the female to build up her fat reserves and convince her of his capabilities as a provider. While foraging the pair will hesitate regularly to call and display. They fly to a prominent perch (usually a tree top) where they will bow to one another, wings raised above their backs and cluck in an increasingly urgent manner.

Once the chicks are about half grown the **female breaks out** of the nest, dressed in a newly emerged set of feathers, and together she, the male and the chicks reseal the chicks into the nest. The parent birds then feed the chicks together. The chicks keep their tails erect while in the nest to conserve space inside the cavity while they grow. This also protects their vital flight feathers from damage.

The specifications for a **prime piece of hornbill real estate** include a hole at a height above the ground of about 4 m. The cavity must be 20 cm wide with the floor of the nest about 10 cm below the entrance lip, which should only be about 2,5 cm tall. It is of paramount importance that a chimney is present in the cavity into which the chicks may crawl to hide from danger. So important are these specifications that hornbills may reuse nest sites year after year. The chicks and female keep the inside clean by climbing up to the entrance and defecating with force out of the slit.

After the **chicks finally break** out of the nest cavity at the end of their epic nesting experience, the family remains together for a couple of weeks during which time the adults continue to feed the chicks. After 3 weeks they become independent.

Southern yellow-billed hornbill

Nests

Blue waxbill
Blue waxbills construct their delicate ball-like nests from the finest of grass materials, usually blue seed grass (*Tricholaena monachne*). These are carefully placed in the outer branches of thorn trees and shrubs which offer the nesting pair a degree of protection from predators. Blue waxbills also often build in proximity to active wasp nests to further ward off would-be predators.

Doves
Doves are unusual for passerines (perching birds) in that they make very rudimentary nests and their nest sanitation is poor. Where other passerines carry the faecal sacs of their young away from the nest, doves allow their nestlings' excreta to accumulate as it glues their primitive platform of sticks together reinforcing it as the chick grows larger.

Holes
Many bird species use holes in trees as their nesting places but only a few species are able to excavate their own. The most obvious of these is the woodpecker, but barbets are also astute hole-makers. Black-collared and **crested barbets** are both monogamous species (breed as an exclusive pair) and both species take turns to excavate the nest-hole preferring dead wood as the medium.

The **black-collared barbet** constructs an entrance about 40 mm wide and then digs a tunnel up to 9 cm deep into the trunk before it turns downwards for 30 cm into a cavity where the eggs are laid on woodchips. Such a large investment of energy is not only expended to create a nesting place but the holes are also used nightly as roosts. Once abandoned by the barbets, smaller hole-nesting species will take over the site.

Nests

Red-knobbed coot

Red-knobbed coots build nests that float on water from pieces of aquatic vegetation. While they are not in attendance of the nest, they will cover the eggs with plant debris to conceal the eggs. Usually the nests are not anchored to anything, as this would heighten the possibility of the nest flooding. **African jacanas** make similar floating nests.

Paradise flycatcher

Long-billed crombec

Cobweb

Spider's web is one of the strongest natural fibres that exists being stronger than steel at the same thickness. It is no wonder then that birds have incorporated its use into the construction of their homes. The **paradise flycatcher** builds a tiny cup-shaped nest from the pliable fibres of inner bark, which it binds together with spider's web and then decorates with lichen. The white-crested helmet-shrike is another user of cobweb. It also constructs a cup-shaped nest from strips of inner bark but then plasters the outside with cobweb until it is smooth. It also connects the nest to the branch of a tree with cobweb. The cobweb is collected on the trademark erectile facial feathers of the helmet-shrikes.

Sunbirds, crombecs and penduline-tits also use spider's web to weave their unique bag-like nests. The crombec makes a purse at the end of a branch with grass, sticks and spider's web which it camouflages with leaves and reuses season after season. Sunbirds make an oval woven ball called a 'sunbird-type oval' from dry material and cobweb with the entrance off-set to one side near the top. **Penduline tits** make felt-like bags with false-entrances as a decoy for predators. The felty texture is obtained from the use of soft fibres like bits of wild cotton or even sheep's wool knitted together with cobweb.

Precocial and altricial

Altricial chicks are those that are **born naked, blind and unable to move around.** Usually it is the passerines (or perching birds that have a foot structure of three toes forward, one back) that produce these kinds of chicks. Passerines are usually birds that nest in trees or holes and these structures in their diversity of forms provide shelter for the chicks which need warmth and protection while they develop through a protracted nesting period. Altricial chicks need to be supported, fed and kept warm by the parent birds. Passerines are generally small birds, the largest of the group being the crows.

Black-backed puffback

One of the criteria that help ornithologists divide the bird kingdom into different groups is the **condition of their young when they hatch.** Chicks will either be altricial or precocial at birth.

Blacksmith lapwing

Precocial chicks are those that are born with a downy covering, their eyes are open and within a short space of time (usually as soon as their plumage dries) they can move around and even swim. Usually ground- or water-dwelling birds (non-passerines) produce precocial young. It is **vital for the young of such birds to be able to escape danger** from the minute they hatch as their rudimentary nests are on the ground and vulnerable to myriad predators. In order for them to hatch more advanced than altricial birds, precocial species incubate their eggs for longer. Since they are more developed at birth, they are better able to regulate their body heat and do not need to rely on a parent bird to keep them warm. They set to the task of finding food almost immediately.

There is an **intermediate group** of birds known as near-passerines that produce altricial young in nests but do not have feet modified for perching but rather for clinging or other functions. Such feet are usually zygodactylous or syndactylous. A **zygodactylous foot** has two toes facing forward and two backwards. This allows birds such as woodpeckers, wood-hoopoes and **mousebirds** to cling to the upright branches of trees while foraging for food. Owls have a toe that may either face forward or backwards depending on the grip required when hunting. A syndactylous foot has the second and third toe fused such as in **kingfishers** and hornbills.

Egyptian geese

African jacana

Raptors do not fit neatly into any of the groups since their young hatch with their eyes open and covered in down feathers but are still helpless, to a large degree being reliant on the parents for food and bound to the nest for safety. This is considered semi-altricial. Other birds that are semi-altricial are egrets and **herons**.

Symbiotic relationships in birds

Symbiosis refers to a protracted relationship between two species where one of the species may benefit from the association, be negatively affected or not affected in any way.

The **fork-tailed drongo** is a bold little black bird with a forked tail (as its name suggests) and a reddish eye. It is well known for its ability and tendency to mimic other birds' calls. The complexity of the tune copied and repeated is one of the criteria for which a female drongo might select a mate. Drongos are particularly adept at mimicking the call of the pearl-spotted owlet. Drongos are aerial hawkers, snapping insects out of the sky with acrobatic manoeuvres. In this respect they use large mammals such as herds of impala or buffalo to their advantage. As the herd moves and feeds, they disturb and flush out insects in the grass which the drongos catch.

They perch around the feeding herbivores in between mouthfuls and wait for more insects to be flushed up. Then with the **swiftness of a small fighter aircraft they dart in** behind the mammals' hooves to snap the insects out of the air. On occasion if things are not happening quickly enough, drongos may even give a false alarm call setting the feeding animals to flight a short distance and then they quickly monopolise on the sudden flush of insects.

The **cattle egret** is the well-known foot servant of buffalo, rhino and eland, patiently following these animals through the grassland. Insects disturbed by the movement of the mammals' hooves through the bush, provide a hearty meal for the egrets. But over and above the feast picked out of the grass, cattle egrets may also land and perch on these large herbivores removing ticks and other ectoparasites much like oxpeckers do. They were originally called 'tick birds' for this habit.

Commensalism is a form of symbiosis. In commensalistic relationships, one of the species gains direct benefit from associating with the other while the second species derives no benefit but is not negatively affected in any way. Birds are masters of opportunism and may use other mammalian species, particularly, to their advantage.

Symbiotic relationships in birds

Mutualism is another form of symbiosis but both species benefit directly from their interaction with one another.

Yellow- and red-billed hornbills enjoy a mutualistic relationship with the **dwarf mongoose** (see p. 112) These species can often be found foraging together. Dwarf mongooses live in groups of about 12 individuals and move through an area together overturning stones looking for scorpions and other invertebrates. They are astute diggers as well. As the troop of mongooses forages, some of their prey escapes or too much is flushed out for the individual to grab. This is where the hornbill benefits. **Hornbills will quickly snap up whatever the dwarf mongooses miss**. In return, the hornbills provide an alarm system warning the mongooses of danger that they may not detect due to being absorbed in feeding. The hornbills even raise the alarm for aerial predators that are only a threat to the mongooses and not themselves.

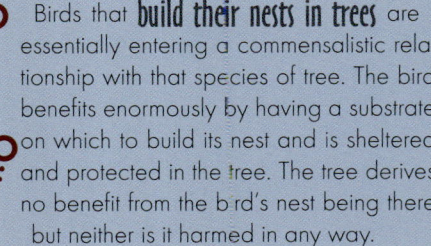

Birds that **build their nests in trees** are essentially entering a commensalistic relationship with that species of tree. The bird benefits enormously by having a substrate on which to build its nest and is sheltered and protected in the tree. The tree derives no benefit from the bird's nest being there but neither is it harmed in any way.

This relationship is so successful that the hornbills will even wait for dwarf mongooses outside their burrows in the mornings, having followed them home the evening before. If the mongooses are slow to rise, the hornbills will call at the termite mound where the mongooses have bedded down in an attempt to rouse them. Although both species benefit from their mutual association, this is not an obligatory form of mutualism, as both species can still exist without the other and their shared relationship.

Raptors

Snake-eagles

The brown (*Circaetus cinereus*) and black-chested (*Circaetus pectoralis*) snake-eagles are common large raptors in the Lowveld and distinguished immediately by their **large yellow eyes** and square-shaped heads.

Unlike other eagles, the snake-eagles have **naked legs** which are covered in robust scales. This is an adaptation to handling snakes as the scales provide some protection from the strikes of snakes inaccurately grasped or not killed on impact.

Snake-eagles lead a relatively **solitary existence** outside of the breeding season.

Snake-eagles **swallow their prey directly into their stomachs** and unlike other birds they do not store their food in their crops first. These eagles do take prey other than snakes including lizards, rodents, insects, birds and even fish and these items may be stored in the crop. Interestingly, the crop (a pre-digestion storage sack in birds) wraps right around the neck of raptors while in other birds it sits in the front of the neck. The black-chested snake-eagle exhibits a great deal of resourcefulness in catching reptiles fleeing fires by aerial perching at the edge of burning areas.

Snake-eagles **feed their nestling chicks on snakes**. These are taken to the nest already swallowed bar a section of the tail which is gripped and pulled by the chick and then swallowed with some contortions of its neck which is believed to allow the snake to seat itself in the stomach.

The **black-chested snake-eagle** is an aerial soarer and locates prey on the ground by hovering intermittently (more correctly called aerial perching, as true hovering involves the ability to move forward or backwards which the snake-eagle cannot do). The black-chested snake-eagle will descend on prey from 450 m high, striking a snake behind the head which is crushed in the talons. Snake-eagles that do not position their grip correctly **are at risk of attack** and even death by the venomous snakes that they hunt.

The **brown snake-eagle** is often seen prominently perched at the top of a tree from where it will descend on its prey. It drops onto a snake and crushes its spine with its powerful talons biting at the same time to crush the head. The **snake is swallowed head first** and may be regurgitated and re-swallowed several times until it is comfortably accommodated in the stomach.

Raptors

Bateleur
Terathopius ecaudatus

The bateleur's **name means marvellous face** (*Terathopius*) without a tail (*ecaudatus*). They are striking eagles with contrasting black plumage, red bills and feet and a very short tail. The name *bateleur* is from the French for tightrope walker or acrobat, due to the side-to-side rocking that results from the bird's lack of tail-induced stabilisation in flight.

Bateleurs are **opportunistic feeders** and being on the alert for meals to either scavenge, pirate or hunt, they fly low (50–150 m above the ground) zigzagging repeatedly over the same area. They will visit areas that have recently been burnt to harvest dead animals or they may follow roads to benefit from road kills. At least a third of their diet includes much-varied hunted prey. The short tail reduces drag during their lengthy foraging flights (estimated at 400 km per day) and provides them with an element of manoeuvrability when they attack prey or in combat with other bateleurs.

It takes **7 years for a bateleur to obtain its full adult plumage**. Juveniles tend to have slightly longer tails, which shortens over successive moults and possibly helps initially to stabilise a young bird learning to fly.

Bateleurs **pair for life** and aggressively defend a territory year round, diving at and even making contact with intruders on the back. They are well known for their dramatic aerial acrobatics associated with courtship during which the male dives headlong at the female who rolls onto her back and demonstrates her talons. Pairs maintain their bond through allo-preening (mutual preening).

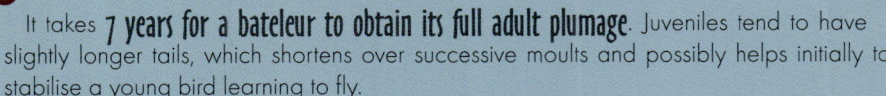

The bateleur is one of the easiest raptors to identify in flight due to its tapering two-toned wings and upturned primaries. **Sexes can easily be told apart** as the black trailing edge in females is much narrower than in males. When perched, female birds have a grey window on the wing below the grey shoulder which the males lack.

Raptors

Martial eagle
Polemaetus bellicosus

The martial eagle is a **magnificent large eagle** and a powerful hunter. It hunts on the wing spending hours of the day engaged in exploratory soaring, covering areas extending 100–1 000 km². It can spot prey 6 km away and will drop upon it surreptitiously by making use of cover in its approach.

Martial eagles sometimes use **ambush techniques** when catching food, perching secretly in a foliaged tree at a waterhole or over a well-used game trail until opportunity presents itself. Although they specialise in eating monitor lizards and to a lesser degree other birds, martial eagles will take very large creatures including hares, rabbits, warthogs, ungulates up to the size of impala, baboons and other primates, jackals, caracals, polecats, dassies, pangolins, mongooses and bats. They **can lift 8 kg** although typically they only lift 1–4 kg. If prey is too heavy to lift to a perch, the martial eagle will feed on it in situ for sometimes up to 5 successive days.

Mobbing

Birds of prey are often mobbed by smaller birds, like the cocky **fork-tailed drongo**. This is a tactic used to encourage the raptor to leave the vicinity. The drongo recognises the raptor as a predatory threat but it is aware that the raptor relies on the element of surprise to attack prey. Being smaller and more manoeuvrable, the drongo is able to dive-bomb perched raptors (or even sometimes those in flight), pecking them annoyingly behind the head, without fear of being caught by the larger bird which has neither surprise nor speed-from-rest to its advantage.

Crow mobbing vulture

Cainism

Cainism (also known as siblicide) is demonstrated by a large number of predatory bird species. This is the phenomenon where adults lay two eggs but the first to hatch is naturally the larger and quickly outgrows its sibling. Having the advantage of size and strength over the later-comer, the older sibling aggressively pecks the younger to death and thereby eliminates any competition for food or other parental attentions. The second egg is simply laid as an insurance policy should the first not hatch. A notorious 'cainism' perpetuator is the Verreauxs' eagle.

Raptors

Wahlberg's eagle
Aquila wahlbergi

In the summer, the **commonest brown eagle** in the Lowveld is undoubtedly the Wahlberg's Eagle (pronounced 'Val'-berg after the Swedish naturalist). **Migrating** to the warmer southern parts of the African continent from its central and more northerly reaches (inter-African migrant), the Wahlberg's eagle comes here to breed during spring and summer. This it does upon a small platform of sticks that it re-bolsters each year and lines with green material. The same nest, usually positioned below the canopy in a main fork of a large riverine tree such as a jackalberry or knobthorn (see pp. 280 and 252) may be used for up to 28 years successively. Usually, however, the eagles have a selection of five different nests within their territories. Remarkably for migrant birds, Wahlberg's eagles remain paired with the same mate for years.

The Wahlberg's eagle is small and has a **long, square tail** when it is perched or in flight. In flight it also carries its head lower than the plane of its body. It has a small crest of feathers at the back of its head. All these features make it easily recognisable. **Two distinct colour morphs** occur which could confuse a novice as being different species: the all-brown form and the **pale morph**, which is almost completely creamy-white with darker streaks on the head and wings.

Wahlberg's eagles are conspicuous for their habit of perching in obvious places and because they soar over their territory regularly to hunt or to advertise their ownership through spectacular aerial cartwheeling. They are also **very vocal** using a mournful whistled call during displays.

The **tawny eagle** (*Aquila rapax*) is the commonest resident brown eagle and occurs in a variety of brown through blonde colours. It is larger than the Wahlberg's eagle with a shorter tail and is separated from other brown eagles by the fact that the gape only extends to the middle of the eye and never beyond. These birds are resourceful predators catching other birds in flight, pirating food from raptors or ground hornbills or scavenging it from carcasses or off vultures.

True eagles
True eagles have feathered legs that extend all the way down to the feet. All the eagles belonging to the genus *Aquila* such as Wahlberg's and tawny eagles are true eagles.

Birds of prey are not always large birds. The **little sparrow-hawk**, the Lowveld's smallest raptor, is the same size as a dove. Sightings of these birds are so fleeting that they can be confused with doves in flight.

Vultures

Vultures have **strong bills** that are adapted to tearing tough flesh. They are curved, have a fingernail texture and grow throughout life. In conjunction to this efficient tool, vultures also have serrated, rough tongues for prying smaller bits of meat off carcasses and bones.

Because of their naked heads and necks, vultures need to have a mechanism to **control their temperature** as heat exchanges easier through naked skin than through the insulation of feathers. When they are circling kilometres up in the sky, ambient temperatures are cold. For this reason they have an **erectable ring of feathers around the base of the neck, called a ruff**. The ruff acts like a scarf. Vultures also pull their necks into their bodies when in flight to prevent heat loss. The naked skin is useful for dissipating heat when on the ground on hot days.

Vultures have **excellent eyesight**. Some sources state that they can see a 6 cm object from 1 km up in the sky. This makes their eyesight eight times better than humans. It is not clear how this could be tested but what is clear is that they are exceptionally astute at spotting even small kills from high altitudes. A vulture's eyes have two lenses: one to see the broader landscape like a fisheye lens and one to magnify objects. Their eyes are large relative to the size of their skulls and bodies and this allows a bigger image to form on the retina thus providing more detail.

Vultures **lack feathers on their heads and necks**. This is because they are inclined to insert these parts of their bodies directly into carcasses and if they were covered in feathers, these would easily become soiled. Soiled head feathers are a 'health hazard' and could cause infection or illness. Furthermore, preening these areas would prove difficult. Vultures are, in fact, very clean birds and most species will bathe regularly to rid themselves of unsanitary debris.

Vultures have **flat feet** and their claws are less curved than those of eagles who rely on their talons to hunt. This is because vultures spend a great deal of time on the ground and they would battle to take the mandatory run-up necessary to take off if their talons were more curved.

Vultures

Vultures generally perch on **prominent, sturdy perches** like the dead anatomies of leadwood trees (see p. 274). Being heavy birds, they require both a solid place to land and a convenient drop-off from which to gain leverage when taking to flight. At night when there are no thermals to facilitate flight, vultures roost in the large trees that typically line river courses.

The **crop** is a distensible storage 'sock' in front of the oesophagus. Since vultures are scavengers and their **food supply is not guaranteed** on a daily basis, they have developed the ability to fill their crops in a very short time (about 2 minutes) with up to 1,4 kg of carrion. This food remains undigested while in storage. If vultures are unduly disturbed or threatened, they will regurgitate their crop-load and the evacuation of the putrid meat both lightens the bird so it can escape easily and acts as a deterrent to the predator. A vulture can lose out on a whole 'banked' meal if it is forced to take this course of action.

Vultures use **thermals to facilitate low-energy flight**. Pockets of rising warm air form when the sun heats the ground during the day and these thermals provide lift to the enormous birds. Vultures are equipped with huge wingspans of up to 2,8 m in lappet-faced vultures, which suit this style of flight. Using thermals prevents the necessity to flap these large wings and thereby the birds save more than three times the energy that would be needed in flapping flight. Vultures use thermals to gain a height vantage to look for food and by moving from one thermal to the next they can survey vast areas while foraging. Vultures can soar at altitudes up to 12 000 m, covering thousands of kilometres at a gliding speed of about 60 km/h but up to 80 km/h. Vultures are restricted to flying during the sunny hours of the day and at night and on overcast days generally find themselves grounded.

White-backed vultures forage using a **grid flight pattern**. By circling in an organised manner, one bird can see when another breaks the formation. If an individual spots something and starts to move downwards, its white back offers an obvious beacon to the other birds that follow suit. Vultures will also watch for other lower-flying species of vultures (like the white-headed vulture) descending on a kill, or scavenging raptors like the tawny and bateleur eagles. They even follow lions and hyenas sometimes. Vultures have been **recorded as achieving diving speeds of 120 km/h** as they literally 'fall' out the sky upon a meal. It is this spectacle of vultures dropping quickly out of the sky in an isolated area that indicates to an observer the presence of a kill. Many people get excited on seeing vultures circling but this is their usual foraging style and in most instances they are merely catching thermals.

Vultures

Four vulture species are particularly common in the Lowveld:

- White-backed vulture
- Lappet-faced vulture
- White-headed vulture
- Hooded vulture

These species tend to fall into a **feeding hierarchy** at a carcass. Although there is some contest regarding the fixed order of this hierarchy, it is clear that the different species do perform different 'duties' at a feeding site. The white-backed vultures are the most numerous and are frantic, noisy feeders hissing and mobbing one another to get their share of the spoils. White-backed vultures are comical birds and new arrivals bound in with wings and neck outstretched and can be seen bobbing from one leg to another, wings spread, to dominate a kill site.

They will feed right inside a carcass, shearing meat from bones with powerful bills. They are extremely opportunistic and attempt to feed even while a predator is still present. They have even been known to chase less aggressive predators like cheetahs right off their kills. Generally, however, most vultures (including the white-backed) have to await the arrival of the lappet-faced vulture in the case of a closed carcass.

It is this 'king of vultures' that is adept at tearing open the skin of a closed carcass with its huge bill to get at the innards. A lappet-faced vulture is the dominant species at a kill due to its size and power. They will eat tough remains such as skin, tendon, hair and ligament. The more solitary white-headed vulture generally remains to one side of the feeding activity, taking bits of meat and feeding a distance away.

The hooded vulture feeds on the softer organs like the eyes or intestines of a carcass. It also tends to hang around the edge of the feast snapping up scraps, which is often all that is available to it due to being pushed aside by the other larger, bossier species. The bill is small and adapted for probing into crevices after the frenzy is over.

The **marabou stork** is often found associating with vultures. Marabou is a French word meaning 'ugly, misshapen old man'. They are unable to shear meat off a carcass with their straight bills and must rely on stealing bits that the vultures have worked free with their sharper beaks.

Vultures

Vultures can be divided into two main groups with regards to their **breeding**.

Where the commoner species in the Lowveld are all tree-nesters, the Cape vulture is a cliff nester. Vultures are all long-lived species that breed slowly.

The **white-backed vulture** tends to form loose colonies in suitable habitat, usually where large trees line a watercourse. Their nests are built at the very top of the tallest trees usually 15–25 m above ground. They prefer to nest in thorn trees as these offer protection from predators. The nest is a sturdy platform of sticks to support the large bodies of both adult and chick and the same site may be reused year after year (up to 15 years in one case).

Due to their messy feeding habits, vultures **drink and bathe regularly** at waterholes. The social species may gather gregariously at their favourite spots and some will spend a whole afternoon near the waterhole often with wings spread to sun themselves and restore the shape of ruffled feathers.

Cape vultures are extremely social and breed in colonies of between 6 and 100 pairs on cliff faces. This provides them with a good position from which to launch their large, heavy bodies into flight. Their grassy nests are positioned on ledges usually where there is some form of overhang. The structure may vary from a few tufts of grass to elaborate structures decorated with sticks stolen from a neighbour. Nests are also used year after year and eventually the cliff faces become distinctively plastered with droppings.

Vultures play a **vital role** in the bush – they clean up dead and decaying carcasses and thereby remove centres of disease. They are often cast as motley, evil birds by the media but vultures have an array of marvellous adaptations that suit them perfectly to their 'job description'.

Sadly, vultures feature prominently in **African muthi** (traditional medicine). They are believed to contain powers of premonition or foresight. The possession and ceremonious use of the bird's skull is believed to transfer the vulture's clairvoyant abilities to a person. Possessing the dried foot of a vulture is also believed to bring good luck.

Owls

Owls are masters of **silent flight**. This skill is necessary so that they can listen for the sounds of their prey while they are in flight and also so that they have the stealth required to surprise and capture prey. Silent flight is achieved in two simple ways. Owls have very large wings relative to the size and mass of their bodies. This gives them a low wing loading and allows them to fly without having to flap excessively. The leading edge of an owl's wings has velvety feathers that are 'frayed'. This splits up the passage of air hitting the edge of the wing and effectively omits the slicing sound associated with other birds in fast flight.

Owls do not essentially have better **eyes** than humans in that they can see the same spectrum of light that we can. An owl's eyes are, however, **designed to collect more light** than humans by having a long optical axis and a much-curved cornea and they are thus able to construct brighter images for enhanced vision in low-light conditions. The eyes are very large with widely dilating pupils. They are well stocked with rod cells (light-sensitive cells) and are subsequently very sensitive to detecting movement. Neither owls nor any other birds can see in total darkness but some species of owl can see so well in low-light conditions that they can detect dead prey in weak starlight.

Owls are often seen **bobbing their heads** when staring at objects. This is a secondary technique that they use to work out the relative positions of objects to one another and this helps them to gauge distance.

Owls enjoy **excellent binocular vision** because they have the most forward facing eyes of all birds affording them a 70 degree overlap. Their eyes are large, which helps with collecting light, but the size restricts their mobility in the skull and owls only have a total visual field of 110 degrees (birds with peripheral vision from side-placed eyes enjoy up to 340 degree fields of vision). To overcome this, owls have very flexible necks which allow them to turn their heads 270 degrees enabling them to even see behind them. Such a contortion of the neck would usually cut off the blood supply to the head by pinching closed the main artery but owls have two such arteries, one on either side of the neck, which provide an uninterrupted blood supply to the brain during neck twists.

Owls

To complement their eyesight, owls have especially **acute hearing**. Owls can detect sounds made by small mammals and insects in the ultrasonic spectrum (higher pitched but not necessarily softer than the human ear can detect). Some species have asymmetrically placed ears that allow a split second difference in the reception of sound in each ear and this allows owls to pinpoint sound precisely, a key feature required to catch prey in total darkness. The ears are positioned on the edge of the facial disc (most prominent in the **barn owls**) and this facial disc acts like a parabola to focus especially the more high-pitched sounds into the eardrums. These high-pitched sounds are further enhanced by air spaces that interconnect the ears. Feathers surrounding the ear openings are soft and do not interfere with incoming sound waves. Barn owls also have a movable flap of skin (an operculum) that helps them direct sounds coming from behind into their eardrums.

Owls are divided into two **main groups or families**, the Strigidae and Tytonidae. The **tytonids** are screeching owls and include the grass and barn owls in southern Africa. These owls have long, slender bills, smaller, dark eyes and a pectinate claw for preening. The **strigids** include all other owls and either hoot or have a whistled call. They have enormous eyes, stouter bills and no pectinate claw.

Southern white-faced scops-owl

Owls

While most owls are **typically nocturnal** hunting under the cover of darkness, some owls use the daylight hours to avoid competition with and predation by their larger counterparts. The **pearl-spotted owlet** is typically crepuscular, meaning that it is active early morning and late afternoon. Because it hunts during the daylight hours, it does not rely as heavily on the use of hearing to locate prey.

The **pearl-spotted owlet** uses startle displays to ward off its enemies. It has two eye-spots on the back of its head that mimic real eyes and a predator would be hard pressed to know for sure which way the owlet is really looking. This technique is used to dissuade attackers, as predators generally will not pursue prey from the front as they then lose the element of surprise critical for effective hunting.

Owls are relatively nonchalant when it comes to **nesting**. Owls generally do not make nests of their own but rely on existing nests made by other raptors and species like hamerkops. The **spotted eagle-owl** nests on the ground in dense vegetation and the smaller species utilise natural cavities in trees or the evacuated nest-holes of barbets and woodpeckers. Because these owlets lay their eggs in the dark, there is no need for cryptically coloured eggs and they lay pure white eggs. **Barn owls** are by far the most prodigious breeders among the owl family. They have been known to lay up to 20 eggs during one breeding season. The laying is staggered and the comical-looking chicks of varying ages share the nest site. As its name suggests, the barn owl is not averse to using human habitations like the eves of barns to nest. Usually owls lay two eggs and raise one chick.

Owls

The feathers that stand erect on top of some owls' heads are known as **ear tufts**. These are not real ears and have a camouflaging function. During the day when owls are attempting to blend into their surrounds to remain unnoticed while they rest, they will erect their ear tufts to help break the outline of their bodies and thereby be more camouflaged. The **African scops-owl** does this especially successfully and its ear tufts help it to mimic pieces of bark or lichen. When owls are nesting (those that do not use holes), they will lie flat on their bellies and also erect the ear tufts to break their outline. In order for this kind of crypsis to be successful, owls have **mastered the art of sitting still**.

Owls generally **swallow their food whole**. The **Verreaux's eagle-owl** has the most voracious diet of the owls, easily taking prey up to the size of scrub hares and vervet monkeys. They will pull this larger prey apart but will not necessarily pluck it first. An owl can use its zygodactylous feet in the same fashion a parrot can, lifting the foot to the mouth. All the indigestible bits of bone and fur are regurgitated in a mucous-covered ball known as a pellet. This is necessary because the food is not chewed and the large particles cannot clear the pyloric opening between stomach and intestine.

Nightjars

Nightjars are the superbly adapted **swallows of the night.** They are often spotted sitting on roads just after sundown. From here they can clearly see insects against the open sky above them and they will fly up to hawk these, returning to the ground between bouts.

To facilitate capturing insects in flight, nightjars have **special modified sensory feathers** on the face, called rictal bristles. These help to channel food into the wide gape.

Nightjars are **built for aerodynamics.** They have narrow, flat wings that taper at the tips, which facilitate the fast flight needed to catch insects on the wing. They rely on flapping to give them the momentum and lift they require to forage. Birds with such an aerodynamic shape are also best suited to migration. Most nightjar species migrate during the autumn when their aerial invertebrate prey begins to diminish to levels that would not sustain the population through winter.

Most insectivorous birds have tweezer-like bills to snap up their invertebrate prey. Nightjars have very **short squat bills** but the design is equally ingenious. They have exceptionally wide gapes (the extent the bill is able to open) and on approach of an insect the nightjar will open its mouth creating a veritable 'black hole' into which the insect is sucked.

The **large eyes** of a nightjar are there to effect good night vision, allowing the maximum amount of light to enter the eye socket in low light conditions. Because they are so large, their shiny eyes are conspicuous by day and nightjars will close their eyes to escape detection when resting up, incubating eggs or if threatened. The reflective layer of cells found behind the retina in these birds' eyes assists with improved nocturnal vision. This shines red in the headlights of an approaching vehicle making nightjars easy to spot after dark.

Nightjars have exquisitely **well-developed cryptic colouration,** their mottled brown patterns merging them perfectly into the leafy litter of the bushveld understorey. During the day it is extremely difficult to find nightjars as they sit unmoving and rely on their crypsis to keep them concealed. So good is the nightjar's camouflage that, unlike many other ground-nesting birds, it does not need to produce cryptically coloured eggs. They will lay pale and even sometimes pure white eggs and then rely on their own body camouflage to conceal them. The eggs are laid directly on the bare ground, as any form of nesting material would compromise their camouflage. The female incubates by day and the male relieves her by night. Should any disturbance threaten the incubating bird, it will flatten its body (eyes closed to eliminate the give-away shininess) reducing its own telltale shadow.

Nightjars have a specially **adapted preening apparatus** known as a **pecten** or pectinate claw. The pecten is a comb device attached to the middle claw of both its feet. It is used in preening and scratching, to remove parasites or to straighten out the rictal bristles.

Nightjar species are very difficult to distinguish between, all of them having similar cryptic colouration. They do vary slightly in features such as the amount of white on the tail feathers but the most reliable way of discerning between species is to use their calls. The **most iconic of African night sounds is the 'Good Lord deliver us...' chant of the fiery-necked nightjar.** The sound of the square-tailed nightjar is also a common night-time sound in the Lowveld. It is a protracted purring noise made at different pitches and it sounds a little like a small engine changing gears.

Ground birds

Double-banded sandgrouse

These are **superbly cryptically coloured** ground birds and they occur in open sandy habitats that perfectly match their attire. They nest in particularly open areas for the same reason, the monogamous male and female sharing incubation duties and concealing their eggs with their own cryptic bodies.

Because of their hot, dry habitat, sandgrouse have developed some unique traits. They have densely packed feathers and thickened skin and scales on their feet. Most uniquely, the **feathers on the belly of the male bird are modified** for collecting and retaining water. The birds visit waterholes at sundown to drink, weaving through the trees to escape attention until they alight at the water's edge. Here the male will wade into the shallows and raising the feathers on his upper belly, will allow them to soak up water in a process known as 'belly-wetting'. These belly feathers are then flattened again before he leaves to return to the nest. Sandgrouse chicks drink the water directly off their father's feathers.

Double-banded sandgrouse are **seed-eaters** and they typically exploit the ephemeral (temporary) abundance of annuals' seeds. Remarkably, the chicks feed exclusively on hard seeds right from hatching and are the only birds in Africa (and most of the world) to do so.

Ground birds

Helmeted guineafowl

These attractive ground-dwelling birds are **found in noisy flocks** of up to 40 birds which occasionally aggregate in good feeding areas to produce groups of hundreds or even thousands. But they are not always together in groups and during the breeding season (and after a good deal of chasing antics to separate a mate from the group) monogamous pairs form and break away to nest alone.

Of all the birds in southern Africa, the helmeted guineafowl is surely one of the **most iconic**, unmistakable for its bony bare casque or 'helmet' on its head, its red wattles and flecked plumage. They are very adaptable birds and they are found abundantly in any open habitat.

The male guineafowl is an **attentive suitor**. He defends his chosen mate, brings her grasshoppers to build up her reserves and shows off to her with the typical guineafowl 'hunchback' display. All this is done at his own expense as he hardly feeds at all **during courtship** and may drop up to 85% of his body mass. The female spends all her time prior to laying eggs preening and feeding and, fortified with her mate's nuptial gifts, she improves her body mass by 15%.

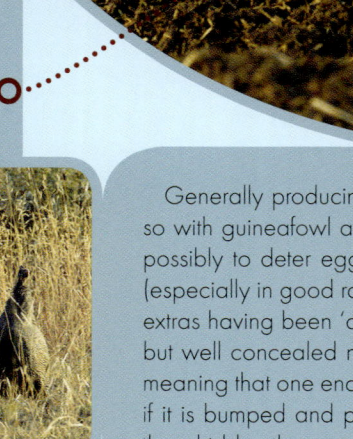

Generally producing eggs is an energy-costly exercise to the female bird but particularly so with guineafowl as they produce the thickest shelled eggs of any bird for their size. This is possibly to deter egg-stealing predators. They also produce **large clutches** of up to 20 eggs (especially in good rainy seasons). Interestingly, a single female may brood up to 50 eggs, the extras having been 'dumped' in her nest by other females. The eggs are laid in a rudimentary but well concealed nest on the ground. The eggs that guineafowl lay are pyriform in shape, meaning that one end is more pointed. This is a design that allows the egg to roll in a tight circle if it is bumped and prevents eggs rolling away. The eggs are a creamy colour and to keep them hidden the parent bird conceals them with her body and sits quite still to avoid detection.

Ground birds

It is **hard to tell guineafowl sexes apart**. Males are slightly larger and the only member of the species to engage in the 'hunchback' display.

During the incubation period, it is the female's turn to fast as she does all the incubating and does not feed much during this time. By the time the brood hatches, the female needs to replenish her reserves and for the first 2 weeks of their lives, it is **mostly the male bird that cares for the keets** (chicks). The keets depart the nest almost immediately on hatching (as soon as their cryptic downy feathers dry) being well developed (precocial) at hatching. They are unable to regulate their body temperature at this stage and are therefore susceptible to hyperthermia. Although they can follow the parent birds around, it is still up to the parents to keep them warm by finding them food to metabolise. The **parents are great defenders** of their brood and will charge and growl at offending predators valiantly. By the time the chicks can fly (at a mere 2 weeks old) the individual family units begin to reassemble into larger flocks, which provide greater protection to the individual.

Guineafowl are **opportunistic in their choice of food** and their diet includes bulbs, seeds and the stems of plants like *Cyperus* sedges. They consume large quantities of protein-rich invertebrates during the breeding season.

Although **guineafowl can fly**, they do not do so very often. They will fly a short distance noisily if startled or they will fly up into trees at night to roost out of harm's way. Guineafowl are very much creatures of habit. They roost at sunset each evening and descend at dawn. They will visit a waterhole in the morning to drink (often parading all in a long line) and here engage in all manner of social and personal hygiene activities including chasing (between males this maintains a flock hierarchy), dust bathing and preening. In the afternoons, guineafowl will feed towards water once more for a repeat of the sociality before roosting for the night.

171

Ground birds

Francolins and spurfowl

Francolins and spurfowl were for a long time collectively referred to as francolins. Although the birds **all look similar**, scientists have discovered that they are **not even that closely related**. Broadly speaking, a francolin is smaller and has yellow legs. It flushes when disturbed from the open areas where it lives and has a musical call. A spurfowl is larger and has orange, red or black legs. It sits tight or runs when disturbed (rather than flushing) and roosts in trees at night. Spurfowl have harsh calls.

Groups of francolins and spurfowl are known as coveys. Usually the **group consists of a monogamous pair and its offspring** which like most ground birds, are precocial from hatching and accompany the parents wherever they go soon after hatching. The young can fly within 10 days, a trait required only in extreme circumstances or for **roosting out of harm's way at night**. When a bird gives the alarm, the covey will fly up noisily and scatter. They **do not fly far** before landing and taking to thick cover (spurfowl fly only as a last resort). Young chicks may scatter and lie flat at the parents' alarm, relying on their cryptic colour to conceal them. The members of a covey reunite after dispersing by using a high-pitched ventriloquial call.

Like other ground birds, francolins and spurfowl **nest** in rudimentary nests on the ground and they conceal their white eggs with their own cryptically coloured bodies.

Francolins and spurfowl are fairly **omnivorous** in their habits and feed on bulbs, seeds, berries, shoots, insects and molluscs. They typically use their bills and feet to scratch around in the leaf litter under vegetation to find food. They produce **large droppings for their size**, which are usually round and slightly smaller than a golf ball. These are smelly due to the omnivorous content. Like other birds, the darker body of the **dung** is coated partly in white. This is uric acid concentrated to conserve body water (and because a heavy water-filled bladder would not be conducive to flight). Birds have only one exit for reproductive and digestive evacuations, known as the cloaca. The white from the urethra is added to the brown faeces on evacuation.

Although many of the species **feed in bushy areas** where they benefit from the cover to conceal them from aerial predators like African hawk-eagles, francolins and spurfowl are often seen feeding on fallen grass seed alongside roads. They are conspicuous by their noisy calls and their habit of chasing one another. This behaviour is thought to be connected to their breeding habits and the maintenance of a territory.

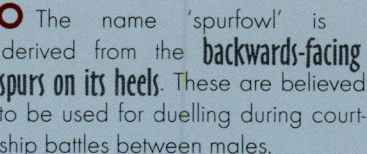

The name 'spurfowl' is derived from the **backwards-facing spurs on its heels**. These are believed to be used for duelling during courtship battles between males.

Ground birds

Coqui francolin: This is the smallest francolin in the Lowveld region but is still fairly conspicuous by its loud and diagnostic call that announces 'Co-qui ... co-qui ... co-qui' as its onomatopoeic name suggests. Pairs remain in particular areas and males will declare their territories by climbing to a high point like a tree stump or termite mound before calling. If flushed, this francolin flies far and fast. Coqui francolins eat more fruit than other francolins and glean ticks off grass stalks.

Crested francolin: This very common francolin is the exception to the 'francolin-spurfowl' rule having the red legs of the spurfowl group and being prone to roosting in trees at night (not on the ground as other francolins do). It also tends to flee danger at a run into thick vegetation rather than being primarily flushed like other francolins. When it does take to the sky it flies low and weaves between the trees until out of sight. Its small size and rhythmical (although not musical) call makes it a francolin. Crested francolins are especially territorial and the monogamous pair proclaims their turf with a duet that supposedly sounds like 'Beer and cognac ... beer and cognac ... beer and cognac'. Outside of the breeding season, these birds may roam widely. They prefer to forage under the cover of thick bush but give themselves away with their noisy habit of scratching in the leaf litter. They frequently disassemble elephant and rhino dung to access seeds and insects.

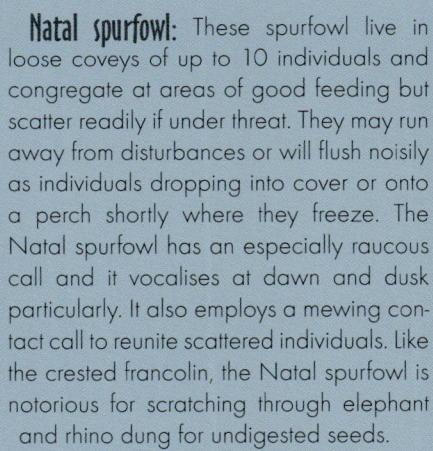

Natal spurfowl: These spurfowl live in loose coveys of up to 10 individuals and congregate at areas of good feeding but scatter readily if under threat. They may run away from disturbances or will flush noisily as individuals dropping into cover or onto a perch shortly where they freeze. The Natal spurfowl has an especially raucous call and it vocalises at dawn and dusk particularly. It also employs a mewing contact call to reunite scattered individuals. Like the crested francolin, the Natal spurfowl is notorious for scratching through elephant and rhino dung for undigested seeds.

Swainson's spurfowl: This is a conspicuous species with a grating call, especially emanated by males at dawn and dusk from their perches atop termite mounds. They live in pairs or family groups and maintain contact through high-pitched mews. They rest during the heat of the day and, unlike other spurfowl or francolins, will feed at night during hot weather (if the moon provides illumination). Swainson's spurfowl are fond of the waste grains on offer in agricultural lands. They are particularly resolute when flushed, taking to cover immediately and not rising up a second time no matter what. They perch low down in trees at night and will typically drink before they go to roost.

Ostrich
Struthio camelus

Ostrich are **the largest and heaviest living birds** in the world standing 2,5 m tall and weighing in at 150 kg (large males). They are also extremely long-lived, surviving in the wild for about 40 years.

Ostriches are **flightless**. They do not possess a keeled breastbone necessary for the attachment of flight muscles. They also have soft, loose feathers that cannot be zipped together for streamlining by means of barbules like other birds' feathers. For this reason they lack a preen gland. Flightless birds are called 'ratites', which is the Latin word for 'raft' referring to their flat breastbones. In spite of being flightless, ostriches do still have very strong wings which are used in displays of aggression and courtship.

Ostriches have an **unusual call.** The male makes a deep booming sound that may be confused with the distant call of lions.

Ostrich
Struthio camelus

The ostrich is the only bird to have only two toes on each foot. This seems to be a useful adaptation as ostriches are the **fastest running birds** reaching speeds of 70 km/h. Ostriches run as a first instinct to escape danger which may come in the form of lions, hyenas or cheetahs. They can cover 4,8 – 7 m per stride and maintain a constant speed for half an hour on the trot. They can also deliver a powerful kick to defend themselves, the blow measuring 500 pounds per square inch (35,15 kg/cm^2). Jumping and flailing of the wings is common in frightened birds and this in itself may cause injury to threatening predators.

Ostriches use their **wings as umbrellas** when it gets very hot. Beneath their wings their thighs are naked. By lifting the wings and back feathers away from the body slightly, the smallest of breezes offers relief by moving hot air away from the skin. They also use their wings to shade their chicks. The feathers can be used in reverse as well, affording them a blanket on cold nights when they will lie down and tuck the naked legs underneath the insulating feathers.

Ostriches are **gregarious** and live together in flocks. Different flocks may even merge their groups of chicks into crèches. This provides safety in numbers and improved vigilance.

At 5 cm wide, the ostrich has the **largest eyeballs** of all birds. Relative to its skull, the eyes are simply enormous and comparable to the size of the eyes found in large mammals with significantly larger heads. Large eyes afford the ostrich excellent vision as more of the image falls on the retina and so a greater amount of detail can be perceived.

In addition to an eyelid, ostriches have a **nictitating membrane** to clean and protect the eyeball.

Ostrich
Struthio camelus

Strangely for ground-nesting birds, ostriches have white eggs. Many **ground nesters** produce cryptically coloured eggs. The ostrich parents provide the concealment. The paler brown female incubates the eggs by day, lowering her neck and flattening herself out if threatened to resemble a rock from far. This is, in part, where the myth comes from that ostriches bury their heads. The black-feathered male takes the night shift, blending in with the cover of darkness. The eggs, when unattended, are also protected from overheating by being white and glossy. They are usually laid in stony, exposed areas and only incubated once the whole clutch has been laid.

Ostriches have the **largest eggs** of all birds but they only constitute 1,5% of the female's weight and are therefore not that large for the bird producing them. By comparison the New Zealand kiwi lays an egg weighing 25% of the female's weight and this is proportionally the largest egg laid by a bird. It takes 2 days for the hard-shelled eggs to form in the female (usually takes 24 hours in other birds) and when they are laid they can weigh in anywhere between 800 g and 1 500 g. The shell is 2 mm thick and the egg has the capacity of 24 chicken eggs.

Jed Bird

Jed Bird

The eggs may be white but the **chicks**, when they hatch, are earthen-coloured and cryptic to escape the attentions of jackals, caracals and raptors like martial eagles, which only a third of them manage to do. Life for an ostrich chick starts out tough and it must struggle its way through the very hard shell of its egg. This initiation has a purpose as the struggling draws a yolk sac into its body in the process and the chick then subsists on this yolk for the first 24 hours of its life. Like a butterfly, helping the youngster out of its incarceration could prove a death sentence, as the sack may then not be absorbed.

Ostrich
Struthio camelus

Courtship in ostriches is a spectacular affair. The males acquire scarlet colouring on their beaks, foreheads, necks and shins. They chase each other around frantically in competition and dance alluringly for the females to achieve dominance. Males will approach females with an exaggerated prancing gait, feathers raised, and then will drop to their knees as if in proposal while waving the wings to reveal their white tips and twisting their necks corkscrew-like.

Ostriches are the only birds (and animals except for camels) that do not exhale moisture-saturated breath like other creatures. The long neck (and trachea) and the wide nasal passages are believed to cool the air being breathed out which reduces the water vapour content to only about 87%. In this way ostriches can **reduce the potential of dehydrating** in the hot, open areas where they live. Their long necks make drinking difficult and as such they must conserve water in their bodies and satisfy most of their water requirements through the food they eat.

Ostriches have a fairly **unique breeding system amongst birds** and are referred to as communal breeders. The male is polygamous (has more than one mate) but within his group of females there is only one major hen, the rest being minor hens. Of the females, only the major hen incubates the eggs and this she does in a shallow scrape in the ground 2 m across. She lays her 8 or 10 eggs first and the minor hens add theirs to her collection (potentially upping the total to 40). Usually the minor hens' eggs are moved to the sides but the parent birds can effectively cover at least 20 eggs when they are sitting on the nest and so there is a good chance that some of the minor hens' eggs will be incubated full term. Excess eggs that may roll out of the nest or be poached by the likes of hyena are likely to be the minor hens' and this is probably a useful insurance policy for the major hen and the reason she allows the others to lay on her turf at all.

Like other birds, ostriches use gular fluttering to cool down on exceptionally hot days. This is the **bird equivalent of panting** but is much less energy expensive. The gular skin sits towards the back of a bird's mouth and is well supplied with blood capillaries. By fluttering this skin with the beak ajar, the blood in the capillaries is cooled by air pumping over the gular area.

Once they do start feeding **ostrich chicks will eat whatever they can swallow**. This is because the gizzard (muscular stomach) where mechanical digestion takes place requires hard objects such as stones to facilitate the mastication of the real food material ingested. Adult birds also deliberately swallow stones to equip their gizzards with grinding tools. Real food for ostriches includes succulent plants, grass, berries, seeds, insects and small reptiles.

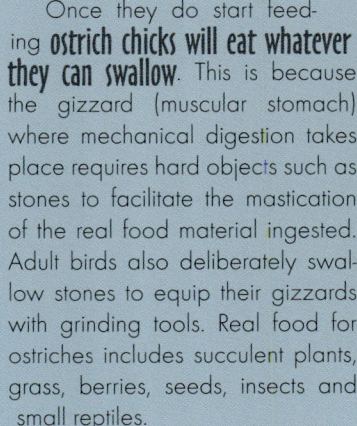

Oxpeckers
Buphagus species

Oxpeckers **live in association with medium to large mammalian herbivores**. The smallest hosts they use are impala and warthog and the largest rhino, buffalo and hippo. These birds spend their daylight hours picking and consuming parasites out of the pelage of their hosts in a win-win relationship known as mutualistic symbiosis. Both species involved gain several advantages from their relationship.

Herbivores benefit greatly by having their coats stripped of blood-sucking invertebrates. In a kingdom where survival is awarded to the fittest individuals, blood loss caused by parasites picked up in habitats carrying high tick loads, constitutes energy loss. Energy loss puts animals at a competitive disadvantage. Not only are animals weaker on a day-to-day basis to find food and avoid enemies but they may also lose critical condition necessary for being the strongest contender to mate. Oxpeckers do not remove all the ticks on an individual but they control the infestations to a large degree and prevent overspill of high loads into the environment from where secondary infestations could potentially occur.

Oxpeckers also benefit their mammalian hosts by affording them an early warning system. Birds are generally more vigilant than mammals and oxpeckers especially fly up noisily if they are startled, hissing and rasping characteristically. Herbivores react to oxpeckers' alarm calls.

Oxpeckers can help **warn humans** of potential danger or alert them to the presence of a large herbivore. Oxpeckers will fly up off the backs of their hosts if startled, indicating the presence of potentially dangerous game. They also descend onto their hosts noisily. The **dipping flight** of a flock of oxpeckers with the accompanying **chip-chip-rasp call** is unmistakable. One can visually track the bird's flight and witness where they descend. At that location it is most likely that there is a host species, like buffalo or rhino.

For the most part the **association between oxpeckers and herbivores** is mutually beneficial but this relationship can degenerate to the point where oxpeckers are almost parasitic. Oxpeckers tend to irritate the edges of old wounds and scars and they often peck open surface irregularities caused by skin parasites. They do this to access small amounts of the host's blood which in itself is not significant enough to be harmful. However, by keeping wounds open, they make them susceptible to secondary infection and due to the lack of opportunity for the wounds to heal, weaken the host animal.

Oxpeckers
Buphagus species

Oxpeckers **line their nests with hair** that they pluck from their mammal hosts. This is placed on top of a few blades of grass in a cup-like form which becomes flattened over time. Any cracks in the walls of the cavity are sealed with dung from their hosts.

Oxpeckers **utilise natural cavities in trees to nest** and they especially favour leadwoods (see p. 274) where old branches have split off from the main trunk and left a hole behind. Holes are located and approved of by the entire flock. Oxpeckers scout for holes during inspection flights from the backs of their hosts. Once a suitable hole has been located, the site may be used consecutively year after year due to stiff competition from other hole-nesting species like starlings.

Oxpeckers are classified into the genus *Buphagus*. This **Latin term** is derived from the words for 'ox' and 'to eat' and refers to their habit of eating ticks off the backs of large mammalian species like buffalo.

Oxpeckers are **cooperative breeders** with only one pair in the group (usually comprising about five birds in total) that actually court and breed. Mating usually takes place on a host animal after a showy performance where the courting pair encircles one another with spread wings, shivering and beaks ajar. Only the dominant pair incubates the eggs but the other members of the flock, known as 'helpers', help to feed the brood and remove telltale signs of the nest like eggshells and faecal sacs. Many of the helpers are offspring from previous broods. All the members of the group are related and so kinship selection ensures that the individual's gene-line is still perpetuated.

Oxpeckers have **short legs and very sharp claws** which help the birds to cling to the fur of their hosts while they forage for parasites.

Two species of oxpecker occur in southern Africa. The commonest is the red-billed oxpecker (*Buphagus erythrorhynchus*). This oxpecker uses its more slender bill in a scissor-like action to glean parasites off the coats of their hosts. The yellow-billed oxpecker (*Buphagus africanus*) is much rarer and at one stage was thought to be on the brink of extinction. Its numbers have improved dramatically and these birds, which use stouter bills in a pecking beak-action, can usually be spotted on giraffe and buffalo.

Oxpeckers have **specially adapted retrices** (tail feathers). These are stiffened and act in the manner of a tripod to help prop the bird up against the bodies of their hosts while they feed.

Naas Rautenbach

Kingfishers

The pied kingfisher is **adept at hovering** in order to look for food in the water. This is achieved by using a figure-of-eight wing-stroke (effectively reversing the wing-beat on the up-stroke to stay in the same place). This is a very costly form of flight and cannot be sustained for very long. True hovering involves the ability to move forwards and backwards (like the hummingbird), which the kingfisher cannot do – the kind of hovering it practises is termed aerial perching.

The **bill of the kingfisher is straight and sharp** – an adaptation for catching fish, which is grabbed with the tip of the bill before being taken back to a perch where it is beaten and swallowed head first. Piscevores like the malachite kingfisher swallow their fish food head first to avoid choking. Head first the fins, scales and tail align the correct way, helping the fish simply slip down the kingfisher's throat.

Kingfishers enjoy well-wooded areas in the vicinity of water but **not all kingfishers fish!** The malachite, giant and pied kingfishers are piscevores (fish-eaters) while the striped, woodland, brown-hooded and pygmy kingfishers eat invertebrates, but will also take lizards, frogs and even snakes, scorpions, rodents and the occasional bat. Insects are often more numerous in the vicinity of water and proximity to water is advantageous for hygiene purposes too.

While most other species of kingfisher are monogamous, the **pied kingfisher is the exception to the rule**. They practise a form of cooperative breeding and are generally found together in more gregarious groups, nesting in loose colonies. A particular pair of breeding pied kingfishers may have a number of helpers, mostly males assisting them with tasks such as feeding and incubation. These may be either offspring from a previous year (called primary helpers) or may in fact be totally unrelated to the breeding pair (called secondary helpers). Secondary helpers are permitted to do fewer duties than primary helpers, effectively expending less energy than primary helpers do on the collective breeding effort. This is because primary helpers are actual kin (and have a genetic investment in seeing the young raised successfully) while secondary helpers assist purely to enhance their chance of breeding in the same place the following season (and potentially with the female in question).

The pied kingfisher has **eyes adapted to correcting** for refraction so as to be able to determine the exact position of fish under the water and also to make adjustments for last-minute deflections by the fish. When it dives, the pied kingfisher will also close its nictitating membrane (transparent eyelid) to help with underwater vision.

Kingfishers have **syndactyl feet**. This is where the second and third toes are fused; the reason for this is poorly understood and is a trait shared with only the hornbills.

Kingfishers have **weak perching legs** and seldom land on the ground, as they do not have the power to 'jump' into flight again rapidly should danger threaten. This is particularly true when they are bathing and to compensate for this handicap (with the added weight of wet feathers), they rather plunge bathe from a perch.

Kingfishers

Most of the kingfishers are **tunnel nesters** excavating holes into banks on road verges or over rivers. This they do by digging with their bills and then using the bill and wings as props, they kick dirt out with their feet. Remarkably, these tunnels penetrate 30–60 cm into the hard earth and in the case of the **giant kingfisher** up to 1,8 m into the bank. At the end of the tunnel is a small, unlined chamber where the eggs are laid.

Keeping tunnel nests clean is problematic and they become progressively fouled throughout the nesting period. The malachite kingfisher's nest is a particularly foul establishment with faeces typically leaking down the passage and out of the entrance. This does have the benefit of putting off predators but adults are often forced to dip-bath in water after leaving the nest to rid themselves of the grime and parasites. The chicks are clothed in spiky quills, which are in fact sheaths that protect their feathers from soiling.

Brown-hooded kingfisher

Kingfishers **regurgitate pellets** of indigestible material in the manner of owls. These pellets contain particles too large to pass from the stomach to the intestine through the pyloric valve. The pellets are much smaller than those produced by owls and crumble away quickly.

Striped and **woodland kingfishers** go against the grain and nest in holes in trees like the disused cavities created by woodpeckers and barbets.

Kingfishers are **conspicuous birds** in the Lowveld thanks to their bright colours and noisy, active habits. There are 10 species that occur in southern Africa of which 9 occur in the Lowveld (7 commonly so). They vary in size from the minute 12 cm pygmy kingfisher to the 45 cm giant kingfisher.

Whether kingfishers are piscevorous or insectivorous influences whether they **migrate** or not. Fish occur in a more or less constant supply all year round while insects are most abundant in summer, diminishing into the winter season. The insectivorous pygmy kingfisher is an intra-African migrant while the similarly sized **malachite**, a fish-eater, is resident.

Most species of kingfisher are **strictly monogamous** (one male and one female pair up). The males defend territories and establish a pair bond with the female through visual displays and courtship feeding. The **woodland kingfisher** has a particularly elaborate display in which it opens its wings and, pivoting on a branch, displays the white and then the blue side of the wing alternately, all the time vocalising loudly. A female taken by his exhibitions will be further convinced to pair up with a male depending on the nuptial gifts he brings her. Some bird species (including the kingfishers) engage in courtship feeding where the male proves his ability to care for a female and her brood by bringing her morsels of food. This also serves to build up the female's reserves before she must produce and then incubate an egg.

The **bright blue** of some of the kingfishers' feathers is the result of tyndal scattering. This is where the layers of structural keratin that make up the feathers are interspersed with air spaces and reflect particular wavelengths of light to appear blue. There is no colour pigment in the feathers.

Woodpeckers

Woodpeckers have **long, straight powerful beaks** for chiselling and drilling into wood. Due to the wear and tear involved, the beak grows continuously to replace keratin that flakes away. The base of the bill is broad and acts like a shock absorber.

The **skull** of a woodpecker is sturdy to absorb the blows of hammering wood. There is a special hinge between the nasal and frontal bones of the skull that dissipates the shock and the delicate brain is cushioned within the skull so as to counter these effects as well.

The **neck muscles** of a woodpecker are well developed to power the drilling strokes of the neck and head.

Woodpeckers have **zygodactylous feet** with two toes facing forward and two backwards. This foot structure is a modification to clinging in the way a woodpecker must against bark. Having the additional support of two toes facing backwards instead of one (like perching birds) makes them agile climbers.

Woodpeckers have **reinforced retrices** (tail feathers) the shafts of which are thicker and more rigid than in other birds and are used to help prop the birds vertically up against the trunk of a tree while they forage, in the manner of a tripod.

Hugh Chittenden

Woodpeckers

Woodpeckers are remarkable for their **ability to chisel into bark and wood** in search of insect larvae or to create their hole-cavity nests during the breeding season. Despite the shock involved in making headway through bark and into solid wood, woodpeckers do not suffer from concussion and are in fact precisely equipped to deal with their lifestyle.

Holes on the surface of trees are typically left behind after woodpeckers have been foraging there.

Woodpeckers have **exceptionally long tongues**. The tongue muscle starts behind the eye and stretches over the skull of the bird before entering its mouth cavity. This may help with insulating the skull against shock. The tongue is able to extend well beyond the end of the bill to probe for buried insect larvae under bark. A sticky salivary covering ensures that prey sticks to the woodpecker's tongue before it is drawn back into the mouth. The **Bennett's woodpecker**, which spends much time foraging for termites on the ground, has particularly glue-like saliva. Woodpeckers also have barbs on their tongues to facilitate the capture of their prey.

Woodpeckers use a **unique form of communication**. Apart from having individual species calls, they also employ a technique called drumming. The bearded woodpecker is especially adept at drumming and choosing a log with good resonance will thump out a rhythm with his sturdy bill to advertise territory or attract a mate. Individual birds can even be identified through their drumming signatures. Drumming is much louder and better coordinated than the noises made when woodpeckers forage.

Woodpeckers are one of only a few families of birds that are **able to make their own holes in trees for nesting**. Although many bird species nest in natural cavities in trees, few are actually able to drill out the adequately large nesting holes that woodpeckers do. Usually they use dead trees for this purpose and the circular entrance is only ever wide enough for the adult to squeeze through, omitting the possibility of larger predators gaining entrance. Remarkably, woodpeckers make new nests every year. The old ones are then taken over by other hole-nesting birds like starlings.

Woodpeckers save energy when flying by **using a bounding flight pattern** that is characteristic and makes the family easy to recognise in flight. Between bouts of flapping (which help the bird gain lift and momentum), woodpeckers close their wings and 'free-wheel' a short distance descending slightly as they 'fall'. Another bout of flapping then ensues and the pattern is repeated until the bird reaches its destination.

Reptiles and amphibians

Lizards, snakes and frogs are far from 'big and furry' and for this reason are seldom high on the wish-lists of many people visiting the bush. Although their behavioural resumes are perhaps less extravagant than mammals and birds, they are no less remarkable for their array of adaptations. With 500 species of reptile and 130 species of amphibian to speak of in southern Africa and an evolutionary history in excess of 300 million years (not to mention the vital roles they perform ecologically), these (mostly) small knobbly creatures are certainly worth a mention. Being ectothermic, reptiles rely on basking to heat up their bodies and as such are often detected where they are lazing about on rocks, termite mounds or alongside waterholes. Frogs and toads are particularly conspicuous during the rainy season for their frantic and raucous breeding cacophonies. The information in this section focuses on the more generic life histories of reptiles and frogs common to most species but it also supplies specific commentary on the fascinating adaptations and lifestyles of the species especially likely to be encountered in the Lowveld. The section is more mosaic in nature than the preceding ones and the photographs serve to both illustrate the text and to provide a reference for identification where appropriate. Since identifying reptiles and frogs is a little trickier than the larger animals, some focus has been given to the actual recognition of species in text.

Reptiles

Leopard tortoise • *Geochelone pardalis*, page 190
Terrapins, page 192
Tree agama • *Acanthocercus atricollis*, page 193
Flap-neck chameleon • *Chamaeleo dilepis*, page 194
Monitors • Family Varanidae, page 196
Moreau's tropical house gecko • *Hemidactylus mabouia*, page 198
Bushveld lizard • *Heliobolus lugubris*, page 198
Striped skink • *Mabuya striata*, page 198
Giant plated lizard • *Gerrhosaurus validus*, page 199
Common flat lizard • *Platysaurus intermedius*, page 200
Mozambican spitting cobra ('M'fezi') • *Naja mossambica*, page 201
Spotted bush snake • *Philothamnus semivariegatus*, page 201
African rock python • *Python natalensis*, page 202
Boomslang • *Dispholidus typus*, page 204
Vine (twig) snake • *Thelotornis capensis*, page 205
Black mamba • *Dendroaspis polylepis*, page 206
Puff adder • *Bitis arietans*, page 207
Nile crocodile • *Crocodylus niloticus*, page 208

Frogs

Banded rubber frog • *Phrynomantis bifasciatus*, page 215
Grey tree frog (foam nest frog) • *Chiromantis xerampelina*, page 216
Brown-backed tree frog • *Leptopelis mossambicus*, page 216
Bushveld rain frog • *Breviceps adspersus*, page 217
Painted reed frog • *Hyperolius marmoratus*, page 218
Eastern olive toad • *Bufo garmani*, page 219
Guttural toad • *Bufo gutturalis*, page 219
Bubbling kassina • *Kassina senegalensis*, page 220
Plain grass frog • *Ptychadena anchietae*, page 220
Russet-backed sand frog • *Tomopterna marmorata*, page 220
Tremelo sand frog • *Tomopterna crytotus*, page 220
Mottled shovel-nosed frog • *Hemisus marmoratus*, page 221
Tropical platanna • *Xenopus muelleri*, page 221
Common river frog • *Afrana angolensis*, page 221
Ornate frog • *Hildebrandtia ornata*, page 221
Snoring puddle frog • *Phrynobatrachus natalensis*, page 221

Reptiles

Reptiles in the Lowveld are represented by three groups (Orders):
- Tortoises and terrapins (Chelonia)
- Lizards and snakes (Squamata)
- Crocodiles (Crocodylia)

Reptiles are **ectothermic**. This means that they rely on the external environment to regulate their body temperature. They cannot control their body temperature internally via metabolism (like mammals) and are sometimes called 'cold-blooded' because of this. Reptiles employ a number of warming up and cooling down techniques, the simplest of which is basking in the sun to gain heat, and retreating into the shade to cool down. They may alternate these behaviours to keep their body temperature constant once initially warmed up. During cold conditions, reptiles become sluggish.

Male vs. female

Telling male and female reptiles apart can be tricky. With some lizards and snakes, generally the male is the more varied and brightly coloured individual.

The chelonians (tortoises and terrapins) have different plastrons (the lower part of the shell). In males the plastron is concave to accommodate the female's shell during mounting. Females' plastrons are flat. Males also have longer tails than females.

Amongst the animal kingdom, the Squamata reptiles possess unique genitals. They have two penises called hemipenes. Only one is used at a time for copulation and it must be everted for use out of the tail base where it is usually stored.

Characteristics – what makes it a reptile?

- **Horny scales** to cover the body and prevent water loss. In the evolutionary scheme of things this allowed reptiles to move onto dry land and they need not even rely on water to breed as frogs do.
- **Ectothermy** – the need to regulate body temperature from the external environment.
- **Ovipary** – reptiles are egg-laying (although some species hatch inside the mother's body just before birth). The eggs are usually leathery but some are hard-shelled (e.g. geckos). Reptiles exhibit little to no parental care of their progeny.
- **Internal fertilisation**.

Reptiles in South Africa **do not hibernate** in the true sense of the word. This involves a dramatically reduced metabolism in response to extreme temperature drops more typical of northern hemisphere winters. Reptiles in southern Africa aestivate. This is a form of dormancy induced more by the lack of moisture during winters that are not exceptionally cold. In the Lowveld, winter is more commonly referred to as 'the dry season'. During winter, reptiles still respond to cooler temperatures and enter a state of torpor (state of inactivity) during which time they rely on internal nutrient stores built up during the plentiful wet season. They will, however, still emerge from their burrows and shelters to sun themselves if opportunity arises.

Different birth techniques

Viviparous: These animals give birth to live young which develop inside the female's body (mostly mammals).

Oviparous: These animals lay eggs that hatch outside the female's body after a period of incubation, for example a chameleon.

Ovoviviparous: This is a combination of the above where eggs hatch inside the mother's body and appear to be born alive or alternatively they hatch immediately on laying, for example a puff adder.

Basic biology

Differences between the members of the Chelonia family

Tortoise	Terrapin	Turtle
Terrestrial (lives on land)	Aquatic – lives in fresh water	Aquatic – lives in the sea
Vegetarian	Omnivorous	Carnivorous (eats squid)
Retracts head directly into shell	Retracts head sideways	Cannot retract head
Feet with claws	Feet webbed with claws	Flippers
Domed carapace – patterned	Flattened carapace – unpatterned	Flattened carapace – patterned or unpatterned

What is the difference between the lizards?

There are different families within the lizards' taxonomical sub-order (Sauria). This means that there are a number of different common names for the generic 'lizard':

- **Agamas** are squat lizards with triangular heads and obvious tympanums (ear discs). They are similar to chameleons, have rough body coverings and cannot shed their tails.
- **Geckos** lack eyelids and instead are able to lick their eyes clean. They have fine scales on their skin and they can shed their delicate tails. They have specially adapted adhesive feet for climbing vertical rock faces.
- **Skinks** have smooth, shiny scales that overlap and are reinforced to facilitate their burrowing lifestyles. They have small heads and no real neck.
- **Lizards** usually refer to the Old World lizards. These species have well-developed legs and claws, and long tails. They have granular scales on their bodies and can shed their tails.

Other families within the lizards' sub-order include chameleons, monitors and plated lizards.

Forms of defence exhibited by reptiles

Autotomy: This is a form of self-mutilation where the reptile will shed a body part in order to escape predation. An abscission zone with modified muscles and blood capillaries facilitates the loss of the body part. This is typically demonstrated by geckos, which exhibit caudal autotomy and easily lose and then regenerate their tails. Some lizards have a number of fracture planes so the whole tail need not be lost but rather only the segment gripped by the predator. The shed tail continues jerking after separating from the reptile in order to distract the predator while the victim makes its escape.

Thanatosis: This is the act of feigning or shamming death and is performed by reptiles to trick predators. Generally predators prefer to kill living creatures, stimulated to attack by their movement. Unless a particular threat happens to be a scavenger, the ploy of acting dead may be adequate to put a predator off its meal.

Reptiles

Snake senses

Snakes have **good eyesight** that is especially sensitive to detecting movement. They have no eyelids but the eye is protected by a spectacle that is sloughed with the rest of the skin to allow a scratch-free lens to emerge.

Snakes have **no external ears** and can therefore not hear sounds carried in the air. They do, however, have a well-developed auditory nerve that responds to vibrations carried through the ground.

Smell is excellent and the **forked tongue** retracts into a sheath that deposits air particles collected during 'flicks' into the organ of Jacobsen. The tissue lining this organ is similar to the epithelium found in a human's olfactory canal and as such, snakes can smell much the same as humans can. The fork in the tongue allows the snake to track specific scents like the chemical trail laid by a female ready to mate. By having two branches to its tongue, the snake can determine which path to follow by which side has the stronger olfactory clues.

Nostrils are present but reserved for breathing.

Snake locomotion

Snakes use four different types of movement.

Serpentine locomotion is the typical snake-like motion where the body winds in an S-shape as it moves and is especially effective for quick movement.

Rectilinear locomotion is where the snake moves directly forward in a caterpillar-like fashion using muscular contractions and tension between the ground and its belly scales. Puff adders are especially known for this type of locomotion.

Side-winding is utilised by desert-dwelling snakes and only two parts of the body touch the ground at any one time as the snake throws itself sideways. In this way the snake minimises its contact with hot ground.

Concertina locomotion is employed when a snake is in a tight spot and this calls for the anchoring of the head and the rest of the snake is then dragged forward.

Snakes generally do not exceed 5 km/h.

Snake anatomy adaptations

- They have very long backbones with more than 200 vertebrae (humans have 26).
- Snakes have no limbs, eyelids or external ears.
- Snakes have only one lung (the right one).
- The liver and kidneys are elongated.
- The heart is positioned near the front of the body.

Swallowing food in snakes

To swallow food, snakes have had to develop a fair amount of adaptations. The jawbones are particularly modified with the lower jaw not connecting in the front except via an elasticised ligament. They can also dislocate these from the skull to allow food to enter their mouths. The upper jaws are only loosely connected to the skull to further accommodate large prey. Prey is moved into the throat with help from the teeth and once there the throat will stretch allowing the prey to pass through and be transported into the gut of the snake by peristaltic movements. Snakes can breathe during this mouth-stuffing performance by means of a forward-placed windpipe (trachea).

Basic biology

Snakebite

There are many old wives' tales with regards to treating snakebite. With the modern medical technologies and treatments available, the primary concern of the caregiver is to get the patient to a medical facility as soon as possible and follow basic first aid procedures (especially keeping the airway open).

It is never advisable to try to self-treat snakebite with anti-venom unless an expert both in snake identification and bite treatments. The most recommendable course of action is to apply a pressure bandage (except for cytotoxic bites). This is applied from the distal part of the limb towards the injury, i.e. if bitten on the ankle, start the bandage from the thigh down. The firm bandage slows the circulation in the affected limb and retards the spread of the venom. Do not attempt to tourniquet the limb. This has the effect of concentrating venom in that limb and in the case of cytotoxins may, in fact, speed up the tissue damage.

It is always important to reassure the patient and keep them as calm as possible. A rapid heartbeat will circulate the venom more quickly.

It is not necessary to catch or kill the snake that inflicted the bite. It is always helpful to suggest to the doctor the species of snake responsible but snakebite is treated symptomatically so risking a second bite by chasing the snake down is unnecessary.

It is interesting to note that not every snakebite necessarily contains venom (or is envenomated). Snakes can inject venom voluntarily via control over their venom glands.

Sloughing

In order to grow, reptiles, like invertebrates, need to shed the outer layer of skin to make room for the expanding body. The rigid nature of the scaly body covering makes expansion difficult otherwise. This moulting process is called sloughing in reptiles (pronounced 'sluffing').

In order to loosen the skin to begin the process, snakes particularly rub their noses on a hard object. The skin peels off inside out and in one piece. Even the eye coverings come off and because the reptile may lose a degree of vision prior to shedding, they will hide up during this time.

Front-fanged

Back-fanged

Solid toothed

A comparison of snake denture and venom (rule of thumb)

Fang type	Type of venom	Effect of venom	Classic example
Hinged front fangs	Cytotoxic	Affects the cells causing tissue damage and necrosis	Puff adder
Fixed front fangs	Neurotoxic	Affects the nervous system causing paralysis and respiratory failure and heart stoppage	Cobras and mambas*
Back fangs	Haemotoxic	Prevents blood clotting and causes internal haemorrhaging	Boomslang and vine snake
Fangless (solid toothed)	Venomless	None – bite wound must be kept clean to prevent infection	African rock python

* Mozambican spitting cobras have a mixture of cytotoxic and neurotoxic venom. Black mambas have a combination of neurotoxic and cardiotoxic venom.

Of the 120 snakes found in southern Africa, only about 10% are dangerously venomous to humans.

Leopard tortoise
Geochelone pardalis

The leopard tortoise is the most common tortoise in the Lowveld and probably in the whole of southern Africa. It is also the **largest** – reaching a maximum of 70 cm and 40 kg. It is the only tortoise known to be **able to swim.**

The leopard tortoise can be recognised by the absence of a small tile that usually fits between the two scutes in the front of the carapace on a tortoise. This is called the **nuchal scute**.

Males have longer tails than females and a concave plastron that allows them to mount females during mating. Females conversely have flat plastrons.

The leopard tortoise is a slow grower and only reaches sexual maturity at between 10 and 15 years old. They weigh about 1 kg at 7 years of age but then body weight doubles every second year thereafter, provided good conditions prevail. They can live up to **75 years**.

The leopard tortoise is called such because it has similar colouration to its namesake. Unlike leopards, however, tortoises do not have teeth nor do they eat meat. The leopard tortoise has a serrated, horny, **beak-like upper lip,** which it uses to secure its vegetarian food including grass, flowers and the young leaves of small annuals and succulents.

The **shell** of a tortoise is divided into two halves. The upper part is called the **carapace** while the lower part is known as the **plastron**. The shell is covered in scutes (horny scales) and these show seasonal rings formed as the tortoise grows. They cannot, however, be aged accurately from these rings as they are prone to rubbing smooth in the centre. Slower growth spurts occur during winter or in times of drought as well.

Leopard tortoise
Geochelone pardalis

The **sex of tortoise hatchlings** is determined by the temperature at which they incubate in their chamber under loose sand and rotting vegetation. Those subjected to temperatures between 26–30°C become males while those exposed to 31–34°C heat become females. The reverse is true of crocodile hatchlings.

The shell of a tortoise is its transportable **protective body armour**, a necessity to accommodate for its slow locomotion. The shell is formed from a modified, fused ribcage and skeleton, the most unique part of this being that the shoulder blades and hips are borne inside the ribcage to allow the tortoise to walk. When threatened, the tortoise draws its head directly back into its dome by means of a specialised, flexible neck and then seals off the opening by pulling in its scaly legs.

To sustain their high calcium requirements necessary for shell maintenance and the production of hard-shelled eggs, leopard tortoises **practise osteophagia** (the chewing of bones) and a rare form of coprophagia (consumption of faeces) – they eat hyena scat to absorb the excess calcium excreted by these bone-devouring predators.

Tortoises are eaten by numerous **predators** despite their protective shells. Leopards and hyenas break the domes with their strong jaws. Rock monitors eat juveniles and ground hornbills feast on individuals that are caught in veld fires. In many parts of Africa humans consider tortoise meat a delicacy and since they are easy to catch, they feature regularly on the menu. As a result of this and an unchecked pet trade, leopard tortoises are **endangered in the wild** and one must now obtain a permit to keep one privately.

The other tortoise found (less commonly) in the Lowveld is the **Speke's hinged tortoise** (*Kinixys spekii*). A flexible 'hinge' towards the rear of the carapace allows the adult Speke's hinged tortoise to close off the back of the shell and so protect its rear-end from predators. Its shell is flatter than the leopard tortoise's and unlike the leopard tortoise its diet comprises animal proteins in the form of giant land snails, beetles and millipedes. It also eats mushrooms.

The leopard tortoise has a device for storing water known as a **bursa sac**. This stored water is needed during times of drought or to moisten soil to more easily dig a pit in which to lay eggs. If a tortoise is threatened, it will urinate profusely and dispel the contents of its bursa sac as a repellent to the predator. After such an occasion, the tortoise is at risk of desiccating.

Terrapins

Two species of terrapin are common in the Lowveld – the marsh terrapin (*Pelomedusa subrufa*) and the serrated-hinged terrapin (*Pelusios sinuatus*).

The **marsh terrapin** has a broader, flatter shell and it cannot close its shell, so one eye is often visible once it has retracted inside. These terrapins are usually found in ephemeral (temporary) pans where crocodiles are absent and can often be seen moving between pools after rain. They will overstay unfavourable times by burying themselves underground.

The **serrated-hinged** terrapin has a jagged edge to its shell. It also has a hinge on its plastron (unlike the Speke's hinged tortoise whose hinge is on the carapace) and this allows it to seal off its shell in the front. Terrapins classically draw their necks in sideways and the legs do not close their heads in to protect them in the manner of tortoises. Serrated-hinged terrapins tend to frequent permanent waterholes and are often found basking in the sun on logs or rocks.

Terrapins are essentially **omnivorous** eating both plant and animal substances but they do have quite voracious carnivorous habits and will eat almost anything they can ambush and overpower, from insects, fish, frogs and mussels to birds that come and drink at the water's edge. Serrated-hinged terrapins are notorious for biting the ticks off the rumps of wallowing rhino!

Terrapins are rather **smelly creatures** that bite readily and as such are best left unhandled. The musky liquid secreted by particularly the marsh terrapin when it is threatened, is designed to deter predators. Crocodiles are the biggest threat to these water-dwelling chelonians.

Tree agama
Acanthocercus atricollis

The **bright blue head** of the male of this large lizard is unmistakable. They can be seen on the sides of trees sunning themselves or nodding their heads to attract females. They are very territorial lizards and chase and fight off intruders often becoming scarred in the process.

Reptiles (except for snakes who have no external ears), have primitive ears called **tympanums** or tympanic membranes. These are obvious on the sides of the tree agama's head.

The agama has a device called the **pineal organ** on the top of its head. This organ apparently reacts to changes in day length associated with seasons.

The tree agama is the largest of southern Africa's agama species reaching 40 cm in length.

Unlike skinks and geckos, tree agamas **cannot shed their tails** and instead they use a tactic whereby they keep the trunk of the tree between themselves and any posed threat, circling if need be, all the way up the stem of a tree. If cornered, they will open their mouths to startle predators with the bright inner lining. They can also **inflict painful bites** and have two fang-like teeth for this purpose.

Agamas' **closest cousins are chameleons.** This is not hard to imagine as both have squat bodies covered in rough scales and exhibit bright colours.

Flap-neck chameleon
Chamaeleo dilepis

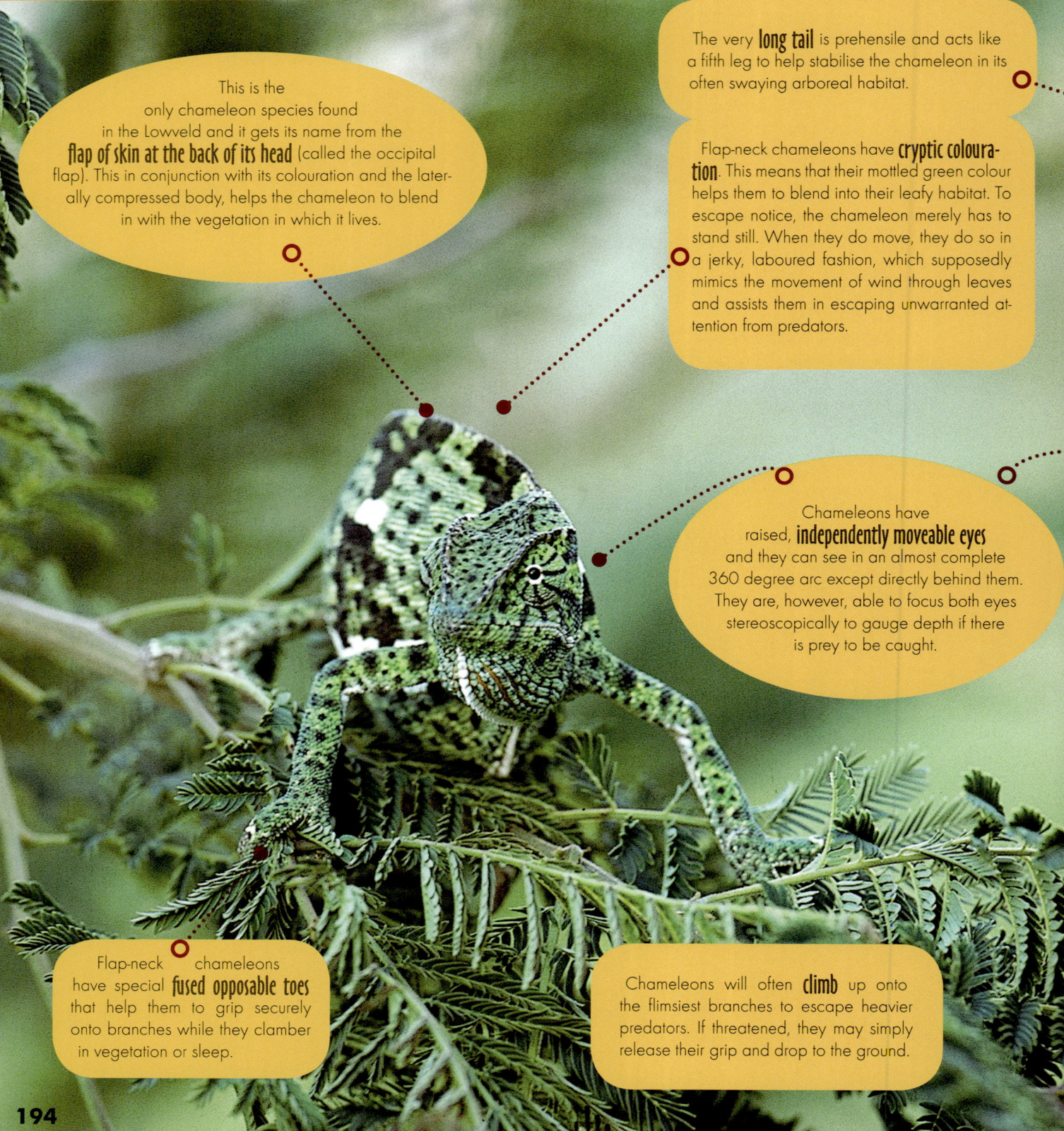

This is the only chameleon species found in the Lowveld and it gets its name from the **flap of skin at the back of its head** (called the occipital flap). This in conjunction with its colouration and the laterally compressed body, helps the chameleon to blend in with the vegetation in which it lives.

The very **long tail** is prehensile and acts like a fifth leg to help stabilise the chameleon in its often swaying arboreal habitat.

Flap-neck chameleons have **cryptic colouration**. This means that their mottled green colour helps them to blend into their leafy habitat. To escape notice, the chameleon merely has to stand still. When they do move, they do so in a jerky, laboured fashion, which supposedly mimics the movement of wind through leaves and assists them in escaping unwarranted attention from predators.

Chameleons have raised, **independently moveable eyes** and they can see in an almost complete 360 degree arc except directly behind them. They are, however, able to focus both eyes stereoscopically to gauge depth if there is prey to be caught.

Flap-neck chameleons have special **fused opposable toes** that help them to grip securely onto branches while they clamber in vegetation or sleep.

Chameleons will often **climb** up onto the flimsiest branches to escape heavier predators. If threatened, they may simply release their grip and drop to the ground.

Flap-neck chameleon
Chamaeleo dilepis

Chameleons in the Lowveld are **preyed on** by a number of species including ground hornbills, shrikes, starlings, vervet monkeys, monitor lizards, spiders, insects, boomslang, vine snakes and raptors of which the cuckoo hawk is a chameleon specialist.

The chameleon's famous ability to **change colour** is controlled by nerves, operating special cells called 'melanophores' that can be flooded with black pigment called melanin. Contrary to popular belief, chameleons change colour in response to mood or temperature stimuli and not for reasons of camouflage (as they are already cryptically camouflaged). Typically, stressed flap-neck chameleons change to brown or black, aggressive chameleons change to contrasting light and dark colours and at night chameleons are pale. Courting chameleons – especially Madagascan varieties – exhibit a number of vivid colours during courtship. The male flap-neck develops pearl-white throat skin at these times.

Chameleons **eat** mostly beetles and grasshoppers. They capture their prey using their **telescopic tongue** which is able to extend the chameleon's full body length out of its mouth and then some. The tongue is controlled by muscular contractions that propel the collapsible tongue off its bony spike (or hyoid apparatus) at the back of the mouth at a speed of up to 5 m/s. The end of the tongue is broad and moist and acts like a suction cup to secure the prey.

The name *chameleon* literally means **'dwarf lion'** and refers to the chameleon's **rather ferocious defensive behaviour**. Threatened individuals inflate themselves, hissing and lunging forward to surprise their enemy. The inner lining of the mouth is brightly coloured and the occipital flap is erectile. This collective behaviour, known as a startle display, is intended to afford the chameleon a few seconds to escape while the attacker regains its composure. Although they typically move slowly, chameleons can 'scamper' quite rapidly in emergencies. Both sexes are very territorial and will utilise similar behaviour to ward off intruders, head butting them and biting if necessary.

The only time a chameleon is likely to be found **on the ground** is when they are seeking mates or when gravid females are looking for soft soil in which to lay their eggs. Breeding in chameleons is a protracted process all round for such small creatures. Mating takes about 30 minutes, the eggs take 2–3 months to develop, the female lays 20–35 eggs (up to 60 eggs if the female is older) over a period of 24 hours and the eggs take about 10 months (sometimes over a year) to hatch.

Chameleons live for about 5 years in the wild.

Monitors
Family Varanidae

The monitors are the **largest lizards** in Africa and indeed the world. Two species occur in the Lowveld: the rock (or white-throated) monitor (*Varanus albigularus*) and the water (or Nile) monitor (*Varanus niloticus*).

The **rock monitor** is a dull grey-brown colour with yellowish blotches above, yellowish spots on the limbs and a yellowish belly. The tail has bands of brown and cream. Juveniles have a black throat while adults have a white throat (as their alternative name suggests). The rock monitor is less attractive than the water monitor and often has scrappy patches of unshed skin on its body and ticks in the soft skin on its face and leg joints. It lives in tunnels under rocks or in tree cavities.

Water monitors are smaller than rock monitors. They are greenish-brown in colour with darker blotches and yellow bands on the body and spots on the legs. Young are striking black and yellow in colour. The water monitor's tail is longer than its body and laterally flattened to act as a rudder when swimming. Their teeth form rounded pegs which are needed to crush crabs. They live along rivers and are often seen sunning themselves on rocks.

Male monitors establish their territories and status through **wrestling matches.**

Monitor lizards have powerful laterally flattened tails, strong limbs and claws, and flexible necks. These traits make them **formidable predators** and they are especially adept at defending themselves. If trouble threatens monitors will thrash out with their tails, they will bite bulldog-like without release, and even feign death (known as thanatosis). If gripped behind the head, they eject the contents of their cloaca (rectal opening) and then on release make a hasty retreat – the water monitor usually taking to water at the first opportunity. The rock monitor's biggest threats are the **martial eagle** and the honey badger. The water monitor is preyed on mainly by pythons and crocodiles.

Monitors have a **forked tongue** much like snakes. They use their tongues to smell out prey. The tongue retracts into a sheath on the roof of the mouth where chemical and olfactory clues are brought into contact with the organ of Jacobsen. The fork assists the monitor in determining where the scent is strongest.

Monitors
Family Varanidae

When it comes to **breeding**, monitors are shy and are seldom 'caught in the act'. The gravid female water monitor cleverly monopolises on the constant temperature of termite mounds to incubate her eggs. Once the soil has been softened by the first spring rains, she bores a hole into the mound where she lays up to 60 eggs. The hole is small enough for the termites to repair without consequence to them. They continue their underworld comings and goings while the monitor eggs develop inside their mound under constant climate conditions. Up to a full year later when the soil of the mound is again softened by spring rain, the young monitors dig out together.

Monitors have **voracious appetites** and will catch and eat whatever they can. The menu is a long one featuring small mammals, snails, millipedes, crabs, mussels, frogs, fish, insects, smaller lizards, snakes, baby tortoises, eggs of various species, birds and even carrion. Food is mostly sized to be swallowed whole but larger prey is taken and shredded with the sharp claws.

Monitor lizards are sought after for human use. The flesh is edible while the fat is used in traditional medicine. The skins are attractive and many have been slaughtered in the past to satisfy fashion demands. **Monitors are protected in South Africa** in this regard.

Moreau's tropical house gecko
Hemidactylus mabouia

This commonest of geckos in the Lowveld is often spotted in camps clambering the walls around lights to catch insects attracted by them. Geckos are able to **tolerate lower temperatures** than many other reptiles and tend to be active at night – an unusual trait for a creature that relies on the external environment to regulate its body metabolism.

To clamber on walls, the tropical house gecko has some help from its **specially adapted feet**. Pads on the toes called scansors are made up of tiny hairs (setae) arranged in rows (lamellae). These setae provide traction on even the smallest of defects on a surface allowing the gecko to scale vertical walls and even overhangs.

The tropical house gecko produces **hard-shelled eggs**. Other lizards have leathery-shelled eggs. Consequently, geckos have higher calcium requirements than usual and are forced to eat old eggshells and store the calcium for future use in glands in the neck.

The gecko family is known for its ability to **vocalise** usually in the form of distressed clicks. Vocalisation is uncommon in reptiles.

Bushveld lizard
Heliobolus lugubris

Although the adults of this species of lizard are **cryptically coloured** to match their sandy environments and avoid the attention of predators, their young are dark with pale yellowish spots or blotches on the back. While the adults concentrate their time on catching small insects with a swift dash from cover, the youngsters are occupied with a **clever deception**. Moving with a stiff-legged gait, the juvenile bushveld lizard mimics the 'oogpister' ground beetle (*Anthia* sp.), which is known for squirting acid at its predators. For this reason many predators, including birds and mongooses, avoid this foul-tasting beetle and apparently also the look-alike baby lizards.

Striped skink
Mabuya striata

The skinks are a family of medium-sized lizards that generally have **strong legs**, a small head without much of a noticeable neck and **shiny scales**.

The striped skink is a very common, easily spotted reptile in the Lowveld bush regions and cities. It is often seen darting rapidly across rocks between patches of sun and shade. This it does to **thermoregulate**. Being ectothermic (cold-blooded), reptiles rely heavily on the temperature of the external environment to regulate their internal metabolism. The skink needs to 'warm up' sufficiently to have the necessary energy to catch its insect prey which requires an active pursuit.

The striped skink has a lithe, flexible body which helps it to operate efficiently in a rocky habitat. It has strong overlapping scales and the skin is reinforced with 'osteoderms', tiny bones found under the scales of some reptiles. Spiny scales on the **soles of its feet** also help with grip on the rock surfaces.

The striped skink is a lizard **capable of losing its tail** to escape danger. This technique of voluntary 'self-mutilation' is known as caudal autotomy. When pressure is applied to the tail, it severs along an abscission plane from where it will regenerate again.

Giant plated lizard
Gerrhosaurus validus

Probably because of their large size and comparatively short legs on which to transport themselves, plated lizards are prone to **sliding down banks on their bellies** toboggan-like.

This **giant of the lizard family** – reaching 70 cm in length – is only smaller than the monitor lizards.

As its name suggests, the plated lizard has square plate-like **scales** that abut one another rather than having the overlapping scale arrangement that facilitates movement in other lizards such as skinks. Since this kind of body covering is restrictive, the plated lizards have a **fold along their sides** made up of smaller scales. This expands to accommodate a **fat belly** after a good meal or the eggs of gravid females.

Like crocodiles, plated lizards **store fat** in their tails.

At first glance the giant plated lizard is drably coloured but they do in fact flaunt striking costumes at specific times of their lives. The juveniles are strikingly coloured in black with yellow spots and stripes. The male becomes washed with purple on his chin, throat and sides of the head when **breeding**.

Giant plated lizards are probably fairly unique among lizards in that they are **omnivorous** and not strictly carnivorous. In conjunction with insects and small vertebrates like baby tortoises, the giant plated lizard eats fruits (like figs), leaves and flowers.

The **black-lined plated lizard** is the smaller cousin of giant plated lizard and usually found on termite mounds.

Giant plated lizards live in loose colonies on broken rocky ground, specifically on granite koppies. To **escape danger** they will flee into rock crevices where they inflate their bodies and jam themselves in. Once this has happened, a pursuer would be hard pressed to free the lizard. They also practise autotomy (they are able to shed and regenerate their tails).

Common flat lizard
Platysaurus intermedius

This lizard is most conspicuous in the Lowveld due to the vividly coloured males and the fact that they live in colonies and so are usually present in large numbers where they occur. Weathering rocks are the common flat lizard's favoured habitat and they shelter under the pieces that flake off. There are nine races of this species and each varies in colour.

Mozambican spitting cobra ('M'fezi')
Naja mossambica

Usually, a spitting cobra will warn you of its presence by **rearing its head up** and fanning out its impressive hood. This in itself is often enough of a startle display to send threats away.

This snake is notorious for its ability to **spit venom** over 2 m at its enemies. This it does with specially modified fangs. Cobras have forward positioned hollow fangs and these have a grooved opening on the front surface through which the venom can be spat forwards.

A snake's eyes become glazed and opaque just prior to sloughing (moulting).

The Mozambican spitting cobra has unique venom which comprises both **neuro- and cytotoxic venoms**. Usually cobras have mostly neurotoxic venom. The cytotoxic-rich combination in the spitting cobra is to make the spat venom more effective as neurotoxins would have little effect landing on a surface. Venom to the eyes is immediately painful. These cobras do also bite readily causing such severe tissue damage that skin grafts are usually necessary.

Spotted bush snake
Philothamnus semivariegatus

This is a very attractive snake and although it is easily confused with a boomslang at first glance, it is in fact harmless. Bush snakes get their name from their habit of climbing expertly into low plants which they do while looking for their tree-dwelling prey, especially tree frogs, geckos and chameleons. They are well equipped for their lifestyle having keeled belly scales that give them traction against the bark of trees, good eyesight and they blend in well. To help them do this they may sway their heads and necks while keeping the remainder of the body still. In this way they resemble swaying branches.

African rock python
Python natalensis

This is the **largest snake** in the Lowveld – it can reach a length of 6 m and a weight of 50 kg. In other areas, rock pythons have weighed in at a remarkable 100 kg and 8–9 m in length.

Although not strictly an aquatic snake, pythons **love water** and take to it readily from where they may hunt or they may simply remain underwater to thermoregulate (control body temperature). They are prone to basking for thermoregulation too, especially after a good meal!

Pythons are one of very few reptiles that exhibit any kind of **parental care**. The female will coil herself around her 30–50 eggs during incubation (which can last up to 80 days) to protect them from the likes of mongooses and monitor lizards. Her coils also provide warmth which helps the embryos' development. Once the eggs hatch, the young may remain with the female for a few days but after this no further care is provided.

African rock python
Python natalensis

Pythons are **ambush predators** and rely on crypsis or more commonly the cover of darkness to hunt. They are able to take extremely large prey including small antelope and primates but once they have done so, they become vulnerable to attack themselves. Wild dogs and hyenas have been known to eat engorged pythons.

Pythons are **long-lived** and can reach 30 years of age. The larger specimens make a hearty meal for large mammalian predators and opportunistic lions and leopards will not shun pythons as a possible meal. Smaller pythons are susceptible to predation by raptors such as the snake-eagles.

Pythons are **fangless but not toothless**. They have jagged rows of fixed teeth on both jaws which are capable of inflicting nasty wounds and they bite readily in self-defence. Although they do not possess venom, the wound is susceptible to infection due to the unsanitary condition of its mouth.

Pythons have **heat-sensitive pits** around their mouths which detect infrared radiation believed to help them find warm-blooded prey in dark conditions.

A python's skeleton still has vestigial thighbones and these miniature femurs are used as charms and medicinal ingredients in **cultural rituals**. Various other parts of the python including its spinal column, skin and fat are used for a multitude of traditional magical-medicinal reasons.

Pythons kill their prey via **constriction**. The method is simple: the prey is held securely in the python's coils and each time the prey exhales the python tightens its grip reducing the size of breath that the prey is thus able to take. Eventually the victim suffocates at which point the snake will consume it. Large pythons can swallow more than 50 kg at one sitting. They are also capable of going without food for extremely long periods, using up stored reserves – one record mentions a two and a half year fast in captivity!

Boomslang
Dispholidus typus

These snakes rely on **cryptic colouration** to camouflage themselves in foliage. The boomslang varies from dull bark-brown (females) to bright foliage-green (males). They will sway slightly to look like swaying branches.

Boomslang are easily recognised by their **enormous eyes** containing round pupils. They consequently have excellent binocular vision and are able to distinguish and identify immobile prey, a trait shared with the twig snake but otherwise unique amongst snakes.

The boomslang has no English name but translated directly from Afrikaans it literally means 'tree snake' which is where it lives.

The boomslang uses **startle displays** to deter their own predators by inflating the neck to expose vividly coloured skin.

If a human gets envenomated by a boomslang, there is **specific anti-venom** (monovalent) that should be administered to counteract the effects. The standard polyvalent used for most other venoms is ineffective against haemotoxic venom. As this is generally in short supply where it is usually needed, a blood transfusion is usually the only alternative. Symptoms may be latent for up to 48 hours but fortunately boomslang are shy and bites are very rare.

Boomslang mainly **hunt chameleons** and birds as these are common where they live. They actively hunt down their prey during daytime and then chew on them with their short back-positioned fangs to inject adequate **haemotoxins** (blood-clotting venom).

Although the vine snake can be swift if it needs to be, it relies on **slow movements** to complement its cryptic colour and ambushes prey which it subsequently swallows hanging downward. Vine snakes eat a more varied diet than the boomslang including lizards, frogs, birds and other snakes.

Like the boomslang, the vine snake has **large eyes** and excellent vision. It has **keyhole-shaped pupils** which provide stereoscopic vision and can thus distinguish and identify immobile prey, a trait unique amongst snakes (except for the boomslang).

These snakes are **masters of camouflage** and they rely on their cryptic colouration to blend them into their arboreal habitats. As their name suggests, they convincingly resemble twigs of vegetation or the branches of vines. They are very skinny snakes with long tails and brown bodies. The top of the head is green with darker markings.

No anti-venom exists for the treatment of vine snake bites and a blood transfusion is the only option to replace the clotting agents destroyed by this haemotoxin. As with the boomslang there may be a latent period of up to 48 hours before symptoms appear.

To seem more intimidating to predators, the vine snake **inflates its neck** when threatened.

Black mamba
Dendroaspis polylepis

The black mamba got its name from the colour of the inside of its mouth, not as one would imagine, from the colour of its body, which is dull grey. When threatened the black mamba swells its neck region and exposes the **black mouth lining**.

The front-positioned fangs are like hypodermic needles and in a swift strike the mamba injects its quarry with a serious dose of combined **neuro-cardiotoxic venom**. It is dubious whether the mouse or bird even feels the blow but the venom quickly paralyses the animal and arrests its breathing at which point the mamba will consume and digest it quickly. Mambas will strike repeatedly until the venom takes effect.

The black mamba is able to **lift one third of its length off the ground**. It does this when threatened throwing its body ahead of itself to make a quick getaway or to change direction.

This is a large snake that reaches a length of 2-3 m and in exceptional cases grow 4,5 m long. Young snakes will achieve a length of 2 m in their first year. This is the **largest venomous snake in Africa**.

The black mamba takes to trees to hunt its warm-blooded prey of either birds or small mammals. They are **active hunters** and do not take already dead prey or cold-blooded creatures.

Black mambas have **large venom glands** and each bite can inject up to 400 mg of venom although only 10-15 mg is needed to kill a human. Their large front fangs afford them easy grip and they bite readily and repeatedly. They are, however, **shy** preferring to retreat from threats. They do not induce confrontation or attack unprovoked as is sometimes believed.

A black mamba's bite should be treated as a **medical emergency** as the venom attacks the heart and nerves resulting in paralysis and respiratory failure. Nowadays thorough treatment is available and most victims survive.

These snakes are **territorial** and they use regular haunts such as termite mounds or rock crevices.

Puff adder
Bitis arietans

Puff adders get their name from their **propensity to puff** or hiss if disturbed. By this point, the snake will have assumed its 'ready-to-strike' poise and will attack readily.

The puff adder is a beautifully coloured and patterned snake that blends in superbly with the mottled floor covering of any habitat. It relies on its **camouflage to ambush prey** (mostly rodents) and to escape the attention of its own enemies. As a result puff adders are easily trodden on and cause the majority of incidental snakebites in South Africa.

The young of puff adders are **born alive**. This is known as ovovivipary. The leathery-shelled eggs are carried to full term inside the female and subsequently hatch there so that the youngsters emerge 'alive'. Ovovivipary is beneficial as the eggs are not susceptible to predation or desiccation as is the case with oviparous (egg-laying) creatures. Newborn puff adders are fully equipped with fangs and venom!

A puff adder female from East Africa holds the **world record** for producing the most offspring in one sitting – an astounding 156! The norm is 20 to 40.

Puff adders are **sluggish snakes** but possess a lightning fast strike delivering a painful, deep bite with long, hinged front fangs. It has been discovered that puff adders can generally strike faster than the shutter of a camera. One should never be deceived into handling a puff adder because it appears lethargic! The snake has cytotoxic venom responsible for cell damage and ultimately tissue necrosis.

Puff adders move with **rectilinear locomotion**. The lateral contraction of muscles causes the adder to move like a caterpillar in a straight line, the scales of the underbelly creating traction with the ground. The track of a puff adder is unmistakable in this regard; it is straight, deep and the tail drags through the middle leaving a thinner line.

Horned adder

Puff adders enjoy an **occasional swim**. They are also prone to lying on roads at night to warm up.

Nile crocodile
Crocodylus niloticus

Crocodiles differ from **alligators** in their teeth arrangement. When a crocodile's mouth is closed, a tooth (the fourth mandibular) sticks up on either side. In alligators this tooth is not visible.

Crocodiles have **clawed feet** and webbed hind feet. These help the crocodile to function in both of its elements, water and land. The webbing helps the crocodile manoeuvre itself for well-timed attacks and the claws are vital for traction on land and for digging during the breeding season.

Crocodiles normally only dive for a few minutes but they can **stay underwater for 30 minutes** if threatened. If they remain inactive while underwater, they can hold their breath for up to 2 hours.

The **tail** of a crocodile is a very powerful rudder. It is flattened laterally and propels the crocodile effortlessly through the water when it swims. The tail also acts as a fat reservoir, storing essential sustenance for times of forced fasts.

Crocodiles are unlike other reptiles in that they have a **four-chambered heart** (usually only birds and mammals have four chambers). The chambers are specially arranged to accommodate the necessary equalisation of pressure between the arteries and veins during long dives in deep water.

Nile crocodile
Crocodylus niloticus

The thick, scaly body covering insulates the crocodile for life in the water. The **sides of the body are expandable** to accommodate breathing and pregnancy. The skin apparently contains special sense organs that are believed to react to water pressure changes.

Crocodile **breeding is rather elaborate** for a reptile. The process begins in May at which time males establish their dominance by bellowing, bubble-blowing and fighting. In the crocodile world dominance is simple: **the older a crocodile, the larger a crocodile, the more dominant a crocodile.** The 10-minute mating affair takes place in the water in June to July and 2 months later the female digs a pit in the riverbank where she deposits about 50 eggs. For the following 3 months the guarding mother only leaves the site of her incubating eggs to cool off. High-pitched chirping sounds from underground start in December and alert the mother to the arrival of her brood. She breaks open the sand-covered chamber to assist the hatchlings out of their shells by rolling the eggs between her tongue and palate. The young are then transported in her mouth and released at the water's edge. Her parental guard duties last only 2 more weeks after this.

Being ectothermic creatures (i.e. they rely on the temperature of the environment to regulate their body temperature), crocodiles are prone to spending many hours **basking in the sun** to warm up. But with crocodiles, basking may also be used for the opposite function of cooling down. By lying on sand banks with their mouths open, they allow themselves to lose heat by evaporative cooling from the moist inner parts of their mouths.

The sex of a hatchling is determined by the temperature of the soil in which they were incubated. Lower temperatures between 26-30°C produce females and higher temperatures of between 31-34°C produce males. The reverse is true in tortoises.

Hatchlings are about 30 cm long at birth. For the first few years the young grow about 30 cm per year and then the growth rate subsides. At 2 years the hatchlings will be about 1,2 m long. A 2-3 m crocodile is usually between 12-15 years old and should weigh in at about 90 kg. Crocodiles continue to grow throughout life. The maximum size of a crocodile in southern Africa is 5-6 m in length which may mean the animal exceeds one ton in weight. They reach 60-80 years but **occasionally may get to be 100 years old**.

Nile crocodile
Crocodylus niloticus

Crocodiles live in the water and they rely on the water to act as cover when they **ambush prey**. To this end, crocodiles have their eyes, ears and nostrils positioned on top of their heads so that if need be only these vital senses stick out above the water while the rest of the body and head is concealed.

Contrary to popular belief crocodiles **eat mainly fish**, the most common source of food in Lowveld rivers. These they swallow whole. Crocodiles are important in river ecosystems for controlling the numbers of barbel (catfish). They are, however, opportunistic hunters and will ambush mammal prey coming to drink at the water's edge particularly in the dry season. Crocodiles have been known to **launch 2 m out of the water** to grab prey with a sideways movement of the head.

Surprisingly crocodiles are quite **agile on land**, walking high-legged on their short limbs. They are even able to gallop and can reach speeds of up to 13 km/h over short distances. When threatened, a belly-slide back into the water is the favoured form of locomotion.

Nile crocodile
Crocodylus niloticus

The **valved nostrils** also prevent water getting into unwanted places while the crocodile dives underwater.

Crocodiles are predominantly **nocturnal** and to accommodate for this habit they have vertical pupils which narrow or broaden according to the available light to facilitate **improved night-vision**. Like other nocturnal animals, crocodiles have a tapetum lucidum which is a reflective membrane that bounces light back onto the retina, also for improved night-vision. At night, crocodiles' eyes shine as if spotlighted because of this tapetum.

Crocodiles have thin, transparent **nictitating membranes** in their eyes. These structures are like underwater goggles and they protect the crocodile's eyeball underwater while allowing it a degree of underwater vision. The membranes pull inwards over the eyeball from the inside corner of the eye while the normal eyelids are open.

There are **gular flaps** at the back of a crocodile's mouth that it can close so that it can **swallow underwater** without choking or drowning.

Crocodiles' teeth do not articulate against one another in the manner that mammals' teeth do. Because of this, crocodiles cannot bite with any kind of slicing effect and to consume prey that they have caught, crocodiles must employ a technique known as the **death roll**. Clamping firmly onto a piece of a floating carcass with its gripping teeth, the crocodile will then spin itself laterally until the chunk of meat comes free. Then with a few chomps of the jaws to flatten the mouthful (not chew it), it gulps the piece down.

A crocodile's **teeth** are replaced continuously throughout its life with new ones growing up from below while the older ones are forced out.

Frogs

Frogs are **amphibians**. This word is derived from *amphi* meaning two and *bios* meaning life and refers to the two phases in its life cycle – the juvenile aquatic tadpole stage and the terrestrial adult stage. Frogs undergo **metamorphosis** to change from the one form into the next. This process is driven by hormones in the pituitary and thyroid gland and is quite remarkable. The tail, fins, mouthparts and oxygen-extracting gills of the tadpole as well as the internal organs that are designed to cope with a diet of predominantly algae are completely replaced by a full vertebrate skeleton and muscles, a tongue, eyelids, proper skin and a digestive tract capable of processing a carnivorous diet. Once they are adults, frogs **moult their skins** as they grow. Frogs usually swallow the old skin once it has pulled free from the body. In some cases, the shed skin provides a capsule in which burrowing frogs (like bullfrogs) can overcome dry conditions.

Frogs have **long, sticky tongues** that they use to capture prey, which they subsequently swallow whole as for the most part they lack teeth. The tongue is attached in the front of the mouth and, facilitated by a lunge in the direction of the victim, is flicked out of the mouth. The food item is swallowed with the aid of the eyeballs, which push down on the mouth's contents with each blink.

A frog's **eyes and nostrils** are positioned high on its head to accommodate vision and breathing above the water surface when it is submerged. Although the eyes are fairly fixed in their sockets, frogs are able to bulge their eyeballs to improve their field of vision. The eyes are large as are the pupils to facilitate good night vision. They are protected by eyelids and in some cases also nictitating membranes.

Eastern olive toad

Because amphibians form the evolutionary transition between aquatic and terrestrial-adapted creatures, **body covering and breathing** mechanism poses a problem. The thin skin, which is permeable to water and allows for the absorption of oxygen in aquatic habitats, dries out if continuously exposed to the dry conditions typical of terrestrial environments thus arresting gaseous exchange. To overcome this frogs have mucous glands in their skin to keep themselves moist while on land, facilitating the absorption of oxygen. Frogs also take the occasional swim to rehydrate and usually hide up in humid habitats during the heat of the day. Frogs are also able to respire using lungs. These are primitive and the absence of a mammalian-like diaphragm means that the air must be circulated by palpitations of the throat.

Frogs have well-developed **legs for jumping**. The larger hind limbs provide the propulsion for each leap. The forelimbs help to absorb the shock during landings. They are also used to manipulate food and to grip females during mating.

Among native cultures, frogs have been used **traditionally as medicinal remedies** or as a source of protein. Bullfrogs, particularly, provide a substantial meal and are typically fried. Medicinally, small bits of toad's skin are ingested to correct heartbeat irregularities and a string used to hang a toad is implicated in rituals to treat tonsillitis. Burnt frogs in combination with selected herbs provide treatments for chronic oedema and asthma.

Frogs

Snoring puddle frog

Frogs use **sounds** to communicate and find mates. As such they have well-developed ears. Although they possess no external ear, the tympanum (eardrum) is large and resembles a disc. This increases in diameter the lower pitched the frog's song.

After the first substantial spring rains, the Lowveld becomes a cacophony of sound thanks to the millions of frogs that leave their wintertime hiding places and begin calling to attract a mate. **Frog breeding** is an urgent process, as they must complete the cycle before the temporary water provided by the showers dry up. Most species choose ephemeral pools in the form of puddles, rock pools and inundated grasslands to breed, as these sources of water tend to lack the majority of predators (to both frog and eggs) found in more permanent water sources. However, there are species that utilise almost every kind of wetland habitat.

Frogs call or sing by moving air backwards and forwards (using the same breath) between the lungs and the **vocal sac**. The sound is produced by the vibration of the vocal chords in the larynx and is resonated in the vocal sac (also called the resonance chamber), which is formed by a thin balloon of skin (or a pair of these) under the chin. Like many other creatures, frogs have different calls to signify different things.

The most common, incessant and often deafening calls heard at night are the **advertisements** of the males singing to attract females. These calls are unique to individual species and attract members of similar species to a particular area and then help the males to space themselves out relative to one another. Although the resultant sound is somewhat frenzied (and confusing to predators wishing to isolate a single frog as a meal), the group chorus does have a degree of order. Two nearby callers will in fact alternate their sounds so that they do not interfere with one another. This is called **timeshare calling** and it makes it easier for females to isolate their choice of mate, which will depend on his pitch, a deeper tone usually representing a bigger and genetically superior male.

Should one male intrude on another individual's turf, he may utter **aggressive calls** to denote his hold over that territory. These are usually heard early on in an evening while the frogs are still establishing their calling sites for the evening. **Prime calling sites are in demand** – females will select mates based on their calling sites since genetically superior individuals are likely to secure the best sites. To this end, males will even fight, wrestling and kicking, to displace one another. Some males maximise on the efforts of the individuals in better calling sites (or with stronger calls) by remaining silent and then **intercepting females** attracted to these males in prime positions. This is called satellite behaviour.

Females produce a specific call, called a **release call**, to indicate to the male that they have completed laying and that he can let go. Sometimes when males are mistakenly grabbed by other males, they too will utter release calls. Distress calls are given by both sexes should they be seized by predators. This is often adequate to startle the predator, which then releases the frog.

Grey tree frog

Frogs

Ecologically, frogs are a **vital part of the food chain** and play an important role in controlling pest insects. They in turn provide food to other creatures such as snakes, birds (like **hamerkops** and herons), fish, small predatory mammals (like mongooses) and even spiders and insects. Since frogs are soft-skinned and sensitive to absorbing ecosystem pollutants, they are a vital indication to scientists regarding the health of a particular habitat. The disappearance of frogs is the first sign that an ecosystem is under stress.

Frogs **require water as a medium** to breed since fertilisation is external and the resultant eggs soft and prone to desiccation. In order for fertilisation to take place, the male must straddle the female to allow their genital openings to lie close to one another for simultaneous deposits of eggs and sperm. **The clasping of a female** by the (usually smaller) male **is known as amplexus** and different species exhibit different types of amplexus. The most conventional grip is whereby the male clasps the female behind her forelimbs using special nuptial pads on his thumbs and forearms. This is known as auxillary amplexus. More primitive species like platannas use inguinal amplexus whereby the female is gripped lower down around her waist and just in front of her hind legs. Some species of frog (like rain frogs) have limbs too short to actuate either kind of grip and must rely on sticking to one another to achieve mating and fertilisation. This is called adhesion.

Banded rubber frog
Phrynomantis bifasciatus

Their colour is not the only conspicuous feature of this frog. Banded rubber frogs produce an easily recognised **high-pitched rolling 'prrrrrr'** sound at night (during the rainy summer months). They call about every 5 seconds with each purr lasting about 2 seconds. This they do from a hidden location alongside the ephemeral (temporary) pans or rock pools where they breed. Banded rubber frogs are **explosive breeders**, each female producing about 600 eggs. She entangles her eggs in the submerged vegetation of her chosen breeding site and these eventually hatch as transparent filter-feeding tadpoles and subsequently each frog may live for up to 10 years.

The banded rubber frog is the most conspicuous **aposematically coloured frog** in southern Africa. The shiny black and red skin is a bold warning to predators and other frog species of its toxic glandular secretions which can even cause symptoms in humans such as skin rashes, respiratory difficulty and nausea, just from handling it (especially if there are abrasions on a person's skin).

Banded rubber frogs **do not hop**. Rather they walk in a lumbering manner and when threatened this gait becomes more exaggerated as the frog puffs itself up on its skinny spotted legs to appear more intimidating.

During the day, banded rubber frogs **escape detection by hiding** in hollow logs or in underground burrows which they dig with their specially unwebbed feet. In spite of the lack of webbing they are still accomplished swimmers and can also climb well, scouring tree trunks or rocks for their favourite prey of ants and termites. They seem totally impervious to ants' formic acid defences.

Grey tree frog (foam nest frog)
Chiromantis xerampelina

As their name suggests, grey tree frogs are **arboreal** (live in trees). To facilitate a life in vegetation, they have broad pads on the ends of the toes which help the frog when leaping. They are also able to change the colour of their skin from cryptic grey for **camouflage** against bark to pale white to thermoregulate (control heat). They are also able to 'sweat' droplets of liquid to reduce their temperature by evaporative cooling during excessively hot weather. Grey tree frogs are able to absorb water rapidly through their skin which allows them to remain out of the water and in their arboreal habitat and they further conserve water by excreting concentrated uric acid.

The **brown-backed tree frog** (*Leptopelis mossambicus*) also occurs in the Lowveld but is of a different family to the grey tree frog. This frog is brown in colour with a distinct darker 'horseshoe' on its back. Both species have unique, easily identifiable calls. The grey tree frog makes a number of inharmonious chirps and croaks. The brown-backed tree frog produces a distinct quack-quack sound often accompanied by a buzzing noise.

The alternate name for the grey tree frog is **foam nest frog** and this is derived from its **breeding strategy** which is also focused in the arboreal world. After good rains, foam nest frog females choose an ephemeral pool over which hangs some form of vegetation (or sometimes a rock face). Here, with the assistance of an amplexing male as well as multiple male 'bystanders', the female will use her hind legs to whip up a protective froth, derived from an oviduct secretion, to surround her eggs as they are laid and fertilised. Often she must clamber down to the water below to rehydrate several times during the process. An attendance of males may mean that on each return she pairs up with a different male. Other males not achieving amplexus with her may simply add their sperm to the mixture relying on sperm competition to fertilise some of her eggs. This improves the genetic viability of the brood.

Grey tree frogs are often found in human habitations.

The resultant **foam nest is usually the size of a small melon** and resembles a hanging meringue (sometimes adjacent nests will fuse to create massive ones). It dries around the eggs to protect them from the sun and from predators and to provide constant incubation conditions. Once the tadpoles have hatched and grown a little (reach 1 cm), the nest will begin degenerating (after about 4 or 5 days) and the tadpoles will drop out the bottom and into the pool of water below.

Bushveld rain frog
Breviceps adspersus

The bushveld rain frog is a **terrestrial frog** that burrows into sand and only emerges to breed after a heavy rain shower has softened the ground adequately. It has no **reliance on pools of water** in order to breed like other frogs but rather the mating pair digs directly back into the soil from which they themselves have emerged, to lay their eggs in a **subterranean chamber** 40 cm below the surface. The eggs are deposited in a thick jelly coating which protects them and keeps them hydrated while they develop. The tadpoles remain inside the jelly once they hatch and they survive by feeding on a sack of yolk within the egg case until they metamorphose into froglets and finally hatch out.

The very **rotund bodies** of the rain frogs make it difficult for them to mate. They have short legs which further complicates normal amplexus (mating clasp). In order to establish a suitable grip to enable fertilisation, the **male actually becomes adhered to the female's back** through secretions she oozes in that region. Until such time as she releases a solvent to reverse the adherence, the male is unable to move from his position, short of tearing his flesh.

The scientific name *Breviceps* means 'short head' referring to the fact that one can hardly determine the head from the rest of the body. This feature in conjunction with the very round body makes the rain frog unmistakable. The bizarre anatomy of this frog is exaggerated comically when it is threatened as it **inflates itself to intimidate predators**. This habit led to its Afrikaans name 'blaasop' or 'blow-up'. In spite of this evasive action, bushveld rain frogs are relished by both bushpigs and monitor lizards.

Bushveld rain frogs and their other southern African relatives are **endemic** to southern Africa meaning they are found nowhere else in the world. Males differ to females in having black throats.

Rain frogs have special **hard digging apparatuses** on their heels called tubercles. They use these as well as their unwebbed toes to excavate burrows which they dig backwards into sandy soil. These burrows provide safety from predators, protection from the elements and a sheltered position from which to provide their nightly whistled serenades. A male calling from the entrance to his burrow elicits a chain response from other rain frogs. Eventually both sexes will temporarily abandon their posts to physically seek one another out. They call incessantly even while roaming and should two males encounter one another they will continue to call while they **tussle each other** with their vocal sacs.

Painted reed frog
Hyperolius marmoratus

This is a **small frog** of only about 2,5 cm but is conspicuous for its **dazzling colouration** and high-pitched piping whistle that creates a notable cacophony when many call in chorus. Painted reed frogs are common in the Lowveld but the species also occurs throughout the eastern part of southern Africa in a variety of different races (up to 16) each possessing unique colours and patterns, which have caused great consternation amongst scientists with regards to classification. The colour form present in the Lowveld is strikingly striped in black, white and yellow on the upper side and the flanks and limbs are fringed with red patches. To create further confusion, painted reed frogs are able to bleach their colouration completely during the day in order to thermoregulate (reflect heat).

The inner sections of the hind legs are infused red and this is used as an anti-predatory device known as **flash colouration**. A threatened individual will leap up, exposing the bright red colour obvious to the predator, which then focuses on this. As the frog lands, the red inner leg is instantly tucked away and the predator no longer has its target in sight and may then struggle to relocate its quarry should the frog remain motionless.

As their name suggests, reed frogs make use of the **tall reed beds** that fringe pans to breed. The males climb right to the top of the reeds to emanate their shrill calls. Reed frogs have flat toe pads to assist in climbing the reeds. Each **call site is defended** from other males and reed frogs are notorious for screeching and kicking to displace a rival. During the day reed frogs may hide in trees taking shelter in the axils of leaves. If no tree cover is available, they will simply remain on the reed stalk sometimes in exposed positions. Their small bodies and hunched posture allows them to minimise evaporative losses at these times.

Eastern olive toad
Bufo garmani

The **difference between a frog and a toad** is sometimes a disputed issue. Basically the term 'toad' is used to refer to a group of frogs that have particularly granular and glandular skin. The Bufonidae family to which these frogs belong, all have large parotid glands behind the head and a cardio-toxic substance (called bufotoxin) is secreted from these as a deterrent against predators. Toads are explosive breeders with some species producing up to 20 000 eggs. These they lay in a string and not a clump as other frog families might.

Two toads occur commonly in the Lowveld most notably the **eastern olive toad**. Olive toads are **cryptically coloured** to blend into the terrestrial environment in which they live except during the breeding season at which time they will make long-range overland migrations to pans and dams to enter the mating fray. Like the painted reed frog, the inner linings of the legs are coloured red to enact **flash colouration** to confuse predators. These toads rely on their crypsis to avoid detection since they are both poor jumpers and swimmers.

The **eggs** of the olive and other toads are counter-shaded. This means the upper portion is darker than the lower portion of the egg. From the point of view of a predator above the water, the eggs blend in with the dark underwater environment. From a predator's below-the-water perspective, the eggs are pale and blend in with the light and sky above. The squat tadpoles hatch and develop quickly and within a year or two reach maturity. **Toads can live for 40 years**.

The **guttural toad** (*Bufo gutturalis*) is also found in Lowveld. The two species can be told apart by looking at the patches on the snout and head. The patches on the head of the guttural toad creates a pale cross while the olive toad has no patches on its snout and those behind the eyes are not fused but present two separate patches. The guttural toad snores and the olive toad utters a quacked bray.

Other common frog species

Some of the other more common frog species likely to be encountered after a Lowveld downpour include the following:

Plain grass frog
Ptychadena anchietae

This frog is often detected in flooded grassy areas. It is easily identified by its sharp snout, long legs, plain pink back and large tympanic membrane positioned just behind the eye. The eyes have broken black marks running over them and down the sides of the frog.

Bubbling kassina
Kassina senegalensis

This frog makes a high-pitched liquid call that sounds like a bubble popping. It is a characteristic sound of the Lowveld summer nights. Males call ventriloquistically from concealed locations and the call of one male causes a chain reaction from others.

Russet-backed sand frog
Tomopterna marmorata

At first glance this frog might be confused with the plain grass frog but is more likely to be found on the sand banks of rivers. This sand frog has an orange-pink back with a pale shoulder patch, grey sides and green patches in the folds of its hind legs. The head is blunter than the grass frog and it has round tubercles on its hands.

Tremelo sand frog
Tomopterna crytotus

This is another common sand frog which occurs in a variety of habitats. It is recognised by its squat body with mottled patterns and a pale patch between the shoulders like the russet-backed. There is a stripe down its back all the way from the snout and another two less prominent ones down the flanks. Behind the jaw is a granular ridge.

Other common frog species

Mottled shovel-nosed frog
Hemisus marmoratus

This frog is notable for its insect-like buzzing call and for its primitive-looking form. The head is very small and the nose sharply pointed with a yellow chin. Overall the frog is mottled grey-brown and yellow above and pink-white below. One can expect to find mottled shovel-nosed frogs in muddy areas abutting pans or rivers.

Tropical platanna
Xenopus muelleri

The platanna is a grey, primitive-looking frog which is distinctly fatter towards the hind part of the body. Orange webbing between its toes and on the underside of the legs will identify the species as a tropical platanna. It has an obvious tentacle under the small eyes. Hamerkops feed almost exclusively on platannas and their tadpoles as they occur in permanent bodies of water.

Common river frog
Afrana angolensis

This common frog is found in permanent streams and has very long legs, very long webbed toes, a streamlined body and a sharply pointed muzzle. It is usually pale green with dark spots. It calls while partially submerged and takes to water if disturbed.

Ornate frog
Hildebrandtia ornata

This attractive frog is covered with different tones of brown patches on the body and the legs are banded brown, black or green. A prominent bright green stripe runs down the back. It has paired vocal sacs.

Snoring puddle frog
Phrynobatrachus natalensis

As its name suggests, this frog makes a snoring sound when it calls. The frog is squat and warty with mottled patches on the body and sometimes a stripe down the back. They breed in inundated grassy areas and call earlier in the evening rather than later.

Insects and other invertebrates

Despite their small size, insects perform vital functions ecologically – pollinating flowers and dispersing seeds, acting as vectors to spread disease, feeding on plants as well as each other and other pests, removing wastes of various descriptions and recycling nutrients. They are the most abundant form of animal life on the planet and as such one cannot expect to visit any destination on earth without encountering them. The bushveld is no exception. Southern Africa has about 80 000 species of insects. This section intends to showcase a colourful assortment of the most common insects in the Lowveld and offers brief snippets of the most fascinating facts on each. Also included in this section is a mosaic of images and short write-ups on other invertebrates (not of the class Insecta) that one is likely to come across in the Lowveld. Particular species of invertebrate may be especially conspicuous or form essential driving forces in the savanna ecosystem affecting its function. As such more detail is provided on these topics in the same flowchart manner of the mammals or birds sections.

Insects

Antlions, page 224
Fireflies and glow-worms, page 224
Horn moths, page 224
Butterflies and moths, page 225
African monarch butterfly, page 225
Bagworms, page 226
Processionary worms, page 226
Mopane worms, page 226
Cicadas, page 227
Spittlebugs, page 227
Assassin bugs, page 227
Blister beetle, page 228
Bombardier beetles, page 228
Ground beetles, page 228
Tenebrionids, page 229
Stick insect, page 229
Grasshoppers and katydids, page 230
Mantids, page 230
Dragonflies, page 231
Matabele ants, page 232
Mosquitoes, page 232
Cocktail ants, page 233
Velvet ants, page 233
Fig wasps, page 234
Other wasps, page 235
Dung beetles, page 236
Termites, page 238

Spiders

Venomous spiders, page 242
Community nest spider, page 242
Golden orb-web spider, page 243
Garden orb-web spider, page 243
Dewdrop spider, page 244
Tropical tent spider, page 244
Kite spider, page 244
Funnel-web spider, page 244
Bark spider, page 245
Baboon spider, page 245

Other invertebrates

Solifugid, page 246
Millipedes, page 247
African giant land snail, page 247
Scorpions, page 248

Insects

Antlions

Antlions are part of the lacewing and owl fly family (Neuroptera). The adult form (which resembles a dainty dragonfly) looks completely different to the larval form (which has a rounded abdomen and large pincer-like mouthparts).

The larvae are predatory and can be found in the soil or free-living on bark or vegetation. They vary in size, the largest reaching up to 2,5 cm. Typically, antlion larvae **form conical pits in soft sand** which are particularly conspicuous along road verges. These they construct by circling backwards into the sand and then anchoring themselves at the bottom of the pit with backwards facing hairs. They lie in wait for prey, especially ants, and when they fall into the pit, the collapsible sides of the pit make it difficult to escape. The antlion will **flick sand over the struggling ant** to further impair its escape and will then grab it with its pincer-like mouthparts that act like hypodermic needles to suck the liquid out of its prey.

Antlions only **defecate once in a lifetime**. During the larval phase, the antlion has no anus and the intestine is blind. After pupation, it will drop a stored faecal pellet but does not ever do so again as the adult form does not feed. Adults may have impressive wingspans of up to 16 cm.

Fireflies and glow-worms

Fireflies have developed a unique method of attracting mates by the use of **flashing light in their abdomens**. This light production is similar to cold fusion and has not yet been harnessed by mankind!

Fireflies and glow-worms are essentially the same thing. The **female** of most species is wingless and **grub-like, resembling a worm** (hence 'glow-worm') while the male has wings and resembles a fly (hence 'firefly').

The **light is produced in special cells** on the abdomen of the insect. A layer of reflective uric acid crystals helps to amplify the illumination, which occurs when the chemical called luceferin is oxidised by the enzyme luceferase, both present in these special cells. A healthy supply of nerves voluntarily controls the pulses of light by regulating the oxygen supply to the illuminating cells. **Each species has a particular pulse rhythm**, which is how males in flight scout for and recognise potential mates on the ground. Sometimes the females of a particular species may mimic the light pulse pattern of another species and then prey on the unwary males that respond to her signals.

Horn moths

The worm-like protrusions found on old antelope or buffalo horns are formed by the larvae of a horn-eating moth. The tubes are reinforced with the larvae's excrement as it gnaws its way through the keratinous horn material. The tube provides protection to the young moth from the sun and predators until it pupates, sometimes up to 2 years later. The process of eating keratin is known as keratophagia and gives the horn moth its genus name of *Ceratophaga*.

Insects

Butterflies and moths

Butterflies and moths have **holometabolic life cycles**. This means that they have four stages in their life cycle (egg, larva, pupa and adult) and a complete metamorphosis occurs between the larval and adult forms. Females lay their eggs on an appropriate larval food plant and on emerging the caterpillars start to feed. Because they have exoskeletons, the larvae must ecdyse (moult) in order to grow. They undergo ecdysis a number of times while in larval form and each phase is called an 'instar'. Eventually the caterpillars have fattened themselves enough to pupate and attach to a branch by a silk thread and support cord.

The **process that then takes place inside the pupa is not fully understood** but it is suggested that the larvae become liquefied, supporting bundles of suspended cells. Slowly the cells that translate into the butterfly form replicate and bunch together to become the adult while the caterpillar translation cells diminish. Several weeks later an adult butterfly emerges from its cocoon. It will locate a mate and the whole cycle will start over. Some common Lowveld butterflies are shown here.

Scarlet tip

Guineafowl

Citrus swallowtail

Broad-bordered grass yellow

Foxy charaxes

Spotted joker

Acraeas

Blue pansy

White-cloaked skipper

Brown-veined white

Club-tailed charaxes

The **African monarch** caterpillar **feeds on the milkweed plant**, which is extremely toxic. It does not negatively affect the caterpillars in any way and in fact they **assimilate the poisons** from the toxic plant, becoming poisonous themselves to potential predators like birds. The larvae have voracious appetites and feed continuously until they have built up adequate food reserves to pupate into the adult butterfly form. The butterfly is attractively coloured in vivid black and orange. These colours are considered aposematic and warn predators of their toxicity and unpalatability.

The **female diadem butterfly mimics the colouration** of the African monarch to gain immunity from predation. Predators confuse the palatable diadem butterflies with the unpalatable monarch as the only difference is small black dots on the hind wing. This is known as Batesian mimicry and is only effective if the diadem population is smaller than the monarch population otherwise the toxic butterfly population would be diluted by the non-toxic one and predators would then not ignore either as a potential food source.

Insects

Bagworms

The larva of the bagworm moth constructs a case or 'bag' from plant material (including *Acacia* thorns) bound together with strong silk. The bag is portable and the bagworm takes its shelter with it while it feeds so that, should danger threaten, the bag can be pulled down over its head for protection. Some species are exceptionally cryptic and effectively mimic *Acacia* thorns. Others have obvious cases but these are not necessarily identifiable to predators as a potential meal except to one species of Ichneumonid wasp that parasitises bagworms to brood its young.

Processionary worms

The caterpillars of the processionary moth are gregarious and occur together on larval food plants. When it is necessary to transfer to a new tree, the worms will move in a procession, head to rear, following a leader and leaving a silk trail as they move. They move imperceptibly slowly and the resultant effect is that the **procession resembles a snake or a stick** and is ignored by their usual predators like cuckoos. The caterpillars pupate collectively (up to 600 together) in a purse-like 'bagnet' and emerge as small cream and brown moths.

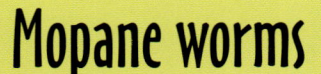

Mopane worms

The mopane worm is the larval form of the *Imbrasia bellina* moth of the emperor moth family. The mopane moth is an impressive creature – large, brown to pink in colour and adorned with lovely eyespots on its wings. The caterpillars are also attractive, being brightly coloured in black, red, white and yellow and may plague mopane trees in the summer months (see p. 269). An audible crunching can be heard as they strip whole tracts of mopane woodland of its leaves. The mopane's leaves contain high percentages of protein (12–15%) and consequently, the caterpillars assimilate this into their own bodies. Humans in rural areas may collect thousands of these worms where they occur and they are consumed as a protein supplement.

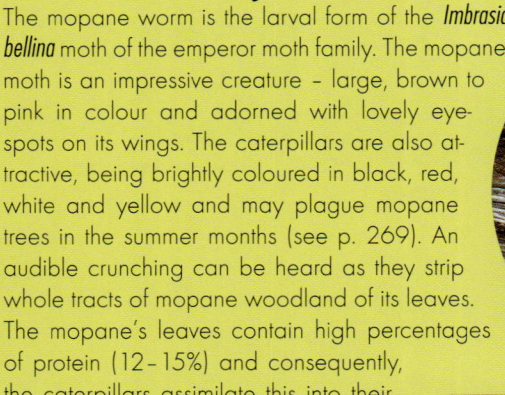

Insects

Cicadas

The high-pitched and **incessant buzzing sound** of the cicada is synonymous with early summer time in the bushveld and has led to the colloquial name for this insect, 'Christmas beetle'. The name is somewhat misleading, however, since cicadas belong to the bug family (Hemiptera) and are in fact not beetles at all.

The **calls are produced by the males** of the species and rally together all the males and females in localised areas to breed. These individuals crawl out of the soil during early November and climb up trees to ecdyse for the final time from their last nymphal instar into adults. The nymphs feed on root sap under the ground and sometimes enjoy very protracted nymphal stages. An American species is often called the 17-year bug for its 17-year incarceration as an underground nymph.

The sound produced by cicadas is produced differently to the stridulating legs or wings of grasshoppers and katydids. A cavity positioned ventrally on either side of the abdomen comprises a convex 'tymbal' (sound-producing membrane). A muscle connects to the tymbal and contracts or relaxes **to move the tymbal in and out**. The effect is similar to popping the lid of a paint tin in and out. This produces a high-frequency noise of up to 7 000 Hz. The sound is amplified by other folded membranes in the cavity and a structure called the mirror, and the sound resonates within the cavity.

Assassin bugs

The assassin bug gets its fearful name from its **powerful, recurved mouthparts** that resemble and act like the knife of an assassin and which is used to perform the same function, namely to pierce the body of its quarry. The assassin bug's proboscis can deliver an exceptionally painful bite to humans. To assist with the capture of prey, the assassin bug has legs that are especially modified for gripping firmly.

In spite of their **nasty predatory habits**, assassin bugs exhibit some family spirit. The male of some of the assassin bug species is one of few insects that exhibits **parental care of sorts** and will guard the female's eggs until they hatch and even the nymphs for a period after hatching. Nymphs will subsequently avoid danger by covering themselves cryptically with soil and other camouflaging debris.

The assassin bug is also involved in a **form of mimicry** known as Müllerian mimicry. Its black, red and yellow aposematic (warning) colouration pattern, which warns predators of its defensive weaponry, is similar to that used by the **cotton stainer bugs** to alert predators of their distastefulness. This shared aposematic pattern has the effect of transmitting the 'stay clear' message to predators once off. Assassin bugs also feed on cotton stainers and the similar colouration may allow them to get advantageously closer when hunting.

Spittlebugs

Marius Swart

Spittlebugs live on the stems of trees such as the weeping wattle or rain tree (see p. 297). The nymphs of the species have mouthparts modified for **sucking sap** which they do at remarkable speeds. Some of the moisture is excreted at almost the same rate as it is ingested and is frothed up into a bubbly body covering referred to as 'cuckoo spit'. The froth affords the nymphs protection from predators and desiccation. Often the fluid being excreted is more than that required for protection and this simply drips off the tree to provide the 'tears' or 'raindrops' that give the particular host tree its common names.

Insects

Blister beetle

The blister beetle gets its name from the symptoms of its defensive strategy, which is to release the chemical cantharidin when disturbed. Once in contact with human skin, blisters form. Cantharidin has been traditionally used in southern Africa to produce the aphrodisiac Spanish fly. The supposed effect of inducing sexual stimulation is in fact mistaken and rather an irritation of the urinary tract occurs. Blister beetles are also known as CMR beetles since their black and yellow bodies closely resemble the uniform of the Cape Mounted Rifles.

Bombardier beetles

These beetles are also known as 'bombardier ant's guest beetles'.

Bombardier beetles are notorious for their ability to **produce miniature explosions** of corrosive, volatile substances (called hydroquinones). They do this to defend themselves. The explosion originates from a specialised compartment on the end of the abdomen and can be heard as it occurs.

Bombardier beetles **associate with ants**, living amongst colonies until it is time to breed. The ants consume scented secretions produced by glands on the beetle and the bombardier beetle and their brood feed on the ant larvae.

Bombardier beetles can easily be recognised by their **broad and flat antennae**.

Ground beetles

Ground beetles are large black predatory beetles that are particularly fast, frenetic movers as they search for prey. They have sharp well-developed jaws, which are not the only weapons for which prey or enemies need to be on the look out. Ground beetles employ chemical warfare as their defence strategy and are able to squirt acid-containing liquids from glands at the rear of their abdomen quite accurately from some distance.

Insects

Tenebrionids

Tenebrionid beetles are large black beetles that are usually flightless because their wing covers (elytra) have fused. Their ground-dwelling life determines their feeding habits which are to scavenge on dead plant material or dead insects.

The **large armoured darkling beetle** is particularly conspicuous in the Lowveld in summer and can be seen scuttling between vegetation and across roads. It is easily recognised by its grooved carapace (body).

The **tok-tokkie beetle** is equally conspicuous but for a different reason. These tenebrionids get their name from the male's habit of rhythmically tapping his abdomen on the ground to attract a female mate. Should the tok-tokkie become threatened it will use thanatosis (feigning death) to dissuade its predators.

Stick insect

The stick insect is the **master of predator avoidance** and has a whole array of techniques and adaptations to its credit. Most notably the stick insect employs very effective mimicry with its whole body modified to **resemble a stick**. If for some reason it is detected by a predator where it hides motionless, then the stick insect will do one of three things. Firstly it might **startle its predator** by suddenly flashing open its streamlined wings noisily to reveal a burst of bright colour. This technique is geared to buying the insect enough time while the predator comes to its senses to use its wings to carry it to safety. The red colour will disappear when the stick insect lands and further complicates the possibility that the predator will relocate it. If this does not work, the stick insect may **play dead** (called thanatosis) as many predators will not pursue dead prey. Alternatively, stick insects are **able to shed limbs** in order to get away from danger (autotomy). The leg severs easily along an abscission plane and can be regenerated. Stick insects are the longest insects in southern Africa reaching lengths of up to 25 cm.

Insects

Grasshoppers and katydids

Grasshoppers and katydids produce their **characteristic sounds** through a process known as stridulation, whereby they rub modified body parts together and in so doing produce sound. Some species will rub the edges of the hind and forewings together while others use the leg femur to rub against a thickened surface on the forewing. The **rain locust** is a common summer presence and sounds a little like sprinklers in a garden and may appear to be pedalling while it stridulates – if you can locate one on a tree branch due to its excellent cryptic colouration and ventriloquist abilities.

The **elegant grasshopper** is common in the Lowveld as well as widespread throughout southern Africa. The bright colours that result in its name are a warning to predators to stay clear. They are able to produce frothy distasteful chemicals if this warning is not heeded.

Plain green **or brown** grasshoppers often have **red inner wings** which are flashed if the grasshopper takes to flight and act as flash colouration disappearing when the insect lands and making it hard for a predator to notice where it landed.

Katydids, like grasshoppers, make use of cryptic camouflage to conceal themselves. The leaf katydid even possesses convincing leaf-like venation on its wings and legs.

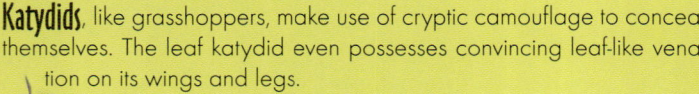

Mantids

Mantids are masters of camouflage and different types either **mimic flowers, leaves or bark** to escape detection as they remain motionless to ambush prey. Some species will even sway like leaves to make their camouflage more convincing.

The praying mantis, named so because of the poised position in which it holds its front legs, is an **effective predator** and is often attracted to lights where it is sure to locate other insects to eat. They have large, mobile heads and enormous compound eyes both of which facilitate the detection of prey and the gauging of distance to attack successfully. The legs are spiny and the coxa is enormous. These adaptations ensure that prey is grasped securely while chewing mouthparts then quickly shred the victim up. These vicious mandibles are also used to **bite off the head of the male** during copulation. This is said to facilitate mating. Eggs are laid in a white, celled purse-like cocoon called an oothica.

Insects

Dragonflies

Dragonflies are a familiar sight at most sources of water, their multicoloured bodies and powerful flight making them particularly conspicuous. Dragonflies are **accomplished hunters** and their **huge compound eyes and strong wings** equip them well for this task. Dragonflies have large wings that cannot be folded away; they hold them horizontally when at rest. This arrangement is called 'palaeopterous' and is the feature that differentiates dragonflies from damselflies, which fold their wings over their bodies when at rest. Dragonflies **can move their wings independently** and this means the insect can fly forward or backward – a useful feature when catching prey on the wing. They scoop up small insects, tadpoles or fish off the surface of water in a catching basket formed by extensions on their forward placed legs.

Male dragonflies are **exceptionally territorial** and they patrol and defend stretches of a river and mate possessively with females who enter their turf. They will guard a female after copulation and during egg-laying to ensure no other male attempts a sneaky mating as the last sperm to be received is that most likely to fertilise her eggs. Mating is an elaborate affair and in order to cling to the female while **flying in tandem**, the male must grab her behind the head with claspers on the end of his abdomen. Once the courting pair come to rest, the female will curl her abdomen into the 'wheel position' in order to make contact with a special receptacle on the male's second abdominal segment into which he would have transferred sperm. He does this to ensure his abdomen is free for clasping her. The tandem flight resumes as the female **lays her eggs by dipping them into the water** where the water-based nymphs will develop.

Dragonflies have an **incomplete life cycle** (hemi-metabolic) in which the naiads (nymphs) grow through a series of moultings (ecdysis) terminating in the adult form. No pupa phase exists. The nymphs look different to the adults and live in a different environment completely. The nymphs are aquatic while the adults are terrestrial. This reduces competition between members or stages of the same species. The nymphs breathe through their anus which is where the gills are stored. The lower lip is modified into the mask – an extendible apparatus used for grabbing their prey, which includes insect larvae, tadpoles and even small fish. The movement of **hunting dragonfly nymphs** is responsible for the interesting patterns often seen in the sand at the bottom of shallow pools or left behind when ephemeral water dries up.

Insects

Matabele ants

Matabele ants are the **main predators of termites** and perform a vital role in bushveld ecology in this respect.

They depart form their colony in **raiding parties** consisting of ants marching two to ten abreast and in columns sometimes 1,5 m long. A single scout will first locate potential food sources and then lay a pheromone trail which the raiding party then follows. Matabeles are large black ants and there are **two size morphs** (one 17 mm, the other only 10 mm) in the raiding party, both adult. This is probably an adaptation for getting into different sized spaces. The ants penetrate termite colonies from access holes created by foraging aardvarks. They will collect termites by stinging and paralysing them and then carry them off to their own colonies as food.

If disturbed, the Matabele ants break rank and **make intimidating hissing sounds**. These warnings are best heeded as they can inflict painful stings.

The Matabele ant **gets its name from the Matabele tribe** (native to Zimbabwe). This tribe is an offshoot of the Zulu people who absconded from the tyrannical Shaka Zulu. Like the ants, the people also used to attack their enemies in raiding parties and would then carry off the possessions of the subdued tribe and incorporate the survivors into their own ranks.

Mosquitoes

The *Anopheles* mosquito is the **host to the disease malaria**. It can be recognised by the abdomen which is held at a 45° angle when the mosquito is at rest. Only the female is bloodsucking (males suck nectar) and therefore is the transmitter of the disease. Mosquitoes have mouthparts that pierce and suck. An anticoagulant is released into the host to allow for a free-flow of blood while feeding. This produces the red bump and itching afterwards. Malaria produces headaches, fever, nausea and the aches, stiffness and other symptoms synonymous with flu. The disease takes between 10 days and 6 weeks to incubate in a human before symptoms are noticeable and it is treated with a 10-day course of quinine and antibiotics. Malaria can be fatal and is a major illness experienced throughout Africa.

Insects

Cocktail ants

Cocktail ants are named as such because they 'cock their tails' when threatened. They have no sting but the intimidating pose is best heeded as they contain an irritant-secreting gland instead. Cocktail ants are best known for the huge carton nests that they construct in trees, made from chewed vegetation glued together with saliva. These resourceful ants 'farm' aphids for the sweet and nutritious honeydew they provide.

Velvet ants

Velvet ants are actually the wingless females of a **wasp** species. They have a petiolar waist much like ants, hence the name. They are, however, capable of administering the **very painful stings** characteristic of wasps. Their maroon thorax and black abdomen with white dots is aposematic (warning colouration) to alert predators of their pain-inflicting capabilities.

Velvet ants are **brood parasites** to ground-nesting bees and wasps (or immature stages of flies, beetles, moths and cockroaches), laying their eggs inside the developing larvae of these insects. When the egg hatches it will consume the host larva and its own stored-up food reserves. Velvet ants can be spotted frenetically moving about on the ground searching for the nests of appropriate hosts to parasitise. The male is winged and will locate a female on the ground, lift her up into the air with him where he mates with her before dropping her off on the ground again.

Insects

Fig wasps

The fig wasp (or fig insect) of the Agaonidae family is the **smallest** of Lowveld insects. This is a necessary feature to enable it to perform its crucial role which is to **pollinate the fig's flowers**. The flowers of a fig are actually enclosed within the fig itself – a hollow, thickened stem with a tiny opening at one end surrounded by small bracts. The fig wasp is the only insect small enough to crawl through the opening of the fig and each species of fig has just one or a few species of wasp that can fit through this opening in a lock-and-key manner. The incentive for the wasps to enter the fig is to lay their eggs in the sanctity of the female flowers' ovaries. In the process they deposit pollen collected from the fig in which they themselves hatched and thereby pollinate the fig flowers.

Males are wingless and live their entire lives inside the fig receptacle. Their role is to mate with newly brooded females. This they do by boring into the female's galls before they even hatch. They then make holes in the external walls of the fig to improve the oxygen concentration inside the fig and also reduce carbon dioxide levels. This has the two-fold effect of stimulating the female wasps' development and departure from their galls and enhancing the development of the fig into a fruit (since the ovaries of the flowers have been fertilised in the process).

The **female fig wasp** departs from her natal fig via the narrow opening collecting pollen from the male flowers as she does so. When she re-enters another fig (on the same or different tree) she deposits the pollen before selecting a female flower in which to lay her eggs. This relationship is called obligatory mutualism. Both the wasp and the fig benefit but furthermore, the wasp could not reproduce without the secure location of the fig and the fig could not reproduce without the services of the wasp.

Insects

Wasps

There are a myriad wasp species in the Lowveld and each has unique and interesting breeding and survival tactics. Most species parasitise prey of one sort or another to provide food for their young on hatching.

The noisy **spider-hunting wasp** chooses a large spider like a baboon spider to paralyse and then places it in a sealed underground chamber with a single egg laid upon it. The large black and yellow **mason wasps** paralyse caterpillars and incarcerate them in carefully constructed mud chambers with their eggs. The **cuckoo wasp** takes advantage of the hard work of other wasps laying her eggs in the brood chambers of other species. The larvae then eat both the stored-up food supplies and the developing larvae of the host wasp species. This is called kleptoparasitism. **Ichneumonid wasp** females have long, threadlike ovipositors which they use to pierce the bags of bagworms and lay their eggs inside the worm or may penetrate the walls of the mason wasps huts for the same reason as the cuckoo wasp.

Paper wasps are social species that build paper-like celled nests from wood pulp and saliva. These are attached to a sheltered overhang by a tough stalk of fibre coated in ant repellent. A fertilised female or 'queen' begins the construction and is then joined by other females, which form a small colony. The females add more concentric circles of cells to the nest and lay eggs at the bottom of each cell. They defend the nest aggressively and instead of the parasitised food provisioned in other wasp species, the larvae are fed directly on a diet of chewed-up caterpillars. A division of labour occurs between the older and younger females whereby the older wasps lay eggs while the younger are tasked with hunting. Once the larvae are ready to pupate, a paper-like lid is placed over their individual cells. Newly emerged females remain with the colony and integrate into their caste roles while males do not do any work but are fed by the females until required for mating after which they perish.

Dung beetles — Insects

There are about 7 000 species of dung beetle described worldwide, of which southern Africa houses the widest variety including about **780 species**, from a few millimetres in size up to 5 cm.

Dung beetles are **astute navigators** and can detect fresh dung within seconds, having it fully colonised within minutes and completely removed within a day.

In one pile of elephant dung there could potentially be 16 000 dung beetles. It is thus important to take care not to drive over elephant dung.

Dung beetles can bury more than 1 metric ton of dung per hectare per year. In this regard they are **exceptionally important ecologically** being responsible for the removal of wastes to under the ground and consequently they destroy the eggs of internal parasites and reduce populations of pest species like flies. They simultaneously return nutrients to the soil and inadvertently facilitate the germination of seeds caught up in the dung they bury.

The most conspicuous dung beetles are the telecoprids (ball rollers). They typically **roll balls of dung for different purposes**.

A pair may roll a ball of dung together to eat. This is called a **food ball**. The male may roll a **'nuptial ball'** for a female into a hole in which they will mate and then consume the ball together. The **'brood ball'** is rolled as a larder for the dung beetle's larvae. The male will roll the brood ball upon which the female will sit to lay a single egg. This she pats down into the ball with dung giving the finished ball a pear-shaped appearance. The ball is buried and the outer shell hardens to keep the insides moist. The larva, on hatching, will begin to feed on the reserves and thereafter pupates in its underground dung-walled chamber. Up to 60 eggs can be laid per female per season meaning that the male must roll 60 of these brood balls alone.

Ball-rolling dung beetles generally **roll balls 50 times heavier** than themselves, occasionally up to 80 times.

Some dung beetles are flightless due to fused elytra (wing coverings). These populations are extremely endangered, as they cannot disperse easily. A particularly healthy population inhabits the Addo Elephant National Park.

Insects — Dung beetles

There are **four different groups** of dung beetles according to what they do with the dung they collect.

The *endocoprids* or 'dwellers' remain inside the pile of dung, living and breeding in situ.

The *paracoprids* or 'tunnellers' bury dung directly underneath the pile of dung as their larval food supplies.

The *telecoprids* or 'rollers' are the species that roll balls and take the dung away from the original site to be eaten or buried elsewhere, effectively reducing competition with the endocoprids and paracoprids. The ball is pushed with the beetle's hind legs while standing on the forelegs.

The *cleptocoprids* steal balls from the telecoprids in which to lay their own eggs.

Adult dung beetles can live for 2 years or more but they are preyed on by a **host of predators** including baboons, honey badgers, civets, hornbills, owls and rollers. Robber flies and wasps may catch the smaller species. The larvae of the beetles are primarily dug out of the ground and consumed by honey badgers but civets and mongooses may also do this.

Dung beetles are superbly **adapted for their lifestyles**. They are large and robust, often with a lovely metallic sheen. They have stout front legs which are serrated and able to cut through compacted dung. The front tibiae are broad and toothed and together with the flattened head are used for digging and raking together dung and patting it into a ball. The antennae are fanned and club-shaped and probably related to detecting and navigating to dung piles.

African dung beetles have been **translocated to Australia** in an attempt to reduce the plague-like fly population. The flies breed rapidly in the copious piles of unprocessed cow dung. Indigenous species of dung beetle cope only with smaller kangaroo droppings. The project failed initially as Australian regulations imposed sterilisation on the batches of beetles coming in from South Africa. Research eventually revealed that by doing this they were destroying a mutualistically symbiotic microscopic organism that facilitated the dung beetle's navigation ability. Once introduced without sterilisation, the African dung beetles quickly set about the task of burying the cow dung which resulted in a drastic drop in the fly population. Unfortunately in some areas the invasive cane toad has wreaked massive predation on the beetles.

Dung beetles may have **preferences for different types of dung**. Some species specifically colonise coarse elephant and rhino dung while others may utilise buffalo, zebra or smaller animals' dung. Some 72% of all dung beetle species prefer herbivore or omnivore dung to carnivore scat.

Dung beetles are scarabs, the same family as **rhino beetles**. Rhino beetles get their names from the miniature rhino horns adorning the males' heads.

Termites

Termites live in **complex colonies** that practise a caste system. This means that there are **different forms or castes**, individuals that look completely different from one another despite being genetically identical, and each caste performs a different function in a process known as **division of labour**. Each member of the colony is the offspring of one king and queen and no individual can survive independent of the colony.

Termites are herbivores and **eat dead and decaying organic material**. Because most termite species do not possess pigmented bodies, they forage under the cover of mud tunnels or consume wood from the inside out leaving a protective sheath. The biomass of termites in the bushveld exceeds that of large herbivores and they are an **ecological force** to be reckoned with and vital in the bushveld for the services they provide. Termites break down wastes and recycle material, returning nutrients to the soil. They aerate the soil through their excavating habits and add moisture and minerals to the surface soil by bringing them up from deep underground. Seeds of trees such as the weeping boerbean (*Schotia brachypetala*), jackalberry (*Diospyros mespiliformes*) and the nyala tree (*Zanthacercis zambesiacum*) (see pp. 301, 280 and 309) germinate readily on termite mounds and optimise on these fertile island habitats, which are also protected from fire due to their elevation. Once large trees become established, thickets of smaller species may form and provide attractive microhabitats to many animals, including predators like lions and leopards seeking refuges to hide their cubs.

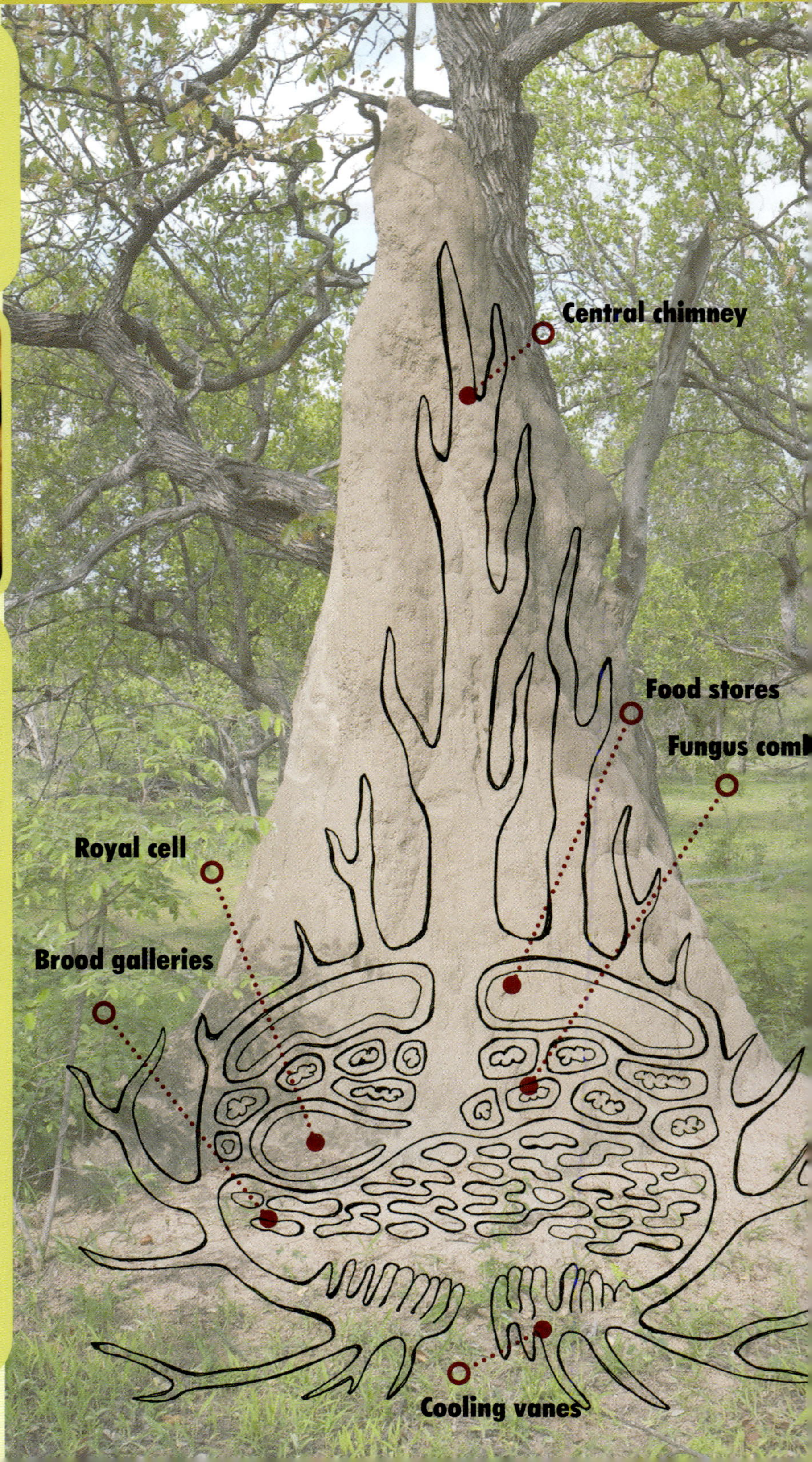

Insects — Termites

The fungus-growing termites responsible for the **enormous spired mounds** that dot the Lowveld do not possess micro-bacteria in their guts (as other animals do) to break up structural cellulose found in the cell walls of all plant material. To overcome this, they have developed a novel technique. Food collected by the workers is chewed and swallowed but once back at the colony the partially digested material is excreted in neat piles and fashioned into combs. Soon miniscule white dots appear. These are a type of fungus that the termites cultivate to the exclusion of any other kinds, which are weeded out. The workers reconsume the combs when they are fully 'digested' by the fungus and regurgitate some for the soldiers who cannot feed themselves. The fungus balls themselves are fed to the queen and nymphs directly. The **fungus gardens** are tended constantly to ensure a constant supply for the colony. Sometimes, after rain, spores of the fungus are carried outside the mound and allowed to grow there, possibly as a backup supply or to facilitate dispersal of spores. The relationship between the fungus-growing termite (*Macrotermes* spp.) and the fungus is an obligatory mutual symbiosis where both parties benefit and in fact cannot exist outside of their relationship with one another.

With the thousands of individuals in a termite colony, the body heat and carbon dioxide build-up in the mound is excessive, especially in the hotter summer months. To combat overheating, the fungus-growing termites use their impressive spired mounds to achieve a **highly effective air-conditioning system** that results in a constant temperature of 32°C. A central chimney goes up the middle of the mound and side vents radiate outwards to just below the external surface of the mound. Rising hot air is exchanged and cooled at the surface and then the heavier, cooled air is forced down alternative vents by the hot air coming up from below. The cooler oxygenated air is further cooled on vanes below the central nest cavity which are kept moist by the workers. Termites will tunnel deep down to the water table to access adequate supplies.

Fungus-growing termites (*Macrotermes natalensis*) build massive mounds that contain tons of soil which is carried particle by particle as it is displaced during foraging from below the ground and constructed over their subterranean nest site. Mounds may tower up to 2 m high and have bizarre pinnacles. Older mounds may become covered with vegetation but this does not necessarily mean they are inactive. A colony that is still active is easily identified by the presence of newly constructed clay particles on the upper reaches of the mound (especially after rain). **Colonies that have gone extinct** erode to reveal a honeycomb effect, the terminal points of the usually covered ventilation shafts, or may become totally covered by vegetation.

The primary **nest cavity** is at or just above ground level, is spherical in shape, 60–90 cm across and comprises several compartments. The thick-walled royal cell is at the heart of the nest, below the clay shelves where the fungus gardens are cultivated and just above the brood galleries where the eggs are cared for. Cooling vanes are positioned under the brood chambers, at the base of the nest cavity. Other irregular chambers are used as 'housing space' by the rest of the termites.

Termites Insects

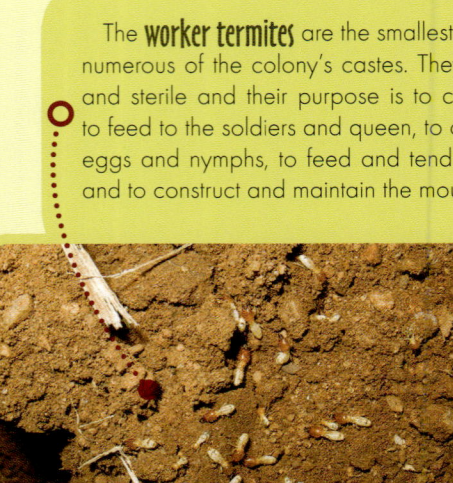

The **worker termites** are the smallest but most numerous of the colony's castes. They are blind and sterile and their purpose is to collect food to feed to the soldiers and queen, to care for the eggs and nymphs, to feed and tend the queen and to construct and maintain the mound.

The **soldiers are the colony's defence force**. They are equipped with large heads and strong weapon-like mandibles to ward off attackers and are also able to squirt an irritant which makes ants, their primary enemy, curl up. Soldiers constitute only about 5% of the colony and are reliant on the workers to feed them.

The **king and queen** are the only reproductive members of a colony of termites. Once mated for the first time, the queen's body swells to about the size of a human thumb and she simultaneously becomes permanently incarcerated in the royal cell, unable to move.

The royal chamber is located at just below ground level in the centre of the mound and is the command centre for the operation of the colony. From here the queen performs her duties as an egg-laying factory (laying about 30 000 eggs per day). The queen is long-lived, surviving for up to 50 years. Sometimes at the end of her life, the workers will lick her to death and bury her shell. A nymph will then be fed a chemical which stimulates her to become the new queen. The new queen can be told apart from the old one as she will be winged due to never having completed a nuptial flight.

The smaller king remains in the royal chamber with the queen to keep her fertilised. He may hide underneath her body if threatened.

Abandoned mounds or those compromised by **aardvark excavations** are regularly taken over by burrowing animals. These animals generally favour the raised sites termite mounds offer as this reduces the chance of flooding. The mound also provides a good insulated location for raising young. Aardvarks create **homes for up to 27 different species** (including 17 mammals). Cavities left over from the aardvarks may be enlarged or excavated according to personal specifications by mammals such as warthogs, porcupines, spotted hyenas and wild dogs. Snakes, frogs and birds like pygmy kingfishers and spotted eagle-owls make use of the holes too. The honeycomb chambers of eroded mounds are used by dwarf mongooses while rock monitors use still active mounds in which to lay their eggs.

Insects | Termites

Due to the queen's incarceration, she relies on **chemical communication** to run her kingdom. Workers exchange food, saliva and excreta with all other members of the colony and with the queen herself. In so doing crucial pheromones circulate and the queen can detect fluctuations in her colony. Stimulated by the queen, the colony will subsequently produce the appropriate counter-measures to restore equilibrium. For example, if there has been a breach in the mound and a notable amount of soldiers were destroyed, the queen will pick up this information from the workers' chemical cues when they groom her and when they feed her with food containing less of the 'soldier pheromone'. She will then begin to produce more soldier eggs. This chemistry is also responsible for the production of winged alates at the appropriate time of the year when pheromones produced by the queen are fed to the nymphs. Workers will also lay chemical scent trails to new food sources. Soldiers alert the colony of danger by tapping on the walls of the tunnels.

Termites reproduce by establishing new colonies and the vectors for this task are the **winged reproductive castes called alates**. After a good drenching summer rainfall, the workers open special guarded entrances to allow the fertile alates to exit the mound in an event known as the **'nuptial flight'**. This happens only once a year for each colony and the nuptial flight is short-lived. The female will land and flag the tip of her abdomen in a dance-like manner to release pheromones that attract a partner. As males and females from different colonies find each other and pair up, their wings are shed. On the ground, the male follows the female and in tandem the pair then searches for a new mound site where they dig shallowly under the surface of the ground and begin the production of the new colony. The female's body expands and she begins to lay eggs.

Termites are the descendents of a type of cockroach and in spite of their physical similarities they are not related to ants, which are descended from a primitive type of wasp.

When winged termites or alates disperse from their colonies after the first rains, they **provide a major food source** to myriad creatures including birds (especially raptors), lizards, snakes, frogs, mongooses, aardwolves and even people. The termites are high in nutrients.

Spiders

Broadly speaking, spiders are divided into two groups: Araneomorphs and Mygalomorphs.

Araneomorphs are predominantly **web-bound spiders** that have sideways striking chelicerae (a small pair of appendages near the spider's mouth used for grasping and biting). They have only one pair of book lungs.

Mygalomorphs are usually **ground dwellers**. They are more primitive than the Araneomorphs and have two pairs of book lungs. Their chelicerae strike downwards.

Venomous spiders

There are only **six very venomous spiders in South Africa**. The neurotoxic black and brown button spiders and the small baboon spider and the cytotoxic violin, sac and six-eyed crab spiders. Although the neurotoxic spiders may **affect heart and respiratory function** and cause symptoms like headaches, chest pain, body temperature fluctuations and anxiety, few deaths have resulted from these bites. A neurotoxic spider bite is painful. The cytotoxic spiders cause localised ulcerations and secondary necrosis of the tissue which may be accompanied with fever and result in **scarring but not death**. The six-eyed crab spider has the most virulent cytotoxic venom and damage to tissue is not localised around the site of the bite but spreads and destroys tissue throughout the body, which can potentially lead to death.

Community nest spider
Stegodyphus species

Community nest spiders make large **untidy web constructions** that superficially resemble bird's nests. Many spiders, including males, females and young, live together on the web but each may recline into a separate one of the many tunnels and chambers present. The nest is made of silk manufactured from the cribellum, which is a plate-like structure placed in front of their spinnerets. This is called cribellate silk and is woolly in texture.

Surrounding the 'house' of the web and often assisting with the suspension of it between two trees is a **multi-angled catch web**. This part of the web is designed to entrap prey, which is immediately overcome by a hunting group of the community nest spiders which drag it back to the retreat where it is shared by all the members of the nest.

Community nest spiders can be fairly large (up to 2 cm) but they are harmless Araneomorphs.

Spiders

Golden orb-web spider
Nephila species

The golden orb-web spider is an **attractive spider** with its fat black, yellow and white abdomen and long, elegant legs. It is made more conspicuous by the female's habit of constructing giant-sized (up to 1 m across) three-dimensional webs between bushveld trees in the summer, the threads of which have a golden colour to them, especially the main rope-like bridge line. She sits head-down in the middle of her web amidst bundled debris from old prey. Despite her conspicuousness, she is a shy spider and will rush off her web into vegetation if disturbed.

The obvious **golden colour of the main strands** of the orb-web are believed to act as a 'household insurance policy' to the spider by advertising its presence to large creatures such as birds so that they do not damage it by flying through inadvertently. Building such elaborate webs is energy expensive and so preventing large-scale damage to the web is important. Some theories suggest that the UV properties of the silk attract insects in the same way that the UV pathways leading to nectar in flowers do.

The **male** golden orb-web spider is **hundreds of times smaller** and less impressive than the female and he lives cautiously on the 'outskirts' of her web to avoid being eaten. When he wishes to mate with the female, he will wait until she is distracted with feeding and then very swiftly move in to deposit sperm from his sperm-laden pedipalps into her oviducts before making a hasty retreat. The female will store the sperm until she needs it and she can produce four egg sacs in a season. Once the **spiderlings** hatch, the female has nothing further to do with them and they disperse by a process known as 'ballooning' whereby they float away on an extended piece of silk.

Like insects, spiders grow by ecdysis (moulting).

Garden orb-web spider
Argiope species

The garden orb-web spider is similar-looking to the golden orb-web spider although they are not closely related. The garden orb-web spider has an abdomen with serrated edges and which is banded in yellow and black. The garden orb-web spider also makes an enormous web but this lacks the golden threads of the golden orb-web. Instead, the garden orb produces a **zigzagged stabilimentum** down the centre of her web. This is white in colour and is produced from specialised silk. The stabilimentum is thought to act as a stabiliser to the web and an advertisement to large creatures so that they do not damage her construction.

Spiders

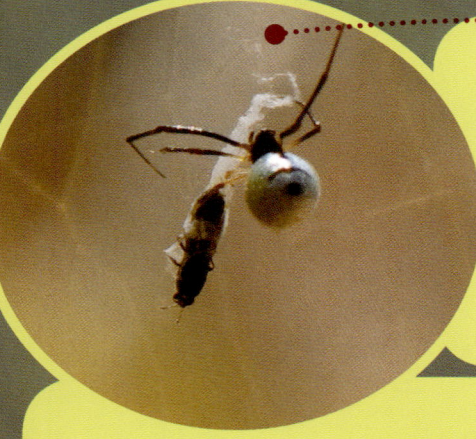

Dewdrop spider
Argyrodes species

Dewdrop spiders are kleptoparasites and **scavenge or steal the remains of food** items off the webs of orb-web spiders. They are tiny silver spiders that resemble drops of dew (or mercury) on the web. Dewdrop spiders belong to the same family (Theridiidae) as the venomous black button spider.

Tropical tent spider
Cyrtophora species

The tropical tent spider weaves a **unique web** easily noticed early on summer mornings when they are dusted with dew. A seemingly random tangle of threads creates a globe-like web which provides the knock-down lines. In the centre of the globe is a horizontal layer of web pinched up in the middle to **resemble a pitched tent**. The spider hangs upside down (known as negative geotaxis) beneath this 'tent-like trampoline' layer waiting for insects to become tangled in the knockdown lines and land above it. Biting through the horizontal layer, the spider subdues its prey.

Kite spider
Gasteracantha species

The kite spider is a common and noticeable spider for its habit of building fine-stranded webs between two trees and then suspending itself in the centre of its almost invisible web like a kite suspended in the sky. True to its name, the kite spider **bears bright red and yellow colours** and its abdomen is appropriately decorated with spiny protrusions.

Funnel-web spider
Olorunia species

The funnel-web spider builds a mat of silk (50 cm wide) flat on the grass in which to catch insects. It **hides itself away in an open-ended funnel** that leads onto the ground and into the safety of a clump of grass or rock should it need to escape. The webs are conspicuous early in the morning when the sun highlights dew that has collected upon the webs. The spider rushes out of her funnel to collect entrapped prey but returns to the safety of the funnel chamber to feed. Funnel-web spiders have long and obvious spinnerets protruding from the rear of the abdomen.

Spiders

Bark spider
Caerostris species

The bark spider is a **superb mimic** spending the daylight hours pressed up against the trunk of a tree pretending to be a piece of bark. This it achieves by pulling its tell-tale spider legs in tight next to its rough, uneven body and then just sitting still. Each evening the bark spider gets active and to capture its dinner it constructs a large orb web which it spans between two trees, sometimes 2 m apart. In the morning, the web is dismantled bar the bridge line and the silk is reabsorbed so as not to waste energy.

Baboon spider
Family Theraphosidae

The baboon spiders (of which there are many species) are Mygalomorphs which **live underground** in silk-lined burrows that afford them protection from the heat of day. They are nocturnal, rising to the entrance of their burrows at night where they patiently sit and wait to ambush prey. A rim of web spreads out from the lip of the burrow entrance and alerts the spider to the approach of prey. Baboon spiders **eat predominantly insects** but will overpower and consume other spiders, solifugids, scorpions, millipedes, reptiles, amphibians and snails. Baboon spiders never stray far from the safety of their burrows unless in search of a mate. In this regard the male must be careful and he taps out a **Morse-code message** in vibrations on the silk at the entrance of a female's burrow so that she does not deem him a meal.

Baboon spiders come in brown, grey, yellow and black. They are large (up to 9 cm) and very hairy which in part has led to their name. The pads on the spider's tarsi (end of leg) are said to **resemble in colour and texture that of a baboon's foot pads**. The last two segments on the spider's leg are also said to resemble a baboon's finger.

Baboon spiders defend themselves with a **powerful and painful bite** from their large fangs (on the chelicerae). If harassed, a baboon spider may rear up lifting its forelegs into the air to show its aggression. In this position the black underparts and red hairs on the chelicerae become obvious and serve as a form of startle behaviour to bide time for the spider while the predator comes to its senses from the surprise. If removed from the safety of their burrows, adult baboon spiders cannot dig another one as they lack a rastellum (the group of teeth on the head of the chelicerae) that are present in the young. If a baboon spider loses a limb, it can replace that. This it does at the next moult though the new limb will initially be a bit skinnier than the last.

A baboon spider lives for up to 25 years.

Other invertebrates

Solifugid

A solifugid or red roman or sun spider as they are also called, is not a true spider as it **lacks both venom glands and spinnerets**. It is an arachnid, however, and is able to administer a painful bite. This is understandable when one considers that a third of its body length comprises head and jaws!

The solifugid **navigates** using tactile stimuli. The pedipalps are extended ahead of the creature as it moves to detect prey. The small eyes are not much use for this. The pedipalps also have adhesive pads to enable the solifugid to climb vertical faces. It may grab prey, cup the pedipalps to drink water or seek out sensitive points of attack on an intruder with these sensory appendages. A solifugid also has specialised **sensory organs** on the 'soles' of its rear legs.

These large eight-legged invertebrates are heavy bodied but are light on their feet, qualifying as one of the **swiftest terrestrial invertebrates** in southern Africa. They are active predators and wander widely searching for prey, which includes anything they can overcome such as insects, small reptiles, spiders and scorpions. Prey is dispatched with the modified jaws (chelicerae). Each of the two chitinous finger-like jaws has two movable parts. These are curved, pointed and toothed or bristled and effectively secure and shred the hapless victim until it is liquidised sufficiently to ingest.

Being so **aggressive** and well equipped with **powerful jaws** makes courtship a risky business for the male. He will only succeed if he can induce a trance on the female. He may stroke her gently to achieve this or simply stun her with an all-out rush. Once she is calm the male quickly deposits his sperm on the ground. Using his jaws, he then opens the female's genital orifice and inserts the sperm with his pedipalps before making a quick exit.

Other invertebrates

Millipedes

The name 'millipede' literally means 'a thousand legs' but although this may seem like the case when it moves, millipedes have nowhere near as many legs. They do, however, have two pairs of legs per segment of the cylindrical body. These work in waves with some legs performing a pushing stroke while others ready themselves for the next stroke. The body is strong, reinforced with a **calcareous shell** and **adapted to pushing through humus** and soil, powered by the wave-like movements of the legs. The strong outer shell also helps protect it from ants. Millipedes are **detritivores** and play an important ecological role in consuming rotting vegetation and fungi. Food is first prepped with an oral secretion before being chewed. It locates food (as well as mates and enemies) by tapping its antennae on the ground ahead of itself while it moves around slowly. When threatened the millipede coils its body up to protect its vulnerable underside. It can also **secrete cyanide** and other chemicals, which deter some potential predators from eating it (but not civets or scorpions!). Millipedes are commonly called *shongololos* in South Africa, derived from the Zulu name for the creature.

Although at first glance **centipedes** seem similar to millipedes, they differ significantly in both body structure and lifestyle. A centipede has a brightly coloured (aposematic) flattened body with only one pair of legs per segment and it moves with a rapid serpentine motion. It is a carnivore and is equipped with venomous claws used to grip and kill prey like earthworms and snails, but also frogs, snakes, mice and birds. The terminal pair of legs is enlarged to perform sensory functions but is also able to pinch in defence. Centipedes can also flick toxic substances to defend themselves.

African giant land snail
Achatina achatina

The African giant land snail is the **largest snail** in the Lowveld and in fact in the world (that we know of). It grows to an average size of about 20 cm and is commonly seen during the wet season. Because snails have soft bodies they require moist habitats and conditions to proliferate and as a rule they move around at night to avoid desiccation, hiding in damp vegetation during the day. The large and sometimes quite colourful shell is borne on a large, muscular foot that actuates the snail's locomotion through undulating contractions. The specialised foot is well supplied with mucus, which lubricates it against the substrate.

Unlike its vegetarian cousins, the African giant land snail is a **scavenger** and eats carrion, providing a useful ecological 'clean-up' service. Food is scraped up with a unique mouth apparatus known as a radula. This is a conveyor-like ribbon membrane with backwards facing teeth for rasping. Ecologically the land snail also provides food to myriad creatures including reptiles, birds and mammals. Giant land snails are sought after by humans for their value as food and have even been exported to other countries for use as escargot.

Snails exhibit a relatively unique configuration known as **torsion**. This is where the anterior and posterior ends of its body are contorted to the point where head and anus are positioned at the same end. This arrangement means that the mantle cavity (a space into which the anus opens) now sits above the head and allows for the head to be retracted into the mantle cavity (and hence shell) when protection is required. To prevent fouling of the mantle cavity, water is always brought in on the left-hand side and washed out on the right-hand side, taking with it anal wastes. The giant land snail is a **hermaphrodite** meaning that one individual contains both the male and female reproductive organs. Two snails do still exchange sperm bundles in order to cross-fertilise each other. They then lay eggs which hatch as miniatures of the adults.

Scorpions — Other invertebrates

Scorpions are unmistakable arachnids (eight legs) with their **large pincers and sting-bearing tails**. But the size of each of these features differs according to their lifestyles and how venomous they are. The family Scorpionidae has large pincers and small stings (telsons). They rely mostly on their pincers to catch their prey and hence their large size. Since the sting is of secondary importance, these scorpions do not produce very toxic venoms. The Buthidae family has small pincers and large stings. These scorpions rely on their venomous injections to overcome their prey and therefore have large telsons which produce copious quantities of often noxious venom. The pincers are of less importance so they are small. The sting of a Buthidae scorpion is exceptionally painful to humans and some members of this family (especially the *Parabuthus* genus) produce symptoms that require medical intervention.

The **venom of a scorpion is the strongest known**. It is produced in venom glands and can be injected via the telson (sting) to subdue prey or enemies at will. Sometimes scorpions will sting their mates to calm them down during courtship (they are immune to their own venom). Scorpions can regulate the amount of venom they inject through muscular contractions. The venom is neurotoxic and sometimes specifically designed to target particular animal species.

Scorpions are remarkable creatures and through an **array of adaptations** are able to inhabit a diversity of habitats and temperature extremes and thrive as successful predators. They are masters at making use of microhabitats such as burrows and crevices in and under rocks and bark, which shields them from the desiccating (or freezing cold) elements. They are also masters of ambushing and overpowering creatures often superior to them in size including insects, spiders, other scorpions and in larger species small vertebrates, snails, reptiles, mammals and amphibians.

Scorpions have **poor eyesight** but the eyes they do have can detect light and gauge depth. Their pedipalps are modified at the terminal points into pincers that are used in defence, to catch food, to seize objects and to facilitate courtship. A scorpion may have one of many types of leg modifications, from stiff spines which aid in traction during burrowing, to arched claws which enable them to traverse surfaces upside-down. Scorpions are talented navigators and are said to be able to orientate themselves in a number of ways, including the use of wind direction, scent trails, landmarks and other visual objects and possibly even the stars.

Other invertebrates

Scorpions

When it comes to **breeding**, scorpions certainly pull out the stops as far as invertebrates go. The male will use his sensory pectines to locate a female who will have left a pheromone trail for him to follow. He will then communicate with her via tapped out vibrations that he is not a potential meal before moving closer and linking pincers with her. The male and female then **engage in an apparent 'dance'** during which time they may move over large areas (up to 25 m) until the male locates a suitable surface on which to deposit his spermatophore. The spermatophore is a sealed capsule of sperm with a hook on the upper side. The male will carefully glide the female over the site until she is in the correct position for the spermatophore to connect with her genital opening at which point he may lift and drop her upon it using her weight to trigger the release of the sperm.

In spite of their formidable adaptations and defences, **scorpions are food themselves** to a variety of creatures including hornbills, owls, frogs, snakes, some bats, monitor and other large lizards, centipedes, solifugids, spiders, baboons, honey badgers and mongooses. Baboons and solifugids rid the scorpion of its dangerous sting before eating it while centipedes attack them with their own toxic venom.

Scorpions spend **most of their time totally inactive**. This is a survival trait which means that they are able to lower their metabolic rate and go unfed for protracted periods while escaping unfavourable conditions above ground.

Young scorpions are born alive after 2 – 18 months of gestation (longer than large mammals!). Some species have eggs that **hatch inside the mother's body** before emerging (ovoviviparous) while others actually have a form of placental development (viviparous), an extremely unusual trait outside of the mammal class. The mother collects the young (one by one) as they emerge by stilting (body raised and tail arched) and positions her legs to form a basket. From here the **grub-like young climb onto the mother's back** where they will remain and be cared for until their first moult (ecdysis). Scorpions may live for up to 30 years although 10 years is more usual.

The pectines are a **unique comb-like apparatus** found beneath the scorpion. They are sensory organs that help the scorpion to read its environment by picking up clues about temperature, humidity and substrate. Scorpions also use their pectines to follow pheromone trails left by females. Aside from the information gathered this way, scorpions have an acute sense of touch. They **detect vibrations** through organs on their tarsi (feet) and feel the touch of an object against them via microscopic slit organs on the legs. Hairs on the body help to decipher both physical and chemical stimuli.

Scorpions, like other invertebrates, must **shed their protective exoskeleton** to accommodate body growth. Immediately after ecdysis (moulting) scorpions lack the fluorescence they usually have under UV light.

Contrary to popular belief, scorpions do **produce sound**. They do this by stridulating (rubbing body parts together). Some species have special rough surfaces on the tail which are rubbed with the sting to produce clicking noises believed to startle predators. Other species rub bristles on the mouthparts over special ridges on the body.

Plants

For some, identifying plants is easy and a delight, for others it is a nemesis. For the most part however, naturalists of all descriptions show a great interest in the cultural, medicinal and ecological uses of trees and other plants once the task of identifying them has been conquered. Since there are innumerable guidebooks available to describe in minute detail the 700-800 odd tree species in the Lowveld, this chapter focuses on the 'meaty' interpretative information on the most popular trees and shrubs. Working around a central definitive photograph of each showcased species, close-up images and blocked text packages offer the most interesting scoop on the different parts of the plant. Where it has been relevant to do so, hints for easy recognition have been provided. Also included in this section is a mosaic of images and short write-ups on the common grasses, wildflowers and other small plants found in the Lowveld.

Icons

Leaf type
- Scale-like
- Simple
- Imparipinnate
- Paripinnate
- Bipinnate
- Bilobed
- Bifoliolate
- Trifoliolate
- Palmately compound

Leaf arrangement
- Alternate
- Tufted
- Opposite
- Whorled

Duration
- Evergreen
- Deciduous
- Semi-deciduous

Leaf margin
- Entire
- Serrated, toothed, scalloped

Trees

- Knob thorn • *Acacia nigrescens*, page 252
- Fever tree • *Acacia xanthophloea*, page 254
- Umbrella thorn • *Acacia tortilis*, page 256
- River thorn (robust thorn) • *Acacia robusta* subsp. *clavigera*, page 258
- Torchwood (green thorn) • *Balanites maughamii*, page 259
- Baobab • *Adansonia digitata*, page 260
- Tree wisteria • *Bolusanthus speciosus*, page 263
- Shepherd's tree • *Boscia albitrunca*, page 264
- Velvet corkwood • *Commiphora mollis*, page 266
- Matumi • *Breonadia salicina*, page 267
- Sjambok pod (long-tail cassia) • *Cassia abbreviata* subsp. *beareana*, page 268
- Mopane • *Colophospermum mopane*, page 269
- Red bushwillow • *Combretum apiculatum*, page 272
- Russet bushwillow • *Combretum hereroense*, page 273
- Leadwood • *Combretum imberbe*, page 274
- Large fever-berry • *Croton megalobotrys*, page 276
- Zebrawood • *Dalbergia melanoxylon*, page 277
- Sickle bush • *Dichrostachys cinerea*, page 278
- Jackal-berry • *Diospyros mespiliformis*, page 280
- Magic guarri • *Euclea divinorum*, page 282
- Rubber euphorbia • *Euphorbia tirucalli*, page 284
- Large-leaved rock fig • *Ficus abutilifolia*, page 285
- Sycamore fig • *Ficus sycomorus*, page 286
- Bushveld gardenia • *Gardenia volkensii*, page 287
- Sandpaper raisin • *Grewia flavescens*, page 288
- Apple-leaf • *Philenoptera violacea*, page 289
- Red spike-thorn • *Gymnosporia senegalensis*, page 290
- Common spike-thorn • *Gymnosporia buxifolia*, page 291

Sausage tree • *Kigelia africana*, page 292
False marula • *Lannea schweinfurthii*, page 294
Cork bush • *Mundulea sericea*, page 295
Jacket plum • *Pappea capensis*, page 296
African weeping-wattle • *Peltophorum africanum*, page 297
Wild date palm • *Phoenix reclinata*, page 298
Round-leaved teak • *Pterocarpus rotundifolius*, page 300
Weeping boer-bean • *Schotia brachypetala*, page 301
Marula • *Sclerocarya birrea*, page 302
Tamboti • *Spirostachys africana*, page 304
Black monkey-orange • *Strychnos madagascariensis*, page 306
Common star-chestnut • *Sterculia rogersii*, page 307
Silver cluster-leaf • *Terminalia sericea*, page 308
Nyala tree • *Xanthocercis zambesiaca*, page 310
Buffalo-thorn • *Ziziphus mucronata*, page 311

Grasses

Foxtail (blue) buffalo grass • *Cenchrus ciliaris*, page 314
Narrow-leaved turpentine grass • *Cymbopogon plurinodis*, page 314
Saw-tooth love grass • *Eragrostis superba*, page 314
Carrot seed • *Tragus berteronianus*, page 315
Natal red top • *Melinis repens*, page 315
Tassel three-awn • *Aristida congesta* subsp. *congesta*, page 316
Spear grass • *Heteropogon contortus*, page 316
Blue-seed grass • *Tricholaena monachne*, page 317
Eragrostis species, page 317
Guinea grass • *Panicum maximum*, page 318
Red grass • *Themeda triandra*, page 318
Herringbone • *Pogonarthria squarrosa*, page 319
Gum grass • *Eragrostis gummiflua*, page 319
Common reed • *Phragmites australis*, page 319

Small plants and wild flowers

Monkey or baboon's tail (black stick lily) • *Xerophyta retinervis*, page 320
Mother-in-law's tongue • *Sansevieria aethiopica*, page 320
Wild basil (wild anaseed) • *Ocimum canum (americanum)*, page 321
Leopard orchid • *Ansellia gigantea*, page 321
Poison apple • *Solanum panduriforme*, page 322
Wild sesame • *Sesamum triphyllum*, page 322
Wild foxglove • *Ceratotheca triloba*, page 322
Devil's thorn • *Dicerocaryum eriocarpum*, page 323
Cape honeysuckle • *Tecomaria capensis*, page 323
Mistletoe • *Plicosepalus kalachariensis*, page 323
Wild dagga • *Leonotis leonurus*, page 324
Lion's eye • *Tricliceras mossambicense*, page 324
Impala lily • *Adenium multiflorum*, page 324
Ruby gnidia • *Gnidia rubescens*, page 325
Purple pan weed • *Sphaeranthus incisus*, page 325
Red-star zinnia • *Zinnia peruviana*, page 325
Morning glory • *Ipomoea* species, page 325
Flame lily • *Gloriosa superba*, page 326
Abutilon angulatum, page 326
Flannel weed • *Sida cordifolia*, page 327
Blue water-lily • *Nymphae nouchali*, page 327
Cornflower vernonia • *Vernonia glabra*, page 328
Caterpillar bush • *Ormocarpum tricarpum*, page 328
String-of-stars • *Helitropium steudneri*, page 328
Wild melon • *Lagenaria sphaerica*, page 329
Hibiscus • *Hibiscus* species, page 329
Crinum (vlei) lily • *Crinum delagoense*, page 329
Potato bush • *Phyllanthus reticulates*, page 329
White-berry bush • *Flueggea virosa*, page 330
Justicea • *Justicea* species, page 330
African wild violet • *Aptosimum lineare*, page 330
Dwarf papyrus • *Cyperus papyrus*, page 330
Num-num • *Carissa* species, page 331

Knob thorn
Acacia nigrescens

The **pods** of the knob thorn are typical bean-like pods that hang in clusters on the tree. They are indehiscent (do not split open). Pods are also nutrient rich and are eaten by giraffe.

The knob thorn **gets its name** from the woody knobs that cover the stems of younger plants and the younger branches of older trees. These protrusions are thorn-tipped and used by the tree as defence against herbivores.

A **hemi-parasitic mistletoe** grows in the canopy of knob thorn trees. Sometimes elephants push the knob thorn over to get to the mistletoe that produces nectar-rich flowers and sticky fruit. The flowers and fruits are also relished by birds. The fruit digests in their guts rapidly and then the seed is regurgitated and wiped onto the branches of a tree where they germinate.

The **leaves** of the knob thorn have the largest leaflets of all the *Acacias*. The pinnules (smallest leaf unit) occur in pairs that look like small butterflies. Even the leaves have small hooked thorns on them to deter herbivores.

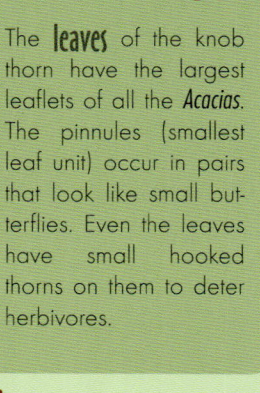

The **knobs** on the knob thorn are reputed to have several uses, from pain relief to eye infections and breast enhancement formulas to aphrodisiacs. In all cases the knobs are powdered.

The **bark** of older trees tends to be dark and fissured while the bark of younger trees has a yellowish colour and is flakier. The bark is used for tanning leather as it contains 15% tannin. The Australian relatives to the African *Acacias*, the wattles, are commercially the best for tanning.

Because knob thorns grow along rivers and because they grow tall, they are often chosen by white-backed vultures as **nesting sites**. These vultures like to nest high up and the fact that knob thorns are thorny adds an element of protection to the nests.

The **inner bark** of the knob thorn braids into a good twine.

The **wood** of a knob thorn is exceptionally hard and was used extensively for mine props and railway sleepers in the past. Walking sticks and knobkerries (traditional clubs) are made from the wood nowadays. Although hard, the knob thorn, like other *Acacias*, is susceptible to woodborers if the bark gets damaged. These are the grubs of longhorn beetles which eat the wood and bury themselves in tunnels in the wood. They have special digestive enzymes that allow for the breakdown of cellulose.

Knob thorn
Acacia nigrescens

18 m

Knob thorn trees **grow very tall** and the poles from these trees are often planted as lightning conductors.

The knob thorn is a firm **favourite of the giraffe** and its diet comprises 40% knob thorn throughout the year and during the short flowering season, a quarter of the giraffe's food intake. Knob thorn trees often take on a characteristic hourglass shape due to browsing pressure from giraffe.

Acacias are highly nutritious trees. One reason for this is because of a symbiotic relationship that the tree enjoys with bacteria. Trees generally cannot absorb atmospheric nitrogen and must rely on decomposition and various processes in the soil (including lightning strikes) to convert pure nitrogen into absorbable nitrogen compounds like nitrates or ammonia. In nodules on the roots of leguminous plants (pea-like pod-bearing plants) such as *Acacias*, there are **nitrogen-fixing bacteria** called rhizobium which convert nitrogen directly into an absorbable compound for the tree roots to absorb. In return the bacteria have a safe and appropriate habitat in the nodules they form on the roots of the *Acacia*. Because of the high fertility of soils under trees like the knob thorn, one often finds stands of nutritious grasses like guinea grass, *Panicum maximum* (see p. 318) growing under the trees.

The knob thorn has **paired hooked thorns** all over the branches of the tree. These are produced to deter herbivores. They do not prevent antelope from feeding on the trees as all antelope have adaptations to overcome the thorny obstacles, but they do limit the feeding time on any given tree. *Acacias* are considered 'fine-leaved trees' and usually occur lower down on the clay soils of the catena. Their counterparts, the 'broad-leaved trees' of the poorer sandy soils up the slope use chemical defences which are more effective against insects, their primary predators. Thorns are more effective against herbivores, fine-leaved trees' primary enemy. Because they grow in fertile soils, fine-leaved trees can also afford more losses and replace leaves easier than broad-leaved ones.

Giraffe (see p. 64) are believed to be the **mammal pollinator of the knob thorn tree**. This is unique as no other large mammal pollinators of plants are known. The job usually belongs to the likes of birds, bees and bats. The knob thorn produces profuse creamy-yellow flowers at the end of the dry season (usually around August) a veritable feast for giraffe that by this time are confined to river courses to seek nutritious food. At this time no other trees are flowering and there are few insects around. While feeding on the trees, the giraffe becomes dusted with pollen on its head and neck. Vast quantities stick to the giraffe's fur, which it then deposits on the next tree it visits. Although it would seem costly to the tree that the giraffe is eating all its flowers, the knob thorn actually produces sterile flowers that dilutes the amount of reproductive flowers that the giraffe eats. The flowering season is also short and giraffe cannot eat all the flowers in this time. Where insect pollinators may have the advantage of being able to fly and widely disperse the pollen they collect, giraffe remarkably can cover 16 km per day between stands of flowering knob thorns visiting many different trees per hour.

Knob thorns **grow on fertile alluvial** soils and the leaves are very nutritious as a result. They are favoured by elephants and giraffe but also eaten by other browsers like kudu. Despite the knobs on the trunk, elephants easily strip bark off knob thorns at the end of winter. They do this to access the nutritious inner bark. The cambium (vascular tissue) houses the nutrients and moisture being pumped up to the canopy for the early flowering season. Knob thorns are the first to flower at the end of winter, offering a feast to animals like giraffe during hard times. The tree has shallow roots so they are easily pushed over in winter by elephants keen for those same nutrients in storage in the roots. Once pushed over the trees do not grow again. This is not as destructive as it seems. In spring, grasses grow up through the thorny canopy now lying on the ground and create a tangled microhabitat that is subsequently used by smaller creatures looking for shelter. These might include rodents, small birds like blue waxbills, and scrub hares.

Fever tree
Acacia xanthophloea

The **leaves** are characteristically (for *Acacias*) twice compound but are particularly feathery in nature. The leaves and young branches are eaten by particularly giraffe and elephant.

The fever tree is a member of the *Acacia* family and like all other southern African members of the family bears **defensive thorns** (modified stipules). The fever tree's thorns are long and white. They may vary from 10-85 mm in length and occur in pairs growing from a common base. The thorns help deter browsers from browsing excessively on the nutritious leaves.

The fever tree is aptly named for its **yellow-green bark** – peeling and powdery to touch, it certainly makes the tree look ill. Remarkably, the bark is in fact used to treat fevers and even sore eyes. The fever tree is popular in gardens for its strange appearance and its habit of growing quickly (provided it is planted in clay soil).

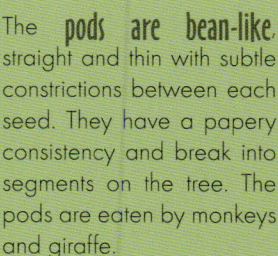

The **pods are bean-like**, straight and thin with subtle constrictions between each seed. They have a papery consistency and break into segments on the tree. The pods are eaten by monkeys and giraffe.

The fever tree has **hard, heavy wood** but in spite of these traits is regularly damaged by a large borer beetle. Sometimes unspoiled sections of wood can be used as general-purpose timber but care should be taken, as these are prone to cracking.

The **flowers** of the fever tree are typically *Acacia*-like. The tree bears small (1 cm diameter) yellow pom-pom balls close to the branches in the axils of the thorns. The flowers are sweet-scented and attract butterflies and vervet monkeys.

Fever tree
Acacia xanthophloea

10–30 m

Branches that have died turn black and these contrast sharply with the rest of the insipid-coloured tree. Often these dead branches are in fact **sacrificial branches** – lower lying limbs in which the tree deposits wastes and toxins until the dump site eventually dies from the noxious accumulation. Because the branch is low down on the tree and not as crucial for photosynthesis as the higher ones, the fever tree can afford to 'sacrifice' the limb for the sake of getting rid of its wastes.

Early pioneers named the fever tree such because they associated it with the **acquisition of malaria**. The tree of course was not making people sick but rather the *Anopheles* mosquito which breeds in the same habitat where fever trees grow – wet, swampy areas.

The fever tree was immortalised by **Rudyard Kipling** in his children's story *The Elephant's Child*. Here he describes the 'Great grey-green greasy Limpopo River all set about with fever trees'. Indeed the northern reaches of the Lowveld that abut the Limpopo floodplain are privy to magnificent fever tree forests.

The height of the fever tree as well as its thorny defence makes it a **good nesting tree** for birds. **Red-billed buffalo weavers** especially favour this tree. The buffalo weavers are useful in indicating direction as they tend to build on the north-western side of the tree.

Primates such as bushbabies and monkeys may also visit fever trees to harvest the **gum** that oozes from injuries on the tree.

Umbrella thorn
Acacia tortilis

The **leaves** of this tree are very nutritious because they grow in fertile clay soils at the bottom of the catena. The tree is thus equipped with thorns to deter herbivores from over-utilising the leaves. Thorns do not prevent animals from browsing the tree but they do reduce the amount of leaves that any individual herbivore will eat before moving on to another tree. Because they grow in fertile soils, *Acacia* trees generally are able to replace lost leaves more readily than trees growing on sandy soils that must rely on chemical defences to deter herbivores. Thorns are modified leaves (or stipules) and the umbrella thorn employs both small hooked thorns (called prickles) and large straight thorns arranged in pairs to deter herbivores.

The umbrella thorn with its **characteristic umbrella-shaped canopy** is an icon of the southern African bushveld.

Acacia **means thorn**. The word is derived from the Greek word 'akis' meaning 'a point' or 'a sharp point'.

The **wood** of the *Acacias* is hard and utilised in the production of curios, an entrepreneurial industry that has emerged in communities as a result of tourism. Sometimes large trees are cut down indiscriminately to make into larger curios and this is not a sustainable practice.

The **wood** of the umbrella thorn is very hard but is susceptible to infestations of the grubs of longhorn beetles, known as *mabungu* grubs. These grubs are large (measuring about 1,5 × 6 cm) and are considered a delicacy by humans and are eaten for their protein. Unfortunately they bore quite deep holes into the tree trunk, metabolising the wood and cellulose with special enzymes and weakening the stem. It is thought that this may be the reason why the trees usually break when being pushed over by elephants.

Umbrella thorns have an **extensive root system** which may be another reason they do not always just pull free from the soil at root level when elephants push them over. Elephants seek out umbrella thorn roots to access the nutrients and water in them, especially during the dry season. The tree is useful in stabilising damaged and eroded areas because of its spreading roots.

The **pods** of the umbrella thorn are **contorted** and the species name *tortilis* refers to this characteristic trait. These are high in protein (19%) and are eagerly browsed by giraffe but also by antelope, monkeys and baboons.

Umbrella thorn
Acacia tortilis

18 m

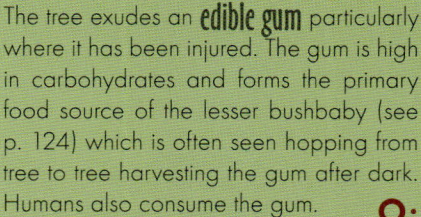

The tree exudes an **edible gum** particularly where it has been injured. The gum is high in carbohydrates and forms the primary food source of the lesser bushbaby (see p. 124) which is often seen hopping from tree to tree harvesting the gum after dark. Humans also consume the gum.

The umbrella thorn (and other *Acacias*) uses a survival tactic called **allelopathy**. This is where the tree will release a chemical into the soil that prevents the germination of other seeds under the tree, including its own. This is to eliminate competition for growth space and conditions.

The **leaves** of the umbrella thorn are unmistakable as they are the smallest of all the *Acacias* (3 cm long) with tiny feathery pinnules (smallest leaf unit).

The **bark** forms deep fissures in older trees and is red-brown in young trees and covered in white marks. Elephants eagerly strip the bark of the trees along the full length of the trunk often causing the trees to die. The inner bark or cambium contains the vascular tissue responsible for transporting nutrients and water between the roots and leaves. A strong rope can be made from this inner bark.

The **flowers** of the umbrella thorn are the small creamy balls characteristic of *Acacia* species. They are sweet-scented, rich in pollen and relished by monkeys and baboons.

It is common to find **community nest spiders** in umbrella thorns (see p. 242).

The umbrella thorn is a species that readily becomes a **native encroacher** in over-utilised areas and is often found growing in impenetrable thickets alongside those of sickle bush (see p. 278) to the exclusion of other plants including grasses. The wood is commonly used as a source of fuel, particularly after bush-clearing operations. It is often made into charcoal.

Mike Amm

River thorn (robust thorn)
Acacia robusta subsp. *clavigera*

25 m

Like other *Acacias* the river thorn is equipped with defensive weaponry in the form of **long thorns** (modified stipules) that deter herbivores from spending protracted periods of time feeding off its nutritious leaves. Like other *Acacias*, the river thorn enjoys clay soils particularly along rivers and drainage lines as these soils are fertile and as a result the tree produces abundant and nutritious leaves. In the case of the river thorn, its paired white thorns may be excessively long (sometimes reaching 10 or 15 cm in length) while smaller, underdeveloped, paired thorns (of only 5 mm) may occur on the same branch.

The river thorn is conspicuous by its lovely **bright green foliage** when it flushes early in spring and by its well-built upward reaching branches and dense canopy which give it a generally robust appearance (as its specific name *robusta* suggests).

The **leaves** of the river thorn are dark green in colour, well formed and closely ranked, having the 'robust' appearance of the rest of the tree. They are not as fine and feathery as many other *Acacia* species. The leaves **cluster on spiky cushions at the base of the thorns** (as do the round creamy flowers) and this feature helps with identification. The river thorn is readily browsed by animals like kudu and nyala.

The **bark** of the river thorn is similar to many other *Acacias*, being dark, rough and fissured on older parts of the stem (younger branches are smoother). The river thorn shows a **reddish colouration in the cracks**. The bark is used for tanning leather. The inner part of the bark is used to make twine.

The **wood** of the river thorn is relatively heavy but little used, except as fuel. It does support the grubs of wood-borer (or longhorn) beetles, known as *mabungu* grubs. These are edible and an important source of protein to some rural people.

The river thorn has narrow linear **pods** that are slightly sickle-shaped and woody in texture.

258

Torchwood (green thorn)
Balanites maughamii

10–20 m

The torchwood tree gets its common name from its **seeds** which yield excellent oil, much like olive oil but without colour or flavour. This oil is highly flammable, igniting into brilliant flames, hence the traditional use of dried torchwood kernels as torches.

Young torchwoods often grow around older torchwood trees. These new shoots look haphazard giving the older tree a messy appearance. **Young branches grow in a zigzag fashion.** These two features can help with identification.

Sangomas (traditional healers) concoct a mixture including the roots and bark of the torchwood tree as a potion to keep evil spirits at bay. The liquid is tossed over the roof of an abode ensuring the entrance becomes doused in the ritual. This is performed three times a day after the frothy scum on the potion has first been licked.

The tree bears pairs of round **grey-green leaflets** that are finely hairy to touch but become leathery with age. These are eaten by browsers like giraffe and elephant in particular.

The **bark** of the torchwood is smooth and grey and is relished by porcupines, which chisel it off with their massive incisors. Humans use a decoction of the bark as an emetic or add the bark to bath water for a stimulating soak. The bark of older trees assumes an irregular blockiness.

The **fruits are brown and hairy** resembling large dates. They turn yellow when ripe. They do not contain much flesh but what is present around the hard core is sticky and bitter and favoured by baboons, monkeys, kudu, duiker, warthogs, porcupines, steenbok and impala. Humans can eat the fruit but they are not a popular choice. If the fruit should fall into a pool of water, they have a very fast-acting potent effect on some forms of aquatic animals. Tadpoles, some fish and the water snails that harbour bilharzia have all been known to die from torchwood fruit poisoning water. Sometimes farmers will plant torchwoods around dams to prevent bilharzia in localised areas.

The **trunk** of the torchwood becomes **significantly fluted** as the tree gets older. The wood of the tree is fine-grained and long lasting and is used to make implement handles and gunstocks.

The **Zulu people believe** the torchwood tree has magic properties and can improve a person's sight. The customary procedure to acquire this improved vision involves the removal of the root-bark of the torchwood which is then mixed together with parts of the potato bush (see p. 329) and stirred vigorously to produce foam. This is then licked off the surface of the solution by the 'patient' without the aid of his hands.

The alternative common name for the torchwood is **'green thorn'**. The tree produces prominent hardy forked spines that are green in colour. These grow up to 7 cm long sometimes with one arm exceeding the other in length.

Baobab
Adansonia digitata

If one tree should be considered **iconic of the bushveld**, the baobab would be it. Myth has it that this enormously stout tree with root-like branches was planted upside down by the hyena. The gods had issued the animals with seeds to cultivate the earth and displeased that it had been left until last the hyena took its seeds, those of the baobab, and planted them upside down.

The **fruit** of the baobab is a large mango-shaped fruit covered in green to brown velvety hair, depending on how ripe it is. The pith of the fruit as well as the seeds contains tartaric acid and the baobab is known as the 'kremetartboom' in Afrikaans (cream-of-tartar tree). The fruit is also rich in vitamin C and a refreshing drink is made from the pith mixed with water. This drink is used medicinally to treat and relieve fevers. During World War I the fruit pulp was used as a substitute for bread yeast and nowadays the fruit shells are collected for use as snuff-boxes. Baboons and monkeys eat the fruit.

The **leaves** of the baobab are distinctive being palmately compound – they radiate out from a central point like the fingers on a hand. The leaflets closest to the petiole are smaller than the central ones. The specific name *digitata* refers to this digit-like arrangement. The leaves, like other parts of the tree, are nutritious and are eaten by browsers once they have fallen to the ground and are thus reachable. Humans use the leaves as spinach. The leaves contain tannins and mucilage (glutinous carbohydrates) and like the fruit, are also used in the treatment of fevers as well as diarrhoea.

The **roots** of the baobab also have nutritional value and particularly the roots of younger trees are edible. The bulbs at the ends of the roots are dried and crushed to produce flour or meal for porridge.

The **heartwood is very pulpy** and fibrous and has no use as 'wood'. It does hold a large amount of moisture (about 40%) and elephants utilise the heartwood material (and the moisture-rich bark) extensively during droughts to obtain water. They may completely ring-bark baobabs but remarkably, the trees are able to recover from such destruction. Humans and other animals may also chew on the fibre for moisture during dry times despite its bitter taste. The pulpy wood is sometimes used to make paper or as floats for fishing nets. The ash from the burnt wood provides a useful substitute for table salt.

Baobab
Adansonia digitata

25 m

The **flower** of the baobab is as unique as it is lovely. The 20 cm wide cup-shaped white flower comprises a bundle of pollen-rich stamens in the centre, flanked closer to the peduncle by waxy petals. The flowers hang downwards. This arrangement is not random and perfectly suits the flower to its pollination tactic, which is to be visited by straw-coloured fruit bats (the largest bats in Africa). The flowers open just before dark when the bats are beginning to get active and the strong carrion scent attracts them to the flowers. The central 'paintbrush' dusts the bats' furry bodies with pollen as they visit each flower. This is then transferred between flowers in subsequent visits. The flowers last a mere 24 hours at which time they drop to the ground and are enjoyed by herbivores like impala, kudu and bushbuck.

The **bark** of the baobab is shiny, grey and smooth except where it has been wounded and the tissue (which easily repairs itself, unlike many other trees) has formed dimples. The bark is harvested extensively for its fibrous qualities. Strips are pounded and then rolled into a tough yarn that is used to weave items such as sacks, fishing nets and even clothes or is employed as rope to bind things or create snares to catch animals. The twine is also used occasionally for the strings of musical instruments.

The **seeds** within the fruit can be sucked to relieve thirst. They are roasted and ground up as a substitute for coffee or caked and kept to use in soups. The seed is as high in protein as commercial nuts and yields 12% oil. A traditional substitute for asparagus is obtained by harvesting the shoots of germinating seeds.

Parts of the heartwood may die off naturally and the inside of these **cavities** forms a lining of bark. These natural holes may be large or small and play a vital ecological role. They serve as homes to birds, reptiles and arboreal rodents or bats. The cavities become reservoirs filled with rainwater and many animals, including leopards and genets, as well as humans will access water at these sites. The presence of appropriate sized holes as well as the water also encourages **bees to form hives**. Humans access the water as well as the honey in hives by knocking pegs into the soft wood of the tree to act as a stepladder. The hollows serve alternate human functions by acting as granaries, kilns, hide-outs, abodes, burial sites or prisons.

Baobab
Adansonia digitata

The baobab is **held in high esteem** amongst Africans. It is believed that spirits congregate under the trees at night and that one should never pluck a flower from the tree as the spirit dwelling in it during the blossoming season will cause a lion to consume you. Resa, the lord of the rain, is said to live in the upper branches of a baobab and is supposed to hold the sky up with his arms. As such, the tree is considered the 'fertility tree'. African women in the process of brewing beer are forbidden to eat the fruit of the baobab, as this will apparently negatively influence the brewing process.

For such ancient trees their **death and breakdown is remarkably rapid**. Baobab trees simply crumple into a pile of papery fibre when they die. A hot fire at this time would probably eliminate all evidence that the tree had even existed.

Although it is fairly certain that larger specimens of baobabs may be in excess of 4 000 years old, **aging the trees** exactly has proven difficult. The reason for this is that depending on the season and climatic conditions baobabs may expand or shrink due to the high water content in their tissues. The suggested guideline is that a tree of 5 m diameter is about 1 000 years old and one of 8 m diameter is more than 3 000 years old. Another extenuating factor with regards to aging the baobab is that trees seem to grow fastest for the first 250 years, quickly reaching a diameter of 2 m. Thereafter the growth rate slows down considerably.

Tree wisteria
Bolusanthus speciosus

4–10 m

The tree wisteria is most conspicuous at the end of the dry season when it flushes with **great clusters of mauve flowers** often up to 30 cm long that resemble bunches of grapes. The flowers are relished by baboons and vervet monkeys.

Braam van Wyk

The **wood** of the tree wisteria is suitable for carpentry; it has a good finish and was used extensively to make furniture by a **well-known carpenter called Van Wyk**, so much so that the tree became known in Afrikaans as 'Vanwykshout' (Van Wyk's wood).

The species name *speciosus* literally means **beautiful**, referring to the spectacular flowers. This tree makes a wonderful garden ornamental.

The tree wisteria **grows upright** with longitudinally fissured **bark**. The inner bark is sometimes dried and used as a remedy for abdominal pain. The tall trunks are suitable for building or as fencing posts as they are termite and fire resistant. Tree wisteria logs were also used historically to build ox-wagons.

The **leaves are bright shiny green**, compound and hang down on droopy branches giving the whole crown a narrow appearance. Each individual leaflet is obviously asymmetrical – if a leaf is folded down the main vein, one side is significantly smaller than the other.

The **roots** of the tree wisteria have emetic properties (they induce vomiting) and have been used in traditional medicine for this purpose.

263

Shepherd's tree
Boscia albitrunca

The **leaves** of the shepherd's tree are small and leathery without any obvious, protruding venation. They spiral around the branchlets, often terminating before the tip of the branch giving the canopy a spiky appearance.

Despite its usefulness, the shepherd's tree is **sensitive** to destruction. Growing in harsh conditions means it recovers slowly from being damaged and if cut back too much, trees may die.

The leaves of the shepherd's tree are **high in both protein (14%) and vitamin A**. The tree is heavily browsed by herbivores and sometimes the bark is eaten as an anthelmintic. Frugivorous birds visit the tree when it is fruiting.

The **wood** of the shepherd's tree is heavy and tough, but is most frequently only fashioned into household utensils. Traditional folklore suggests that should wood from this tree be burnt cows will produce only bull calves.

The fruit of the shepherd's tree is a **small ovoid green berry**. It is believed that should fruits wither before the ripening of the millet crop then the harvest is going to fail. Unripe fruit is used commercially as an epilepsy remedy.

The **roots** of the shepherd's tree are **very nutritious**. During the Anglo-Boer War roots were cut, dried and roasted to produce a coffee-substitute. Although this was often a desirable substitute, sometimes the flavour was not pleasant at all. By boiling pieces of root in water, sweet syrup can be extracted or the roots can be eaten raw as a vegetable. The roots are also dried and ground by locals to produce fibreless flour which is then cooked into porridge or boiled (without any bark remnants) to produce a sweet, refreshing drink. Pulverised root has preservative properties and is added to milk or butter to improve the shelf-life. It also inhibits the growth of mould on citrus, bread, tomatoes and potatoes. A decoction of the root is used to treat haemorrhoids.

Shepherd's tree
Boscia albitrunca

7 m

The **common name** 'shepherd's tree' comes from the fact that in the drier parts of its range (these trees are especially abundant in Namibia), herdsmen use the tree for shade when tending their flocks as there is little else on offer. The leaves are highly nutritious and branches are cut down and fed to domestic stock when little else is available. Unfortunately, too much foraging on the leaves taints cows' milk.

The **Afrikaans name** 'witgat' means 'white hole' and refers firstly to the white bark and secondly to the propensity of older trees to become hollow. These cavities collect water and are an important resource to people living in drier areas.

The **Latin** species name *albitrunca* is derived from 'albi' for white or pale (as in 'albino') and 'trunca' which refers to the trunk of the tree, i.e. pale-trunked.

The shepherd's tree is **very obvious** where it grows due to its white trunk and flat almost umbrella-like canopy. It usually grows in arid or sandy, story areas where it stands out all the more.

Pickled young **flower buds** are a pleasing substitute for capers.

The tree has many human uses and is colloquially referred to as **'the tree of life'** for its ability to provide so much to people living in dry places. The shepherd's tree is so valuable a resource that local culture protects the tree, forbidding its destruction.

Velvet corkwood
Commiphora mollis

8 m

The velvet corkwood superficially resembles a marula tree (see p. 302) but on closer inspection you will notice that the **bark is sickly looking**, peeling in shades of green, yellow and pink and the stems are fluted. The tree is not as large as a marula and the canopy is much more matted and twiggy.

The corkwood, true to its name, has **soft wood** and is used to make basic household utensils like cups.

Elephants push over velvet corkwoods to access the **succulent roots** and sometimes the leaves higher up on the crown. The dense tangled canopy, once at ground level, forms a useful microhabitat for nesting birds and small ground creatures such as rodents and reptiles. If part of the rootstock remains anchored in the soil, the tree will continue to produce green foliage while it is horizontal. This is part of the reason the tree is sometimes called a 'kanniedood' (cannot die) in Afrikaans. The family generally is referred to as 'kanniedood' for its prevalence in arid areas where little else survives.

Yellow-billed hornbills relish the **fruit** of the velvet corkwood and are surprisingly adept at using their huge bills to remove the seeds from inside their fleshy jackets. The seed is a black stone partly coated with four fingers of a fleshy red pseudo-aril, which the hornbill removes before discarding the seed.

Sometimes there is a prevalence of **hairy caterpillars** on velvet corkwoods. It is not advisable to camp under one of these trees in summer for this reason. The migrant cuckoo species, however, relish hairy caterpillars and will visit velvet corkwoods for this their specialised food source.

The **leaves** are compound but fairly small with the terminal leaflet and last lateral pair of leaflets forming a trifoliate-like (three joined at the base) arrangement. The petioles and rachis are red in younger leaves. The leaves may have two to six pairs of lateral leaflets but commonly have only two or three. The lower pairs of leaflets are always smaller than those towards the apex (tip).

The velvet corkwood **gets its name** from the velvety hairs that coat the tips of new branchlets and leaves.

The corkwoods belong to the **myrrh family** (Burseraceae) and most of them exude aromatic resins. An Arabian corkwood, *Commiphora myrrha*, is the source of the substance myrrh used for medicine and incense. Another Arabian species, *Commiphora gileadensis*, is tapped for its medicinal resin known as 'balm of Gilead'.

Grubs of an insect known as a flea-beetle feed on the leaves of one of the velvet corkwood's relatives, the **poison-grub corkwood** (*Commiphora africana*). The grubs fall off the tree and then pupate under the ground. These cocoons were harvested by Khoisan hunters for use as an arrow poison. To apply the poison, the hunter would roll the cocoon between thumb and index finger to liquefy the grub (taking care not to get any on himself). The binding thread between the shaft and the arrowhead is then coated with the toxic albumin present in the entrails of the larva. Eight or so of these cocoons are needed to make an arrowhead lethal. Many cocoons were harvested at the end of summer and stored for later use. The poison remains active for a long time while the grub is still in the cocoon.

Matumi
Breonadia salicina

40 m

The **most notable feature** of the matumi as far as human utilisation goes is its wood. The matumi has a hard, heavy, oily wood with a distinct smell (reminiscent of linseed oil) and a yellowish colour uniform throughout the sapwood and heartwood. In the past the wood was used extensively for parquet flooring and boat building. The tall stems of the trees made them suitable for use as structural beams as they did not have to be joined.

The **wood** was also used for railway sleepers and in Malawi to produce dugout canoes. The tree can be grown in commercial plantations and is desirable nowadays for furniture especially dining room tables and chairs, benches, side-tables and trays. The oiliness of the wood makes it especially suitable for cheese and breadboards as it prevents the wood cracking when it is exposed to repeated washing.

The matumi is **protected** in South Africa. This comes as a result of previous over-utilisation of this majestic tree which is commonly found adorning the banks of rivers, sometimes overhanging the water gracefully.

The **bark** of the matumi is greyish-brown in colour and rough in texture often becoming grooved with age. It is often covered with lichen because of the riverine habitat in which it grows. Extracts of the bark are used medicinally for curing stomach complaints or may be given to children as a tonic.

The **specific name** *salicina* means 'leaves like a willow' referring to the typical lanceolate (strip-like) leaves of the tree which bunch and spiral at the ends of the branches resembling the leaves of a pineapple fruit. They are bright green, waxy in texture and adorned with an attractive bold yellow midrib.

Sjambok pod (long-tail cassia)
Cassia abbreviata subsp. *beareana*

5–10 m

The sjambok pod is at its **most spectacular** at the onset of spring when the tree **flowers** profusely in an otherwise dry landscape. Each bright yellow flower is relatively large (measuring up to 5 × 7 cm) and is borne on a long stalk. These cluster together towards the ends of the branches producing spectacular sprays (up to 20 cm in length) that have a sweet fragrance. This feature makes the tree popular as a garden ornamental.

The sjambok pod is widely revered as the tree that can cure blackwater fever. The remedy is prepared from **extracts of the bark** or a decoction of the roots. The effectiveness of this traditional treatment was observed in 1902 by Dr O'Sullivan Beare who subsequently had these medicinal liquids made available on the commercial market. The sub-specific name *beareana* is derived from Dr Beare. Another subspecies is found outside the Lowveld.

The sjambok pod has a rough, ridged **grey bark** that is often flaking slightly. The bark is used medicinally in infusions with the root to treat various ailments including abdominal pain, toothache, constipation and diarrhoea. In a powdered form it can be applied to abscesses or is administered to patients to cure bilharzia, apparently quite successfully.

The common name of the tree is derived from the **long, brown, cylindrical pods** which may reach 90 cm in length and are rather rough to the touch. They are said to resemble sjamboks – sturdy whips made out of rhino or hippo hide. The pods remain on the tree for some time after they first appear as it can take up to a year for them to ripen.

The **leaves** of the sjambok pod appear on the tree simultaneously or shortly after the flowers. They have a bright green colour and a thin velvety texture at first, but quickly fade to a smooth, dull-green surface. The leaves droop prominently. They are browsed by giraffe, kudu, nyala and elephant but not popularly so.

On ripening the **pods dehisce** (burst open), releasing the seeds from their bed of sticky green substrate. The fruit pulp and seeds are then relished by birds, including grey go-away birds, brown-hooded parrots, barbets and hornbills. Humans may suck the seeds as a tonic.

The sjambok pod is believed to have **magical powers** and the people of the Shangaan tribe will cook over coals from the tree to ensure a successful hunting trip. The smoke from burning branches is believed to be effective against headaches. The wood is used for fashioning various household articles as it is hard and works easily. The wood is, however, often damaged by wood-boring insects.

The sjambok pod regularly **grows on termite mounds**. These sites are fertile compared to the surrounding soils due to the activities of the termites, which aerate and moisten the soil and incorporate organic material into it. The tree benefits from these localised favourable growing conditions.

Mopane
Colophospermum mopane

18–30 m

Dry leaves that have fallen to ground maintain about 40% of their original protein content and are an important source of fodder to wild animals (and domestic stock) during times of drought.

The high protein levels are obviously attractive to herbivores and to dissuade them from over-utilising the tree, mopane produces **high levels of tannin**. This gives the leaves a characteristic turpentine smell when crushed. It is also distasteful. Tannins are proteins that bond to useful proteins and prevent their absorption by herbivores' digestive tracts. The evolutionary arms race between plants and herbivores has seen to it that herbivores can and do overcome the effects of tannins but they still act as a deterrent to excessive herbivory.

Plants that contain tannins usually make good dyes to tan leather. This is true of mopane. The tannin in the leaves is also quite effective in relieving stomach upsets.

The **leaves** of a mopane tree are very **high in protein** as far as plants are concerned (they contain 12-15% protein in the growing leaves).

Usually broader-leaved trees such as *Combretum* species (see pp. 272-275) use **chemical defence** against herbivores while finer-leaved trees like *Acacias* (see pp. 252-258) use structural defences like thorns. This is because *Acacias* are more nutritious than *Combretums* because they grow in more fertile soils. As a result they are eaten by large herbivores like antelope and giraffe whereas the less-nutrient rich *Combretum* leaves are eaten more by insects. Chemicals are a better defence against small invertebrate feeding apparatus while thorns are more effective to dissuade large antelope mouths.

In the case of mopane, the chemical defence probably plays a dual role. Since mopane usually grow in low-lying clay soils and have a high protein content, they are probably equally attractive to larger mammals and to smaller invertebrates such as the brightly coloured mopane worm. At some times of the year these worms occur almost as plagues on the trees. The **caterpillars** are the larvae a large moth, *Gonimbrasia belina*, from the **emperor moth** family. In their vast numbers they can completely strip trees bare and produce an audible 'munching' sound as they do so! Because their food source is rich in protein, the worms themselves become rich in protein and are harvested by locals wherever the trees occur in southern Africa, providing an important meat supplement in rural areas. The worms are eaten roasted, dried or simply sans heads and innards in a small ball of traditional 'mieliepap' (stiff maize meal porridge).

Elephants are astute about choosing the best plants to eat at different times of the year. They are also adept at knowing which part of the plant to eat for the best nutrition. Mopane is a favourite of elephants and the leaves and bark are eaten all year round. The palatability of mopane leaves changes seasonally and at the start of the rainy summer the tannins decrease and the nutrients improve. At these times the young green leaves are especially edible to elephant. Mature green leaves are most palatable during the wet season with tannin levels at their lowest but elephants are eating mostly tannin-free grass at this time anyway. The nutritional quality of mopane leaves decreases with age (as the season progresses) and elephants then turn to the more palatable inner bark (or cambium) going into winter. Because mopane loses its leaves irregularly throughout the dry season, the senescent leaves are still utilised at a time when other trees have shed theirs and may supplement the elephants' diet for the short period before the flush.

Mopane
Colophospermum mopane

The Damara people of Namibia use mopane exclusively to **construct their traditional huts**. Mopane **wood** is hard and termite resistant – good traits of a building material. It is, however, also a flexible wood and poles are compliant to bending. Each post is bowed inwards towards a central point where it is fastened with a strong rope, also made from the mopane using the fibrous inner bark. Eventually a dome-shaped structure emerges. Sometimes smaller branches and leaves are strewn over the top to create better shading.

The **termite resistance of the mopane pole** is well known. This along with the fact that mopane usually grows very upright, makes them suitable for use as all manner of posts, from fence posts in cattle kraals to lantern posts along pathways in modern game lodges. The wood is also used medicinally to cure eye infections.

The kidney-shaped mopane **pods** are produced profusely during the dry season, often giving the tree the appearance of being laden with small ornaments. The pods can be found strewn on the ground throughout most of the year. Each pod contains one seed that has a number of folds on its flat surface and obvious resin-filled glands. This resin is oily and flammable and the Latin genus name of this tree, *Colophospermum*, literally means 'gum-producing seed'. Tree squirrels feast on mopane seeds during the dry season.

The **bark of the mopane is characteristically rough and fissured**. The inner bark produces a strong rope and is used in a cure for venereal diseases.

Generally mopane **dominates** areas where it grows. It occurs in different growth forms but no matter the height, these stands are usually homogenous. Where conditions are ideal, mopane grows into tall woodland with thick-trunked trees reaching up to 20 m high. In other places mopane is stunted into a scrubby-looking shrubland. Some opinions ascribe these shrublands to poor growth conditions. There is evidence that some of these shorter stands are maintained by elephant feeding behaviour (they repeatedly browse the regrowth on damaged trees). Fire also contributes to maintaining the lower form of mopane woodland.

Mopane is a natural **encroacher species**. An 'encroacher' is an indigenous plant that tends to grow aggressively and dominate areas where it occurs to the exclusion of other natural species. They have shallow root systems and easily out-compete undergrowth for moisture in the upper soil surface. They are also a species that coppices easily, producing several stems where one may have been broken off. In this way they overcome the often destructive feeding habits of elephant. Mopane prefers clay soil but tolerates poor soils better than most other species.

Mopane
Colophospermum mopane

Mopane have what are known as bifoliolate **leaves** and this gives the leaf the appearance of butterfly wings. The word 'mopane' (both the common and species name of this tree) is actually the Shona word for butterfly. Shona is one of the languages spoken in Zimbabwe where large tracts of mopane occur.

The two **leaf blades** of the mopane leaf, each with characteristic fountain-like venation, are joined by a small gland. This causes the blades to close and hang down during extreme heat and on windy days. By closing the leaf blades, the tree reduces the surface available to transpiration losses. In this respect mopane does not make a particularly good shade tree.

Mopane trees lose their leaves irregularly through winter and some trees may still have foliage right at the end of the season. In this way they provide important forage throughout the dry season. The **leaves change colour** from bright green to golden-yellow and then turn brick red when dry. This transforms huge tracts of usually monotonous mopane woodland into a vivid spectacle during the autumn-winter season. At some point towards the end of winter, all the trees will shed their leaves and stand barren briefly. They tend to flush quickly, independently of the onset of rain. This flush usually precedes other woody trees budding, once again providing an important source of forage before the onset of spring.

Mopane trees are prone to **natural cavities** and this provides a myriad hole-nesting species, from barbets and hornbills to tree squirrels, with viable home options. Tree squirrels are so abundant in mopane woodland that they are sometimes even called 'mopane squirrels' (see p. 78).

Another creature that makes use of the mopane's cavities is the **mopane bee**. This tiny 4 mm member of the bee family is sometimes referred to as a 'mopane fly' because of its irritating habit of buzzing close to people's eyes and noses in pursuit of moisture. These tiny bees are stingless but they do make honey. Due to the size of the insect, the honey production is much less than that of honeybees but just as desirable. Many mopane trees in the Lowveld bear the scars of an axe used to penetrate honey-rich mopane cavities.

Red bushwillow
Combretum apiculatum

10 m

Like the other members of the Combretum family, this tree has exceptionally **hard wood**. The red bushwillow is rivalled only by zebrawood for the densest wood in southern Africa, weighing in at 1 230 kg/m³. Coals from burning logs last for up to 12 hours.

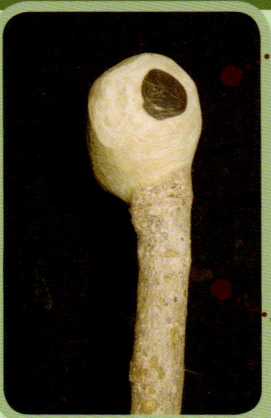

Red bushwillow knobkerrie (club)

Because of the exceptionally **hard wood**, red bushwillow timber is termite resistant and has been used for mine props and railway sleepers. It is a very hard wood to work for furniture although it is sometimes used for this purpose.

As with all *Combretums*, the red bushwillow produces **four-winged pods** that shelter a single seed in the middle. The centre of the pod is a light red colour when it ripens. The pods are favoured by brown-hooded parrots.

Although the red bushwillow usually has a relatively **formless canopy**, its secondary branches do tend to grow at right angles off the central beam and this feature can assist with recognition of the tree.

A **refreshing tea** can be made from an infusion of the pods and leaves. The wings of the pods must be separated and the seeds removed as they are poisonous and may induce **prolonged hiccupping**.

The **bark** is usually dark grey to red-brown. On the younger branches, fibres may flake off in stringy bits.

The **leaves** have a characteristically pinched and twisted apex (the tip of the leaf) to which its species name *apiculatum* refers. Red bushwillows are responsible for a wonderful autumn show of colour across the tracts of bushveld where they occur.

Red bushwillows prefer the **upper slopes** of the Lowveld catena, growing in the sandier soils just off the crests. In areas that have been disturbed through overgrazing and other forms of over-utilisation, red bushwillows become bush encroachers growing aggressively to the exclusion of other native species (particularly encroaching dehydrated seeplines downslope from their usual habitat).

A **decoction** of the leaves is traditionally used as an enema for stomach ailments.

Russet bushwillow
Combretum hereroense

3–10 m

Russet bushwillows earned their name from their tendency to appear completely **rusty brown** when laden with copious bunches of red-brown **pods** towards the end of summer and into autumn. The pods stay on the tree for a protracted period of time. The young branches and undersides of the leaves are also covered in fine reddish-brown hairs. So spectacular is the overall effect that the trees can easily be picked out of a landscape from a distance.

The **leaves** of the russet bushwillow are relatively small and oval shaped, and are dark green above and paler below. The underside of the leaf is diagnostically **littered with either russet-coloured hairs or scales** on the raised veins. Sometimes the dried leaves are included in the infusion when making bushwillow tea. They are also browsed readily by herbivores including kudu, impala, giraffes and elephants.

Like other bushwillows (*Combretum* species), the russet bushwillow has **four-winged pods**. They are relatively small (smaller than the red's but larger than leadwood's). Herbal tea much like rooibos can be produced from the pods if they are soaked or boiled briefly in hot water. The seed must be removed from the centre of the pod before brewing.

The largest of the bushwillow pods belong to the **large-fruited bushwillow** (*Combretum zeyheri*) another common bushwillow in the Lowveld. A similar species with slightly smaller rosy-coloured pods is the **variable bushwillow** (*Combretum collinum*).

The russet bushwillow is a somewhat raggedy plant being multi-stemmed with a rather **shapeless canopy**. Usually one or two branches are fairly curved and the newer stems grow very erect from these.

Although nothing much to look at, the **flowers** of the russet bushwillow attract butterflies, wasps and other insects. These in turn encourage an abundance of insect-eating birds in the vicinity of the trees.

The **bark** of a russet bushwillow is rough and fissured and generally grey or dark brown in colour. Extracts of the bark are used in treatments for heartburn and heart disease. The younger stems may be in any phase between green, red and grey. While young and reddish, the **younger bark tends to peel in fine stringy strips** which helps with identification. Dried out, the younger shoots are used in traditional cures for coughs or tonsillitis.

True to family nature, the russet bushwillow has very **hard wood**. It is resistant to termites and is borer proof so it is particularly suitable for use as structural supports in mines. It is also used to make solid, long-lasting furniture, especially chairs and side-tables but the hardness of the wood makes it difficult to work. In the past russet bushwillow stems were used as wheel spokes for wagons. The branches are fairly straight and have been used as pick handles and walking sticks. Walking sticks are known as 'kieries' in Afrikaans, hence the Afrikaans common name 'kierieklapper'. Coals from any bushwillow wood fire are long lasting and produce wonderful cooking or heat fires.

Leadwood
Combretum imberbe

The **leaves** are small to medium sized (they vary from tree to tree) with a typically wavy margin. If you look closely at both the upper and lower leaf surfaces you will see they are **covered in tiny grey speckles** that resemble pixels on an out-of-focus TV screen.

Sacrificial branches are characteristic of leadwood trees. These are lower branches on the tree that are used as toxic waste depots. Since the branches are lower down and not serving as vital a photosynthetic function as the higher branches, the tree can afford to 'sacrifice' the branch in order to have a site for waste disposal. These branches eventually die but remain on the tree due to their durability.

Leadwood **bark** is easy to recognise. It is a pale grey colour, which often makes the tree stand out amidst its surrounds (particularly in early morning or afternoon light). The bark is also very blocky and the texture resembles the scale pattern on a reptile's back.

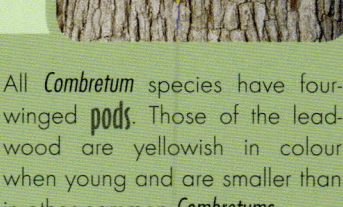

The young trees have **small side branches** modified as defensive spines. This is because the younger leaves in particular are browsed by animals like kudu, giraffes and elephants.

All *Combretum* species have four-winged **pods**. Those of the leadwood are yellowish in colour when young and are smaller than in other common *Combretums*.

The leadwood has many **medicinal uses**, for example inhalation of the smoke from burning leaves is used to relieve coughs and the common cold.

7–15 m

Leadwood
Combretum imberbe

Leadwood is one of the **heaviest woods** found in the Lowveld with a weight of 1 200 kg/m³. As a result, this wood sinks in water! It is a member of the Combretaceae family, all of which have very hard wood, the red bushwillow (*Combretum apiculatum*) being the hardest (see p. 272).

Because of the great density of the wood, it **burns slowly and for a very long time**, producing long-lasting coals (sometimes lasting up to 12 hours). The ash produced is high in lime and abrasive, hence its use by local people as a substitute for toothpaste. When mixed with milk, leadwood ash also makes an effective whitewash. After a veld fire it is easy to spot where a leadwood used to grow. The intense, slow fire produced by the wood often renders a perfect white 'ghost anatomy' on the charred ground. If the leadwood was still standing, you may be surprised to discover it smouldering weeks after the fire passed by.

Due to the **density** of leadwood, the tree is termite and borer resistant. As a result a leadwood will **remain standing for hundreds of years** after it has died. These sturdy anatomies provide ideal perches for large birds of prey and vultures. **Vultures** especially, require strong perches to support their weight. Also the dead leadwood is free of the entangling foliage likely to interfere with their huge wingspan when they are trying to take off from a living tree. Where side branches have fallen off, cavities remain which may be colonised by hole-nesting bird species.

Leadwood is by no means an easy **wood** to work and is ill suited to furniture making. It is, however, well suited for use as heavyweight traditional tools like **grain mortars**. In the past it was also used for mine props and railway sleepers. Before the advent of steel hoes, leadwood was used to hoe fields. Obtaining the wood for all these purposes is hard work – **cutting a leadwood with a band-saw produces sparks!**

Some leadwoods have been **carbon-dated** by scientists to over 1 000 years old.

Leadwood is considered an indicator of **sweet veld** and good grazing.

Large fever-berry
Croton megalobotrys

5–15 m

The large fever-berry is unmistakable where it grows along watercourses for its **leafy, evergreen foliage**. The leaves have a triangular, almost heart-shape to them and attach to the tree with long stalks. When plucked these ooze watery latex but this does not deter browsing antelope or elephants. Younger leaves are velvety on the underside where silvery hairs are present but with age these disappear. Both young and old leaves are conspicuously veined with up to five principal veins originating from the base of each leaf.

Dr John Maberley of the Klein Letaba Goldfields Hospital published an account in 1899 of an elderly prospector who claimed to have been **cured from malaria** by an African doctor who prescribed the seeds and bark of the large fever-berry (at the time an unidentified tree). The man had kept some of the seeds and passed them on to Dr Maberley who subsequently treated fever effectively in his own patients with them. Twenty years later the source plant was identified as the large fever-berry and although Africans traditionally have and still use the bark and seeds of the tree to treat fevers (and even as a prophylactic against malaria), no further research was ever done into the value of this plant as a potential commercial cure for malaria.

The **bark is smooth and grey** with corky spots (lenticels). Younger branches are green and hairy but also marked with lenticels. The bark of the large fever-berry can be crushed and used as a fish poison. Locals catch fish by introducing the powdered bark to an isolated pool of water. This results in the fish becoming paralysed and they simply float to the surface where they may be scooped off.

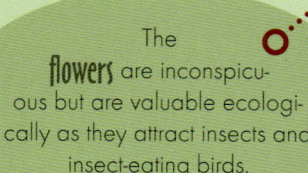

The **flowers** are inconspicuous but are valuable ecologically as they attract insects and insect-eating birds.

The generic name *Croton* is the Greek word for 'tick' and this describes the shape of **fruit** which is a 3,5 cm large yellowish-brown, pear-shaped capsule. Tree squirrels relish the oily seeds found inside the fruit and doggedly chew their way through the hard capsule to get to them. The seeds are collected and used by humans as a purgative. They comprise 50% oil which is extracted for its medicinal value as a purgative and is known as 'croton oil'. This oil can also be used in soap-making.

An infusion of the **roots** of the large fever-berry is known to relieve stomach ache.

Although the tree seldom gets very large, the **wood** is used for household articles and shelving. Traditionally it was used as the lower part of a device to make fire by friction.

Zebrawood
Dalbergia melanoxylon

5–7 m

The **heartwood** of the zebrawood is purple becoming black when cut or dried and the sapwood is light. Sometimes the dark and light are laid down irregularly and when the wood is cut it shows black and white striping, which resembles a zebra's markings, hence the common name.

Due to the lovely colouration (and scent) of the **wood**, the zebrawood is popularly used for **making ornaments**, jewellery, woodwind instruments, chess pieces and walking sticks. The wood is very hard and the pieces seldom very large due to the small size of the trees, which makes it suitable for only smaller woodwork items. However, occasionally broad enough planks are produced which are incorporated in furniture items.

The **Latin genus name** *Dalbergia* comes from Nils and Carl Dalberg, well-known Swedish botanists in the 1900s, and *melanoxylon* refers to the black heartwood.

The **pods** of the zebrawood are flat and thin with just a bump over the seeds. They grow in profuse bunches on the tree for a protracted time and have given rise to the alternative name of 'zebrawood flat-bean'.

The zebrawood is a **multi-stemmed, straggly tree** with an old appearance even though it only really grows as a shrub or small tree.

The **roots** of the zebrawood are used medicinally to relieve toothache and to treat headaches.

Traditional arrow tips are produced from zebrawood due to the **hardness and durability of the wood**. Local people also use it to make hammers to beat bark cloth.

The **leaves** are compound with alternating leaflets and they cluster droopily at the base of the spines or off dwarfed side shoots. The lower leaflets are smaller than those towards the apex (tip of the leaf) with the terminal leaflet being largest. They are eaten by giraffe, impala and kudu despite the mean spines.

The **spines** on a zebrawood are vicious and multi-pointed. The hardness of the wood renders the spines (modified branches) equally hard and it is hazardous to one's tyres to drive over a zebrawood branch. In spite of these formidable defensive structures, elephants favour the roots and leaves of zebrawood trees and regularly disfigure the trees so that they have a scrambled, untidy appearance.

277

Sickle bush
Dichrostachys cinerea

The **flowers** of the sickle bush are the most unique and striking of bushveld flowers. The bush produces two-tone spikes with pink on the top and yellow below. The genus name *Dichrostachys* refers to this characteristic of the tree. The flowers look like miniature Chinese lanterns and the tree is sometimes referred to as the Chinese lantern tree. The decorative flowers are present on the tree (quite appropriately) over the Christmas season.

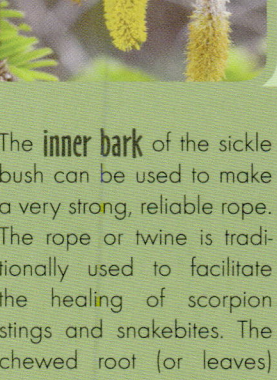

The **inner bark** of the sickle bush can be used to make a very strong, reliable rope. The rope or twine is traditionally used to facilitate the healing of scorpion stings and snakebites. The chewed root (or leaves) is applied to a scorpion sting or snakebite and then bound onto the wound with the twine from the tree. The same treatment can be given to irritating insect bites.

The sickle bush is one of the **major native encroachers** in the bushveld. It quickly colonises disturbed areas particularly those that have been overgrazed or previously cultivated. This tree gets the competitive advantage over other indigenous species because it can grow in all soil types, it coppices readily from any small piece of the root and the seeds are not digested when they get eaten. The seeds pass out of an animal's gut untouched and are deposited in a ready-made pile of compost, especially if deposited by elephants!

Bush clearing programmes are often initiated to clear the impenetrable thickets that eventually form from this aggressive encroacher. Fortunately the wood produces excellent coals and so the cleared stems can be sold as firewood (or charcoal) and the money recycled back into the rehabilitation of the land.

Sickle bush **branches** are often used in brush or mattress packing operations to **reclaim eroded or barren areas**. By placing the branches over the surface of the ground they serve to trap windblown debris and to slow the flow of water over the surface of the soil. The slowed water is then able to infiltrate the ground and also allows soil particles and seeds to be deposited. Eventually enough of a deposit will allow the seeds to germinate in the improved growing conditions of the area. The **spines** on the branches prevent unwanted passage over the area by animals and also shelter the newly germinating seeds. The branches break down over two or three seasons leaving a transformed area.

Sickle bush
Dichrostachys cinerea

5–7 m

The sickle bush's **bark** has long fissures. By powdering the bark, skin conditions of various kinds can be treated. The inner bark is used to treat toothache and stomach complaints.

The sickle bush is the **A-Z of medicinal plants** – it has antibiotic properties and is used successfully for numerous conditions including stomach complaints, pneumonia, abscesses, dysentery, gonorrhoea and intestinal worms to name a few.

Sickle bush produces very **strong, hard wood**. It is one of the best woods for making tool handles because of this. The pieces are seldom very thick but always strong. Sickle bush wood burns well in spite of the thinness of its trunks.

The **hard wood** means that sickle bush poles are termite resistant and long lasting. They are often used to substitute iron uprights in fencing as they can even withstand fire.

The **leaves** of the sickle bush are soft and feathery. Like other parts of the tree, they are nutritious and are also used in a number of medicinal applications. They make an effective local anaesthetic for topical application. They can even be ingested to relieve internal aches and pains. Toothache can be relieved by boiling the roots and leaves and inhaling the steam; chest complaints can be relieved by burning the roots and leaves and inhaling the smoke.

The **clusters of contorted pods** produced by the sickle bush are unmistakable and are relished by animals for their high nutritional value. Eyewash can be made from an infusion of the seedpod to relieve eye irritations and sometimes the pods are collected for decorative purposes.

The sickle bush is sometimes grown in the vicinity of homes to **ward off evil spirits**. Charms from the tree are also kept for the same purpose.

The sickle bush is often confused with the *Acacia* trees but the sickle bush is not an *Acacia* because it does not have thorns but rather spines. **Spines are defensive spikes** produced by the tree through the modification of branches whereas thorns are modified leaves. Both *Acacias* and the sickle bush are considered fine-leaved trees and tend to occur in the lower part of the catena (in the more fertile soils). The sickle bush is a very nutritious plant and virtually the whole plant is eaten by animals, especially elephants. It produces these hard spines to limit the amount of herbivory taking place on the tree.

Jackal-berry
Diospyros mespiliformis

Jackal-berries are **massive, impressive trees** that grow along rivers or upon termite mounds. Termites enrich the soil with organic material and aerate it with their tunnelling activities. This in conjunction with access to the water table, make termite mounds ideal fertile islands for some species of trees to utilise away from their usual habitats. Jackal-berries may germinate and grow in rocky areas as well due to their seeds being deposited there by monkeys or birds but they never reach their full stature growing in these less optimal habitats.

The **canopy** of the jackal-berry is **dense and shady**. The foliage is dark green with younger leaves having a distinct red colour. **Leaves** on smaller plants may look similar to those of the guarris (see p. 282) but the leaves are only slightly wavy and arranged alternately, unlike the guarris.

Due to the size of the trees, they provide excellent **general-purpose timber**. The wood is frequently used for furniture, flooring or for maize pestles. It is also one of the more commonly used trees for mokoros (dugout canoes) in the Okavango Delta.

The **bark** of the jackal-berry is black and looks as if it has been burnt, with a distinct white wash over the top. An infusion of the bark will produce a black dye.

In some parts of Africa, the jackal-berry is called the **ebony tree**. This name comes from the dark wood of some of the jackal-berry's more commercialised family members. Ebony and ivory were the most highly valued commodities of the early colonial traders in Africa.

The jackal-berry is known for its **antibiotic properties**.

Jackal-berry
Diospyros mespiliformis

25 m

The jackal-berry is **high in tannins** and these can be extracted from the leaves, fruit and roots. These tannins are used medicinally to treat dysentery. Tannins are also used to tan leather. They stabilise the protein in animal skins to prevent them rotting and hence convert them to leather. Leaves and twigs are used to treat wounds as these supposedly improve the production of scar tissue. Decoctions of the bark and leaves treat ringworm, internal parasites and are combined with other plants for a leprosy cure.

The jackal-berry's common name arises from the fact that the tree produces grape-sized fruit that, once fallen to the ground, are relished by myriad creatures not least of which is the omnivorous **black-backed jackal**.

A **superstition** regarding the jackal-berry suggests that a man away from home should not eat of the fruits of this tree lest he be inhabited by evil spirits.

Diospyros means 'pear of the gods' and the **ripened fruit** is relished by humans too who eat it as is or make it into fruit preserves, beer and brandy. Sometimes the pulp is dried into flour or used to make porridge.

The **berries** can be used as paper glue before they ripen. By peeling away some of the flesh, the fruit oozes a sticky sap and this is effective in adhering pieces of paper together.

Frugivorous birds such as the green pigeon are often found in fruiting trees. So too are baboons and monkeys which knock the sought-after fruit down to warthogs, kudu, impala and civets. Fruit may persist on the tree for a full year before it ripens.

Magic guarri
Euclea divinorum

The evergreen nature of the magic guarri renders its **tough leathery leaves** fairly firmly attached to the branches. Leafy branches are plucked and used as brooms, tick-swats and fire-beaters because of their robustness. Women carrying water in open buckets upon their heads will often place guarri branches on the surface to seal the surface and act as a lid to prevent the water splashing out onto them.

The **leaves** of the magic guarri are shiny green and have very wavy margins which make them easy to recognise. These are high in chemical tannins which make the plant undesirable to most browsers.

The magic guarri is a conspicuous **evergreen shrub** that grows especially abundantly in **sodic areas** (usually at the base of the catena where there is an inordinate accumulation of sodium and other salts in the clay, producing compact subsoil and highly erodable topsoil). Other plants do not grow easily on sodic sites as their roots are eroded by the hard ground as it expands and contracts.

Although the thinly **fleshy purple berries** are relished by hornbills, they have a purgative effect on humans. They may be eaten during times of famine if little else is available and are used to produce alcohol. Boiled, the fruit is used to produce a purple ink.

The root of the plant is widely used in **traditional remedies**. An oral application of infused root is taken for constipation, abdominal or pregnancy pains and to treat infertility in women. The infusion is dropped directly into the ear to cure headaches. An ointment prepared from root material is rubbed over the body to control convulsions or in powdered form can be added to porridge to treat diarrhoea. A decoction of the root cures toothache or a depressed fontanel in babies. A dark dye is also extracted from the roots of the guarri.

The **wood** of the magic guarri is tough and can be used to fashion smaller household articles. The Zulu people believe that cutting the whole tree down will result in the destruction of their entire kraal.

Magic guarri
Euclea divinorum

8 m

The magic guarri is **highly regarded by Africans** who hang branches over their doorways or build the wood into the crossbeams of the kraal entrance to ward off evil spirits and witches. Zulu hunters carry a piece of the plant as a good luck token during the hunt.

The magic guarri is named so due to its use in **water divining**. A Y-shaped branch held with the shorter parts in each hand and the tail facing outwards, is said to lead a man with divining skills to water, the tail dipping downward to indicate its position in the ground. The *divinorum* part of the Latin name alludes to this trait too.

The magic guarri is sometimes colloquially called **'the toothbrush tree'** as an effective toothbrush can be fashioned from the young twigs. After peeling the bark away from the base of a broken-off twig, the fibres of the wood can be separated by chewing the end of the branch. The end of the twig takes on a brush-like appearance and can then be used to polish one's teeth with the toothpaste ash of the leadwood (see p. 274). The twig may also be used as a paintbrush.

The similar **Natal guarri** (*Euclea natalensis*) also occurs in the Lowveld and may be confused with the magic guarri (or even a young jackal-berry), but the leaves of the Natal guarri are less wavy and are coated in a fine hairy covering (especially underneath). The apex curls over and the upper surface of the leaf is dark green and shows a leather-like patterning. The fruit of the Natal guarri is more edible than the magic's fruit. Like the magic guarri, the Natal guarri can be used to make toothbrushes or to extract dye from the roots for colouring straw mats. The roots are also used to treat leprosy, headaches and toothache.

Rubber euphorbia
Euphorbia tirucalli

10 m

The rubber euphorbia is unmistakable for its **bizarre growth form** which resembles a tangle of green spaghetti emanating from a solid main trunk. **The branches of this tree are modified** into cylindrical photosynthetic organs. The process of synthesising glucose food from carbon dioxide and water is usually the role of the leaves, the part of the tree usually endowed with green chlorophyll (which traps the sun's energy and powers the food-making process). The leaves of the rubber euphorbia are, however, scale-like in appearance and virtually non-existent.

All parts of the rubber euphorbia are well supplied with an **extremely toxic milky latex** which bleeds profusely from the tree should it be damaged in any way. This latex has been used traditionally as a fish poison and in traditional cures for sexual impotence. For use as medicinal treatment it has to be administered with extreme care as even a small excess of ingested latex can result in death by internal bleeding. Animals such as black rhino and even nyala eat the stems of the tree without ill effect.

The **flowers** are borne on the ends of the spaghetti-like branches and thereafter develop into three-lobed capsule fruits which ripen to an attractive pink colour.

The poisonous nature of the rubber euphorbia has led to its cultivation as a **hedge to enclose homesteads** and protect them from unwanted intruders. Sometimes the rubber euphorbia is also known as the 'rubber-hedge euphorbia' for this reason. Rubber euphorbias are believed to repel moles and insects and are useful around homesteads to keep these kinds of pests at bay.

The rubber euphorbia generally grows in rocky areas but shows a **great deal of resilience** in its habitat requirements. Early traders took specimens home with them to India and the Far East where the plants have flourished.

Megan Emmett

Another euphorbia that is fairly common in the Lowveld is the **Lowveld or lesser candelabra euphorbia** (*Euphorbia cooperi*). This tree is said to have the **deadliest latex of all the euphorbias** and will irritate the skin and throat of a person merely standing close to a plant that is seeping latex. This euphorbia is shaped like a candelabrum, each 'candle-stick' comprising separate heart-shaped constrictions and the main stem decoratively dimpled by old branches that have died and fallen off. The flowers and fruit are borne on the tips of each branch and are yellow and red respectively, creating the impression of candles that have been lit. Despite the poisonous properties of the plant, baboons and doves eat the flowers and fruit.

Large-leaved rock fig
Ficus abutilifolia

The large-leaved rock fig is often obvious for its habit of **growing on bouldered outcrops** or rock faces. It is a gnarled, spreading tree whose creamy coloured meandering root system makes it an attractive feature in the Lowveld.

Like all figs, the large-leaved rock **fig's fruit are edible** and utilised by myriad frugivorous (fruit-eating) creatures including baboons, monkeys, bats, civets, bushpig and antelope. Birds include green pigeons, brown-headed parrots, mousebirds, grey go-away birds and barbets.

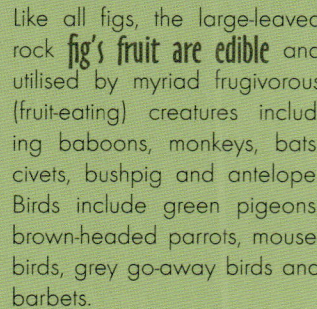

Mike Amm

The **figs** are sweet but not very palatable to humans due to the presence of tiny wasps inside the fruit. These wasps breed inside the fig and in return pollinate the flowers of the fig, which are contained inside the fleshy receptacle. Each fig tree species is pollinated by a particular species of fig wasp, the size of the wasp relating to the size of the opening at the tip of the fig (see also p. 234).

The **bark** of this tree is creamy white in colour which makes it even more spectacular as a landscape feature when illuminated by the afternoon or morning light. A sap derived from the bark is used by locals to produce a strengthening tonic for men.

The large-leaved rock fig has the **largest leaves** of all the figs (measuring 15×20 cm). The leaves are attractive with pale, well-defined venation that sometimes takes on a reddish tinge. The main vein is conspicuously raised under the leaf. The leaves of the small-leaved rock fig can be told apart from the large-leaved species due to their slightly smaller size and their coarser, hairier texture.

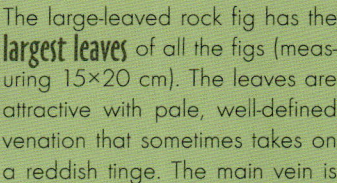

The tree relies on nutrients derived from the soil. The **roots of the tree find passages through cracks** in the rocks to reach the soil below. When the plant is newly germinated it appears 'root heavy' having a disproportionately large spaghetti-like root system for a small underdeveloped plant bearing only one or two leaves. Once the roots take anchor, the plant begins to grow into its roots.

The large-leaved rock fig produces copious amounts of **non-toxic milky latex**. Latex is produced by all the members of the fig family.

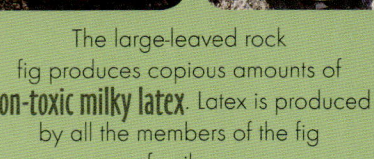

The large-leaved rock fig is an important **natural weathering agent**. The spaghetti-thin roots that force their way through the thinnest of cracks expand as the plant grows. The pressure of the expanding root splits and breaks up the large boulders on which the fig grows.

285

Sycamore fig
Ficus sycomorus

30 m

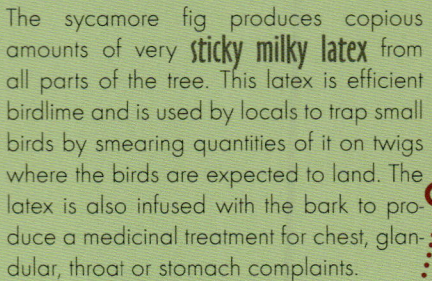

The **wood** of the sycamore fig is soft, dries quickly and is easily carved. It is most typically used to make drums. Small planks have also been used extensively as the base plates for traditional fire-starting drills. Sometimes the wood is also used to fashion mortars or mokoros in the Okavango Delta.

The **leaves** of the sycamore fig are almost round. They are relatively large and have the rough texture of a cat's tongue. In spite of this sandpapery feel, they are exceptionally good forage and are browsed by whichever herbivores can reach them before they grow out of reach. Farmers have been known to feed the nutritious leaves to their cows to improve milk production.

The sycamore fig produces copious amounts of very **sticky milky latex** from all parts of the tree. This latex is efficient birdlime and is used by locals to trap small birds by smearing quantities of it on twigs where the birds are expected to land. The latex is also infused with the bark to produce a medicinal treatment for chest, glandular, throat or stomach complaints.

A **strong rope** can be made from the inner bark.

The **plum-like figs** of the sycamore fig are borne directly off the main branches. They are initially green in colour but ripen to a pleasant pale pink colour at which time they are sought after by all manner of animal life. Hornbills, barbets, rollers, green pigeons, brown-headed parrots, bushbabies, monkeys, baboons, bushpig, warthog, rhino, civets, porcupines, antelope and fruit bats all make use of the sycamore's figs and the tree is generally a hive of activity. Even fish eat fruit that is knocked into the water below. Conveniently for the wildlife, the sycamore fig has ripening fruit on its boughs all year round and can produce up to four crops annually.

Humans use the figs fresh but need first to wash out the **small fig wasps** which breed inside the figs. Although pesky at times, these wasps are crucial for the pollination of the tree (see p. 234) and neither wasp nor tree could perpetuate without the other. The Tonga people prefer to dry the fruit, which then taste more like sultanas and are longer lasting. A gin-like spirit can also be distilled from the figs.

The sycamore fig is a spectacular and iconic member of the Lowveld's riverine forests. Towering in height, it is conspicuous by its **yellow-coloured smooth bark** and contrasting dense, dark green crown, especially in the late afternoon light. The stems are buttressed and look fairytale-like growing alongside streams. The sycamore fig is a popular bonsai species for these features.

Bushveld gardenia
Gardenia volkensii

10 m

The **flowers** of the bushveld gardenia are large, sweet smelling and extremely attractive when they cover the tree in early spring. They begin white when they emerge at night and age to yellow relatively quickly before shrivelling up only to be replaced by another. The tree is often covered in flowers of different hues, imparting their pleasant fragrance to the immediate area. For this reason, gardenias are popular garden trees.

The **branches** of the gardenia are fairly distinct. The smaller branches tend to branch at right angles to one another mostly in splits of three. This creates an interesting dense, tangled canopy.

The **bright green leaves** occur in whorls of three around the smaller branchlets. They are balloon shaped and slightly scalloped along the apex (top point). They are also variable in size.

Gardenias make good **bonsai** specimens.

The **bark** of the gardenia is pale cream in colour and flakes off to leave behind yellow-coloured bark.

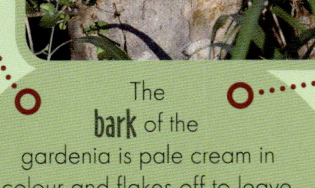

The **fruit** of the gardenia is grey-green, between the size of a large egg and an apple, hard and ridged. It is conspicuous for its uniqueness. It is not edible to humans and has emetic properties (it is used to induce vomiting for medicinal purposes). Baboons and kudu are known to eat the fruit.

Bushveld gardenias are **protected** trees in South Africa and may not be cut down. In the past the wood was used for smaller household utensils like spoons or ornaments.

Bushveld gardenias are sometimes planted at the entrances to kraals and homesteads to **ward off evil spirits**. They may also be planted on graves for this purpose.

Sandpaper raisin
Grewia flavescens

1–5 m

The members of the raisin family are named as such for their small **raisin-sized fruit** which in some cases turn black like a raisin on ripening. The sandpaper raisin fruit is brown in colour, two-, three- or four-lobed and covered with a rough skin which is removed by humans prior to eating the fruit. The fruit is fibrous with little flesh to chew but is sweet to the taste and is also favoured by animals such as baboons and civets. Crushed the fruit produces a tasty drink which can also be fermented into an alcoholic beverage.

Medicinally sandpaper raisins are used to cure nosebleeds and syphilis, to disinfect wounds, to restore energy after childbirth and to treat measles (by dropping an infusion of the leaves into the nose and ears!).

The **wood** of the sandpaper raisin is very strong and is often used to make walking sticks. The raisin species generally are used by the San to make the shafts of their arrows, the structural part of their bows or fire-sticks.

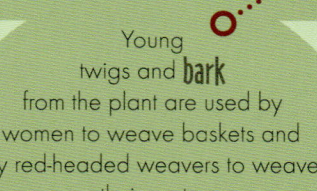

The **leaves** of the sandpaper raisin are rough to the feel and give the plant its common name.

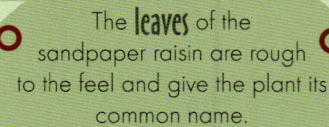

The specific name *flavescens* refers to the **colour yellow** of the delicate and profuse star-shaped **flowers**.

Young twigs and **bark** from the plant are used by women to weave baskets and by red-headed weavers to weave their nests.

The sandpaper raisin is unique for its obvious **square branches** (a trait shared only with the far less common climbing raisin, *Grewia caffra*).

Many **other Grewia** species occur in the Lowveld. Most of them are very similar looking, similar-sized bushy shrubs that form the medium level of vegetation in woodland and wooded grassland. The silver raisin (*Grewia monticolor*) white raisin (*Grewia bicolor*), brandy bush (*Grewia flava*) and giant raisin (*Grewia hexamita*) are the most common species and told apart by slight variations in the margins and symmetry of the leaves. All have round stems and small yellow flowers.

The Shangaan people use the square branches of the sandpaper raisin to conduct **traditional punishments**. Three equal lengths of a relatively thick branch are placed between the fingers of the offender while the hands are held palm-to-palm and fingers ajar. Once in position, the person conducting the punishment will squeeze the fingers closed. The fluted edges dig painfully into the finger nerves and the offender is expected not to flinch. As this exercise is often done as part of initiation ceremonies, the young candidate should show no pain if he truly is ready to become a man.

Apple-leaf
Philenoptera violacea

18 m

The apple-leaf gets its name from the **large, leathery leaves**, which when crushed, sound like someone biting into a crunchy apple, especially the drier leaves. Once crushed the leaves also have an apple-like scent to them.

The **leaves** are compound with characteristically large leaflets that are tough and leathery. There is usually one very large terminal leaflet and only one set of lateral leaflets (sometimes two, rarely three). The leaflets are typically damaged by insects and wind.

The apple-leaf produces profuse bunches of flat **pods** which decorate the tree for a protracted time.

The apple-leaf is sometimes also called the **rain tree** due to the presence of **spittlebugs or froghoppers** (*Ptyelus grossus*) (see p. 227) on the stems of the tree. Both the adults and larvae of this small insect species suck the sap from the tree's younger stems to extract nutrients. This they must do at such a rate to accumulate enough sugars that the excess fluid is emitted at almost the same speed it is ingested. As the liquid exits the insect from both its anus and special pores, it runs over the insect's head-downwards body, which the spittle-bug then froths into a foam that it uses to protect itself from the sun and from predators. Due to the excessive amount of froth, some of it drips down from the tree creating 'rain'. In extreme cases, pools form under the tree and the moisture can then be reabsorbed by the tree's roots.

The **bark** is pale grey and somewhat rough, peeling in small blocks to reveal a more yellow under-bark in older trees.

The apple-leaf is a *phreatophyte* – it indicates the presence of ground water, as its **roots** penetrate down to the water table. Most other bushveld trees have an adventitious root system that only penetrates 1 – 2 m under the ground and utilise the moisture in the soil surface, since the water table is generally quite deep under the ground.

It is believed to be exceptionally **bad luck** to cut down an apple-leaf. A split in the family is said to result from such action! If one is brave enough to risk this superstition, the wood can be used to make tool-handles, carvings, grain mortars and even dugout canoes. Hole-nesting birds like barbets and rollers seem to favour the apple-leaf as a choice of home.

The **flowers** are a pale violet colour to which the species name *violacea* refers. These hang in bunches off the tree (resembling bunches of grapes) in early spring. As the trees start to lose their flowers they form an attractive confetti-like mat around the tree.

Mike Amm

The apple-leaf has a **single, meandering trunk**. The main branches also undulate characteristically.

The **roots and bark** of the apple-leaf contain poisons and it is possibly this trait that keeps them from the devastation inflicted on other trees by elephants pushing them over. The tree is used as a fish poison by local people – throwing the toxic root or bits of bark into an isolated pool, the gills of trapped fish are arrested and the fish then float to the surface where they can be easily scooped up. Since the toxins affect the gills of the fish only, the flesh remains untainted and can be eaten. The roots are also burnt and inhaled to relieve the symptoms of the common cold.

Red spike-thorn
Gymnosporia senegalensis

3–8 m

The **leaves** of the red spike-thorn are leathery in texture and thick. The edges are fringed with fine serrations which feel much like the one side of a zip if one runs a finger against the margin. Biting into the leaf produces a distasteful dryness in the mouth as a result of the presence of tannins. The leaves, if folded carefully along the mid-vein and then blown into, produce an effective whistle.

The **spines** of the red spike-thorn are useful to local people wishing to stretch drum-skins. They are used as the pins to secure the taut skin over the body of the drum. The common fiscal bird finds the spines useful as butcher hooks and commonly stashes its prey in red spike-thorn larders.

Red spike-thorns have been used traditionally against **snakebite**. It is believed that if the head of the offending snake is burnt together with the root of the red spike-thorn and then mixed with a little oil and applied to the bite wound and tongue of the patient, he will be instantly cured.

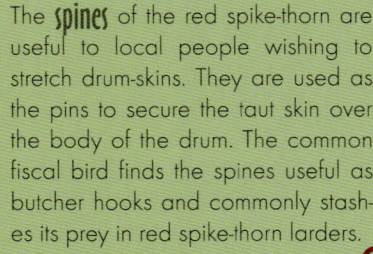

The red spike-thorn is sometimes called the 'confetti tree' because of the profuse and delicate nature of its **flowers**. When it blossoms, the red spike-thorn is quickly covered with sweetly scented many-flowered axillary clusters. The flowers do not last long and fall to the ground as they finish, creating a carpet around the bush. Handfuls of the fallen blossoms can be scooped up much like handfuls of confetti.

Due to the haphazard **shrub-like growth** form of the red spike-thorn, the tree does not produce useable pieces of timber. The wood is, however, hard and the straight branches have been used by locals as the drill part of their fire drills.

Common spike-thorn
Gymnosporia buxifolia

4–6 m

The tree's common name is somewhat misleading as the plant has neither spikes nor thorns but rather **spines** – stems modified into defensive armoury to protect it from overuse by animals. The younger branches, spines and midribs of leaves are tinged with pink, hence the 'red' part of the name.

The red spike-thorn is a **native encroacher** species and easily colonises disturbed areas to the exclusion of other indigenous species.

The **bark** of the red spike-thorn is smooth and grey. This trait makes it easily distinguishable from the similar common spike-thorn, which has **rough and deeply fissured bark** usually profusely covered with lichen.

Incidentally, the lichen growing on the trunks of trees can help determine direction in the bush when navigation is difficult due to overcast conditions. Lichen (like moss in wetter areas) grows on the cooler side of the tree, which in South Africa is the southern side. Obviously one should take care that the tree is not shaded on a particular side by other vegetation which would thus bias where the lichen grows!

The red spike-thorn is most commonly encountered growing in thick tangled stands along **riverine areas** or may be conspicuous in its evergreen form during winter amongst the dry grass of open areas.

The similar **common spike-thorn** (*Gymnosporia buxifolia*) is sometimes also called the pioneer spike-thorn for its propensity to grow in disturbed areas as a pioneer species. It has **greyer, more coarsely serrated leaves** than the red spike-thorn and these typically cluster at the base of the spines and occasionally emanate off the spines. The red spike-thorn's leaves generally occur singly or in pairs off the stems and spines. The common spike-thorn also has profuse flowers but unlike the red spike-thorn these are unpleasantly fragranced. The wood of the common spike-thorn is used for engraving or as handles for tools.

The **roots** of the red spike-thorn exhibit a multitude of medicinal traits. Boiled the roots are used in poultices to treat chest pains and the liquid can be added to porridge and fed to invalids. Chopped up and added to beer, the root is said to be an effective aphrodisiac and powdered and added to mustard oil it is used as a treatment for lice. A decoction of the roots can treat menstrual problems, cramping and prevent abortion. Roots combined with the thorns are implicated in the treatment of colds and coughs, pneumonia and tuberculosis.

Sausage tree
Kigelia africana

The **leaves** of the sausage tree are rough and leathery but still browsed by elephant and kudu. The young leaves are a lovely bright, shiny, green colour. The leaves can be used to produce a poultice to treat backache.

The **wood** is relatively soft but it is strong and does not crack and so it is used for planking, yokes, fruit boxes, oars and dugout canoes. It provides a poor fuel but the fruit can be dried and burnt successfully when there is a shortage of firewood.

The **bark** is light brown and smooth. In older trees it peels off in patches and the trunk becomes gnarled and grooved. The bark, like the fruit, has numerous medicinal uses. An extract is used to treat wounds and a decoction as a gargle for toothache. An infusion of the bark and root can be swallowed to relieve pneumonia and an infusion of the bark alone applied to the head to combat epilepsy.

Megan Emmett

The flowers are borne on long **hanging stems** that may be a full metre in length. The fruit subsequently grow on the ends of these stalks and there may be more than one sausage per stalk.

The **flowers** are conspicuous when they cover the tree in spring. They are large (15 cm across), deep red with yellow veins and trumpet- or cup-shaped with crinkly petals. They hang in groups of three off long stems with up to 12 on each stalk, creating the impression of an elegant candelabrum. The flowers appear just before the new leaves start and they have an unpleasant smell which does not deter nectar-eating animals like monkeys, baboons, sunbirds and insects, particularly *Charaxes* butterflies. It would appear that the tree is pollinated by bats which are probably responsible for knocking the flowers onto the ground where terrestrial mammals can access them. The flowers are eaten by impala, kudu, nyala, duiker, civets, bushpig and porcupines.

Sausage tree
Kigelia africana

25 m

The sausage tree with its giant **mushroom-shaped, dense canopy** is valuable as a source of shade and shelter for both wild animals and humans. The trees grow very quickly and are easy to cultivate in gardens but they do have rather invasive root systems. In parts of South Africa and Australia, sausage trees are planted as street trees down avenues. The sausage tree is considered holy by some African tribes but as attractive as they are as a site for religious meetings, picnicking or parking a car, care should be taken as the fruits tend to fall off the tree once ripe and may potentially cause some harm!

The sausage tree gets its name from its **enormous elongated fruits** that can reach proportions of up to 1 m by 18 cm and can weigh up to 12 kg. Hanging for a protracted time on the tree, these fruits resemble giant sausages hanging in a butcher's shop.

Megan Emmett

The sausage-like **fruit** is poisonous to humans while it is green and inedible even once it has ripened, although the fruit are regularly baked and then used to aid fermentation in the beer-making process. The seeds are imbedded in a fleshy pulp inside the fruit and these can be extracted and roasted to eat during times of famine. While humans avoid eating the 'sausages', many **animals utilise them as a food source** including monkeys, baboons, porcupines, bushpig, zebras, tree squirrels and hippo (in spite of them being grazers!). Even giraffe have been observed chewing comically on the young fruit like oversized sweets.

The fruit is used in an array of **traditional magico-medicinal treatments**. Unripe fruit is used in poultice form to cure syphilis and rheumatism. In powdered form, the sausage fruit is applied to skin sores and ulcerations and is effective against acne. A decoction (boiled solution) of the fruit and bark is administered orally or as an enema to children suffering from stomach complaints. Milk production in lactating women is said to improve once the fruit or a powder thereof is rubbed on the breasts; powdered fruit is applied to babies to ensure they become fat and healthy (avoiding the head area as application in this region is believed to cause hydrocephalus). Fruits are often strung up inside tribal huts to ward off whirlwinds and red dye can be extracted by boiling the fruit. There are rumours of the fruit being involved in genital enlargement ceremonies.

False marula
Lannea schweinfurthii

10 m

The false marula is named as such because it so closely **resembles the marula tree**, *Sclerocarya birrea* (see p. 302). However, it belongs to a completely different family.

The false marula's **bark** peels off in longish strips and is a uniform grey colour. It does not have the mottling of the marula's bark that leaves a whitish under-colour when the circular discs peel off. An infusion of the false marula's bark is used for tanning leather giving it a purplish colour.

Like the marula, the false marula **grows quickly** and does not have a very dense wood. The wood is generally only used for making household items such as wooden spoons.

False marulas make good **bonsai** specimens.

The easiest way to tell the false marula from the marula is by looking at the leaves. Both trees have compound leaves but the leaflets of the false marula are unstalked and attach directly onto the rachis (the main stalk of the leaf). Each marula leaflet has a long stalklet (called a petiolule) which attaches it to the rachis. The marula's leaves are blue-green in colour while the false marula has bright, shiny, green leaves with a waxy appearance. The terminal leaflet (at the end of the rachis) is often larger than the rest of the leaflets on the false marula and it has fewer pairs of leaflets (up to three pairs) than the marula (up to seven pairs).

Mike Amm

The **fruit** of the false marula is wine red and bunched together like grapes. They are edible to man and beast (including antelope, baboons, monkeys and warthogs) and relished by birds such as mousebirds and the grey go-away bird. The fruit taste a little like mini mangoes.

The false marula is **dioecious** meaning that male and female flowers are found on separate trees.

The false marula is often found growing on **termite mounds**. The mounds act as fertile islands amongst less nutritious soils and the tree's roots find their way more easily into the ground via the tunnels the termites have made. These often penetrate directly down to the water table. The movement and processing of organic material by the termites renders the soil nutrient-enriched.

The Swazi people call the false marula the 'tree of forgetfulness' as it is used in a **traditional ceremony** where enemies come together and forgive one another their grudges.

The **leaves** of the false marula have been used traditionally as a poultice. By chewing the leaves, the paste can be applied to skin abscesses to treat the infection.

294

Cork bush
Mundulea sericea

2–5 m

The cork bush is a very attractive plant. It has **pale grey leaves** embedded with fine silver hairs that give the whole plant a shiny appearance. When in flower, the cork bush turns **vibrant purple** with dense bunches of pea-like flowers.

The **bark** of the cork bush is thick, furrowed and corky which is where its common name comes from. It contains rotenone which acts as an insecticide. The bark (and seed) is also used extensively as a fish poison, actually killing fish when it is crushed and introduced to isolated pools of water. It does not merely stun the fish as many other fish poisons might. The **Zulu people** use the bark of the cork bush to treat poisoning in humans as it has an emetic effect (it causes vomiting).

Like the leaves, the **flat brown pods** are velvety in texture. The Latin species name *sericea* means 'silky' due to the nature of the leaves and pods.

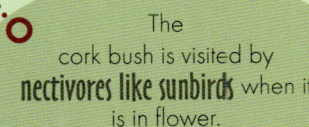

The cork bush is visited by **nectivores like sunbirds** when it is in flower.

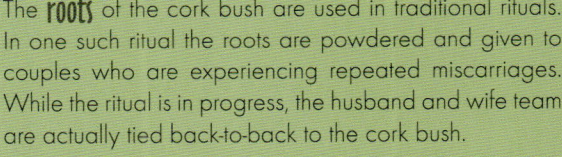

The **roots** of the cork bush are used in traditional rituals. In one such ritual the roots are powdered and given to couples who are experiencing repeated miscarriages. While the ritual is in progress, the husband and wife team are actually tied back-to-back to the cork bush.

Jacket plum
Pappea capensis

10 m

The jacket plum is often called the **indaba tree**. 'Indaba' is the Zulu word for meeting and the tree was traditionally used as a meeting place. The boughs of a fully mature tree droop down towards the ground but do not become dense around the trunk. Tribal chiefs would hold meetings under the boughs of the jacket plum as they could be screened from view but could still see out through the branches to keep an eye on their village. The tree does not have a dense canopy generally and the hot air easily rises up from below, sucking in cooler air from the sides and providing a well air-conditioned conference facility.

The *Pappea* part of the **botanical name** comes from Carl Pappe who was a professor of botany at what is now UCT (University of Cape Town). He also founded the herbarium at the South African Museum.

The **wood** of the jacket plum is used traditionally for making spoons and yokes. More recently it has been used for making furniture but decent sized planks are hard to come by.

The jacket plum has a **small plum-sized fruit** which has a hard but velvety green skin. When it ripens, the fruit splits open along a clean seam revealing juicy red flesh which makes the fruit look as if it were wearing a dinner jacket.

The **bark** of the jacket plum is distinctive and an easily identifiable feature of the tree. The bark is **mostly smooth** and looks as though it has been sponged down with two tones of grey paint. Older sections form rougher, blacker blocks that resemble small bricks on a peeling plastered wall. The bark has been used in the past to cure venereal diseases.

The **bright scarlet flesh** of the **fruit** is tasty and is eaten by many fruit-loving species from baboons and civets to mousebirds, barbets and starlings. Humans may eat the fruit as is or may stew it up into a jelly preserve. Vinegar and an alcoholic beverage are also made from the fruit.

Inside the **fruit** is a hard seed. This contains a great deal of viscous oil which may be extracted from the roasted seeds. Traditionally this oil was used for curing baldness and ringworm; more recently it has been used by farmers to oil their rifles. The oil is edible but may have a purgative effect if consumed. It is also used for soap making and as a lubricant.

The **leaves** of the jacket plum are oak-like in texture. They have either smooth margins on the older leaves or roughly toothed margins on the younger ones. The combination of both margin-types is a useful identification feature. Infusing leaves of the jacket plum is said to help ease sore eyes.

10–15 m

African weeping-wattle
Peltophorum africanum

The weeping-wattle gets the weeping part of its **name** from the fact that it **harbours spittlebugs** (see p. 227). These small sap-sucking insects tap moisture from the stems of the weeping-wattle so rapidly that it is excreted almost as quickly as it is ingested. Some of the fluid is frothed into a protective coating against the sun and predators but the copious liquid drips off the spittle-bugs and gives the impression that the tree is weeping.

The **flowers** are bright yellow with crinkly petals and create a spectacular show when they emerge in clusters on the trees. They are also sweet smelling and these features make the tree a particularly suitable specimen for growing in the garden (in frost-free areas). Nectar-loving insects such as bees visit the tree when it is in flower as do insectivorous birds which feed on the insects.

The **wood** of the weeping-wattle is fairly versatile and is used to produce furniture as well as finer articles such as ornaments or functional tools like axe handles.

The weeping-wattle has very **large, feathery, twice-compound leaves** that have a lovely velvety feel to them. It has been suggested that the leaves are the most suitable of all bushveld trees for use as toilet paper due to their softness. One does have to consider using more than one ply however and be careful not to confuse the tree with one of the thorny *Acacias* which may have similar leaves!

The **bark** of the weeping-wattle is dark and fissured lengthways and the younger stems are covered in red-brown hairs (as are most of the other parts of the tree). The bark is traditionally chewed to relieve colic and a decoction of the bark and leaves helps to expel internal parasites. The steam from a hot decoction of the bark is used to treat sore eyes.

The **pod** is a woody tear-shape with a bulge where the seed sits in the middle.

This is **not a particularly popular browse plant** and few indigenous herbivores use it extensively. Cattle and goats are fairly partial to the younger leaves and will eat the pods.

The **root** of the weeping-wattle has many traditional medicinal uses. Powdered it can be applied to wounds to speed up healing. As an infusion it may be consumed to relieve stomach problems or cure infertility in women. As a decoction it may be used as a gargle to treat sore throats or swallowed as a remedy for venereal disease. A sprinkling of the decoction in the home is said to keep witches at bay. A body wash can be made from the infused root and is said to cure oedema (body swelling); a wash made from the whole plant is used to treat the insane.

Wild date palm
Phoenix reclinata

The midribs of the **leaves** of the date palm are dried and used to weave mats. Fibres taken from young leaves are crafted into sunhats, carpets, brooms and ceremonious kilts. The leaves are not as tough as those of the lala palm and are not used for basket weaving as the lala palm leaves are.

The wild date palm is common wherever there are **watercourses or drainage systems** and it is often found growing in the actual water channel. It is obvious for its reclining growth form, which gives rise to the species name *reclinata*.

The **dates** of the wild date palm ripen bright orange at which time they are sweet and edible to humans. The pulp is, however, very thin. Local people use the fruiting stems, after they have lost their dates, as brushes for sweeping.

The wild date palm is particularly **popular with elephants** that ransack stands of the plant to raid the sweet dates or feed on the roots and leaves. Baboons also favour the fruit and fruit-loving birds such as mousebirds will also frequent fruiting plants.

The **root** of the date palm produces an edible gum which is popular with local children. A brown dye can also be obtained from the root.

Both the wild date palm and the lala palm are prone to forming **dense stands**.

Wild date palm
Phoenix reclinata

10 m

The **giant-sized, feather-like leaves** of the wild date palm originate out of the top of the palm's stem and usually obscure the stem completely from view, except in the odd case where a tree grows particularly tall. Up to a hundred leaflets occur on one leaf of which the lower ones are modified into spines which protect the base of the leaves and fruiting stems. The other palm found in parts of the Lowveld, the **lala palm** (*Hyphaene coriacea*), can be told apart by its grey-green, fan-shaped leaves.

The **palm swift** relies on the presence of palm trees to breed. These delicate birds use sticky saliva to glue their feathered nests onto the underside of palm leaves (usually lala palms are favoured, but date palms are sometimes used as well). Two eggs are laid which are also glued onto the palm leaves and the parent will then incubate its brood in a most unusual vertical position.

The lala palm contains milk much like coconut milk within its fruit. The pulp of the fruit is housed in a very hard skin (exocarp) but is still relished by baboons and elephants, which are believed to assist the seed in germinating, as does fire. Inside the fruit is also an **exceptionally hard 'vegetable ivory'** (endosperm) which is commonly used to fashion ornaments and buttons.

Sap is extracted by locals and used as a refreshing drink. Unfermented it has a ginger flavour. Once fermented the sap becomes an **intoxicating wine**. The sap is tapped from the stem just before the plant flowers, as there is an increase of sap rising up towards the flower heads at this time. The plants are burnt before they are tapped to increase the rate at which the sap rises and also to remove the spiny leaves. The stem is cut near the tip and the leaf blades are inserted into the incisions to act as spouts. The sap oozes out gradually and is collected in vessels placed below. During the tapping process, the stem is covered with other leaves to prevent the sap from drying up. Unfortunately, although the burning hardly affects the tree at all, the incisions often result in the tree dying afterwards. Lala palms are also tapped for their sap in this way to brew a particularly potent alcoholic beverage.

Round-leaved teak
Pterocarpus rotundifolius

1–20 m

This tree has multiple **common names** but all begin with 'round-leaved' because of the conspicuously round glossy leaflets it bears. It is called the round-leaved teak, the round-leaved kiaat and the round-leaved bloodwood. The specific name *rotundifolius* also refers to the round leaflets.

The generic name *Pterocarpus* means 'winged fruit' and refers to the **flat pods** that occur in clusters on the tree in summer. They are brown in colour (when mature) with a seed in the centre skirted by a lighter-coloured membrane that aids in dispersal.

Round-leaved teak uses its **propensity to coppice** to combat the effects of fire to which it is relatively sensitive. Frequent burning results in the prevalence of stunted, multi-stemmed plants and large trees are then seldom found. Dead branches tend to protrude from the canopy of the round-leaved teak after fires.

The **bark** of the round-leaved teak is brown, rough and fissured in older trees peeling away in places. Younger bark is greyer in colour and has a velvety texture.

Round-leaved teak **wood** is a good general-purpose timber when large enough specimens are grown. The wood has a pale yellow colour with brown markings that led to one of its colloquial names 'round-leaved bloodwood'. The wood is durable and insect-resistant although it has an unpleasant smell when it is first sawn up. The wood has been used for articles varying from wagon wheels to picture frames. It is a popular furniture wood especially for kitchens.

The **flowers** are yellow in colour, pea-shaped with crinkly petals and pleasantly scented. They occur in profusion after rain and provide a good source of nectar for insects and their avian predators. Bee farmers utilise round-leaved teaks extensively for their value as a nectar-producing plant.

The **leaves** of the round-leaved teak are borne on long stalks and the leaflets bear herringbone-like parallel venation which makes identification easy. The underside of the leaflets is covered in velvety hairs. An infusion of the leaves is traditionally applied to sore eyes to effect relief.

Round-leaved teaks are a **favourite food plant of the elephant** which is prone to damaging the plants in pursuit of the leaves and young branches. Impala, kudu and even stock animals are also fond of the round-leaved teak. The tree is equipped to deal with heavy browsing pressure by coppicing readily. It is this trait (in conjunction with overgrazed conditions) that contributes to the plant's habit of encroaching and forming almost pure stands of teak. These clusters of teak provide valuable cover and nesting sites for animals and birds.

Weeping boer-bean
Schotia brachypetala

25 m

The 'weeping' part of the **common name** comes from the bright red flowers that cover the trees at the beginning of spring. The **flowers produce such profuse nectar** that it drips out of the flowers and makes the tree appear as if it is weeping. Every nectivorous bird in the vicinity will be attendance of the tree when it is in flower and the squeaky-toy trills of the white-bellied sunbird are particularly prominent at this time. Monkeys and baboons eat the **flowers**, as do antelope, warthogs and civets which will pick up what the primates drop. There are also a host of insects that drink the nectar, out of the flowers or from the pools on the ground. These in turn attract insect-eating birds. *Brachypetala* means 'short petals' because the flowers have virtually no petals.

The 'boer-bean' part of the common name comes from the fact that the early Dutch settlers and Voortrekkers, who were sometimes known simply as 'the Boers', tried numerous plants out for their value as a **coffee substitute**. The seeds of the weeping boer-bean, they discovered, could be ground into a very palatable coffee and the tree hence became known as the 'boer-bean'. The seeds can also be roasted and eaten.

The **wood** makes a good all-purpose timber and is used in furniture production because of the decent-sized planks it produces. It makes particularly good benches. Sometimes the wood is used for floor boarding.

A **decoction of the bark** is used as a treatment for heartburn or is drunk to relieve hangovers.

The weeping boer-bean **grows along rivers or upon termite mounds** where they access well-aerated and fertile soil created by the termites' organic earth-works. The trees grow very large on these island habitats.

The **leaves** are often easily recognisable by the flat or winged rachis onto which the leaflets attach. The leaves can be used to curb nosebleeds if they are burnt and the smoke inhaled.

The **bark** contains tannin which is used for tanning leather. Tannins stabilise the protein in animal skins to prevent them rotting and hence convert the skin to preserved leather.

Marula
Sclerocarya birrea

Marulas are probably best known for the **delicious fruit** they produce. The plum-sized fruit fall off the tree green and ripen to yellow on the ground where elephants, baboons and antelope feast on them during the later summer months (Jan–Mar). The fruit has a lovely citrus flavour and has been used by humans to make jams, jellies, port, juice, beer and Amarula liqueur. They are many times richer in vitamin C (6,9 mg/100 g) than an orange even though the fruit contains significantly less flesh and juice than an orange!

There is an **exceptionally hard kernel inside the fruit** that has two to three caps that enclose the nuts. Nuts are high in protein and oil. The nuts taste like almonds and are collected by locals to be eaten (fresh or roasted) or pressed for the oil, which serves as a meat preservative and is also used in women's facial cosmetics as a moisturiser. Although humans battle to pop the caps off the stone to extract the tasty flesh, squirrels do not share this problem and feast on marula pips.

The kernel of a marula fruit passes untouched out of an elephant's stomach (elephants only digest 40% of what they eat and only the easiest material at that!). It is believed that the passage of the seed through the **gut of the elephant stimulates germination** which is further facilitated by the fact that the seed is deposited in a pile of compost.

Some suggestions have been made that elephant bulls tend to feast on marula fruit for the vitamin C to boost their immune systems before entering musth. In summer there is seldom a fruiting marula tree without an elephant bull in attendance. Once the fruit on the ground have all been scooped up, elephants are known to shake the tree to release more from the canopy. **It is not true that elephants (or baboons) become intoxicated from eating marula fruit**. Their digestive systems do not facilitate that kind of fermentation and this would be improbable with their rapid digestive systems anyway. Elephants would also have to eat an inordinate amount of fruit to achieve inebriation.

Elephants eat the leaves and roots of marulas pushing the trees over in times of food shortage to access these parts. They will strip the bark to access the **cambium (inner bark)** which comprises the vascular tissue. This is the part of the tree that transports water and nutrients from the roots to the leaves (and in reverse during autumn) and is understandably sought after by elephants. They often ring-bark the trees, which have the unusual ability to repair themselves (a trait shared with the baobab) and it is commonplace to see scarred marula trunks.

Marula
Sclerocarya birrea

7–18 m

The tree is **dioecious** and houses the male and female parts on separate trees. This means that cross-pollination is obligatory and keeps genes vigorous. The obvious way to tell the tree's sex is by the presence of fruit on the female tree. This is only reliable for a few months of the year. The locals have a tradition regarding the sex of a marula that can help determine the gender of an unborn child. If a family wishes to have a boy, the pregnant woman is given tea from the powdered bark of the male tree and should they wish for a girl, tea from a female tree.

The **leaves** of the marula are grey-green in colour. When new, they show a lovely pink rachis and petiolules (stalks on the leaflets).

The marula is **held in high regard** amongst the indigenous people of the Lowveld both for its yields and for its spiritual uses. Marriage ceremonies are associated with the marula and the tree symbolises fertility and tenderness. It is known to the Shangaan people as 'elephant tree' for its links to these animals, and diviners of this tribe use marula nuts as dice.

The **wood** is soft and used to make mokoros (dugout canoes) in the Okavango Delta.

The **inner bark** of the marula has antihistamine properties and is used successfully against the stings of hairy caterpillars in particular. A pinkish dye can be extracted from the inner bark and is generally used to dye basketwork. A brandy tincture made from the inner bark is also used as a traditional malaria prophylactic.

The marula is the larval host plant of the **lunar moth**. Local people use the cocoons of the lunar moths to make ankle rattles, achieved by filling them with small pebbles.

The **bark** of the marula tree is easily recognisable by the fact that it peels in circular discs revealing a white undercolour. The tree looks as if someone has taken an ice-cream scoop to it.

Marulas generally grow on the **crest of the catena**, thriving on the well-drained sandy soils found there and the uninhibited access to light.

The **roots** contain a significant amount of water. If a portion of root is cut and hung upside down, a fair deal of liquid will drip out and can be drunk. But one has to wonder if it is worth the effort, as digging up the root of the tree in the first place would be cause for some serious sweating!

Tamboti
Spirostachys africana

Tamboti **leaves** are a lovely fresh, green colour but the older leaves turn bright red and a number of these can be seen mixed into the canopy in an almost decorative fashion. A picked leaf exudes milky latex which should not be brought into contact with the eyes or mouth.

The tamboti tree is notorious for its **poisonous properties**. It contains toxic latex that causes blistering, eye irritation and even death if ingested in quantity. Burning the wood on campfires leads to diarrhoea and severe headaches, especially if meat is barbequed on the coals.

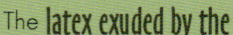

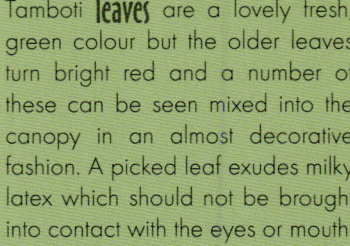

The **latex exuded by the leaves** has been used as a traditional treatment for toothache. Just one or two drops should be applied to the gum at the site of the sore tooth and this numbs the pain in this area.

The **latex is used as a fish poison**. By adding some of the toxic liquid to an isolated pool of water that contains fish, one can effectively stun the fish and thereby harvest a catch from the surface of the pool since the fish simply float to the top. The flesh can be eaten without ill effect as the poison interrupts the functioning of the gills and does not contaminate the rest of the body.

The tamboti tree is easily recognised by its very **straight, upright growth habit**. The trees sometimes occur in groves or stands along drainage lines where the preferred clay soils are to be found.

The **bark** is unmistakably black and blocky. Young trees are quite different, however, and have smooth, pale white-grey bark and side branches that are modified into protective spines. The paler young branches are still visible on the older trees towards the top of the canopy.

Tamboti
Spirostachys africana

18 m

The fruit of the tamboti consists of a small, three-lobed capsule. The fruit are dehiscent (they burst open) and the sound of the 'explosion' is actually audible in summer. The seeds of the tamboti are eaten by ground-feeding birds like doves, francolins and guineafowl. The seeds also become infested with the larvae of the knotthorn moth (*Melanobasis* spp.). The movement of the larvae inside the seeds makes them jump, particularly when they lie in the sun. The seeds are consequently known as jumping beans.

The tamboti's flowers are quite inconspicuous and the spikes consist of red female flowers at the base of the spike and yellow male flowers at the end. The fruit emerge from the female flowers while the male ones are still persisting.

The wood is an attractive reddish-brown colour with a lovely smell and it works well. It is popularly used for furniture, gunstocks and smaller carved items such as knife handles. One is advised to use a mask and eye protection when working with tamboti wood as even the sawdust causes eye irritation and numbness.

The wood is used as an effective insect repellent and blocks of this can be placed in cupboards to deter pests like fish moths. It has a more pleasant smell in a linen cupboard than mothballs!

The bark is used as a purgative in very small amounts.

Despite its poisonous properties, the tamboti tree makes up a large percentage of the diet of the black rhino, which suffers no ill effect from eating it. Porcupines relish the bark from the base of the stems and frequently ring bark the trees this way. Elephants eat tamboti for its purgative properties. Browsing antelope like nyala, impala and grey duiker eat both the fresh leaves and those on the ground without any trouble.

Black monkey-orange
Strychnos madagascariensis

6–15 m

The black monkey-orange bears a **fruit** about the same size as a commercial orange (up to 10 cm diameter), which starts out green-blue in colour and ripens to a dull yellow colour. Despite their size and thick rinds, the fruits are eaten by herbivores such as kudu, eland and nyala. Baboons, monkeys and bushpig will also eat the fruit (and manage them a little easier than the antelope). Because of their appeal to wildlife, local people bury monkey-orange fruit until they are ripe and ready to eat.

Humans may eat the fruit fresh (only when ripe) or dry and powder it in which form it may be kept for weeks. Drying the fruit with fire is said to increase the sweetness and for this task the silver cluster-leaf (see p. 308) is the favoured wood. The shells of the fruit are used as sounders on traditional musical instruments or may be used as decorative calabashes and placed in fruit baskets in modern game lodges and homes.

The **potent poison** strychnine is extracted from an Indian *Strychnos* species.

The **seeds** have a purgative effect if ingested.

The **stems** grow very erect and appear bunched as if tied together by an imaginary rope.

The **leaves** of the black monkey-orange are variable in size. The key distinguishing feature is the obvious three veins which originate from the base of the leaf. The side veins follow the margin of the leaf in parallel almost to the apex. The leaves are velvety in feel, shiny green on the upper side and borne in clusters off knobbly side-shoots, which resemble spines but are not. The leaves are held close to the branches and do not create a spreading canopy.

The **presence of spines** would probably indicate that the plant in question was in fact the similar green monkey-orange (*Strychnos spinosa*).

Common star-chestnut
Sterculia rogersii

The common star-chestnut has delicate, **trumpet-shaped yellow flowers** decorated with red lines. These usually cover the tree before it regains the leaves that it sheds in early autumn. The fruits occur on the tree at the same time as the flowers.

The **leaves** of the common star-chestnut are typically chestnut-shaped (three-lobed) and velvety. They have a dull grey-green colour.

The common star-chestnut is an unusual looking tree which is hard to miss with its **fat trunk** that resembles molten material both in shape and its grey-pink colour. Although it is not a very tall tree, the low branches make it a rather spreading specimen.

The **bark** is paper-like in texture and peels away to reveal a lighter red or yellowish under-colour. The under-bark is very fibrous and this is harvested for use as twine for weaving fishing nets or sewing sleeping mats.

The **common name** of 'star-chestnut' is derived from the peculiar fruit which consists of three to five velvety boat-shaped carpels which are arranged in a star-like pattern. Each carpel is velvety to the touch, about 5 cm long with a prominent beak. They are dehiscent and burst open to reveal the black seeds which are embedded in long, fine hairs. The seeds are edible but one should take care not to touch the hairs, which sting like those found on a hairy caterpillar if they come into contact with the skin.

Silver cluster-leaf
Terminalia sericea

The cluster-leaf trees belong to the Combretaceae family. The **wood** of all members of this family (which includes the red bushwillow and leadwood tree) is hard and termite-resistant. The silver cluster-leaf is no exception and its long-lasting wood is suitable for various purposes, from furniture and household items to fence poles and axe handles. The wood burns well as fuel too.

The **lowveld cluster-leaf** (*Terminalia prunoides*) is another common cluster-leaf found in the Lowveld but usually occurs most abundantly in the drier regions. It has a **fountain-like appearance thanks to its drooping branches** which carry clusters of small leaves on reduced side-shoots. The flowers of the Lowveld cluster-leaf have an unpleasant smell and a tree in bloom can be detected a good distance away. Usually unpleasantly scented trees rely on insects such as flies and moths to pollinate them as opposed to bees which usually pollinate sweet-smelling flowers. Like the silver cluster-leaf, the Lowveld cluster-leaf has hard wood that is used to construct kraals or fashion handles for implements.

Unlike their close relatives from the *Combretum* genus, trees from the *Terminalia* genus have two-winged **pods** (as opposed to four-winged pods). These are pink in colour and the dried-out pods persist on the tree for a long time.

The **lowveld cluster-leaf** (*Terminalia prunoides*) has wine-red pods, giving rise to its alternative name 'purple-pod terminalia'.

The silver cluster-leaf is often parasitised by a **gall-making wasp**. The wasp stings the tree with a growth hormone which causes the tissue in a localised region to expand, forming a hard, acorn-sized gall. These are often mistaken for fruits. The wasp lays her eggs inside this gall which acts as a safe-haven for the developing larvae.

Silver cluster-leaf
Terminalia sericea

6–20 m

The silver cluster-leaf is the **key identifying feature of seeplines**. These are water-saturated bands of veld that run along the contours of slopes. Underground water moving down the slope hits an impermeable layer (bedrock or dense clay) and is forced to the surface to form a seepline. The silver cluster-leaf is able to deal with the waterlogged conditions and quickly colonises the area. Seeplines are vital during dry times as they provide greenery for animals for longer into the dry season.

The silver cluster-leaf has a practical **common name**. Its long lance-shaped leaves are clustered at the ends of the branches and fine silvery hairs covering the surface of the leaves give them a shiny appearance with the result that the whole tree takes on a silvery sheen.

The **bark** of the tree becomes fissured with age. Extracts of the bark contain tannin and are used in tanning leather or for treating wounds and poisonings. It is sometimes also implicated in diabetes treatments.

The silver hairs on the **leaves** provide ideal glazing material and local people apply the leaves to their clay pots before they are fired to get a glazed effect.

The **bark of the silver cluster-leaf** peels back from the plant very easily and in long strips, which makes it ideal for braiding into rope or twine. This is accomplished by softening the bark and then either rolling pieces together against a thigh or using individual strips, twisting them individually and wrapping them together to form a strong twisted braid.

According to **tradition** the silver cluster-leaf should never be cut down lest the offender wish to bring on violent hailstorms in the area. Sticks removed from the tree are used in rituals to improve crop yield. The sticks are planted into the floor of shrines at planting time or harvesting time to achieve this.

The **root** is used medicinally in lotions and potions that treat stomach disorders, pneumonia or eye ailments.

Nyala tree
Xanthocercis zambesiaca

30 m

Nyala trees **grow along rivers or on termite mounds** where they have access to lots of moisture and fertile soils. This is necessary as the trees grow to be enormous. Spectacular specimens of nyala trees can be seen growing in profusion along some of the major Lowveld rivers like the Shingwedzi and the Levuvhu. They are also prolific in the Tuli Block of Botswana along the Limpopo and Shashe rivers where they are known as mashatu trees.

The **fruit** of the nyala tree is a grape-sized berry that is picked up off the ground and eaten by antelope such as bushbuck and nyala, from which the tree gets its common name. It is also eaten by other animals and humans. Local people make porridge from the dried pulp. Interestingly, the nyala tree is the only leguminous plant that produces berries rather than pea-like pods.

Nyala trees **branch low down** making them appear multi-stemmed and this contributes to their huge appearance. The trunks become elegantly fluted with age.

A typical feature of nyala trees is that the **leaves will grow directly out of the branches** and trunks in an untidy manner.

The nyala tree is a **phreatophyte** – it indicates the presence of ground water.

The **leaves** are compound with those leaflets nearer the petiole (leaf stalk) smaller than those towards the apex (leaf tip), the terminal leaflet being the largest. The leaflets alternate. From a distance, the leaves do not appear compound but merge together into a dense, spreading, shady canopy. Animals such as monitor lizards and baboons take refuge in the giant canopies of nyala trees.

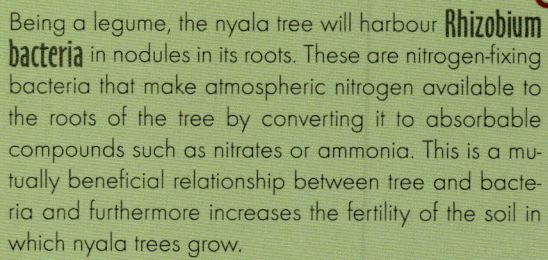

Being a legume, the nyala tree will harbour **Rhizobium bacteria** in nodules in its roots. These are nitrogen-fixing bacteria that make atmospheric nitrogen available to the roots of the tree by converting it to absorbable compounds such as nitrates or ammonia. This is a mutually beneficial relationship between tree and bacteria and furthermore increases the fertility of the soil in which nyala trees grow.

The nyala tree has a distinctive rough, **yellowish bark** that cracks into smallish squares.

The **wood** of the nyala tree is hard and can be worked, finishing with a smooth appearance, but it irritates the nose and throat in the process.

Buffalo-thorn
Ziziphus mucronata

up to 17 m

The buffalo thorn is also implicated in a **burial ritual**. If a man dies away from home, a friend or family member will travel to where he died, taking with them a branch from the buffalo-thorn to represent the soul they are going to fetch. During their journey, they will buy two of everything – two bus tickets, two meals – one for the traveller and one for the departed soul. Once the body has been retrieved, it will be buried with the buffalo-thorn twig. If there is no body to retrieve, the twig alone will be buried to represent the body. In this manner, the soul is returned to its native land. The hooked thorn is said to have captured the soul and the straight thorn directs it to heaven. Sometimes buffalo-thorns are planted on graves to protect them from animals.

The buffalo-thorn is the **source of many cultural beliefs**. The Zulu people call this the 'tree of life' and liken its zigzag branches with one's passage through life. At each zigzag junction there is a pair of thorns, one hooked, one straight (responsible for the second part of the tree's Afrikaans name 'wag-'n-bietjie' meaning 'wait-a-while'). The Zulus believe that at every junction in life we need to make decisions and the straight thorn resembles the future and looking ahead while the curved thorn cautions us to remember our past.

A **poultice of chewed leaves** is applied to skin sores. A poultice of the powdered and baked roots is applied to any area of pain. It is believed to enhance the treatment if the patient eats the poultice after topical application.

Buffalo-thorns make ideal **hedges** and are planted around homesteads for thorny protection.

The lovely **shiny green leaves** (responsible for part of the tree's Afrikaans name 'blinkblaar wag-'n-bietjie', meaning 'shiny leaf wait-a-while') are edible directly off the tree much like a salad herb or cooked up into nutritious spinach. Giraffe favour the leaves of buffalo-thorns and a browse line is often evident on these trees. Many other browsers also use it for its nutritious leaves.

The **fruit** ripen into red berries and can be eaten by humans if the birds and monkeys have left any behind. These can also be collected, dried and cooked into porridge. The seeds inside are ground up and used as a coffee substitute.

The buffalo-thorn is one of the **most useful trees** in the bushveld. Practically every part can be eaten or used to some advantage.

The buffalo-thorn is believed to **protect a person from lightning** should he take shelter underneath it during a storm. This is possibly because lightning tends to strike the tallest trees in a landscape and buffalo-thorns are typically shorter trees.

It is very **bad luck** to cut a buffalo-thorn down after the first rains, and drought is sure to ensue.

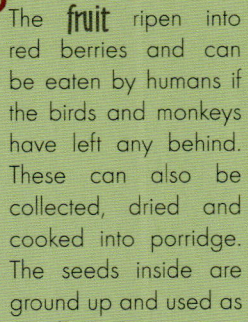

The buffalo-thorn's **roots** have been used rather successfully in the treatment of diarrhoea and dysentery probably due to high tannin contents.

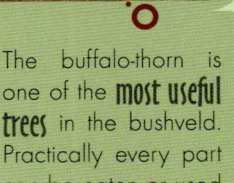

Grasses

By way of simple explanation, the **savannah (bushveld) biome** is the combination of grassland and woodland existing in a dynamic equilibrium. The **grassy layer** competes with the trees and shrubs to become pure grassland but is prevented from doing so by fire and grazing animals. The **woody layer** competes with the grass to become pure woodland (or ultimately forest) but is prevented from doing so by the foraging actions of browsing animals, including elephants, by fire and by seedling competition with the grass.

Because of its structure, bushveld supports a vast diversity of animal life. Creatures adapted to woody habitats, those adapted to grassy habitats as well as those that utilise both sorts, inhabit the bushveld.

Grass is adapted to being **utilised by grazers** or even to being burnt by the inevitable veld fires which are an integral part of the bushveld ecosystem.

The growth points on woody plants are usually at the tips of the shoots. Once removed through browsing, these parts are prevented from growing. Grass has **growth points on the tips of the shoots** as well as close to the ground. This means that a grass plant can be grazed or burnt down to ground level and will continue to grow.

Furthermore, during the growing season while the all-green grass plant is photosynthesising effectively, they are **constantly placing reserves in storage in the roots** and at the base of the culms (stems). As the plants lose their leaves to grazers, they tap into their reserve stores to replenish themselves. Once they have grown adequate green material again to photosynthesise, reserve stores are once again bolstered.

Grass plants are so adapted to being utilised that they actually require it to stimulate their growth. Grazers and fire remove old material, which prevents the grass plant from becoming moribund. A **moribund grass plant** is one that has collected all its own dead leaf material upon itself to the point that the plant begins to 'suffocate'. Water and sunlight do not penetrate the dense tangle and the rootstock weakens to the point that the plant may die.

The **converse is over-utilisation**. After a grass plant has been heavily grazed, it needs time to recover before being used again. Excessive grazing causes the plant to use up all its stored resources so that it cannot re-grow after all. It also weakens the roots so that they can no longer absorb water. In nature, animals migrate or rotate their feeding grounds seasonally and thereby avoid over-utilising their pastures. Over-utilisation generally occurs when small reserves are fenced in and animals cannot migrate or there are too many animals on the reserve. Domestic animals tend to overgraze natural pastures. Drought is also a form of over-utilisation.

Over-utilisation affects the equilibrium between grass and woody vegetation. Since trees and shrubs now have the competitive advantage over the weakened grass layer, bush encroachment often occurs as a result.

Grasses

Grazing value (GV)

The amount of green leafy material that a particular species of grass plant produces is variable. **The ability of a grass plant to generate leaves and the subsequent nutritive content** of these is considered its grazing value. Leaves are nutritious and palatable (digestible) if they have low fibre and contain lots of nutrients absorbed from the soil and produced through photosynthesis. The more green leafy material a grass plant possesses, the more glucose it can produce through photosynthesis. Grazing animals will mostly choose to eat grass species that have high or average grazing values. These are mostly perennial grasses (have a life cycle that takes longer than two years to complete) and will generally grow in moist habitats.

Compare **foxtail buffalo** to **carrot seed** grass.

Ecological value of grass

Grass is vital in the savannah biome because it **provides food on a sustainable basis for animals** such as grazing antelope, zebra, buffalo, cane-rats, seed-eating birds and insects like locusts and termites. It also provides habitat and nesting material for the likes of ground-nesting birds, reptiles and rodents.

Grass is a **vigorous and spreading groundcover that protects the earth** from the erosive forces of wind and rain. As groundcover, grass absorbs the velocity of rain, slowing and collecting the resultant water runoff and allowing it to seep into the ground where it replenishes underground reservoirs. The soil surface is also sheltered from baking by the sun and the removal of particles by the wind. The combined effect is that the ideal growth conditions for seed germination are created. As grass grows, parts of the plant die off and this organic material in conjunction with the excrement left by grazing animals fertilises the soil.

Basic terminology

Culm: Stem of grass plant

Inflorescence: Flowering head of grass plant

Spikelet: Flower unit (bears florets and seeds)

Spike: Unbranched inflorescence with sessile (stalkless) spikelets

Panicle: Branched inflorescence

Raceme: Unbranched inflorescence with stalked spikelets

Community: A group of different species in a common area

Grasses

Ecological status (ES)
Every species of grass has a **specific set of preferred conditions** under which they will grow well. Different types and degrees of utilisation (be it by grazers or by fire) may change these conditions and grass species **react differently to these changes** – one group of grass species may decrease in number while another may increase.

Foxtail (blue) buffalo grass
Cenchrus ciliaris

GS	Climax & sub-climax
ES	Decreaser
GV	High

Foxtail is aptly named for its fluffy spikes that resemble small animal tails. Each spikelet is dressed with wavy, purple bristles that make the inflorescences stand out amongst the grass plant's dense green leaves. Like other climax grass, foxtail buffalo grass has a very high grazing value in spite of its propensity to grow in more arid areas (where it may also act as a sub-climax grass). It grows in well-drained soils and in fertile hotspots like the sides of termite mounds. It also often grows where it can benefit from excess water running off roads. This climax grass has a root system that may penetrate up to 2 m into the soil and is an excellent soil preserver in this sense. It can also endure trampling by animals such as buffalo which may visit pastures for the nutritious leaves. As soon as ideal growing conditions diminish or major disturbances take place, foxtail buffalo grass starts to disappear from the system.

Decreaser: These species **proliferate where there are ideal growing conditions** and diminish or 'decrease' in number as soon as overgrazing (or under-grazing) takes place. They are usually climax grasses and have high grazing value. A large presence of decreasers in the bush is an indication of healthy veld.

Narrow-leaved turpentine grass
Cymbopogon plurinodis

GS	Climax
ES	Increaser I (III)
GV	Low

The turpentine grasses get their name from the turpentine-like smell that the fresh leaves and inflorescences give off when crushed. This scent is as a result of essential oils found in the plant. The oil in narrow-leaved turpentine grass is complex and contains 17 different ingredients. Despite the relatively substantial tuft of blue-green leaves that the plant produces around its base, the oil in the grass makes the plant very distasteful and unpalatable to grazing animals. Narrow-leaved turpentine grass grows in many different soil types and usually reaches a climax when veld is underused.

Increaser I: These species prefer not to be defoliated (leaves removed) and **proliferate where the bush has been under-utilised**. They are usually climax grasses with a low grazing value.

Saw-tooth love grass
Eragrostis superba

GS	Subclimax
ES	Increaser II
GV	Average

Saw-tooth love grass is easily recognised by its large heart-shaped spikelets that resemble large kernels of wheat with jagged edges. The lower parts of the culms are often bent noticeably. This grass enjoys the conditions of relatively overgrazed areas and grows rapidly, improving the prevailing dire conditions. It is a relatively palatable grass earlier on in the growth season but becomes less desirable towards winter as it hardens.

Increaser II: These species **thrive in over-utilised areas** and inevitably colonise disturbed, bare patches of ground. They are usually hardy pioneer and sub-climax grasses.

Grasses

Grassland succession (GS)

Grass species tend to **occur as specific communities depending on the prevailing growth conditions**. Communities are progressively replaced by other communities as growth conditions change in a dynamic process known as grassland succession. Usually preceding communities improve the growth conditions for their successors until a climax community is reached. If disturbances occur that render growth conditions less favourable, succession is retrogressive and weaker pioneer or sub-climax communities again take hold.

The pioneer community

When disturbances take place that expose bare ground, it is a **hardy group of grass species** that move in to colorise the soil. This community is known as the pioneer community. **They are small annual grasses with little leaf growth**. Annuals complete their life cycles in just one year and so all available resources are directed towards producing seeds in which form the plants will survive until the next season. Although small, the pioneers redirect water runoff into the ground and trap seeds. Their roots bind and protect the soil and when the plant dies, they add organic material to the soil. These actions ready the ground for better seedling development and support the next, slightly more substantial community. Because of their low leaf production and poor growing conditions, pioneers have a low grazing value.

Carrot seed
Tragus berteronianus

GS	Pioneer
ES	Increaser II
GV	Low

Carrot seed is a very small, flat grass plant with short wavy leaves and long thin spikes. It inhabits the barest and hardest soil surfaces before anything else is able to. In this regard, carrot seed is considered an indicator of over-utilised or drought-stricken bush. This tough little annual produces copious amounts of seed to ensure it perpetuates into the following season. Each spikelet is barbed and when it dries it adheres to everything it touches, animal hoof and human sock alike. This vigorous reproductive strategy results in a greater number of plants appearing on the barren surface and each one then protects an additional small section of soil and thereby enhances the growing conditions there.

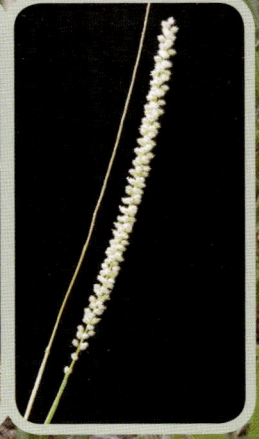

Natal red top
Melinis repens

GS	Pioneer (sub-climax)
ES	Increaser II
GV	Low

Natal red top is a pretty grass with fluffy red inflorescences that change to white once they mature. Stands of Natal red top typically line the verges of roads where they are most noticeable during the early morning and late afternoons when the sunlight illuminates the 'red tops'. Natal red top grows beside roads because it favours the disturbed, well-drained soils that occur there and it plays a vital ecological role in stabilising these areas. So effective is this attractive grass that it may perpetuate to serve as a sub-climax community as well. Although it has only a few meagre leaves per plant, these are in fact palatable to animals.

Grasses

Tassel three-awn
Aristida congesta* subsp. *congesta

GS	Pioneer
ES	Increaser II
GV	Low

The three-awn grasses are easily recognised because the shaft of each spikelet is divided into three portions or awns. The main shaft of the spikelet is twisted in the manner of a corkscrew and this design drives the barbed seed (positioned terminally) into the hard earth where it falls. The effectiveness of the seed's penetration is demonstrated when the seeds come into contact with a human shoe and work their way through both the canvass of the shoe and the sock below to end up wedged in one's skin. Such an aggressive approach is required of a successful pioneer grass. Little energy is invested in the growth and leaf production of the plant, rendering it a very poor grass for grazers but this ensures that the three-awn can perform its role of stabilising disturbed habitats without unnecessary competition by herbivores.

Tassel three-awn is very similar to spreading three-awn grass (*Aristida congesta* subsp. *barbicollis*), however the spreading three-awn has only one or two branches on the panicle whereas spreading three-awn has three branches or more. These plants are subspecies of one another and may hybridise, causing further confusion.

The sub-climax community

The sub-climax community maximises on the improved growing conditions provided by the pioneer community and gradually **takes over from the pioneers**. Sub-climax grasses are bigger, stronger plants as they invest more energy into the growth and structure of the plant so that it might last the duration of its two- to five-year life cycle. Sub-climax grasses are weak perennials but still have more to contribute than pioneer species in the form of the amount of soil each plant can protect and the amount of water each plant can trap. The denser cover shades the soil providing shelter from the baking sun and conserving surface moisture. The sub-climax grasses contribute more organic material to the cycle than the pioneers were able to do and growing conditions improve significantly. Often one sub-climax community is replaced by another for several generations, each benefiting by the improved conditions and contributing more to perfecting the environment to support a climax community.

Spear grass
Heteropogon contortus

GS	Sub-climax
ES	Increaser II
GV	Average

Spear grass is a striking grass where it grows as a stand because of its bright green colour and dark spear-like awns. As the season progresses and the inflorescences dry out, the spikelets twist and bunch together forming matted heads amongst the swathe. The same design which causes the awns to tangle drives the seed (placed at the one end of the awn) into the ground. Spear grass grows on gravelly soils and a hardy seed dispersal mechanism is critical. Spear grass seeds easily penetrate human skin. The grass plants themselves are exceptionally hardy even proving resistant to fires. In spite of its endurance and persistence as a sub-climax grass, spear grass is in fact relatively palatable early in the growing season (summer) and is favoured by waterbuck.

Grasses

Blue-seed grass
Tricholaena monachne

GS	Sub-climax
ES	Increaser II
GV	Average

Blue-seed grass has a delicate, attractive panicle, the spikelets resembling small beads. It is this quality that has led to its use in flower arrangements. The culms are also fine and delicate and used by blue waxbills in the construction of their nests. The plant does not produce much foliage albeit the leaves are palatable and it is thus able to avoid excessive attention from herbivores and play its role in protecting over-utilised areas.

Eragrostis species

GS	Sub-climax
ES	Increaser II
GV	Average

Generally the *Eragrostis* genus of grass, all the species of which have wheat-like spikelets of varying size (some are tiny), fulfils the role of the sub-climax community. Most species colonise over-utilised areas and offer an average grazing value to animals.

Grasses

The climax community

The climax community is the **final stage in grassland succession**. It comprises strong perennial species of grass that thrive under ideal growth conditions and these will continue to grow as long as the conditions continue. The grass plants are usually large and spreading in design and they produce vast quantities of highly nutritious leaves ideal for grazing animals. Climax communities are generally stable and resilient to minor changes and disturbances. They completely fulfil all the functions of healthy ground cover including soil protection, moisture infiltration and retention, seed bank construction and organic recycling.

Guinea grass
Panicum maximum

GS	Climax
ES	Decreaser
GV	High

Guinea grass is a wonderfully lush, leafy grass partly because of its tendency to grow in moist, shady, fertile places often along rivers or under *Acacia* trees where the soils have been enriched by nitrogen-fixing bacteria (see p. 253). It has an enormous value in the ecosystem as a grazing grass and although it is a climax species, it is also able to fulfil the role of pioneer and sub-climax grass in the specific habitats where it grows. The attractive, large open panicle is littered with round green and purple spikelets which provide food for seed-eating birds like finches. An abundance of guinea grass in an area is an indication of healthy veld. So useful is this grass that it is used commercially in cultivated pastures and to make hay.

Red grass
Themeda triandra

GS	Climax
ES	Decreaser
GV	High

Red grass gets its name from the fact that the entire plant turns a rich red colour at the end of the growing season. This appealing grass is made more noticeable for its habit of growing in dense stands. Such areas are exceptionally valuable to grazing animals due to the highly palatable and copious leafy material. Red grass is very persistent as a climax community and even increases when exposed to regular fires. Swathes of red grass amidst the veld are a clear indication that the veld is in a healthy condition. Conversely, red grass will disappear from a system should the veld conditions deteriorate, in other words, it decreases.

Grasses

Seepline indicators

Herringbone grass and gum grass are seepline indicator species. Their concentrated abundance in a particular area is clear evidence that the band where they are growing experiences seasonal water-logging. This is as a result of groundwater rising to the surface due to the transition of sand and clay soil (or bedrock) on the middle contours of a catena (see p. 10).

Herringbone
Pogonarthria squarrosa

GS	Subclimax
ES	Increaser II
GV	Low

The inflorescence of herringbone grass bears red-brown lateral racemes that resemble the cleaned bones of a fish. Herringbone is an erect, sparse, hardy grass that aside from protecting the dynamic soils of seeplines is only really useful for making broom heads.

Gum grass
Eragrostis gummiflua

GS	Subclimax
ES	Increaser II
GV	Low

Gum grass is aptly named for its sticky culms, a result of glands in the upper portion of the leaf sheaths. This gummy substance lowers the grazing value of a grass that should essentially have a moderate grazing value (like the other *Eragrostis* species). Like herringbone, this lack of palatability renders the grass an effective grass cover over the sensitive seepline habitat. The inflorescence is relatively rigid compared to other *Eragrostis* species and the culms are hard. Like herringbone, this grass is well suited to use as broom heads. The nodes and other sticky parts are purple.

Common reed
Phragmites australis

GS	NA
ES	Decreaser
GV	Low

The common reed is very tall, reaching heights of up to 4 m and is attractive when adorned with its fluffy, willowing inflorescences. It is found growing as dense stands near water or even in the water channel. This hardy grass serves numerous important ecological functions in the wetland habitats of the Lowveld (and southern Africa generally). Many animals and birds shelter in the dense stands of reeds especially weavers, warblers and waterfowl. Old buffalo bulls enjoy lying up in reed beds near water. The reeds act as a natural purification system for the waterway, filtering out undesirable contents. They also buffer adjacent areas from flooding. The common reed is useful to humans too. They have been used to construct fences, build huts or as a substitute for thatching grass to roof buildings. Household articles like mats and baskets can be woven with material stripped from the reeds and the hollow shaft was traditionally used to make arrows.

Small plants and wild flowers

Monkey or baboon's tail (black stick lily)
Xerophyta retinervis

This small plant is **aptly named for its dark fibrous stems** that stand erect in the ground and resemble the tail of a monkey or baboon. The leaves of the baboon's tail are grass-like and emerge from the top of the stem like a small fountain. Once these have died, the leaf bases add to the structure of the stem much like a palm's leaves. The resultant stem is non-flammable and is most popularly used by bushmen to carry coals. By removing a small section at the top of a stem and hollowing out the space, a small coal can be inserted and carried a long distance before being used to start another fire. The tough stems are also **used as pot scourers**. Medicinally baboon's tail is implicated in asthma cures and magically as a charm against being struck by lightning. The baboon's tail grows in hot, dry rocky places and is anchored in these formidable habitats by a thick root. It produces sprays of sweetly scented white or mauve flowers at the start of summer.

Megan Emmett

Mother-in-law's tongue
Sansevieria aethiopica

The unique name of this plant comes from the flattened tongue-shaped leaves that emerge directly from the ground and terminate in a sharp point. The usefulness of this derogatorily named plant is extensive. The leaves produce excellent fibre and are used by bushmen to produce string for their bows. Sometimes the mother-in-law's tongue is actually called 'bowstring hemp' due to this feature. The **fibre is also used to weave fishing nets** and sleeping mats or as fishing gut. The fibres are separated from the leaf structure and then the individual strands are rolled together using the palm of a hand against a thigh. Pieces are gradually rolled together to increase the length of the strand and then two strands are woven together for reinforcement.

The leaves are attached to a **sturdy root** below the surface of the ground and this can be **dug up and chewed for moisture** should a person find himself short of water and in need of surviving in the bush. The root was also historically used by European farmers in southern Africa to cure haemorrhoids and the effectiveness of the treatment led to its Afrikaans name 'aambeiwortel' (which literally means 'haemorrhoid root'). The root is cut up and boiled with water or milk and then swallowed. The medicinal treatment causes the swollen veins around the rectum to constrict relieving the pain and pressure of the piles. The root is also used as a traditional treatment for earache and is ritually twisted into the ear. This practice led the Tswana people to name telephones after the plant due to the fact that they are held to the ear and have a twist in the cable.

(Long thin-leaved species = *Sansevieria pearsonii*)

Small plants and wild flowers

Wild basil (wild anaseed)
Ocimum canum (americanum)

Wild basil is conspicuous for its **appealing aroma after the rain**, when damp with dew early in the morning or when the seed heads are crushed between fingers. The aromatic properties of this small herb have led it to be used for a variety of purposes. Wild basil is used as a substitute for commercial basil in cooking and can be used to flavour foods boiling in a pot or being cooked over an open fire. The leaves are also dried and used as a kind of herbal tea which is effective in relieving fevers. The leaves have other medicinal functions including the relief of chest complaints and nose bleeds if the smoke of burning leaves is inhaled. The smoke of the plant is also an effective insect repellent. Dried leaves rubbed on the head repel lice and rubbed on the body act as a **deodorant**. Fresh leaves rubbed on the skin act as a muscle-relaxant and sometimes ointments made from leaves and oil are produced to this end. The oiliness of the fresh leaves is also effective to deter pestilent insects from biting a person. Dead bodies are even covered with wild basil to repel flies and conveniently these mask the odour as well. When embarking on a long walk in the bush, one may consider placing fresh leaves in one's shoes to **alleviate potential foot soreness**.

Leopard orchid
Ansellia gigantea

Orchids are an ancient family of plants comprising about 18 000 species world-over. They are valued for their often spectacular flowers. The leopard orchid is the **largest orchid plant** of the 500 species found in southern Africa and gets its name from its delicately scented flowers, which are yellow in colour dotted with brown like a leopard's coat. Sometimes appearing as a pile of garden rubbish caught in the fork of a large tree, the leopard orchid is not a parasite but rather an epiphyte, meaning it uses the tree for support and access to light but not for food. For this it has aerial roots and establishes a compost heap within the centre of the plant accumulating its own decomposing material. It is thought that leopard orchids establish themselves in the higher boughs of trees by virtue of monkeys' feeding habits. Vervet monkeys eat the seeds and sweet canes of the leopard orchid dispersing the seeds in the process. The Zulu people call the plant 'imfe-nkawu' which means **'sugarcane of the monkey'**. The Zulu people also use the leopard orchid in a **love charm ritual** whereby a desired partner can be caused to think of his or her admirer. To achieve this, a person must chew the roots or canes at midnight and then spit out the masticated bits while saying the name of the person desired. Leopard orchids are also used traditionally to remedy bad dreams and are often planted in homesteads to ward off lightning. Plants are only suitable for use as muthi (traditional medicine) once they are at least 10 years old. The largest clusters may be up to 100 years old.

Small plants and wild flowers

Poison apple
Solanum panduriforme

So poisonous is the poison apple fruit that the consumption of it will cause the stomach and intestines to swell, will induce convulsions and a coma and ultimately **may even prove fatal**. The fruits are most poisonous when they are green as they contain high quantities of solanine, a substance which remarkably is also present in all parts of the commercial potato plant. It is, however, eaten by animals under stressful conditions and is used medicinally for a number of remedies. The **root is used to treat boils** and coughs and is taken orally to cure piles. The mashed plant is used to relieve constipation and where babies are suffering from stomach problems a mother may chew the root and then administer her saliva directly into the infant's mouth. An ointment prepared from the plant is said to remedy rheumatic pains and the fruit mixed in water is applied to sore eyes. Hunters that wash themselves with an infusion of the root of the poison apple are sure to have a successful hunt.

Wild sesame
Sesamum triphyllum

Wild sesame is a herb that grows in disturbed areas where it is noticeable for its tall erect stems adorned with **attractive pink tubular flowers** with deeper pink throats. The leaves have a strong aroma when crushed and produce a glutinous substance that can be used instead of soap. Bushmen use the wild sesame plant to construct shelters in which to sleep or cook. When added to fresh milk, a yoghurt-like liquid results which is drunk by men as an aphrodisiac. Snakebites are treated with the burnt roots of the wild sesame mixed with petroleum jelly.

Wild foxglove
Ceratotheca triloba

The wild foxglove is **attractive for its mauve flowers**, trumpet-like in shape and edged with purple stripes. The flowers open from the bottom of the spike upwards and are ideal for use in decorative pressing. This herb may reach 1,5 m in height growing as a **pioneer plant in disturbed soils**. The leaves are foul smelling and can be used to manufacture insect-repellent sprays. The leaves are also cooked and eaten as spinach, losing their aroma on boiling. They are nutritious being rich in vitamins, iron and calcium. Medicinally the wild foxglove is useful to treat diarrhoea, earache, eye problems, flatulence, menstrual pain, nausea, stomach cramps and to induce abortion.

Small plants and wild flowers

Devil's thorn
Dicerocaryum eriocarpum

The devil's thorn gets its name from its fruit. The small oval is just over a centimetre in size and **adorned with two sharp thorns** which face upwards like the horns of a devil, a design that facilitates dispersal as the seeds thus stick to the hooves of animals. 'Dikera' from which the generic name is derived means 'two horns'. The plant is a creeper that grows on the ground and produces pink trumpet-shaped flowers and bluish-green leaves. These can be eaten as spinach. The most notable feature of the leaves however is their propensity to foam when mixed with water. This is as a result of saponins in the leaves, steroid glycosides that work like an antiseptic or detergent transporting dirt off the surface to which it is applied. In this regard, the devil's thorn is used as a **substitute for soap** or as a lubricant for child or stock birth. Remarkably, the liquid assists with actually causing the birth canal to dilate and can also be taken orally to assist with labour or constipation. Men may opt to bath with the liquid derived from boiling the roots of the devil's thorn to acquire good luck during a hunt.

Cape honeysuckle
Tecomaria capensis

Cape honeysuckle is most often encountered in the understorey of riverine forests or elsewhere along drainage lines or streams where it provides a showy display of ruby-orange flowers and attracts all manner of nectivorous birds and insects. This attractive indigenous shrub is **cultivated broadly** in gardens for these characteristics. When bare of flowers, the shrub can be recognised by its flimsy shiny dark green compound leaves, each leaflet delicately adorned with scalloped edges.

Mistletoe
Plicosepalus kalachariensis

Mistletoe is a **parasitic plant** that grows on the crowns of trees (particularly marula trees and **Acacias**) deriving its nutrients from them by inserting an absorbent organ into the tree's vascular tissue, which works much like a tree-graft. Once established, the plant does produce greenish chlorophyll-endowed leaves and can photosynthesise its own food in part. Mistletoe produces bright pink-orange flowers in winter when little else is in flower. **Nectivorous creatures** such as birds and butterflies visit the flowers which burst open on contact to shower its visitors with pollen, ensuring cross-pollination. Birds also visit the parasite when it fruits, acting as dispersal agents. Once eaten the seeds are either regurgitated immediately (e.g. by barbets and starlings) or defecated out immediately (e.g. by bulbuls and mousebirds). Small bird species may not even swallow the seeds but peck off the flesh and then wipe the sticky seed onto a branch where it germinates promptly. The Afrikaans name for mistletoe is 'voëlent' which means 'grafted on by birds'. The fruit can be used as a **traditional birdlime to catch birds**. The pulp from the boiled fruit is combined with oil and then smeared onto a branch where a small bird is likely to land. Its feet stick to the smeared substance. A similar lotion is also traditionally placed on sticks and pointed at the sky to ward off impending rain.

Small plants and wild flowers

Wild dagga
Leonotis leonurus

The name of the wild dagga immediately leads one to believe that the plant is associated with the hallucinogenic *Cannabis* plant but it is not. Although wild dagga is smoked by many tribes (first recorded by Van Riebeeck as being used by Cape Hottentots) it is **not a narcotic** and in fact causes nausea. It does contain a similar resin to *Cannabis* and when the leaves of the *Cannabis* plant are very young they resemble those of the wild dagga plant. The plant, with its erect stems and ball-like flower structures, gets its generic name from the Latin 'leon' meaning lion and 'ous' meaning ear. The hairy petals are said to resemble a lion's ear. The **orange flowers are rich in nectar** and are visited by butterflies, birds and even sucked by humans. Medicinally the plant is implicated in treatments for elephantiasis, syphilis ulcers, skin problems and tapeworm.

Lion's eye
Tricliceras mossambicense

The lion's eye is a small herb commonly encountered in grassy areas of the bush during summer but most especially early on in the rainy season. Each sparse plant renders a few bright orange flowers atop a very erect but thin stalk which are supposed to **resemble the honey-orange colour of a lion's eyes**. The flowers close up at night but reopen the following morning. The lion's eye is made more noticeable by its attendance of butterflies.

Impala lily
Adenium multiflorum

Spectacular crimson-lined white flowers (5 cm wide) drape the impala lily plant in the middle of winter when the plant is bare of all else, making it stand out vividly amongst the dry landscape. These succulent shrubs generally grow in rocky areas and are solidly anchored to the ground by chunky underground stems. The waxy green leaves emerge in summer once the last of the flowers are gone and cluster towards the ends of the branches from where they are browsed by game despite their supposed toxicity. Fish and arrowhead poisons are prepared from the impala lily. The impala lily can potentially grow up to 3 m high but seldom reaches 1 m tall due to browsing pressure from wild animals.

Small plants and wild flowers

Ruby gnidia
Gnidia rubescens

This **small perennial herb** resembles the flower of the noxious *Lantana* weed but is bright red in colour with yellow highlights and grows as a single stalk amongst the grass. The word 'gnidia' comes from the Greek city Knidos but its association with the plant is not broadly reported. Species of *Gnidia* are used medicinally in curing headaches, fevers and bad dreams as well as for divining torches used to locate crooks.

Purple pan weed
Sphaeranthus incisus

This flat little herb with its **sticky leaves** and round flower heads (indicated by the generic name *Sphaeranthus*) grows in temporary pans where the clay soils tend to retain moisture throughout the year. The purple pan weed **smells like sage** due to the presence of aromatic oils and can be used as an ingredient of potpourri (room-scenting fragrant dried flower mix). The plant is traditionally used to induce abortions and is sometimes drunk as an infusion prior to sexual intercourse to prevent conception. This unfortunately has negative side-effects in the form of headaches and hallucinations.

Morning glory
Ipomoea species

Morning glory is a ground creeper that produces large trumpet-shaped flowers, pink or white in colour. The delicate petals are joined together showing a seam along the join so that it **looks like a star from above**. The plant grows out of a large flat underground tuber that can be used for moisture when one is without water in the bush. This is dug up and scraped clean before being squeezed into the mouth.

Red-star zinnia
Zinnia peruviana

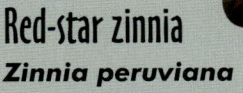

The red-star zinnia is an annual herb that was **introduced from Peru** but has become naturalised in South Africa where it grows in dry river valleys.

Small plants and wild flowers

Flame lily
Gloriosa superba

As suggested by its botanical name, the flame lily is a **spectacular flower** with bright yellow or red flame-like petals. As is often the case, the magnificent flower masks a **lethal poison**. In spite of its toxicity, the flame lily tuber (the most poisonous part of the plant) is regularly dug up and **eaten by porcupines**. Such an action would cause death in a human after severe, albeit delayed, gastro-enteritis. In spite of, or perhaps because of its noxious properties, the flame lily has been used extensively in traditional medicine. It contains colchicines, which is the same ingredient extracted commercially from a European plant for its value as an anti-inflammatory substance, particularly against arthritis and gout.

The roots are used to treat bruises, sprains and toothache and the leaf and root saps are extracted for use as a disinfectant, especially for the treatment of pimples. The corm is believed to have **aphrodisiac properties** and is used in remedies to cure infertility but these remedies have resulted in birth defects because of the toxins. Similarly, the **Zulu belief** that ingesting an infusion of the corm can assist in determining the sex of an unborn child has been discouraged due to subsequent birth defects. Traditionally, corms were selected on their shape and that which most closely resembled the genitals of the required sex of the child would be used to prepare the treatment.

Abutilon angulatum

Abutilon shrubs are common in the Lowveld, growing on riverbanks or alongside roads. Every part of the **plant is velvety** in feel including the fruits. The leaves have a blue-grey colour and are darker above than below. The flowers are yellow.

Small plants and wild flowers

Flannel weed
Sida cordifolia

Flannel weed gets its name from the **texture of its leaves**, which are finely velvety and resemble the feel of a flannel cloth. The specific name *cordifolia* also relates to the leaves of the plant and means 'heart-shaped'. The flannel weed is a small grey-green shrub that grows in disturbed areas and is made noticeable when it is in flower, producing delicate yellow heads. Infusions of these as well as the fruit can be rubbed on the skin as an insecticide. Smoke from the burning plant also repels pests. The flannel weed is useful to extract fibre for making twine and is high in potassium nitrate (also called saltpetre) which can be used as a food preservative or fertiliser and traditionally even to produce gunpowder. The flannel weed is also valuable for its medicinal properties, especially for treating children's illnesses.

Blue water-lily
Nymphae nouchali

The water-lily is a well-known and adored wild flower and a useful one at that. Its **medicinal value is vast** and it is used as an antiseptic and to treat bladder and kidney problems, chest complaints, diabetes, piles, diarrhoea, skin problems and infertility.

Many **animals rely on water-lilies** for their survival. The African jacana is equipped with long toes to enable it to traverse the lily-pads and forage for its food resulting in its colloquial name 'lily-trotter'. Pygmy geese eat the seeds by severing the underwater-housed fruit from its stalk and then pecking it open, dispersing the seeds in the process. Bees and other insects gather nectar and pollen from the flowers and may become trapped temporarily in the plant's clever ploy to ensure cross-pollination. The female part of the flower matures first and a sticky substance is released to attract insects. Once the insect makes contact, it becomes entangled and wriggles about to free itself, depositing pollen in the process. A few days later the stickiness dries up and by this stage the male part of the flower has matured, dusting the struggling visitor with new pollen before it manages to fly away. It is for this trait that the Zulu people have incorporated the water-lily into a love-charm ritual in which a partner can be attracted and a permanent bond established with them by consuming the roots of the water-lily early in the morning.

Animals are not the only creatures that benefit from the water-lily's produce. **Humans eat the fruit** or dry it to mill into flour. The anchoring rhizome can be roasted for a nutritious, albeit bland, meal and the roots are used for dye. The lily-pads can be applied to sunburn to relieve blistering and the sap from the stems and roots provide a natural sun lotion. The plant can be both an aphrodisiac and an anaphrodisiac depending on which part of the plant is ingested – the rhizome as an aphrodisiac and the flower as an anaphrodisiac. The hollow stems of the floating plant can be used to drink up clean water from below the murky surface of a water body and the lily-pads are used to line the floor of a grave to keep the corpse cool. The flowers were used by the shamans of ancient Egypt to bring on trances due to their apparent narcotic effect and Greek mythology featured in the naming of the plant. **Numphaios means 'sacred to the nymphs'** and Nymphe was a Greek water nymph, a minor goddess who presided over water bodies.

A **water-lily bud**, like its developing leaves, begins under the water and rises gradually to reach the surface as it matures. The flower, open only during the day, lasts five days and immediately on pollination is again drawn under the water where the fruit develops. This eventually bursts to release buoyant seeds that begin the life cycle anew.

Small plants and wild flowers

Cornflower vernonia
Vernonia glabra

The cornflower vernonia is a common wild flower and the small purple heads are commonly seen intermingled in grass. Once these dry out they produce small **dandelion-like seed heads**. Cornflower vernonias are ecologically valuable as a food plant for butterflies, providing nectar for these insects later in the year. The brown-veined white and the African monarch are common associates of the vernonia. Humans also value this small herb and it is used to treat gonorrhoea and kidney trouble (with an infusion of root), to induce abortion (by inserting the root into the vagina), as an antiseptic to relieve burns (by rubbing with the ash from leaves) and to remedy infertility (the powdered root is mixed with porridge).

Caterpillar bush
Ormocarpum tricocarpum

The caterpillar bush is named after the shape and texture of its pods. The 4 cm long fruit is covered in rigid hairs that make it **look like a caterpillar**. These appear on the plant between October and March when butterflies and their larvae are also abundant. This shrub (sometimes a small tree) grows on stony ground against hillsides where the conditions are hot. When not in fruit, the plant has tiny compound leaves that cluster on short lateral branches.

String-of-stars
Helitropium steudneri

The tiny delicate white flowers of this perennial herb are notable for their habit of growing alongside one another in rows, as if miniature stars had been bound to a string. The inflorescence is curved in a rainbow-like fashion and sometimes forked with two rows lying attractively beside one another. The flowers appear in summer and the plant grows in disturbed grassland areas. The generic name **Helitropium means 'to turn to the sun'**.

Small plants and wild flowers

Hibiscus
Hibiscus species

Wild hibiscus has large bell-shaped flowers with scarlet throats and the many species that abound in the bush can usually be distinguished by their leaves. These plants act as the **larval host plants for some types of hawk moths**. The flowers are cooked as a vegetable and the root is implicated in a remedy for stomach bloating in young children.

Wild melon
Lagenaria sphaerica

Wild melons are climbing herbs that are **only truly obvious when they are in fruit**. The 10 cm large green balls are dotted with paler patches and drape over other plants, especially in riverine vegetation. *Lagenaria* means 'large flask fruit'. The white velvety flowers attract insects like bees, flies and ants. The plant is used traditionally to cure swollen glands and stomach ache. Despite the large size of the fruit animals such as kudu and nyala relish it and comical contortions of the face result from their efforts to bite and chew them.

Potato bush
Phyllanthus reticulates

The potato bush is **best known for the smell** given off by its small yellow flowers during summer evenings. This clambering shrub typically grows in riverine vegetation or in thickets found along drainage lines and can be recognised by the leaves which have thin red veins on the under surface and appear to be compound but are not. The leaves (and fruit) can be used to treat burns and sores. The black berry produces a black dye used to colour fishing nets.

Crinum (vlei) lily
Crinum delagoense

The *Crinum* is a **spectacular lily** with pink-striped, trumpet-shaped flowers and contrasting broad green leaves that encircle the base of the plant. The plant may be spotted growing on deep sandy soils in early summer and is supported by a large underground bulb (20 cm in diameter). Equally striking are the burgundy-coloured fruits that reach lemon size when mature.

Small plants and wild flowers

White-berry bush
Flueggea virosa

The white-berry bush is a shrub that grows along forest edges or in rocky places and is generally inconspicuous as a plant except for its bright green colour. However, when in fruit, the white berry bush is unmistakable. Small white berries adorn the whole plant in dense clusters along the branches from December until March. The **edible berries have a sweet taste**. Naturally frugivores including baboons, monkeys, civets and birds like grey go-away birds and mousebirds relish the fruit too. The plant is used by browsers throughout the year and also serves as a larval food plant for *Charaxes* butterflies. The wood is flexible and often used in the construction of fish traps.

African wild violet
Aptosimum lineare

The leaves of the African wild violet are thin and grass-like, emerging from a central point like a miniature fountain. The small purple flowers are **reminiscent of the commercial violet flower**, only smaller.

Justicea
Justicea species

Justiceas are **small herbs** that may be noticed growing amongst grass in disturbed places. The different species produce white, yellow or blue flowers. The upright spikes, in which leaf-like bracts enclose the delicate flowers, are typical of the genus. Although small, these plants play an important role in butterfly ecology. The genus is named after James Justice who was a renowned Scottish horticulturalist.

Dwarf papyrus
Cyperus papyrus

Papyrus is a grass-like plant but lacks nodes and has more angular stems than grasses. It **grows in stands in damp areas** around pans or watercourses and remains green year round. Papyrus can be stuffed into the legs of a pair of trousers to produce a float during floods. The Zulu and Tsonga people weave sleeping mats out of papyrus and other tribes construct children's toys with it.

Small plants and wild flowers

Num-num
Carissa species

The num-num is a small multi-stemmed shrub with **red-tipped robust green thorns** that are either single (in *C. edulis*) or forked in a Y-shape (in *C. bispinosa*). They produce star-shaped white or pale pink flowers in clusters before producing fleshy red fruits that are edible and sought after by man and beast, conveniently causing the expulsion of intestinal worms in the process of being ingested. The fruit can be used to make jam and the root is implicated in traditional medicinal treatments.

Tracks and tracking

Tracking is both an art and a skill acquired from prolonged exposure to and experience in the bush. Tracking involves a person observing the physical footprints of an animal as well as the other clues it may have left behind in order to follow and subsequently locate that animal.

A **track** is the physical imprint left by an animal, bird or insect's foot on the ground.

Signs are all the other clues to an animal's presence in an area including broken branches, mud rubbed off on vegetation, drops of blood or saliva and dung.

Types of signs

There are three different categories of sign to look out for.

1. **Aerial signs:** Any clues above the ground or vegetation layer alluding to an animal's presence are considered aerial signs. This may take the form of birds flying up noisily off the backs of animals, like **oxpeckers** (which also descend noisily out of the sky onto animals' backs). Birds like francolin or guineafowl vocalise an alarm when predatory animals disturb them. Animals such as **baboons**, impala and squirrels will also alarm in the presence of a predator, alerting the tracker to its presence. **Giraffe** are inquisitive animals and tend to stare down at predators in the grass. Following their stare may lead a tracker to a lion or cheetah.

   Scent is another form of aerial sign as anyone who has been downwind of an elephant in musth would know! Some animals such as hyenas and mongooses deposit scent-rich pastings from anal glands, the strength of which can help the tracker formulate its time of passing.

Tracks and tracking

2. **Arboreal signs:** Clues left behind on trees and other vegetation are considered arboreal signs. Often animals prone to mud-bathing will loosen old mud against tree trunks or other rubbing posts or simply enjoy a good scratch after a wallow. Warthogs, elephants, rhino and buffalo leave clues behind in this way. Sometimes after a particularly comprehensive mud-wallow, animals will leave wet mud clinging to branches that overhang their pathways simply by passing by. Branches broken by animals, such as elephants feeding, are also considered an arboreal sign. Other animals like giraffe leave conspicuous browse lines where they have fed. Often plant material is bent by the passing animal, particularly larger ones. Usually this bends in the direction of travel of the animal. Cats regularly claw trees to maintain their claws and as a form of visual territorial marking. The physical presence of territorial pastings on bits of grass made by species such as hyena or vegetation moistened by cats spraying urine, are considered arboreal signs.

3. **Terrestrial signs:** This mostly relates to the actual imprint left by the animal walking over a substrate, be it sand, mud or stony ground. All animal species have unique footprints of a certain shape, size and sometimes even pattern. Even animals of the same species have unique individual prints just like no two human feet are exactly the same. Droppings fall where animals walk, as do particles of food they have been engaged in chewing. Both these signs could help with the identification of the species and the aging of the trail. Many territorial animals utilise prominent pathways, including game trails and human roads, as territorial boundaries and subsequently mark these routes with scent (e.g. urine and middens) and also with prominent physical scrape marks of the feet. These are all forms of terrestrial signs.

Wildebeest dung

Porcupine dung

Tracks and tracking

Effective tracking relies on two main skills: **observation and practise**. Constantly being aware of one's surroundings on a level that includes all one's senses is known as 'situational awareness'. This kind of awareness is married to one's powers of observation and these are skills that, like any other, can be learnt and honed with dedicated and ongoing practice.

Golden rules of tracking

1. The best time to look for tracks is early in the morning or late in the afternoon. At these times, the angle of the sun's rays causes the tracks to stand out in greater relief, making them more visible to the observer. In this regard one should always try to **place the track between the sun and oneself**.
2. It is wise to **look ahead about 5 m in front of oneself** when tracking and not directly down at the closest track to one's feet. By looking ahead one does not become so focused on individual tracks that the surroundings are ignored. It is vital to be collecting clues from the environment and noting all the other signs left by the animal while progressing. This is **'looking at the bigger picture'**. Also, by looking ahead, tracks upfront tend to show up better and speeds up the tracking effort as shortcuts can be taken, allowing the tracker to leapfrog from one point to the next.
3. To track an animal successfully it is best to **understand some of its behaviour** in order to 'predict' where it was going or what it was most likely doing. If the animal has passed over hard ground and left no tracks, this could stump a tracker. Being able to venture an educated guess as to what the animal was doing – for example, it was on its way to water or favoured grazing grounds – improves the tracker's chances of picking up the trail again. Animals generally move in fixed patterns and do not usually zigzag all over the place. Understanding an animal's habits will help with predicting where it has gone.
4. It is quite handy to **mark tracks along the trail** by encircling them in the dust with a finger, particularly if tracking in a difficult substrate. Should the tracker reach a 'dead-end', returning to the last evident track (now encircled and made more obvious) is the easiest way to pick up the trail again.
5. A method known as the **'cloverleaf approach'** is useful in determining where an animal's trail has diverted off to. This involves walking in a circle from the last known track in the three directions branching off the trail, i.e. left, right and straight ahead. By circling slowly and gradually enlarging the loop, tracks can be relocated systematically and the search continued.

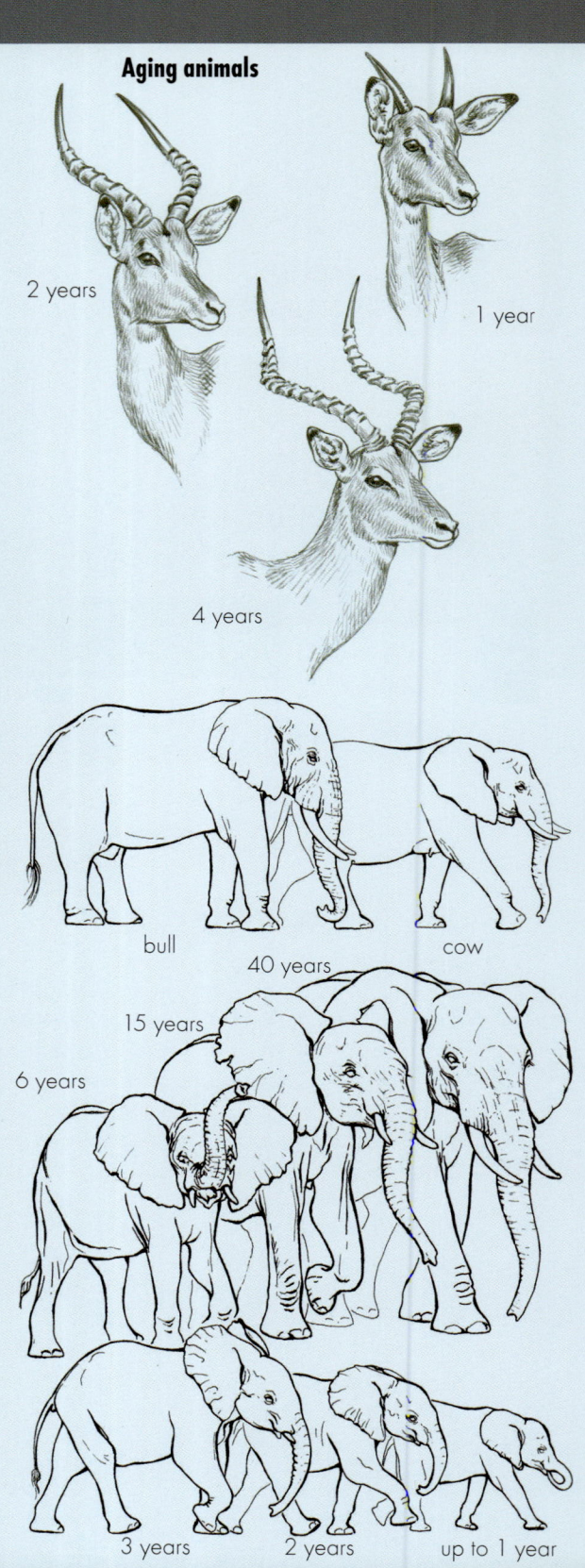

Aging animals

Tracks and tracking

Aging tracks

Being able to age tracks is a skill that develops with experience and exposure to different scenarios. A fresh track is neatly formed with a clear outline. It is almost shiny because of the fresh soil that has been compacted.

By looking at insect trails and the tracks of other animals that have superimposed upon the tracks of the animal being tracked, one can get a general idea of when the track was left. Certain animals, birds and insects are only active at specific times of the day. If, for example, a genet has passed over the elephant tracks which are being followed, this indicates that the elephant passed by before the nocturnal genet became active, indicating the tracks are probably at least as old as the previous afternoon or evening.

Weather plays an important role in aging tracks. Weather such as wind and rain can age tracks, dung and other signs very quickly. Wind will collapse the edge of tracks and rain can obliterate tracks completely. Cool weather will delay the eroding of tracks and signs making them seem fresher than they are. The sun can quickly dry out dung but kicking this open might better indicate the freshness. Tracks can be aged from weather signs like rain droplets. By referring to the time it rained and determining whether the tracks are on top of the rain-marked soil or whether it has rained lightly on top of the track, the relative age of the track can be worked out. Dew in the early morning is also a good indicator of when an animal has passed by. If tracks are covered with dew then the animal passed by in the night or even longer ago. If the tracks are on top of the dew then they are fresh. Sometimes pathways where animals have walked are made more obvious by the disruption of dew-drenched grass.

Plant material is often broken in an animal's passing and subsequently trampled on. Tracks can be aged by the **degree to which the vegetation has withered**.

335

Tracks and tracking

Animal feet and tracks

Within the mammal class, animals have been grouped into three general groups based on their foot structure.

1. Animals that walk on their toes without the heel of the foot touching the ground are said to have **digitigrade feet**. The carnivores fit into this group. Digitigrade feet are an adaptation to walking and stalking quietly, the pads underneath the feet cushioning them and increasing sensitivity to facilitate the exploration of the animal's habitat and to provide traction in climbing.

Lion

Vervet monkey

2. Animals that walk on their whole foot are said to have **plantigrade feet**. Primates have plantigrade feet. They have dextrous hands and feet like humans which they use to manipulate food, hold onto branches or to dig and pick up things. They have five digits on each foot and nails instead of claws.

Wildebeest

Hippo

3. Some animals walk right on the tips of their toes or more correctly, upon hooves which are modified nails or claws. These animals are called **ungulates** and their foot structure is called **unguligrade**. Hoofed animals have the advantage of being able to run very deftly. They have no need to be silent when moving and thorns do not pose a problem to this sort of foot when they are in full flight.

Ungulates are further divided into two groups: those with an even number of toes (*artiodactyla*) like impala (two toes) or hippo (four toes) and those with an odd number of toes (*perissodactyla*) like zebra (one toe) and rhino (three toes).

Impala

Zebra

Tracks and tracking

Animals that do not fit into the first two categories but are also not true ungulates are called **near-ungulates**. Dassies and **elephants** are near-ungulates and both have unique tracks.

The type of foot structure possessed by an animal is recognised in its tracks and will give a tracker a starting point with regards to the broad group the animal may belong to. From there, the field can be narrowed down using size. Most adult animals have tracks of almost the same size. For example, it is reasonably accurate to say that mature elephant bulls have front feet that are 50 cm long and adult impala tracks are 5 cm long. By carrying a ruler of sorts or measuring the different dimensions of one's own hands and feet, it is easy (and crucial) to determine the size of a track and thereby isolate whether the unguligrade track belongs to a small, medium or large sized antelope for example.

Elephant track

The **front feet** of most animals are larger than the hind feet because of the weight of the forequarters and head being carried in the front. The left foot can be told from the right foot by the indentations on one or other side of the track. As with humans, animals step more heavily on the outside curve of their feet. If the larger, more deeply impressed part of the foot is on the left-hand side then that foot is the left foot.

Two important concepts to which a tracker refers are straddle and stride.

Straddle refers to the distance between the hip bones and hence the distance between the animal's left and right feet. In females this is wider than in males. Determining straddle can help with determining the size of a particular animal; this is useful when diagnosing confusing tracks.

Stride is the length between footsteps and can vary depending on how fast the animal was moving. Understanding stride can assist a tracker with working out what sort of gait the animal was using, as the relative position of the tracks to each other differs with different gaits, for example a leisurely walk compared to an all out gallop. When animals move quickly, their toes splay and they do not leave very neatly defined tracks.

Tracks and tracking

Impala midden   **Impala**

Animal droppings

Dung refers to the droppings of a herbivore. The droppings of a carnivore are known as **scat** while those of omnivores are called **faeces**.

Jackal

Baboon

Civetry

Many animals use their droppings to demarcate their territories. This they do by depositing piles of excreta in obvious places or by creating **middens** (in the case of herbivores) or **latrines** (in the case of carnivores) which are enlarged through repeated use. These areas are depots of information for these animals, and trackers as they are loaded with both visual and olfactory messages.

Analysing the contents of droppings may assist with clarifying the identity of an animal that has left confusing tracks. If a print is indiscernible in its detail from another similar species (due to a hard substrate or weather erosion) then the contents of the droppings may hold critical clues as to its identity. For example, if the droppings in question contain large amounts of fruit and millipede rings, then small cat-like tracks are more likely to be from a civet than a serval or caracal which eat mostly rodents and other more 'meaty' foods.

Breaking droppings open will indicate if they are fresh or not. Sometimes the **freshness of droppings** is clearly evident by steam rising off them on a cold morning or just by feeling that it is still warm to the touch.

One should never touch scat (predator dung) with bare hands as it contains harmful bacteria.

Leopard

Tracks and tracking

Members of the **cat family** (*Felids*) usually have very rounded tracks with distinctly three lobes to the main pad. The claws of cats are protractile and do not show up in their tracks, with cheetah being the exception.

Lions are the largest of the cats with their tracks measuring 13–15 cm in length. The track has three lobes on the back pad (hyena have only two) and the toes are slightly oblong in shape and clearly separate (they do not fit together as the hyena's do). Claws do not impress in the track.

Leopard tracks resemble lion tracks but are smaller (9–10 cm) and rounder.

Civet tracks closely resemble jackal tracks in size but they are very round tracks that are about as long as they are wide. If the substrate is soft, the claws may mark but are not always evident. They have two lobes on the main pad of the foot. A civet track is about 5,5 cm long. The activities of civet are often made more conspicuous by the presence of enormous civetries (latrines) that contain many berry and millipede remnants.

Genet tracks (both species) look like miniature versions of the civet track measuring 2–3 cm in length and do not show the claws.

Members of the **dog family** (*Canids*) have claws showing in their tracks and normally a two-lobed main pad. The tracks of a **jackal** are usually elongated (almost rectangular in shape) with the two middle toes placed relatively far ahead of the two side toes. The track measures about 6,5 cm. Sometimes the outline of a jackal track is blurred by the presence of fur around the feet, especially in winter.

Tracks and tracking

Kudu have small feet relative to their size and they walk by placing the hind foot almost directly over where the front foot just impressed. This is known as registering and is an adaptation to walking quietly in thick bush. The family group to which kudu belong, Tragelaphines, all do this. Their tracks are also very oval is shape (almost like a rugby ball), being widest two-thirds along rather than at the back of the track.

Nyala have almost identical tracks to kudu but these are fractionally smaller. Male kudu tracks (forefeet) are about 8 cm long (9,5 cm if the register is included) and female kudu tracks are 7 cm long (8,5 cm if the register is included). Nyala tracks (forefeet) are between 6 and 7 cm long.

Wildebeest tracks are similar to waterbuck but only the hind foot of the wildebeest is heart-shaped (and is 10 cm long). The forefeet have a more square shape and are 11 cm long. The combination of both shapes in a set of tracks helps with the identification of wildebeest tracks.

Waterbuck have broad, spreading hooves to accommodate their lives near water. The track impresses as a heart-shaped imprint with the broadest portion being at the back. Waterbuck tracks are about 9 cm long and can be 5-6 cm wide. Waterbuck tracks often overlap slightly but unlike the typical register of a kudu, the overlapping track is slightly offset to the side.

Hippo have large (26 cm) feet that have four toes. Sometimes these might be confused with rhino tracks (especially in harder substrates) but careful examination will reveal four and not three toes.

Tracks and tracking

Elephant tracks are unmistakable due to their huge size and round shape. The front feet are larger and particularly round (to support the massive head) while the hind feet are more oval and slightly narrower. The cracks in the soles of the feet imprint in the tracks and these can be used to identify individuals (much like fingerprints). The heels of elephant's feet wear smooth at the back of their tracks and leave a shiny crescent shape on the ground. This aids with telling the direction of the track as does the fact that the toes tend to **kick out dust at the front**. Depending on the gait, the hind foot steps into the front foot's track, usually overstepping it slightly. The shoulder height of an elephant can be determined by multiplying the circumference of the forefoot by 2,5.

Fore foot (bull): 50 cm

Hind foot (bull): 58 cm (but narrower than the fore foot)

Rhino have large, three-toed feet. There is one toe in front and one toe either side of it. The heel of the track is constricted at the back and has a distinct 'W' shape. Often the cracks on the soles of the feet imprint in the track. Black rhino tracks are smaller than white rhino tracks and they tend to have a larger gap between the toes. The 'W' shape on the back of the foot is also less pronounced in black rhino. Rhino bulls scent mark by scraping their hind feet backwards and regularly leave two parallel lines in the sand amidst their tracks.

White rhino: 30 cm

Black rhino: 24 cm

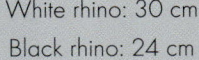

Hyena tracks are obvious from the angle of the main pad, which lies at a 45 degree angle as these animals walk with their feet turned outwards. The back pad has two lobes. The non-retractable claws mark obviously in the track and the outer toes are distinctly kidney-shaped, fitting snugly next to one another. The hyena's front feet are noticeably bigger than the back ones (to support the heavy forequarters) and measure about 11 cm in length.

Tracks and tracking

Giraffe have the largest unguligrade tracks, measuring about 20 cm in length. These are rectangular in shape tapering slightly towards the front end of the track. The tracks of a young giraffe may be confused with buffalo tracks but the latter are much rounder. The presence of giraffe in an area is often made more obvious by a distinct browse line above where tracks have concentrated around a tree. Sometimes bits of material drop out of the giraffe's mouth or branches are broken during foraging.

Warthog have very square unguligrade tracks that resemble the mark left when one pushes the flat section of two bent fingers into the soil. Often the dew claws mark in the soil as well. The track is about 4 cm long (8,5 cm with dew claws).

Aardvark have very distinct tracks. Three elongated toes lie obliquely parallel to one another. The claws are long and imprint ahead of the track. Aardvark tracks are inevitably accompanied by excavations and the soil displaced from a digging generally piles up in one spot. An impression of the tail is often clearly visible atop this pile of earth where the aardvark has stood while digging. Claw marks are obvious in the actual hole. Sometimes the tail dragging behind when the aardvark walks leaves a mark on the ground.

Fore foot: 8,5 cm
Hind foot: 11 cm

Common duiker have very small unguligrade tracks which have a blunt heart-shape and although 4 cm in length, often appear shorter than this as the full track does not necessarily imprint on the substrate, especially hard surfaces. (By comparison, steenbok have very pointed tracks.)

Zebra have hooves which resemble horse's feet but without the shoe. They have one toe per foot which imprints as a semi-circle with a triangular-shaped wedge at the back known as a 'frog'. Zebra are fond of dust-rolling and disturbed earth is often found in association with their tracks. Zebra tracks are 9,5–10 cm long.

Tracks and tracking

Impala have 5 cm long tracks that are typically unguligrade and neatly heart-shaped. Since impala live in herds, generally there are many impala tracks in one location making the recognition of the species easy. Rams make enormous dung middens.

Baboons have hands and feet that resemble those of a human child. The hind foot imprint is double the length of the hand. Baboons walk with their fingers curled into their palms (i.e. on their knuckles). Both the hands and feet of these primates have opposable 'thumbs' which show clearly in the tracks. The folds of skin on the extremities often show up clearly in the track on fine substrates.

Baboon hand: 8 cm
Baboon foot: 15 cm

Vervet monkeys have similar tracks to baboons except that baboon tracks are much larger than the vervet's especially in the width of the track. Often a vervet's tail will drag in the earth where it has been active.

Vervet hand: 8 cm (but thinner than baboon)
Vervet foot: 10 cm

Tortoises make parallel lines of round imprints due to the distance between their pillar-like legs. Their slow movement means that they only take small steps at a time and the impressions lie close to one another or may even appear as drag lines.

Francolin and guineafowl tracks are commonly spotted on the dust roads in the Lowveld as the birds use these as passageways through a landscape, benefiting from the openness to spot predators and picking up seeds knocked down by vehicle and other animal traffic. Both groups of birds have tracks with three toes facing forwards and one smaller toe facing backwards at an angle. Often the constricted surface on the individual toes is evident. Guineafowl tracks are significantly larger (being 10 cm in length) than francolin and spurfowl (which are usually about 7 cm long).

References & further reading

Apps, P. 1994. *Wild ways – Field guide to the behaviour of southern African mammals.* Southern Book Publishers: Halfway House.

Apps, P. and Du Toit, R. 2000. *Creatures of habit.* Struik: Cape Town.

Branch, B. 1998. *Field guide to snakes and other reptiles of southern Africa.* Struik: Cape Town.

Branch, B. 2000. *Everyone's guide to snakes, other reptiles and amphibians of southern Africa.* Struik: Cape Town.

Carnaby, T. 2005. *Beat about the bush – mammals and birds.* Jacana Media: Johannesburg.

Carruthers, V. 2001. *Frogs and frogging in southern Africa.* Struik: Cape Town.

Estes, R.D. 1992. *The behavior guide to African mammals.* University of California Press: London.

Filmer, M.R. 1991. *Southern African spiders – an identification guide.* Struik: Cape Town.

Grant, R., Thomas, V. and Van Gogh, J. 2006. *Sappi tree spotting – Lowveld including Kruger National Park.* 3rd edition. Jacana Media: Johannesburg.

Hall-Martin, A. 1993. *A day in the life of an African elephant.* Southern Book Publishers: Halfway House.

Hine, G. 2004. *Bush knowledge and skills: study material for level I / II / III and trails guide.* The Interactive Wildlife Company: Johannesburg.

Hockey, P.A.R., Dean, W.R.J. and Ryan, P.G (eds). 2005. *Roberts birds of southern Africa.* 7th edition. The trustees of the John Voelcker Bird Book Fund: Cape Town.

Kruger, W. *Inside invertebrate information.* Unpublished.

Lawson, B. and Lawson, D. *Specialist training manual for bird guides.* Lawson's Birding Academy.

Leeming, J. 2003. *Scorpions of southern Africa.* Struik: Cape Town.

Liebenberg, L. 2000. *A photographic guide to tracks and tracking in southern Africa.* Struik: Cape Town.

Liebenberg, L. 2005. *A field guide to the animal tracks of southern Africa.* David Philip Publishers: Claremont.

Little, R., Crowe, T. and Barlow, S. 2000. *Gamebirds of southern Africa.* Struik: Cape Town.

Loon, R. and Loon, H. 2005. *Birds – the inside story.* Struik: Cape Town.

Marais, J. 2004. *A complete guide to the snakes of southern Africa.* Struik: Cape Town.

Mills, G. and Harvey, M. 2001. *African predators.* Struik: Cape Town.

Onderstall, J. 1996. *Sappi wild flower guide – Mpumalanga and Northern Province.* DynamicAd: Nelspruit.

Palgrave, K.C. 1995. *Trees of southern Africa.* 2nd edition. Struik: Cape Town.

Picker, M., Griffiths, C. and Weaving, A. 2002. *Field guide to insects of South Africa.* Struik: Cape Town.

Pooley, E. 1998. *A field guide to the wild flowers of KwaZulu-Natal and the Eastern Region.* Natal Flora Publications Trust: Natal.

Roodt, V. 1998. *Common wild flowers of the Okavango delta – medicinal uses and nutritional value.* Shell Oil: Botswana.

Roodt, V. 1998. *Trees and shrubs of the Okavango delta – medicinal uses and nutritional value.* Shell Oil: Botswana.

Sinclair, I., Hockey, P. and Tarboton, W. 2002. *Sasol birds of southern Africa.* 3rd edition. Struik: Cape Town.

Skaife, S.H., Ledger, J. and Bannister, A. 1979. *African insect life.* Struik: Cape Town.

Skinner, J.D. and Smithers, R.H.N. 1990. *The mammals of the southern African subregion.* University of Pretoria: Pretoria.

Smit, N. 1999. *Guide to the Acacias of South Africa.* Briza Publications: Pretoria.

Steyn, P. 1996. *Nesting birds.* Fernwood Press: Vlaeberg.

Tarboton, W. 2001. *Nests and eggs of southern African birds.* Struik: Cape Town.

Van Oudtshoorn, F. and van Wyk, E. 1999. *Guide to grasses of southern Africa.* Briza Publications: Pretoria.

Van Wyk, P. 1994. *Field guide to the trees of the Kruger National Park.* Struik: Cape Town.

Van Wyk, B. and Van Wyk, P. 1997. *Field guide to the trees of southern Africa.* Struik: Cape Town.

Venter, F. and Venter, J. 1996. *Making the most of indigenous trees.* Briza Publications: Pretoria.

Weaving, A. 2000. *Southern African insects and their world.* Struik: Cape Town.

Index

Page numbers in bold indicate main species entries.

Animals

aardvark **116-117**, 230, 240, 342
aardwolf 102
Acanthocercus atricollis **193**
Achatina achatina **247**
Acinonyx jubatus **94-97**
acraea 225
Aepyceros melampus **36-39**
Afrana angolensis **221**
agama, tree **193**
agamas 187
Agaonidae 234
alligator 208
Anopheles mosquito 230, 255
Anthia species 198
antlion **224**
ants 133
ants, cocktail **233**
ants, Matabele 117, **230**
ants, velvet **233**
Aquila rapax 159
Aquila species 159
Aquila wahlbergi 159
Argiope species **243**
Argyrodes species **244**
assassin bug **227**

babbler, arrow-marked 134, 135, 140
baboon spider 242, **245**
baboon, chacma 37, 45, **86-89**, 237, 256, 257, 259, 260, 263, 281, 284, 285, 286, 287, 288, 292, 293, 294, 296, 298, 301, 302, 306, 310, 332, 343
badger, European 84
bagworms **226**
barbel 210
barbet, black-collared 129, 151
barbet, crested 128, 151
barbets 145, 151, 166, 181, 268, 271, 285, 286, 289, 296, 323
bark spider **245**
barred owlet, African 164
batis, chin-spot 135
bee-eater, white-fronted 138
bee-eaters 131, 132, 138
bees 138, 161
beetle, ant's guest 228
beetle, blister **228**
beetle, bombardier **228**
beetle, Christmas 227
beetle, CMR 228
beetle, darkling 229
beetle, ground 198, **228**
beetle, longhorn 252, 256, 258
beetle, rhino 237
beetle, tenebrionid 229
beetle, tok-tokkie 229

Bitis arietans **207**
'blaasop' 217
'blouaap' 92
boomslang 189, 195, **204**
Breviceps adspersus **217**
brubru 135
buffalo, African 17, **28-31**, 154, 178, 179, 319, 333
buffalo, Cape **28-31**
buffalo-weaver, red-billed 148, 255
Bufo garmani **219**
Bufo gutturalis **219**
Bufonidae 219
bulbul, dark-capped 135, 137
bulbuls 137, 323
bullfrog 212
bunting, cinnamon-breasted 135
bunting, golden-breasted 135
Buphagus africanus 179
Buphagus erythrorhynchus 179
Buphagus species **178-179**
bush snake, spotted **201**
bushbabies 255, 286
bushbaby, lesser **124-125**, 257
bushbuck **47**, 261, 310
bushpig 286, 292, 293, 306
bush-shrike, grey-headed 131, 135
bush-shrike, orange-breasted 135
bush-shrikes 131
bustard, black-bellied 147
Buthidae 248
butterflies **225**
button spider, black 242, 244
button spider, brown 242
button spiders 242

Caerostris species **245**
canary, yellow-fronted 130, 135
Canis mesomelas **108-111**
caracal **106-107**, 110, 176
Caracal caracal **106-107**
catfish 136, 210
centipedes 247
Ceratophaga species 224
Ceratotherium simum **32-35**
Cercopithecus aethiops **90-93**
Chamaeleo dilepis **194-195**
chameleon, flap-neck **194-195**
chameleons 187, 193, 204
charaxes butterflies 292, 330
charaxes, club-tailed 225
charaxes, foxy 225
cheetah **94-97**, 162, 175, 332
Chelonia 186, 187
Chiromantis xerampelina **216**
Choeropsis liberiensis 73
cicadas **227**
Circaetus cinereus 156
Circaetus pectoralis 156
civet **118**, 122, 237, 247, 281, 285, 286, 288, 292, 296, 301, 339
Civettictis civetta **118**
cobra, Mozambican spitting 189, **201**
community nest spider **242**, 257

Connochaetes taurinus **54-55**
coot, red-knobbed 152
crab spider, six-eyed 242
crake, black 130
crocodile, Nile 196, **208-211**
Crocodylia 186
Crocodylus niloticus **208-211**
crombec, long-billed 135, 152
crombecs 152
crows 153
Crocuta crocuta **102-105**
cuckoo, diderick 145
cuckoos 137, 144, 226, 266
Cyrtophora species **244**
cytotoxin spider 242

damselflies 231
dassie, rock **82-85**, 107, 337
Dendroaspis polylepis **206**
dewdrop spider **244**
diadem 225
Dispholidus typus **204**
dove, laughing 135, 147
doves 130, 134, 136, 146, 147, 151, 159, 284, 305
dragonflies **231**
drongo, fork-tailed 129, 135, 154, 158
duck, fulvous 146
duck, white-faced 138
duck, yellow-billed 128, 132
ducks 138, 146
duiker, common **51**, 259, 292, 305, 342
duiker, grey 51
duiker, Grimm's 51
dung beetle, ball-rolling 236
dung beetle, flightless 236
dung beetles 122, 136, **236-237**

eagle, bateleur 157, 161
eagle, black 82, 83, 84
eagle, martial 158, 176, 196
eagle, tawny 159, 161
eagle, Verreauxs' 158
eagle, Wahlberg's 159
eagle-owl, spotted 166, 240
eagle-owl, Verreaux's 148, 149, 167
egret, cattle 62, 154
egrets 132, 153
eland 40, **60-63**, 154, 306
eland, giant 60
eland, Lord Derby's 60
elephant, African 17, **22-27**, 85, 253, 254, 256, 257, 259, 260, 266, 268, 269, 273, 274, 276, 279, 292, 298, 300, 302, 305, 332, 337, 341
Equus burchelli **56-59**

Felis lybica **123**
fig insect 234
finch, cuckoo 144
firefinch, red-billed 135, 145
fireflies **224**
fiscal bird, common 290
fish-eagle, African 139, 146
flat lizard, common **200**

345

Index

flea-beetle 266
flycatcher, paradise 152
foam nest frog **216**
Formicinae 133
francolin, coqui 173
francolin, crested 129, 173
francolins 133, **172-173**, 305, 332, 343
frogs **212-221**, 240
fruit bats 286
fruit bats, straw-coloured 261
funnel-web spider 244

Galago moholi **124-125**
galago, lesser **124-125**
Gasteracantha species **244**
gecko, Moreau's tropical house **198**
geckos 187
geese 138, 146
geese, Egyptian 138, 146, 147
geese, pygmy 327
genet **119**, 122, 261, 339
genet, large spotted **119**
genet, small spotted **119**
Genetta genetta **119**
Genetta tigrina **119**
Geochelone pardalis **190-191**
Gerrhosaurus validus **199**
giant land snail, African **247**
Giraffa camelopardalus **64-69**
giraffe **64-69**, 179, 252, 253, 254, 256, 259, 268, 269, 273, 274, 277, 311, 332, 342
glow-worms **224**
gnu, brindled 54
Gonimbrasia belina 269
grass frog, plain **220**
grass owl 165
grass yellow, broad-bordered 225
grasshopper, brown 230
grasshopper, elegant 230
grasshopper, green 230
grasshoppers 227, **230**
green pigeon 281, 285, 286
grey go-away bird 268, 285, 294
ground birds 169-173
guineafowl, helmeted 133, **170-171**, 225, 305, 332, 343

hamerkop 136, 149, 166, 221
hawk, cuckoo 195
hawk-eagle, African 172
hawk moth 329
Heliobolus lugubris **198**
helmet-shrike, Retz's 135
helmet-shrike, white-crested 135, 140, 141
helmet-shrikes 129, 152
Helogale parvula **112-115**
Hemidactylus mabouia **198**
Hemiptera 227
Hemisus marmoratus **221**
heron, green-backed 137
heron, grey 137
herons 132, 137, 153
Hildebrandtia ornata **221**

hippo **70-73**, 178, 293, 336, 340
Hippopotamus amphibius **70-73**
hippopotamus, pygmy 73
honey badger 97, **122**, 196, 237
honeybees 122
honeyguide, greater 145
honeyguide, scaly-throated 145
honeyguides 122, 144
horn moth 224
hornbill, grey 136, 150
hornbill, ground 140, 143, 191, 195
hornbill, red-billed 115, 133, 136, 143, 150, 155
hornbill, yellow-billed 115, 135, 136, 143, 150, 155, 266
hornbills 133, 136, 150, 153, 180, 237, 268, 271, 282, 286
hummingbird 181
Hyaenidae 102
hyena, spotted 17, 18, 19, 101, **102-105**, 175, 177, 191, 203, 240, 332, 341
hyena, brown 102
hyena, striped 102
Hyperolius marmoratus **218**
hyrax **82-85**
Hystrix africaeaustralis **121**

ibis, hadeda 131
Imbrasia bellina 226
impala **36-39**, 99, 154, 178, 259, 261, 273, 277, 281, 292, 300, 305, 332, 336, 343
indigobird, village 145
indigobirds 144
'iNhlekabafazi' 142
insects 195, 222-241
invertebrates 222-249

jacana, African 147, 152, 327
jackal, black-backed **108-111**, 176, 281, 339
jackal, side-striped 108

Kassina senegalensis **220**
kassina, bubbling **220**
katydids 227, **230**
king cheetah 96
kingfisher, brown-hooded 180
kingfisher, giant 180
kingfisher, malachite 180, 181
kingfisher, pied 180, 181
kingfisher, pygmy 180, 181, 240
kingfisher, striped 180, 181
kingfisher, woodland 180, 181
kingfishers 131, 153, **180-181**
Kinixys spekii 191
kite spider **244**
kite, black-shouldered 128
kiwi 176
klipspringer **52**
knotthorn moth 305
Kobus ellipsiprymnus **48-49**
korhaan, red-crested 130, 147
'kremetartboom' 260
'kringgat' 48

kudu **40-43**, 253, 258, 259, 261, 268, 273, 274, 277, 281, 287, 292, 300, 306, 340

leopard 15, **18-21**, 101, 107, 191, 261, 339
leopard, black 20
Leptopelis mossambicus **216**
Lepus saxatilis **120**
lily-trotter 327
lion **14-17**, 18, 19, 101, 105, 175, 332, 339
lizard, bushveld **198**
lizards 187
lizards, Old World 187
Loxodonta africana **22-27**
lunar moth 303
Lycaon pictus **98-101**

mabungu grubs 256, 258
Mabuya striata **198**
'machiki-chorr' 114
Macrotermes natalensis 239
Macrotermes species 239
mamba, black 189, **206**
mantids **230**
Melanobasis species 305
Mellivora capensis **122**
m'fezi **201**
millipedes 118, **247**
monarch, African 225, 328
mongoose, dwarf **112-115**, 155, 240
mongooses 202, 237, 332
monitor lizard 139, 158, 195, 202, 310
monitor, Nile 196
monitor, rock 191, 196, 240
monitor, water 196
monitor, white-throated 196
monitors 187, **196-197**
monkey, samango 90
monkey, vervet 45, **90-93**, 195, 254, 256, 257, 259, 260, 263, 281, 285, 286, 292, 293, 294, 301, 306, 311, 321
mopane bee 271
mopane fly 271
mopane moth 226
mopane worm **226**, 269
mosquitoes **230**
mousebirds 153, 285, 294, 296, 323
Mustelidae 122

Naja mossambica **201**
Nephila species **243**
Neuroptera 224
nightjar, fiery-necked 168
nightjars 130, 132, 168
nyala **44-46**, 258, 268, 292, 305, 306, 310, 340

okapi 64
Olorunia species **244**
'oogpister' 198
orb-web spider, garden **243**
orb-web spider, golden **243**
Oreotragus oreotragus **52**
oriole, black-headed 133
ornate frog **221**

Index

Orycteropus afer **116-117**
ostrich **174-177**
otters 122
owl, barn 165, 166
owlet, pearl-spotted 154, 166
owls 146, 153, **164-167**, 181, 237
oxpecker, red-billed 34, 75, 179
oxpecker, yellow-billed 179
oxpeckers 34, 36, 140, 154, **178-179**, 332

pansy, blue 225
panther 20
Panthera leo **14-17**
Panthera pardus **18-21**
Papio cynocephalus ursinus **86-89**
Paraxerus cepapi **78-81**
parrot, brown-headed 268, 272, 285, 286
parrots 131
Pelomedusa subrufa 192
Pelusios sinuatus 192
penduline-tits 152
Phacochoerus aethiopicus **74-77**
Philothamnus semivariegatus **201**
Phrynobatrachus natalensis **221**
Phrynomantis bifasciatus **215**
platanna 136, 214, 221
platanna, tropical **221**
plated lizard, giant **199**
plated lizards 187
Platysaurus intermedius **200**
plover, three-banded 130
polecat 122
Polemaetus bellicosus 158
porcupine, Cape **121** 240, 259, 286, 292, 293, 305, 326
Procavia capensis **82-85**
processionary worms **226**
Ptychadena anchietae **220**
Ptyelus grossus 289
puddle frog, snoring **221**
puff adder 188, 189, **207**
puffback, black-backed 129, 135
python, African rock 189, 196, **202-203**
Python natalensis **202-203**
pytilia, green-winged 135

quelea, red-billed 134

rain frog, bushveld **217**
rain frogs 214
Raphicerus campestris **50**
raptors 146, 153, **156-159**, 195
ratel **122**
red roman 246
reed frog, painted **218**
rhino, white **32-35**, 178, 192, 286, 336, 341
rhino, black 35, 305, 341
river frog, common **221**
robber flies 237
robin-chats 129
roller, lilac-breasted 130
rollers 131, 237, 286, 289
rubber frog, banded **215**

sac spider 242
sand frog, russet-backed **220**
sand frog, tremelo **220**
sandgrouse 130
sandgrouse, double-banded 132, 169
Sauria 187
scarab 237
scarlet tip 225
Sciuridae 79
scops-owl, African 167
scops-owl, southern white-faced 165
scops-owls 130
Scorpionidae 248
scorpions 247, **248-249**
screeching owls 165
scrub hare **120**, 253
scrub-robin, white-browed 135
17-year bug 227
shongololo 247
shovel-nosed frog, mottled **221**
shrikes 195
skink, striped **198**
skinks 187, 198
skipper, white-cloaked 225
snake-eagle, black-chested 156
snake-eagle, brown 156
snake-eagles 156, 203
snakes 139, 156, **201-207**, 240
snipe, painted 147
solifugid **246**
sparrow, southern grey-headed 130
sparrow-hawk, little 159
sparrows 130
spiders 195, **242-245**
spittlebug **227**, 289, 297
spoonbill, African 138
spotted joker 225
spurfowl 172-173
spurfowl, Natal 135, 173
spurfowl, Swainson's 128, 173
Squamata 186
squirrel, European 80
squirrel, mopane 78, 271
squirrel, tree **78-81**, 270, 271, 276, 293, 302, 332
starling, glossy 131
starlings 179, 183, 195, 296, 323
steenbok **50**, 259
Stegodyphus species **242**
stick insect **229**
stork, marabou 129, 136, 139, 162
stork, openbill 137
stork, saddle-billed 146
stork, yellow-billed 139
storks 129, 146
Strigidae 165
Struthio camelus **174-177**
sun spider 246
sunbird, white-bellied 135, 301
sunbirds 152, 292, 295
swallows 132
swallowtail, citrus 225
swift, palm 299
Sylvicapra grimmia **51**

Syncerus caffer **28-31**

tent spider, tropical **244**
Terathopius ecaudatus 157
termites 117, 230, **238-241**
termites, fungus-growing 239
terrapin, marsh 192
terrapin, serrated-hinged 192
terrapins 33, 139, 186, 187, **192**
Thelotornis capensis 205
Theraphosidae 245
Theridiidae 244
thrushes 131
'tick birds' 154
tit, southern black 135
toad, cane 237
toad, eastern olive **219**
toad, guttural 219
toads 219
Tomopterna crytotus **220**
Tomopterna marmorata **220**
tortoise, leopard 104, **190-191**
tortoise, Speke's hinged 191
tortoises 186, 187, 343
Tragelaphus angasii **44-46**
Tragelaphus oryx **60-63**
Tragelaphus scriptus **47**
Tragelaphus strepsiceros **40-43**
tree frog, brown-backed 216
tree frog, grey **216**
turaco, purple-headed 131
turacos 131
turtles 187
turtle-dove, Cape 147
twig snake **205**
Tytonidae 165

Varanidae **196-197**
Varanus albigularus 196
Varanus niloticus 196
venomous spiders 242
vine snake 189, 195, **205**
violin spider 242
Viverridae 118, 119
vulture, Cape 163
vulture, hooded 162
vulture, lappet-faced 161, 162
vulture, white-backed 148, 161, 162, 163, 252
vulture, white-headed 161, 162
vultures **160-163**, 275

warblers 319
warthog 37, **74-77**, 178, 240, 259, 281, 286, 294, 301, 333, 342
wasp, cuckoo 235
wasp, fig **234**, 285, 286
wasp, ichneumonid 226, 235
wasp, mason 235
wasp, paper 235
wasp, spider-hunting 235
wasps 233, **235**, 237, 308
waterbuck **48-49**, 316, 340
waterfowl 319

Index

waxbill, blue 134, 135, 151, 253, 317
weaver, red-headed 148
weavers 147, 148, 319
white, brown-veined 225, 328
whydah, paradise 147
whydahs 144, 147
wild cat, African **123**
wild dog **98-101**, 203, 240
wildebeest, blue **54-55**, 57, 340
wolf, Ethiopian 100
woodborer 252, 254, 258
wood-dove, emerald-spotted 135, 147
wood-hoopoe, African 133
wood-hoopoe, green 133, 140, 142
wood-hoopoes 153
woodpecker, bearded 129
woodpecker, Bennett's 183
woodpecker, golden-tailed 135
woodpeckers 145, 151, 153, 166, 181, **182-183**

Xenopus muelleri **221**

zebra, Burchell's **56-59**, 293, 336, 342

Plants

'aambeiwortel' 320
Abutilon angulatum **326**
Acacia nigrescens 65, **252-253**
Acacia robusta subsp. *clavigera* **258**
Acacia species 10, 67, 318, 323
Acacia tortilis **256-257**
Acacia xanthophloea **254-255**
Adansonia digitata **260-262**
Adenium multiflorum **324**
Ansellia gigantea **321**
apple-leaf **289**
Aptosimum lineare **330**
Aristida congesta subsp. *barbicollis* **316**
Aristida congesta subsp. *congesta* **316**

baboon's tail **320**
Balanites maughamii **259**
baobab 143, **260-262**, 302
'blinkblaar wag-'n-bietjie' 311
blue-seed grass 151, **317**
boerbean, weeping 238, **301**
Bolusanthus speciosus **263**
Boscia albitrunca **264-265**
bowstring hemp 320
brandy bush 288
Breonadia salicina **267**
buffalo grass, blue **314**
buffalo grass, foxtail **314**
buffalo-thorn **311**
Burseraceae 266
bushwillow, large-fruited 273
bushwillow, red 10, **272**, 275, 308
bushwillow, russet **273**
bushwillow, variable 273

Cannabis species 324
Carissa bispinosa 331
Carissa edulis 331
Carissa species **331**
carrot seed 315
Cassia abbreviata subsp. *beareana* **268**
cassia, long-tail **268**
caterpillar bush **328**
Cenchrus ciliaris **314**
Ceratotheca triloba **322**
Chinese lantern tree 278
cluster-leaf, lowveld 308
cluster-leaf, silver 10, 306, **308-309**
Colophospermum mopane **269-271**
Combretaceae 308
Combretum apiculatum **272**, 275
Combretum collinum 273
Combretum hereroense **273**
Combretum imberbe **274-275**
Combretum species 269
Combretum zeyheri 273
Commiphora africana 266
Commiphora gileadensis 266
Commiphora mollis 266
Commiphora myrrha 266
common reed **319**
confetti tree 290
cork bush **295**
corkwood, poison-grub 266
corkwood, velvet 136, **266**
cornflower vernonia **328**
Crinum delagoense **329**
Croton megalobotrys **276**
Cymbopogon plurinodis **314**
Cyperus papyrus **330**
Cyperus sedges 171

Dalbergia melanoxylon **277**
devil's thorn **323**
Dicerocaryum eriocarpum **323**
Dichrostachys cinerea **278-279**
Digitaria eriantha 49
Diospyros mespiliformes 238, **280-281**

ebony tree 280
'elephant tree' 303
Eragrostis gummiflua **319**
Eragrostis species 317
Eragrostis superba **314**
Euclea divinorum 11, **282-283**
Euclea natalensis 283
Euphorbia cooperi 284
Euphorbia tirucalli **284**
euphorbia, lesser candelabra 284
euphorbia, lowveld 284
euphorbia, rubber 52, **284**
euphorbia, rubber-hedge 284

false marula **294**
fever tree **254-255**
fever-berry, large **276**
Ficus abutilifolia **285**
Ficus sycomorus **286**

fig trees 234
finger grass 49
flame lily **326**
flannel weed **327**
Flueggea virosa **330**
foxglove, wild **322**

Gardenia volkensii **287**
gardenia, bushveld **287**
Gloriosa superba **326**
Gnidia rubescens **325**
gnidia, ruby **325**
grasses 8, 10, **312-319**
green thorn **259**
Grewia bicolor **288**
Grewia caffra 288
Grewia flava 288
Grewia flavescens **288**
Grewia hexamita 288
Grewia monticolor 288
guarri, magic 11, **282-283**
guarri, Natal 283
guinea grass 49, 253, **318**
gum grass 10, **319**
Gymnosporia buxifolia **291**
Gymnosporia senegalensis **290-291**

Heliotropium steudneri **328**
herringbone grass 10, **319**
Heteropogon contortus 49, **316**
hibiscus **329**
Hibiscus species **329**
honeysuckle, Cape **323**
Hyphaene coriacea **289**

'imfe-nkawu' **321**
impala lily **324**
indaba tree **296**
Ipomoea species **325**

jackal-berry 110, 143, 159, 238, **280-281**
jacket plum **296**
justicea 330
Justicea species **330**

'kanniedood' 266
'kierieklapper' 273
Kigelia africana **292-293**
knob thorn 8, 65, 159, **252-253**

Lagenaria sphaerica **329**
Lannea schweinfurthii **294**
leadwood 161, **274-275**, 308
Leonotis leonurus **324**
leopard orchid **321**
lily, crinum **329**
lily, vlei **329**
lion's eye **324**
love grass, saw-tooth **314**

marula 8, 10, 294, **302-303**, 323
mashatu 310
matumi **267**

Index

Melinis repens **315**
melon, wild **329**
mistletoe 252, **323**
monkey's tail **320**
monkey-orange, black **306**
monkey-orange, green **306**
mopane 63, 226, **269-271**
morning glory **325**
mother-in-law's tongue **320**
Mundulea sericea **295**

num-num **331**
nyala tree 238, **310**
Nymphae nouchali **327**

Ocimum canum (americanum) **321**
Ormocarpum tricocarpum **328**

palm, lala **289**
palm, wild date **298-299**
Panicum maximum 32, 49, 253, **318**
Pappea capensis **296**
papyrus, dwarf **330**
Peltophorum africanum **297**
Philenoptera violacea **289**
Phoenix reclinata **298-299**
Phragmites australis **319**
Phyllanthus reticulates **329**
Plicosepalus kalachariensis **323**
Pogonarthria squarrosa **319**
poison apple **322**
potato bush 259, **329**
Pterocarpus rotundifolius **300**
purple pan weed **325**

rain tree 227, **289**
raisin, climbing **288**
raisin, giant **288**
raisin, sandpaper **288**
raisin, silver **288**
raisin, white **288**
red grass **318**
red top, Natal **315**
river thorn **258**
robust thorn **258**
rock fig, large-leaved **285**

Sansevieria aethiopica **320**
Sansevieria pearsonii 320
sausage tree **292-293**
Schotia brachypetala 238, **301**
Sclerocarya birrea 294, **302-303**
sesame, wild **322**
Sesamum triphyllum **322**
shepherd's tree **264-265**
sickle bush 257, **278-279**
Sida cordifolia **327**
sjambok pod **268**
Solanum panduriforme **322**
spear grass 49, **316**
Sphaeranthus incisus **325**
spike-thorn, common **291**
spike-thorn, pioneer **291**

spike-thorn, red **290-291**
Spirostachys africana **304-305**
star-chestnut, common **307**
Sterculia rogersii **307**
string-of-stars **328**
Strychnos madagascariensis **306**
Strychnos spinosa **306**
sycamore fig **286**

tamboti 121, **304-305**
teak, round-leaved **300**
Tecomaria capensis **323**
Terminalia prunoides 308
Terminalia sericea **308-309**
terminalia, purple-pod 308
Themeda triandra 32, **318**
three-awn, spreading **316**
three-awn, tassel **316**
'toothbrush tree' **283**
torchwood **259**
Tragus berteronianus **315**
tree wisteria **263**
Tricholaena monachne 151, **317**
Tricliceras mossambicense **324**
turpentine grass, narrow-leaved **314**

umbrella thorn **256-257**
Urochloa mossambicensis 32

violet, African wild **330**

'Vanwykshout' **263**
Vernonia glabra **328**
'voëlent' **323**
water-lily, blue **327**
weeping-wattle, African 227, **297**
white-berry bush **330**
wild anaseed **321**
wild basil **321**
wild dagga **324**
'witgat' **265**

Xanthocercis zambesiaca **310**
Xerophyta retinervis **320**

Zanthacercis zambesiacum **238**
zebrawood **277**
zebrawood flat-bean **277**
Zinnia peruviana **325**
zinnia, red-star **325**
Ziziphus mucronata **311**

General concepts

aardvark burrows 50, 75, 99, 104, 109, 116, 117, 121
abortion 39
Acacia tree gum 124, 255, 257
adhesion 214, 217
aerial perching 156, 181
aerial signs 332
aestivation 186

aggressive display 85
aging tracks 335
alarm 27, 30, 43, 45, 47, 52, 59, 81, 89, 91, 114, 128, 155, 172, 178, 332
alates 241
alkaloids 92
allelomimetic behaviour 134, 142
allelopathy 257
allo-grooming 36, 59, 62, 79, 89, 91, 113
allo-mothering 25
allo-preening 133, 141, 146, 147, 157
alpha pair 98, 112, 140, 141
altricial 16, 21, 79, 87, 99, 120, 143, 153
ambushing 248
amphibian 212
amplexus 214, 216, 217
anal gland 79, 105, 113, 118, 119, 122
androgen 103
animal droppings 48, 333, 338
animal tracks 52, 117, 332-343
ano-genital swelling 86
anthrax 105
anting 133
aposematic colouration 118, 215, 225, 227, 230, 233
araneomorph 242
arboreal signs 333
arrow poison 266
Artiodactyla 71, 336
askaris 23
autotomy 187, 198, 199, 229
auxillary amplexus 214

babysitting 112, 113
bachelor groups 23, 31, 38, 40, 49, 54, 60, 69
ballooning 243
barbs 132
barbules 132, 174
basalt 8
basking 70, 72, 83, 113, 202
Batesian mimicry 225
bathing 27
belly-wetting 169
beta male and female 98
Big Five 14-35
bilharzia 71, 259
bill snapping 129
binocular vision 19, 86, 92, 164, 204
bird call 128, 145, 168, 173, 174, 183
bird parties 134-135
bird song 128-129
birdlime 286, 323
body posturing 22
breeding strategy 38, 39, 43, 55, 60, 99, 115, 163, 177, 213, 249
bristles 116
brood parasite 144-145, 233, 235
bufotoxin 219
bulk feeder 56
bulk grazer 30, 73
bursa sac 191

Index

caecotropic faeces 120
cainism 158
cambium layer 23, 253, 257, 269, 302
camouflage 17, 20, 39, 40, 44, 52, 57, 66, 82, 106, 167, 168, 194, 195, 204, 205, 208, 216, 227, 230
canines 15, 70, 73, 93, 74, 103, 111
cantharidin 228
carapace 190, 192
carnassial shear 15, 100, 103, 111
carnivore 14, 85, 102, 112, 118, 122, 136, 336, 338
carotenoids 130, 131
caste system 238
catena 8–11, 253, 256, 272, 279, 282, 303
cheek glands 113
cheek pouches 87
cheek teeth 83, 100
chemical communication 26, 241
chemical defence 118, 122, 228, 247, 269
chemo-receptor 16, 25
chest gland 125
civetone 118
civetry 118, 339
clan 25, 31, 104
clawing trees 333
clay soils 8, 10, 11, 67, 253, 256, 258, 269, 304
cleptocoprid 237
climax community 318
climax grass 314
coalition 14, 94, 104
colchicines 326
colour vision 86, 92
commensalism 154
communal breeding 177
communication 17, 19, 21, 22, 28, 32, 84, 89, 106
community 313
competition 89
concertina locomotion 188
contagious behaviour 15
contour feathers 132
cooperation 14
cooperative breeding 98, 112, 140–143, 179, 180
cooperative hunting 94
coprophagia 77, 120, 191
counter-shading 39
coursing 101, 105
courtship 42, 54, 59, 73, 129, 146, 147, 150, 170, 172, 177, 181
covert feathers 132
crèche 68, 69, 175
crepuscular 43, 166
cryptic colouration 47, 130, 168, 169, 172, 176, 194, 203, 204, 205, 219, 226, 230
cuckoo spit 227
culm 313
cyanide 247
cytotoxin 201, 208

dabble 138
dawn chorus 128
death roll 211
decreaser 314

defensive spines 274, 277, 291
defensive thorns 253, 254, 256, 258, 269
dehiscent 305
destructive feeders 23
detritivores 247
dewclaw 15, 20, 107
digitigrade feet 336
dioecious 294, 303
disembowelment 101
displacement behaviour 35
disruptive markings 20, 40, 44, 46, 57
distress call 213
diurnal 75, 80, 83, 95, 96, 113
division of labour 238
dolerite dyke 11
dominance 105
dormancy 186
dorsal gland 85
down feathers 132
drainage lines 11
Drakensberg Mountains 8
drumming 183 see also tapping
duet 129, 173
dung 52, 117, 173, 333, 338 see also animal droppings
dust bathing 59, 85, 133

ear tufts 167
ecca shales 8
ecdysis 225, 227, 231, 243, 249
ecological status 314
ecotone region 36
ectoparasites 27, 33, 34, 36, 59, 62, 75, 85, 109, 133, 133, 145, 154, 178, 192
ectothermic 186, 198, 209
egg dumping 170
elephant dung 26, 87, 108, 173, 236, 302
elephant graveyard 25
encroacher species 10, 257, 270, 272, 278, 291
endangered species 100, 191
endemic 217
endocoprid 237
endothermic 81
epiphyte 321
erosion 11
Escarpment 8
even-toed ungulates 71

facial expression 89, 90, 106, 119
facial grimace 16, 58, 61
facial markings 106, 107
faecal sac 151
faeces 338
family groups 94, 109
fatty acids 85
feather hygiene 132–133
feeding hierarchy 162
feldspar 9, 11
field signs 332
fighting 17, 26, 29, 34, 49, 59, 60, 73, 125
filoplumes 132
fish poison 276, 284, 289, 295, 304
flagwaving 142

flash colouration 40, 50, 218, 219, 229, 230
flatulence 56
flehmen 16, 31, 34, 58, 61
'follow me' sign 17, 21, 38, 40, 46, 48, 69, 74, 100, 106
food chain 214
foregut fermentation 73
formic acid 133, 215
freezing 114
frog calls 213
frugivore 134, 137
fungus garden 239

gabbro 8
genetic diversity 39, 93, 96
geophagia 26, 33, 52, 65, 77
gneiss 8
godfather 87, 89
Gondwanaland 8
granite 8, 9
grassland 36
grassland succession 30, 57, 315
grazers 138, 312
grazing value 313
gregarious 31, 34, 40, 69, 91, 134, 175, 180, 226
grooming 36, 89, 113
grooming claw 85, 125
grooming contest 115
group cohesion 23
gular flap 211
gular fluttering 177

habitual behaviour 27
haemotoxin 189, 204, 205
handicap hypothesis 147
harem system 49, 54, 59, 73, 82, 89
heaping 82
heat sensitivity 30
heat-sharing 82
helpers 180, 140, 179
hemi-metabolic life cycle 231
hemipenes 186
herbivores 178, 238, 338
hermaphrodite 103, 247
hibernation 186
hiding prey 18, 19, 107
hind-gut fermentation 26, 56, 73, 77, 120
holometabolic life cycle 225
home range 30, 34, 47, 54, 88, 112
hormones 16, 19, 31, 34, 58
hovering 156, 181
huddling 82, 83, 92
hunting 14, 17, 95, 99, 101, 105, 106, 110, 114
hydroquinones 228
hyena scat 104, 191
hyracium 84

incisors 22, 32, 36, 83, 100, 111, 121
increaser 314
infanticide 14, 20, 115
infantile appeasement ritual 101
infantile begging 99
inflorescence 313

350

Index

infrasonic sounds 22
inguinal amplexus 214
insectivore 136, 168
instar 225
interspecific allelomimetic behaviour 134
interspecific competition 110
iridescence 131
ischial callosity 88
ivory 22

jumping bean 305

keratin 33, 131, 181, 182, 224
keratophagia 224
keystone species 23
kin recognition 73
kinship group 25
kinship selection 98, 179
kleptoparasitism 235, 244

lagomorph 120
lateral display 47
lateral presentation 41, 46
latrines 50, 84, 104, 108, 113, 338, 339
Lebombo Mountains 8
leguminous plants 253
lichen 152, 291
locomotion 188
lordosis 16
Lowveld, formation 8-11
Lowveld, topography 9
luceferase 224
luceferin 224
lying-up period 43, 46, 49, 61, 68

malaria 230, 255, 276
mammal pollinator 65, 253
maternity group 69
mating 16, 20, 26, 31, 34, 73, 76, 115, 214, 231, 249
matriarchal society 23, 76
median horn 66
melanin 20, 130, 131, 132, 195
melanistic form 20
melanophores 195
metamorphosis 212, 225, 231
metatarsal gland 39
mica 9
microhabitat 23, 238, 248, 253, 266
middens 34, 39, 55, 108, 119, 338
'middleman' safety effect 38
migration 54, 181
mimicry 74, 97, 129, 154, 198, 225, 226, 227, 229, 245
mixed feeders 36
mixed feeding party 37, 134
mobbing 158
molars 24, 32, 77, 100, 103, 111
monogamy 52, 109, 121, 129, 146-147, 150, 151, 157, 159, 169, 172, 173, 180, 181
mopane woodland 78, 270
moribund 312
moulting 133, 225

mucilage 260
mucous gland 212
mud-wallowing 27, 30, 33, 75, 333
Müllerian mimicry 227
musth 25, 26, 302, 332
mutual grooming see allo-grooming
mutualism 155, 178
mygalomorph 242, 245

nannying 25
natal pack 98
near-passerine 153
near-ungulate 85, 337
necking ritual 69
negative buoyancy 71
negative geotaxis 244
nest-robber 139
nests 143, 145, 147, 148-152, 150, 151, 155, 159, 163, 166, 172, 176, 179, 181, 183
neurotoxin 189, 201, 206, 242, 248
nictitating membrane 175, 180, 211, 212
night vision 124, 164, 211
nitrogen-fixing bacteria 253, 310, 318
nocturnal 106, 166, 211
nomadic 17, 60, 101
non-passerine 153
non-selective feeder 72
nuchal hump 33
nuchal scute 190
nuptial flight 240, 241
nuptial gift 146, 150, 170, 181
nursery herd 60, 73

obligatory mutualism 234, 239
occipital flap 194
oestrus 16, 18, 31, 34, 39, 46, 51, 54, 59, 86, 115
olfactory messages 19, 28, 33, 34
oligarchy 89
omnivore 89, 110, 134, 172, 199, 338
opportunism 17, 18
opportunistic feeder 157
organ of Jacobsen 16, 25, 31, 34, 58, 61, 73, 188, 197
osteoderm 198
osteophagia 52, 65, 77, 121, 191
over-specialisation 95
over-utilisation 272, 312
oviparous 186
ovoviviparous 186, 208, 249

pair bond 52, 109, 129, 133, 141, 146, 147, 149, 150, 157, 181
palatal spots 145
panicle 313
pantries 80
paracoprid 237
parasitism 178, 226, 308, 323
parking 125
passerine 151, 153
passive display 44
passive dominance system 41
pasting 105
paternity competition 79

pathfinder 30
pathways 333
patrolling territory 34
pecten 168
pectinate claw 132, 168
pectines 249
pedal gland 50, 55
peripheral vision 37
perissodactyla 336
phreatophyte 289, 310
pilo-erection 37, 46, 74, 85, 97, 102, 118, 119, 121
pineal organ 193
pioneer community 315
piscevore 139, 180
pituitary gland 212
plantigrade feet 336
plastron 186, 190, 192
play 20, 25, 38, 93, 105, 107
play fighting 27
pollination 234, 253, 261, 285, 286, 303, 308, 327
polyandry 147
polygamy 146, 147, 177
polygyny 147
population bottleneck 96
posturing 29, 34
precocial 51, 55, 58, 85, 120, 121, 147, 153, 16, 171, 172
predator 17, 30, 38, 40, 43, 45, 46, 52, 62, 94-115, 120
preen gland 132, 174
preen oil 132
preening 132
preorbital gland 50, 51, 52, 55
pride cohesion 15
primaries 132
primates 85, 89, 124, 336
promiscuity 86
protractie claws 15, 107
pseudo-penis 103, 105
pseudo-scrotum 103
pure grazer 54

quartz 9, 11

rabies 100
raceme 313
radula 247
rank hierarchy 29, 31, 59, 60, 69, 89, 90, 91, 113, 142
rastellum 245
ratites 174
reabsorption (of foetuses) 39
rectilinear locomotion 188, 208
refection 120
registering 42, 45, 340
regurgitation 99, 105, 109, 181
release call 213
remiges 132
resonance chamber 213
retrices 132, 179, 182
reverse sexual dimorphism 146
Rhizobium bacteria 253, 310
rhyolite 8

Index

rictal bristles 132, 138, 168
ring-barking 23, 121, 260, 302, 305
ritualised behaviour 16, 34, 45, 60, 94, 101, 102
rodent control 107, 110, 123
rotenone 295
royal pair 146–147
rubbing posts 33, 55
ruff 160
rumbling 22
ruminants 63, 73, 77
rut 39, 42, 54, 99

sacrificial branches 255, 274
sandy soils 10, 272
saponins 323
satellite behaviour 213
satellite males 49
scat 108, 113, 338
scavenging 17, 18, 102, 105, 110, 118, 136, 247
scent-marking 17, 18, 19, 21, 34, 50, 51, 52, 55, 79, 82, 90, 94, 101, 105, 113, 118, 122, 123, 125, 332, 341
scrape marks 19, 34, 333
scutes 190
secondaries 132
sectorial 100
seed-eaters 136, 169
seepline 10, 272, 309, 319
seepline indicator 319
selective feeders 54, 66
selfish herds 38
semi-altricial 153
semi-retractable claws 97
sensory feathers 132
sentinel 83, 91, 115
serpentine locomotion 188
sexual dimorphism 28, 41, 44, 146
sexual monomorphism 146
siblicide 158
side winding 188
simple-gut mammals 85
site selectors 54
sloughing 189
snakebite 189, 204, 205, 206, 208, 290
soaring 161
sociality 14, 23, 91, 94, 102, 235
sodic sites 11, 282
sodium 11
solitary 18, 44, 50, 51, 117, 123
Spanish fly 228
spider bite 242
spider's web 152
spike 313
spikelet 313
spoor see animal tracks
stabilimentum 243
stalking 17, 18, 95, 106
stampede 30
startle display 166, 195, 204, 245
statue-pose display 52
stereoscopic vision 205
straddle 337
stress 35

stride 337
stridulation 230, 249
strigids 165
strychnine 306
sub-climax community 316
submission 33, 49
sunbathing 81, 133
super-predators 17
suspensorium 15, 19
sweet veld 275
symbiosis 115, 154–155, 234, 237, 239, 253
synchronised breeding 16, 55
syndactylous foot 153, 180
syrinx 128

tactile hairs 84
tail feathers 132
tannins 10, 92, 252, 260, 269, 281, 282, 290, 311
tapetum lucidum 19, 124, 211
tapping 129 see also drumming
tartaric acid 260
tear marks 95
tectrices 132
teeth gnashing 84
telecoprid 236, 237
telsons 248
temporal gland 26
temporary associations 45, 69
tending bond 42
termite mounds 96, 112, 116, 173, 197, 206, 238, 239, 268, 280, 294, 301, 310
terrestrial signs 333
territorial behaviour 14, 15, 17, 18, 34, 39, 45, 49, 50, 52, 73, 79, 82, 90, 101, 104, 108, 110, 113, 118, 125, 146, 157, 173, 196, 206, 231, 333, 338
testosterone 103
thanatosis 122, 187, 196, 229
thermolabile 83
thermoregulation 25, 27, 37, 52, 55, 59, 63, 66, 75, 81, 83, 108, 113, 160, 175, 177, 186, 198, 202, 209, 216, 218, 239
thicket 40, 46
threat warning 34, 37
throat glands 50
thyroid gland 212
timeshare calling 213
tinaeid moth 24
toothcomb 125
torsion 247
tracking 332–343
tragelaphines 47, 340
trumpeting 22
turacin 131
turacoverdin 131
twins 105
tympanic membrane 193
tympanum 193, 213
tyndal scattering 131, 181
tytonids 165

umbraculum 84
ungulate 85, 336

unguligrade feet 336
unselective feeders 30, 56
uric acid 172, 224
urine testing 61
urine-washing 125
uropygial gland 132

vascular tissue 23
vibrissae 21, 124
visual advertising 86, 92
visual display 44, 91, 100, 106
visual marking 19, 34, 60, 113
viviparous 186, 249
vocal sac 213, 217
vocalisation 15, 17, 18, 19, 22, 43, 45, 46, 59, 68, 73, 76, 79, 81, 84, 89, 91, 96, 101, 103, 107, 111, 114, 119, 125, 128, 198, 213
volcanic activity 8
vomeronasal organ 58

waterlogged soils 10
waterproofing 132
whiskers 84, 93, 124
woodland 36

yolk sac 176

zygodactylous feet 153, 167, 182

SEAN PATTRICK – Photographer

Sue Haughton

Sean has spent most of his life in close proximity to nature. He was schooled in the KwaZulu-Natal Midlands and then studied agriculture at the Royal Agricultural College, Cirencester (UK). After a brief stint in farming, his love of the bush drew him to the field-guiding industry. Sean has guided at and managed some of southern Africa's top private lodges and in the process attained his FGASA Level 3 and SKS (DG) dangerous game qualifications. He is an accredited FGASA guide's trainer and assessor. After years of experience living and working in the African bush, Sean has become an accomplished photographer. He is a versatile artist equally at home hanging from a helicopter shooting elephant and rhino captures, tracking the Big Five for photographic safaris and collaborating with magazine journalists for foreign or local publication commissions.

Sean established his company Natural Exposure in 2002 to offer clients the exposure and experience of wildlife that Sean himself is passionate about. Natural Exposure has a vast image library comprising thousands of Sean's images; some can be seen at www.seanpattrick.com. Sean travels extensively to international destinations and leads unique safaris for Clearly Africa to some of the most pristine wilderness areas in Africa. This together with his photographic workshops means he spends a great deal of time exploring new areas with his guests, something he finds most enjoyable as it brings out the child in all involved. Sean can be contacted at www.naturalexposuresafaris.com.